THE ICON CRITICAL DICTIONARY
OF
GLOBAL ECONOMICS

THE ICON CRITICAL DICTIONARY
OF
GLOBAL ECONOMICS

EDITED BY

ROBERT BEYNON

ICON BOOKS

Published in 1999 by Icon Books Ltd.,
Grange Road, Duxford, Cambridge CB2 4QF
e-mail: icon@mistral.co.uk
www.iconbooks.co.uk

Distributed in the UK, Europe, Canada, South Africa and Asia by
the Penguin Group:
Penguin Books Ltd., 27 Wrights Lane, London W8 5TZ

Published in Australia in 1999 by Allen & Unwin Pty. Ltd.,
PO Box 8500, 9 Atchison Street, St. Leonards, NSW 2065

Cover illustration by Steve Rawlings
Design and layout by Christos Kondeatis
Managing editor Christopher Long
Typesetting by Hands Fotoset, Leicester

ISBN 1 84046 012 1

Printed and bound in Great Britain by
Mackays plc., Chatham, Kent

CONTENTS

v

CONTENTS

vi

EDITOR'S INTRODUCTION

WHAT IS ECONOMICS?

Economics is the study of any material or trading relationships between people. It addresses fundamental questions such as the causes of wealth, poverty, growth, employment, and inflation. It is much concerned with identifying causation, and where possible relies on empirical observation to test its theories; its biggest difficulty is in isolating the effects of particular actions, occurrences or 'shocks', on individuals, economic entities or societies as a whole. Its closest relatives are politics, sociology and business studies.

The development of economics as an intellectual discipline has tended to mirror the increasing complexities of trade and money which have characterized our world over the past couple of centuries since the first industrialization, but its roots are as old as society itself. Like other academic subjects, economics has many broad 'schools' of thinking, some of which are in open conflict, others arriving at similar conclusions via very different thought processes.

Critics of economics question its fondness for making sweeping assumptions about such issues as rationality or competition to facilitate the logical process: how, they ask, can findings be worthwhile if the underlying assumptions do not reflect reality? Others dislike what they see as its pretensions of positivism, accusing its students of ignoring ethical issues such as welfare, distributive justice, and the 'quality of life'. Some attack it for giving a cloak of respectability to greed, waste and anti-social behaviour. Without it, however, policymakers would be short of a prescriptive armoury for the economies they try to manage; although there are many who might argue (from widely differing viewpoints) that this would be a significant improvement!

Perhaps the scepticism concerning the subject is the stronger because of the great increase in popularity that it has enjoyed over the past decade. The expansion of various types of business studies courses, from MBAs to accountancy, from management to IT, has greatly broadened the constituency of economics. Of course there are still the core who study and research pure economics, but the greater number now encountering the subject do so as part of another field of study. Add to them the burgeoning numbers of people worldwide who need to follow economics, business and the markets for professional or personal investment reasons, and you have something of an economics explosion.

This book is aimed at everyone for whom economics is already important, as well as the sceptics, critics, and curious newcomers. It should provide not just a useful grounding in the main concepts, but an excursion into current thinking by academic and professional economists. This is important, because as we shall see, some of the changes to our world are shifting the emphasis of economic thought very rapidly indeed.

THE MAIN SCHOOLS

Any attempt to condense economics into half a dozen areas of thought invites the charge of over-simplification. This brief summary should be used in conjunction with the relevant entries in the dictionary section of the book.

Modern economics is generally held to have started with the Classicals, the eighteenth- and nineteenth-century economists and philosophers (the subjects were regarded as overlapping at the time) who addressed such issues as value, labour, population, and trade. In the works of Smith, Malthus, Ricardo and Marx you can almost feel the curiosity and bafflement that industrialization had created. Theirs was a world which had changed from a predominantly agrarian society to a rapidly growing urban manufacturing machine, whose trade was underpinned by global empires, and whose people experienced extremes of wealth and poverty, as well as more rapid social and technological change than had ever been known before.

Classical economics covered a considerable distance in explaining the mechanics of production in this new world. But it was the need to understand how markets worked, and to develop a theory of price, that took the Classical thinkers into the realm of what is now called neo-Classical economics. Neo-Classical economics is still the basis of much of our understanding of microeconomics (the study of individuals, firms, or economic entities, as opposed to the forces at work in the wider economy, which is macroeconomics). Much of what you will find in this book about supply, demand, pricing, and elasticities is neo-Classical. Now, for the first time, economists felt they could explain why wages, or prices, were at different levels in different circumstances. It had less to do with underlying value, and much to do with supply and demand. Say,

Walras, and others extended neo-Classical thought to macroeconomics. Market-clearing theories held that economies would, if left alone, tend toward a full-employment equilibrium; therefore the trade cycle, which is the tendency of economies to swing between boom and slump, was empirically real but best tackled by least intervention. Without intervention, prices, wages and interest rates would restart or slow down economic activity when such change was needed.

Neo-Classical economics held sway until the Great Depression of the 1930s. The 1920s had been a period of capitalist growth, of industrial and productive expansion to what were at the time dizzying heights. In the United States especially, mass production brought growth, prosperity, and a spectacularly bullish stock market. It all came crashing down, first with the markets, then with world trade and domestic demand. The world seemed mired in a deeper and more permanent recession than it had ever known before. Unemployment reached what at the time seemed catastrophic levels. In Europe some countries turned to fascist or marxist parties who promised (very different) solutions to the standstill.

From Cambridge University came one man who changed the world. John Maynard Keynes provided the desperate policymakers with a body of economic theory that acknowledged the possibility of economic equilibrium at less than full capacity – in other words, the possibility of becoming 'stuck' at any point in the economic cycle. The way out, he argued, was to stimulate demand. Governments could do that: indeed, he argued that they should, vigorously and regularly. The US in particular embraced Keynesian thinking in the 'New Deal' policies of President Roosevelt, with 'public works' – government spending – being used as a way out of the recession. Of course the Second World War soon created temporary command economies with production – and demand – at full capacity, for strategic reasons. Nonetheless, Keynesian policies formed the paradigm for capitalist economies until the 1970s. Pump-priming, demand management, fiscal measures, budget deficits – these were the tools of post-war economics. There was growth, prosperity, and a great expansion of world trade, under what was known as the Bretton Woods system of fixed exchange rates.

Things began to turn sour with stubborn inflation accompanied by high unemployment, then the shock of the heavy increases in oil prices by the OPEC cartel. These were inflationary while at the same time encouraging recession. The whole sorry combination brought a new word to the economic lexicon: stagflation. Policymakers started looking for alternatives. There were two, and they are politically, but not necessarily intellectually, related. Monetarism was a development of neo-Classical economics, much of it stemming from the work of Professor Milton Friedman of the University of Chicago. Unlike Keynesianism, it set great store by nominal variables such as the money supply. Where Keynes had argued that inflation came from excess demand when the economy was at full capacity, monetarists preferred to look at how money itself affected prices. Monetarists tended to eschew fiscal measures, especially if they implied budget deficits. The monetary measure they embraced was control of the money supply so that it never exceeded the growth of output in the economy. The great problem of that central plank of monetarism turned out to be defining the plank – what exactly was the money supply? How broadly should it be measured? It is simplistic, however, to say that monetarism did not work because controlling the money supply proved to be the pursuit of a chimera. As we shall see in a moment, the new consensus has embraced several of the tenets of monetarism.

The other new trend in economic thinking was supply-side measures. Broadly, the supply-siders believe that inflation, and inefficiency, can be squeezed out of the system by improving the workings of the supply elements within an economy, and in particular the labour market. At the time of stagflation in the 1970s, labour union power was strong in many capitalist economies, and many believed that it encouraged inflation through excessive wage demands, leading to a wage price spiral. Supply-siders also firmly rejected government interference in industry, which included support for loss-making entities and protection of markets. Governments which embraced monetarism were also likely to adopt supply-side measures, and the Reagan and Thatcher administrations in the United States and the United Kingdom were perhaps the best examples. Real improvements in productivity followed, but often at the expense of an initial period of high unemployment.

WHERE ARE WE NOW?

Although we are very far from seeing a state of contented peace among the world's economists, there are certain consensus elements among the world's economic policymakers. For a start, the collapse of the state socialist empire in eastern Europe and the former Soviet Union has more or less eclipsed any hardline socialist economic remedies. The choice now concerns what level of management there should be in capitalism: arguably even countries like China are now part of the capitalist club. And what are the best operational methods? There are still disagreements over the finer points of monetarism and modern, or neo-, Keynesian economics, mostly over the working of money, liquidity, and interest rates. But we can sketch out what drives much macroeconomic policymaking at the end of the twentieth century:

- Inflation is an ever-present danger and it must be tackled, ideally, by central banks which are independent of policymakers (the Fed and the new European Central Bank between them will control most of the world's GDP).

- Monetary policy, especially control over interest rates, is best applied a little and often, rather than in traumatic steps.

- Fiscal policy as a tool of demand management should only be used in the context of more or less balanced budgets: the old notion of budget deficits plays havoc with monetary policy, and is also inflationary.

- Managed – or dirty – floating is the preferred policy for exchange rates. That way the markets can react to an economy's fundamentals, but governments can smooth out some of the erratic flows of 'hot money'.

- Free trade is not only desirable, it is the biggest single impetus for global prosperity, and therefore membership of the World Trade Organization (WTO) is a prerequisite for any serious economy.

The main concerns are unemployment, under-development, and the fear of a global economic catastrophe arising from ever more globally interlinked markets. To examine these we should take an overview of some of the key forces at work which when taken together put us at the start of a completely new economic era.

THE NEW ERA: TECHNOLOGICAL, GLOBAL, INDIVIDUAL

The new era is in some ways as important as industrialization, which heralded the machine age. The economic and social implications of current information technology are changing the way we look at growth, employment, trade, and microeconomics. The technological age means that mature economies are less likely to make things, more likely to outsource manufacturing to where labour is cheaper, that companies need to be more flexible in product lines and management, that therefore employment is less long-term and more 'contractual', that markets are more global but that marketing is more individual, that less developed countries can acquire information and expertise at a speed and efficiency that was unimaginable even a decade ago, and that there now exists the possibility of stable economic growth without the most extreme shocks of the trade cycle.

That is indeed a very positive scenario (much too positive, according to some economists). What is important is that – partly because of the technological age, and partly for broad demographic reasons – individuals who previously never took any active part in financial markets are now helping to create them. Ageing populations in most developed countries mean that governments can no longer take sole responsibility for provision of health, retirement, and welfare, simply because the taxable base of the population is not large enough to sustain the transfer payments. Hence the enormous growth of market-related saving, through private pension funds, mutual funds and various kinds of tax-friendly investment vehicles. In Europe this has put millions of individuals in the markets for the first time ever, and in the United States it has encouraged new entrants and greater participation by those who already own equities or bonds. Technology means that getting information, and trading, has never been easier or more universal. From an economic point of view, this is an inflow of savings direct to the company sector, rather than via the banks. This will be important for the policymakers who in the past have used bank credit as an important monetary instrument. What will be critical is whether it will lead to asset price inflation, and perhaps a major downturn, or whether company performance will keep pace with the inflow of funds. The early signs are that today's technology is greatly helping company performance.

The challenge will be to keep economic performance and growth at the sort of level that leads not to massive unemployment in the developed world because of automation and the shift to cheap-labour economies, but that makes employment itself more flexible and highly skilled. The challenge also will be to start growth in the least developed world, and technology will help this in some cases. And the fear of a global financial and economic melt-down? There is certainly a great deal more global liquidity, and shocks are transferred across the globe within seconds. That is a function of deregulated financial markets which have the most detailed information transferred at the speed of light. There is, however, no reason at all to suppose that such markets will do anything that markets have not done since the beginning of time: they will be subject to rumour, fashion and fear; but in the end, they will look at the fundamentals.

The aim of the book

This book addresses the needs of today's economics. It is both a dictionary and a primer, but it is more than this. It is the only publication to put modern economic theory into today's global context. We believe that an understanding of concepts and terms is not on its own enough. They are constantly being developed and modified on the basis of empirical evidence in real markets, in real companies, and in real trade. They are being tested on the basis of increasingly sophisticated models. They are being outflanked, and in many cases overtaken, by the revolution in technology. For that reason the A–Z entries are cross-referenced to and supplemented by essays, to create a true overview for anyone – student or participant – in economics, business, and management.

The Essays

How better to learn about global economics than at first hand from those at the leading edge of academic study or professional practice? We have carefully chosen the contributors to cover the broadest sweep, with the best value for all readers. This section is both rigorous and accessible. It can be seen as a way of putting fundamental economic concepts into lively and current debate. Words in **bold** type in the essays are cross-references to specific A–Z entries, to which the reader can refer for extra guidance on methodology or terms.

The 11 essays are grouped as follows:

● 'The new economics': here we address some of the broadest issues facing the subject today, and what we have selected is designed to be both thought-provoking and challenging. We explore some of the great claims made by Professor Minford and his followers for liberalizing markets, especially labour markets, in the interest of efficiency. Any opinion, from supply-side zealot to industrial *dirigiste*, will find something to chew over in this contribution. In addition we have some new analysis of trade and development by Dr Sanjaya Lall, which takes as its starting-point our current thinking on trade theory, and develops it to answer some of the biggest riddles about why some countries succeed where others fail. Neil Mackinnon, who once helped formulate policy for the UK Treasury, uses his perspective as an independent professional economist to explore the limits to the power of today's global financial markets. And finally Professor Paul

Ormerod has developed his mathematically-based theories of markets, chaos, and economics to tell us what the subject is not and never can be.

- 'The global context': any collection of essays about global economics requires some overview of North America, Europe, and Asia, and how they interact with each other and the rest of the world. Over the past few years much has been written of 'global recession' or 'global meltdown'. We have also seen great attention given to the launch of the euro, and the role of the US equity markets in world economics. In all these areas we have tried to take a cool analytical view of topical events, and found – not surprisingly – that the reality is more complex than the popular headlines. Jeremy Pink carefully traces how the Asian economies have changed from 'economic miracle' to 'recession disaster'. He finds lessons for all policy-makers and students of economic policy. David Hale asks whether the global recession has actually been averted by the extraordinary recent buoyancy of the US economy, largely driven by the equities markets. And Ian Harnett looks at Europe and Euro-land and finds much to fear from unemployment, but perhaps more to gain from the promise of stable trade, efficient production and flexible markets. Running through these three essays, and several of the others as well as the A–Z entries, is the notion that the financial markets are global and largely deregulated, and that individual investors, or banks, or firms, increasingly hold the key to economic prosperity. In other words, the role of microeconomics is now real and measurable on the macro trends. The question then is who are the policymakers, who the regulators, and what should be the parameters of their roles. In one sense, then, 'the global context' illuminates 'the new economics'.

- 'The world tomorrow': if 'the global context' provides a map of the terrain, 'the world tomorrow' is the weather forecast for our economic odyssey. Justin Urquhart Stewart develops the concept of the explosion in personal financial involvement – through equities, bonds, investment devices, all of which have changed our financial markets for ever. This essay serves as an introduction to the whole section. The second great driver of change is technology. Richard Lander shows how no aspect of business and economics – indeed, no aspect of our lives – will be untouched by what we can legitimately call the technology revolution. The changes in technology and investment are reflected strongly in our essays on management and marketing. Robert Beynon looks at the new management ethos – more holistic, contractual, virtual and global than anything in the 'machine age'. And Professor Adrian Payne and Sue Holt rewrite much of what we understand about buying and selling in his contribution on relationship marketing. This is a glimpse of a future in which loyalty, retention, and partnership will be the drivers of economic success.

Each essay is preceded by an editor's introduction which will set it into the context of the book, as well as highlighting, where necessary, some of the key points about the authors' methodologies or intellectual standpoints. This introduction can also be seen as a conduit forward to the relevant A–Z entries. There is also a list of suggested further reading following each essay. We have included brief biographical notes on our contributors in the preliminary pages that follow this introduction.

THE A-Z ENTRIES

We have some 180 entries which cover the main areas of micro- and macroeconomics. These are longer than the entries in many standard dictionaries, so that the book can be used as a primer as well as a basic lexicon. The entries are arranged alphabetically, but they can also be seen in a 'grouped' context in the list which precedes the A–Z section (p. 149). So that someone looking at Trade, for example, would be able to go to the Theory of comparative advantage, Heckscher-Ohlin factor proportions theory, Exchange rate theory, Bretton Woods, Trade organisations, Balance of payments, Devaluation/revaluation, J-Curve and Marshall-Lerner, by using the grouped list. This list would also guide the reader into aspects of the currency markets. The entries can therefore be seen in a context in which the main subjects are clearly defined, with the subsidiary areas laid out in relation to them. Thus the reader can avoid the somewhat haphazard feel of a purely alphabetical approach.

The entries in general are written at a level which will be understandable for a student who is approaching economics for the first time, or needing a refresher or update after being away from the subject. Because every effort has been made to make them clear, starting from first principles, there is no reason at all why they should be difficult to follow for a reader who has not studied economics in its own right. This applies particularly to people who might be involved in work or study which touches on economics, such as management or marketing. There are diagrams where appropriate. Although much of today's economics is taking on an increasingly mathematical flavour, we have not assumed specialist mathematical knowledge, working on the assumption that many of the current concepts can be explained verbally and graphically without needing to resort to complex equations.

All entries are cross-referenced in **bold** type. There are also cross-references to the essays, where relevant. Thus the reader who wanted to explore trade would be pointed toward the essay about trade and developing economies by Sanjaya Lall, as well as being encouraged to dip into those on international wage markets and supply-side economics (Patrick Minford) and the European single currency (Ian Harnett). This is a crucial element in the book: once the principles have been mastered, the reader can then see in practice how they operate, either at the forefront of academic economics, or else in the 'real world' of international markets and business – or, more often than not, in both. We strongly believe that this is the best way to study and understand economics. It is also the most effective way to put the subject into context with other areas such as technology, finance, management, politics, etc., which is the route by which most students encounter economics nowadays.

There is also an index which covers both the essays and the A–Z section. Main entries in the A–Z section are shown in bold in the index, along with the relevant page numbers.

Finally, there is one key message that we have tried not to lose sight of: the sheer excitement of getting close to economics. There is no other subject which can more rigorously and incisively lead us to a scientific understanding of the society in which we live and all its trade and trends. What this book will demonstrate is that there has never before been a time when the study of economics has been so pivotal to our lives and our futures.

The editor wishes to thank two LSE postgraduates, George Bitsakakis and Mohsen Namazi, for their invaluable help with the A–Z entries, and for their interest in the project as a whole. I am also grateful to many of my former colleagues at Dow Jones and European Business News for their useful suggestions and support. The biggest debt is to Sara Holmes, who provided consistent input to editorial, text and graphic elements, as well as the overall framework. Finally thanks to my publishers at Icon, and Duncan Heath in particular, for what can only be described as dogged patience in dealing with my scrambled e-mails from all corners of the globe.

To Sara, for making it happen.

CONTRIBUTORS

Robert Beynon is an independent strategic and management consultant, working mainly in television and new media. His company, MediaNet Worldwide, has clients in Europe, the US and Asia. After studying Economics at Cambridge, he worked at the BBC, ITN, Sky, and the cable and satellite channel EBN: European Business News. He was until recently Director of Programming for CNBC Europe.

David D. Hale is the Global Chief Economist for the Zurich Group, advising the company's US and global fund management operations on the economic outlook and a wide range of public policy issues. He is a member of the US National Association of Business Economists and of the New York Society of Security Analysts. He writes regularly in several business publications, and has frequently testified before Congressional committees on domestic and international economics. He has conducted briefings for senior officials in the US Executive, including those of President Bush, and he is a consultant to the US Department of Defense on how changes in the global economy affect US strategic relationships. He holds a BSc in International Economic Affairs from the Georgetown University School of Foreign Service, and an MSc from the London School of Economics.

Dr Ian Harnett is Director of European Equity Strategy at BT Alex Brown in London. He has been chief economist, European strategist, and director of a number of City-based companies including NatWest Markets, Société Générale Strauss Turnbull, and ANZ McCaughan. He also worked as a specialist economist for the Bank of England and has lectured in Economics at Oxford University.

Sue Holt, BA(Hons), Lic.IPD, MMRS, MBA, is a Doctoral Researcher in the Institute for Advanced Research in Marketing at Cranfield University. Her current research interests are in strategic and relationship marketing, key account management and in customer value, with particular reference to business-to-business markets and services. Previously she was Head of Marketing for the Stationery

Office Ltd's print businesses. She has practical experience at senior management level in strategy, strategic marketing and planning and marketing research. She has also worked as a policy advisor to the Treasury and for the Speaker of the House of Commons.

Sanjaya Lall is based at Queen Elizabeth House, Oxford, and is University Lecturer in Development Economics and a Fellow of Green College at the University of Oxford. He has published widely on international investment, industrial and technological development, and trade policy in developing countries. He has been a staff member of the World Bank, and has consulted for many international organizations. His current research focuses on trade, technology policies and competitiveness, with particular reference to South East Asia and Sub-Saharan Africa.

Richard Lander is a Strategic Technology and Marketing Consultant, with clients in Europe and the USA. He worked for Dow Jones to develop and launch a digitally compressed video and information service for the financial community. He has written several books about technology. He has also worked as a journalist for *The Independent* newspaper, based in London. He has an MBA from City University and an MA from Cambridge.

Neil Mackinnon is a director of the independent economic research group Burke & Mackinnon, based in London. Previously, he was Chief Economist at Citibank. He has worked as an economist for several international financial institutions, and he was on the Economics team at the UK Treasury in the early 1980s.

Patrick Minford is Professor of Economics at Cardiff Business School, University of Wales. He was Professor of Economics at Liverpool University from 1976 to 1997, and remains Director of the Liverpool Research Group in Macroeconomics, which publishes monthly forecasts of all major economies, together with policy and investment advice. Between 1967 and 1976 he held economic positions in the Ministry of Finance, Malawi; Courtaulds Ltd; the UK Treasury; the UK Treasury's delegation to Washington, DC; Manchester University; and the UK's National Institute for Economic and Social Research. He was a member of the UK Monopolies and Mergers Commission from 1990 to 1996, and a member of the UK Treasury's Panel of Forecasters ('The Six Wise Men') from 1993 to 1996. He was awarded the CBE for services to economics in 1996.

Paul Ormerod is the author of two of the most influential recent books about economic theory – *The Death of Economics* and *Butterfly Economics* (1998). Both question the mechanistic assumptions behind much conventional economic thought. Paul Ormerod is currently chairman of Post-Orthodox Economics. He has been Head of the Economic Assessment Unit at *The Economist*; Director of Economics at the Henley Centre for Forecasting, a private UK business and economic think-tank; and a visiting Professor of Economics at London and Manchester Universities. He also has extensive first-hand experience in business, journalism and broadcasting.

Adrian Payne is Professor of Services and Relationship Marketing at Cranfield University, UK. Before joining Cranfield, he was on the faculty of the National Graduate School of Management at the University of Melbourne in Australia, where he was responsible for both the business policy and marketing subject areas of the MBA degree course. His current research and teaching interests are in strategic marketing and management in services organizations. He has published many papers in the areas of strategy, marketing and financial markets. Adrian Payne has practical experience in marketing, market research, corporate planning and general management. He has acted as a consultant to a wide range of organisations in the financial services, professional services, government and manufacturing sectors. He holds an MSc, MEd and PhD.

Jeremy Pink is Managing Editor of www.worldlyinvestor.com, an international personal finance online community. Worldly Investor is also located on America Online. He spent five years as Deputy Managing Editor of the Dow Jones-owned *Asia Business News* (ABN) in Singapore, and also worked as a consultant for Dow Jones in New York. He holds a BA in Economics from the Ohio State University and an MBA from Duke University.

Justin Urquhart Stewart is Corporate Development Director of Barclays Stockbrokers, and a Trustee of the Wider Share Ownership Trust. He studied law, specializing in international law and the European Community. He has worked in corporate finance in Africa and Singapore, and thereafter in electronic corporate cash management and information exchange in Europe. In 1986, he helped establish Broker Services Ltd, which has now become Barclays Stockbrokers Ltd, the UK's largest retail stockbroking and PEP administration firm. His primary role is to develop new business ideas and concepts for the future. Justin Urquhart Stewart is also a regular commentator in the media on market events and developments.

I
THE NEW
ECONOMICS

1

THE SUPPLY SIDE AND THE LIMITS TO INTERVENTION

PATRICK MINFORD

Professor Minford is one of the leading exponents of **supply-side** measures as a way to stimulate economic performance in both developed and undeveloped markets. He is a vigorous supporter in particular of liberalization of labour markets. Here, he takes the example of the UK economy during the government of Margaret Thatcher to demonstrate how changes in the employment market led eventually to a lower 'natural' level of unemployment, and to higher productivity (*see* **employment, minimum wage, Phillips Curve, Expectations-Adjusted Phillips Curve**). Professor Minford then examines the lessons for economies in a global context, and concludes that growth will be faster and productivity greater under the most laissez-faire regimes. To demonstrate this he subjects his empirical tables to a series of 'shocks' and concludes that for the developed economies, free market policies – combined with those that raise education and skill levels – are the best safeguard against rising unemployment, whilst for developing countries they provide the best hope for growth and expanding employment. (*See* **Heckscher-Ohlin Factor Proportions Theory, Laffer Curve.**)

Professor Minford's opinions are expressed in characteristically robust style; behind that is plenty of rigorous analysis and a good insight into how empirical data can be used to test and demonstrate aspects of economic theory. Recently there has been a significant slowdown in some of the previously well-performing Asian economies mentioned by Professor Minford, leading to scepticism about extreme laissez-faire policies. There is also increased interest in some European countries in a more corporatist approach to industry and economic management. So it is important to stress that the Minford approach is not accepted by all economists or policymakers. For different perspectives, read the essay by Neil Mackinnon ('The Limits to Global Markets'), and the more detailed analysis of 'World Trade and Development' in the essay by Dr Sanjaya Lall. Recent developments are examined in the 'regional' essays on Europe, Asia, and the United States, in 'The Global Context' section of the dictionary.

FREE MARKETS AND GLOBALIZATION

Many people complain about globalization and free markets: they impoverish western workers, they undermine governments' power to control their economies, and they widen the gap between rich and poorer countries. This essay argues the opposite. Globalization and free markets are creating huge opportunities for better living standards all over the world: for both rich countries and poor ones, for skilled and unskilled workers in both. The stress is on 'opportunities': for those who do not grasp them, it is a hard world indeed. Poor countries must open their markets, keep their costs low, create law and order and property rights, and erect an adequate infrastructure. If they do, they 'emerge'; if they do not, they can slide backwards, like so many parts of Africa. Poor western workers must get a job and use it as a launching pad for acquiring the many skills firms can offer them: skills (like the team skills in constructing an oven or a car) that are open to those without conventional 'training'. Rich countries must have flexible labour markets so that their workers get this chance. The disciplines go with the opportunities for all the players.

There is any amount of free market theory supporting this thinking. But many policy-makers nervously wonder whether the theory really works. In this article we examine two important pieces of evidence which suggest that it does. First, we will look at the UK's conversion from a lacklustre economy of three post-war decades to the relatively free market of today, with a better-performing economy and greater potential. Secondly, there is a discussion of the past few decades of experience in the world economy: of globalization. It sheds light on how poor countries emerge and how rich countries can thrive on the challenges. It shows that free market policies can work best both in poor and rich countries; and in particular, how trade, rather than aid, is the key to development in poor countries and to full employment in the rich economies.

THE UK EXPERIENCE

At least half the story of economic reform is that of regaining control of **inflation**. This implies the maintenance of responsible **monetary** and **fiscal** policy; and the abolition of any incomes policies which, besides being useless as a tool of inflation control, seriously distort market forces. The focus here, however, is on the **supply side** and its impact on growth and **employment**; macro policies are an essential background but they are not in themselves enough.

Under the Thatcher government, microeconomic policy covered a broad spectrum of measures designed to improve the efficiency of the UK economy during the period from 1980. They included moves toward privatization of state-controlled industries and the associated de-regulation, as well as tax changes designed to bring down marginal rates by reducing government expenditure (*see* **budget deficit**), and by reforming the tax structure towards greater neutrality. Within the two programmes the role of the labour market was of great significance. The labour market is the engine room of the economy; labour is the principal **factor of production** located in an economy with no real chance to move away (land is another, but far less important for the modern economy). The labour market limits the economy's potential both in quantity and quality. Other inputs such as **capital** and raw materials can be hired in to fit with what labour can profitably produce.

The UK economy had performed badly in terms of growth and was beginning to perform badly also in terms of unemployment by 1979 (*see* **stagflation**). This was connected with the stranglehold on industry of many competing labour unions whose demands were buttressed by rising benefits for those out of work and rising tax rates for those in work. It was the break-up of this labour market stranglehold that was the key to the success of the Thatcher microeconomic reforms. The supply-side programme had as its main objective the raising of the economy's potential growth per head, and as a further objective the increase of **consumer** sovereignty and related improvement in the use of the economy's output. If the national statistics of the quality of output are to be believed, then the value of output at constant prices should reflect improvements in the use of output, i.e. in the benefits each unit of output provides. The only omission would be any gains in consumer surplus due to the reduction in distortions such as taxes; unfortunately we have no general direct measures of this so we will have to ignore it in favour of straight output measures.

Arithmetically, we can split potential growth per head gains into gains in:

- output per worker (productivity), multiplied by
- working age population as a share of the total population (demographic and retirement trends), multiplied by
- worker supply as a share of the working age population (work participation), multiplied by
- employment as a share of worker supply (one minus the unemployment rate).

Government policy affects all of these, and the Thatcher programme was designed to raise each measure. Here we concentrate on the first and last, where the changes were most dramatic.

PRODUCTIVITY

We can see a considerable effect on behaviour post-1979 on a wide variety of measures benchmarked against major competitor countries. This benchmarking is necessary because it allows for the opportunities available to all countries from the general environment of technology change.

We can see a clear improvement for manufacturing productivity in the comparison with Germany (Fig. 1). Tables 1 and 2, taken from

Fig. 1 Manufacturing productivity in UK and Germany

Comparative levels of output/employee in manufacturing (UK level in each year = 100)

	1870	1913	1938	1950	1973	1989
UK	100	100	100	100	100	100
USA	204	213	192	263	215	177
Japan	n/a	24	42	20	95	143
Sweden	n/a	102	100	118	128	121
France	n/a	79	76	84	114	115
Italy	n/a	59	49	68	96	111
Germany	100	119	107	96	119	105

Growth of output per hour worked (% per year)

	1960–73	1973–79	1979–89	1989–94
UK	4.14	1.01	4.13	3.95
USA	3.28	1.41	2.34	2.47
Japan	9.59	5.15	4.58	4.18
Sweden	6.25	2.65	2.53	2.87
France	6.55	4.39	3.28	3.04
Italy	6.14	5.60	3.86	3.91
Germany	5.71	4.21	1.83	2.22

Sources: Broadberry (1996) and Oulton (1995), cited in Crafts (1997).

Table 1 Labour productivity in manufacturing

Total factor productivity (TFP) growth in the business sector (% p.a.)

	1960–73			1979–94	
1	Japan	5.5	1	Ireland	2.6
2	Portugal	5.4	2	Finland	2.5
3	Ireland	4.6	3	Spain	1.7
4	Italy	4.4	4	Portugal	1.6
5	Finland	4.0	5	UK	1.5
6	Belgium	3.8	6	Denmark	1.3
7	France	3.7	7	France	1.3
8	Netherlands	3.4	8	Belgium	1.2
9	Spain	3.2	9	Japan	1.1
10	Austria	3.1	10	Netherlands	1.1
11	Germany	2.6	11	Sweden	1.0
12	UK	2.6	12	Austria	0.9
13	Greece	2.5	13	Italy	0.9
14	USA	2.5	14	Australia	0.8
15	Denmark	2.3	15	USA	0.5
16	Australia	2.2	16	Germany	0.4
17	Switzerland	2.1	17	Canada	−0.1
18	Norway	2.0	18	Norway	−0.1
19	Sweden	2.0	19	Switzerland	−0.2
20	Canada	1.9	20	Greece	−0.3

Source: OECD (1996), cited in Crafts (1997).

Table 2 Total factor productivity (TFP) growth in the business sector

Crafts (1997), show improvement compared with a wide group of OECD countries across both manufacturing (Table 1, output per man), and for the non-government (business) sector (Table 2, total factor productivity).

Attributing this improvement to changes in environment is not easy. An attempt has been made by Bean and Crafts (1996) in a statistical analysis of 137 industries' behaviour from 1954 to 1986. They find that the power of multiple labour unions is the major factor responsible for poor productivity; and that the Thatcher union laws and related developments reduced this power virtually to zero. Furthermore this reduction seems to increase the growth rate of productivity, not just its level. Hence we should expect to see this higher growth maintained.

Another element they identify is the shock effect of the 1980–81 recession and the accompanying shift of government and company attitudes towards cushioning labour redundancies. Whereas previously the government had often become involved in efforts to contain redundancies, the new government refused any involvement, preferring to give help instead for relocation and retraining in particularly badly-hit regions. This signalled clearly that efficiency rather than job-preservation would guide employment behaviour; unions accordingly lost influence and power to hold up changing working practices.

EMPLOYMENT

In early 1993 UK unemployment again all but reached the 3 million mark – 10.3 per cent of the labour force. A number of economists suggested at the time that it would not fall much below that rate in the foreseeable future. The implication of such a view was that the UK 'equilibrium' or natural rate was of this order (*see* **Phillips Curve**, **Expectations-adjusted Phillips Curve**). Even in May 1984, when unemployment had fallen to 9.4 per cent, a number of economists (for example, Metcalf, 1984, and Barrell *et al.*, 1984) continued to take a pessimistic view of the natural rate. By mid-1997 unemployment had fallen to 5.5 per cent and the sceptical economists of that time had to abandon their views. Nevertheless few believed that unemployment can fall much further without triggering higher inflation. However, the evidence suggests strongly that not only have the reform policies been responsible for the fall so far, but also that this fall has substantially further to go.

This alternative view is based on the work of my research group in Cardiff and Liverpool, which is embodied in the Liverpool model of the

UK. In brief we would argue that the economic reforms of the 1980s created a new flexibility in the labour market which pushed the natural rate down sharply from the peak of nearly 11 per cent it reached early in that decade.

The natural rate of unemployment in the Liverpool model is calculated as the interaction between pressures driving up wage demands and the wages that employers can offer while still remaining profitable: both wage amounts are defined in terms of purchasing power (i.e. adjusted for inflation), since that is what matters to both parties. At the point where these two forces equate (supply = demand) we obtain an 'equilibrium' inflation-adjusted (or real) wage and employment rate. This can therefore be thought of as the situation in which employment is (just) profitable for firms and wages are (just) worthwhile for workers. The idea can be illustrated in a single supply and demand diagram: Fig. 2. In this diagram demand corresponds to what firms would want when the economy is in its normal state (that is in practice where the balance of payments on current account is not in deficit and where inflation is not unexpectedly high or low). The factors involved are familiar: productivity, taxes on employers, indirect taxes, and the level of world trade (which means more can be sold abroad profitably).

The other curve in the diagram is labour supply, where the factors are less obvious. Unemployment benefits in particular have a direct effect in raising demands in so far as they compete with wages of low-paid workers. But there is a further subtle effect: they act as a floor on wage demands, creating a rigidity downwards in wages. This prevents

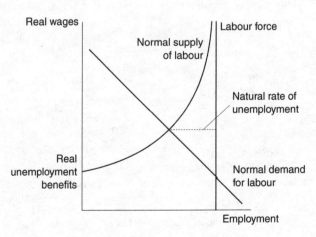

Fig. 2

9

adjustment (or 'flexibility') of wages in response to new shocks requiring wage falls: instead of wages falling, employment falls and unemployment rises. Other factors on the labour supply side include the effect of union power in raising wage demands and taxes on workers (which means that more has to be earned to compete with benefits).

Figure 3a shows the overall natural rate of unemployment we obtain over the last two decades from the model from the interaction of all these factors. From its 11 per cent peak in 1981–83 it has fallen to around 2 per cent.

What were the constituent contributions from the factors we have enumerated to this natural rate estimate? Figure 3b shows the effects, variable by variable. The flat profile of benefits during the 1970s rules them out as having contributed to changes in the natural rate during that decade. However, in the 1980s sharp rises in rents for public housing, fully compensated in unemployment benefits, but only partially in in-work benefits, substantially raised the benefit package. Besides this contributory role, the key role of benefits is in giving wage demands (along the **supply curve** of labour) their relative rigidity, arising, as discussed above, from benefits creating a 'benefits floor' for low-wage workers. The main elements producing change are unionization, followed by taxes of various sorts. The former rises steadily to 1980 before steadily falling back. The tax rates moved in largely offsetting ways until 1983 when their net effect was to reduce unemployment, led by falling employment taxes on labour. Besides these we can see that the trend elements (productivity and world trade trends) produce a tendency to improvement which is reversed by the serious world

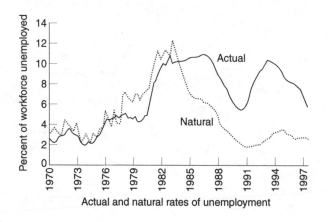

Fig. 3a

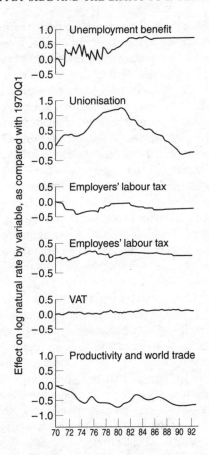

Fig. 3b

recession of the early 1980s. Thereafter the ground is gradually re-captured over the rest of the 1980s.

One way to summarize this story is to say that trends in productivity and world markets managed after the global recession of 1982 to dominate (just) the effect of rising benefits, while 1980s supply-side influences reducing labour union power and lowering taxes had further reduced equilibrium unemployment by 1991 to below the level of 1970, restoring it (at around 2 per cent) well towards the natural rate of the 1950s (put by the annual model at about 1 per cent).

Ultimately, a low natural rate of unemployment depends on policies that permit wages to find a level equal to productivity, especially at the bottom end of the pay scale, where benefits and ideas of social justice put an artificial floor beneath them. These policies are politically hard to implement in any country with a tradition of Christian and social democracy, let alone of socialism or communism. In the United States, with its tradition of decentralized liberalism there has never, except during the Great Depression (*see* **Keynes**) been much pressure to pursue such policies. One might add that the 'productivity' just referred to could be interpreted in trade-theoretic terms as the 'equalized wage for equivalent labour' of the **Heckscher-Ohlin**-Samuelson (HOS) model, which we will proceed to make use of shortly. As we will argue, the downward pressure of low wage costs in 'emerging markets' across the world makes the policy dilemma of European governments more acute; that is true even for a potentially emerging market economy, since for its traded industries to compete internationally its wage costs must reflect these pressures. Yet if social and union intervention puts a floor below wages, the result will be unemployment. In effect the traded sector will contract (or fail to expand) until the marginal industry can pay these wages. Meanwhile, because these wages are well above rural living standards, they attract immigration from rural areas; these immigrants will in effect search for long periods, putting up with immigrants' hardships, for the chance of such good jobs. But the strength of regulation and union intervention prevent wages falling to reflect this excess supply.

The irony for an emerging market is that the global opportunities from free market policies are virtually limitless. By allowing wage costs to fall, the traded industries would expand to create jobs in huge numbers while the attraction of excess urban immigration would fall. Unemployment would drop back to normally acceptable rates. We see this from the success (for much of the 1990s) of emerging market economies like Korea, Singapore, and China.

In the next section we expand on the question of just what these international processes (know as globalization) have been in the past two decades, and how they can be explained in terms of trade and development theory (for a full account, see Minford *et al.*, 1997). We begin by describing the main trends of the past two decades which require explanation; and then describe the way they can be accommodated within a traditional HOS model of the world economy (a model similar in spirit is used by both Wood in his 1994 book, and by Rowthorn, 1995). In particular we consider how far the process of 'emergence' among developing countries and technological bias against unskilled workers in developed countries may have contributed to these trends.

THE LAST TWO DECADES: A GLOBAL PERSPECTIVE

Table 3, left-hand column, shows the key facts from 1970–90 for 'North' and 'South', expressed as average change per annum over the period. (The 'North' is the OECD; the 'South' is all developing countries, that is non-OECD countries except the former Soviet bloc. While some of these are clearly 'developing', their history within the free-market world is too recent and their data too patchy to include.)

In the North there has been deindustrialization: the share of manufacturing in GDP has fallen. In the South there has been industrialization largely at the expense of agriculture. Notice too how

Change p.a. 1970–1990	Actual	Simulations 1	2	3	4	5	6	7	8
North									
Unskilled/skilled:									
Wages	−0.9	−0.75	−1.08	+0.25	+1.84	+0.61	+0.03	+0.28	−0.355
Employment	−4.2	−0.48	−0.66	−0.34	−2.89	−0.43	+0.02	+0.15	+0.019
Shares of GDP:									
Manufacturing	−0.22	−1	+0.3	−0.09	−0.45	+2.19	−0.01	−0.16	−0.049
Services	+0.195	+0.1	−0.2	0	+0.47	+1.07	−0.05	−0.48	+0.12
Primary	−0.075	+0.92	−0.07	+0.08	−0.07	−3.27	+0.06	+0.63	−0.048
Non-traded	+0.1	−0.02	−0.03	+0.01	+0.05	0	0	+0.01	−0.012
Unemployment									
Unskilled	+0.4	+0.1	+0.12	+0.47	−0.18	−0.13	0	−0.02	−0.314
Total	+0.2	−0.22	−0.05	+0.38	+0.1	−0.02	0	+0.03	−0.285
Living standard	+2.2	+0.25	+0.29	−0.32	+0.14	+0.31	0	0	+0.786
South									
Unskilled/skilled:									
Wages	+2.3	+0.76	−1.07	+0.26	+1.83	+0.5	+0.03	−1.04	−0.096
Employment	+1.3	+0.47	−0.11	+0.03	+0.18	−0.08	+0.12	−0.08	−0.004
Shares of GDP:									
Manufacturing	+0.1	+1.31	−0.48	+0.16	+0.66	−2.44	−0.11	+0.18	−0.058
Services	+0.14	+0.05	+0.36	−0.06	−0.69	−1.63	0	+0.69	+0.046
Primary	−0.55	−1.23	+0.07	−0.09	+0.13	+4.37	−0.21	−0.86	+0.002
Non-traded	+0.36	−0.13	+0.05	−0.01	−0.1	−0.3	+0.32	−0.01	+0.01
Living standard	+1.1	+0.32	−0.01	0	+0.02	+0.12	+0.12	+0.01	−0.008
World									
Relative prices:									
Manufacturing/services	−0.8	−0.27	−0.39	+0.09	+0.67	+0.06	+0.01	+0.11	−0.042
Primary/services	−0.3	−0.16	−0.3	+0.06	+0.54	−0.35	−0.01	+0.1	−0.032
North trade balances/GDP:									
Manufacturers	−0.025	−0.93	+0.32	−0.11	−0.43	+1.93	−0.01	−0.12	+0.047
Services	+0.005	−0.01	−0.26	+0.04	+0.5	+1.31	−0.05	−0.51	−0.018
Primary	+0.02	+0.94	−0.06	+0.07	−0.07	−3.23	+0.06	+0.63	−0.02

Simulations
1 Simulated effect of 0.5% p.a. rise in Southern manufacturing productivity
2 Simulated effect of 1% p.a. fall in Northern unskilled wage share across all sectors
3 Simulated effect of 1% p.a. rise in Northern unemployment benefit rate
4 Simulated effect of 1% p.a. fall in Northern unskilled labour supply due to rise in higher education
5 Simulated effect of 0.5% p.a. rise in Southern primary productivity
6 Simulated effect of 0.5% p.a. rise in Southern non-traded productivity
7 Simulated effect of 0.5% p.a. rise in Southern service productivity
8 Simulated effect of 0.5% p.a. rise in Northern general productivity (distributed 0.5 manufacturing, 0.28% primary, 0.625% services, 0.395% non-traded)

* All changes are expressed as % p.a. (average 1970–90), except shares of GDP and Northern trade balances/GDP (% of GDP, change p.a.) and unemployment (% of relevant labour force, change p.a.)

Table 3 Actual data, 1979–90 and simulated shock effects

non-traded production has expanded there; also the large shift to traded services.

In the North, wages of the skilled have risen virtually across the board. We define 'skilled' here as those with higher education (preliminary university education or equivalent). This seems appropriate in view of the emphasis, in modern technology, on knowledge-based, rather than craft-based, skill. 'Unskilled' then becomes the rest of the labour force. The data come from Nickell and Bell, 1995, and Nickell, 1995, gathered by them from other OECD economists.

In the South, unskilled real wages appear to have risen both relative to skilled and in absolute terms. However, we have no data on skilled wages as such; we have had to infer skilled wages from per capita GDP, assuming this grows at the same rate as average real wages. Unskilled wages we have identified with general manufacturing wages. Our ratio of skilled to unskilled wages is consequently of doubtful accuracy.

Employment of unskilled workers has fallen everywhere in the North relative to skilled. Skilled employment averaged about 14 per cent of the total in the North as whole at the start of the period but had risen to around 30 per cent by the end. In the South if we treat manufacturing employment as a proxy for unskilled, we find that it has risen both relatively to total employment and in absolute terms. As with wages however we have no data on skilled employment directly, and have inferred it from total employment. Again our ratio of skilled to unskilled employment is of doubtful accuracy. Per capita GDP growth in the North has been roughly double that in the South.

Unemployment rates among the least skilled have risen everywhere in the North. Absolute rates of unemployment are in the low or high teens across the OECD, virtually without exception. Unemployment rates among skilled workers, again as measured by upper-secondary education or above, have risen as well, so that overall unemployment rates have increased.

There has been a rise in the average skill-intensity of output in the North. This of course must be so, given the large rise in overall relative skilled employment cited above. But it is far from clear that it reflects a rise in skill-intensity in given sectors over time, if the nature of firms' activity is controlled for. Data on the skill-intensity of output in the South are scarce. In both North and South there is the possibility of an aggregation bias, as the nature of output, even by sectors, has changed.

World prices of manufactures exported by less developed countries (LDCs) have fallen relative to those of services and complex manufactures ('services' here), as shown in Fig. 4. Some uncertainty

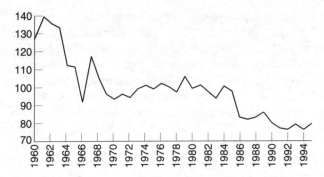

Fig. 4 LDC manufacturing prices relative to services and complex
manufactures

surrounds this index in the years up to 1975, owing to the effects of sharp
movements in non-ferrous metals prices (Rowthorn, 1996, Athukorala,
1993, Sarkar and Singer, 1993). Our index gives an estimate of this trend
from 1960 that is in the middle of this range of possibilities.

Primary product prices rose in real terms in the 1970s and fell in the
1980s: this applies particularly to crude petroleum, but it also applies, if
far less dramatically, to other products. The net effect of these swings
has been an overall increase of about a third in real oil prices but a real
drop of some 40 per cent in other primary product prices. Thus, depending exactly on how one weights these two components one could say that
for primary products as a whole there has been little net real change
since 1970 (see Fig. 5).

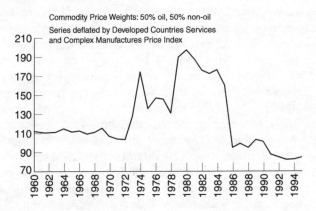

Fig. 5 Real commodity prices

Throughout this period, the North has been a net exporter to the South of complex manufactures and services, while the South has been a net exporter to the North of primary products. During the 1980s the North switched from being a net exporter of basic manufactures to being a net importer. This shift in **comparative advantage** goes hand in hand with a huge growth in total trade between North and South, as a percentage of Northern GDP: the South became much more important as a trading partner for the North. In particular, Southern exports of manufactures (basic and complex) have risen from a negligible 0.2 per cent of Northern GDP in 1970 to 2 per cent in 1992, accounting for over 10 per cent of all Northern visible imports.

SIMULATION

To explain these facts we use a two-country model of North and South. The basic idea in our HOS model is that these have different stocks of resources, fixed, so to speak, within their borders: notably land and labour, which we may divide into unskilled (or with no skills that are in special demand) and skilled. Capital and raw materials do not properly belong in this category because they can be bought or sold on an international market.

These resources are then employed in competitive industries which have fully exploited all increasing returns to scale; hence each has constant costs and its price is driven to equality with those costs. We identify the non-traded sector and three traded industries – primary, basic manufacturing, and complex manufacturing – which we lump together with traded services as being skilled-labour intensive. HOS assumes full employment, but this can be relaxed: if you are willing to pay a resource more to be idle than it is worth at work then you will get unemployment. We allow for this in theory, so that the 'supply' of the resource will not be given merely by physical availability but also affected by such social policy. In particular, unemployment depends on the relation between wages and benefits (the social reservation wage).

Table 3 shows in the left-hand column all the key facts reviewed above about the world economy. To account for trends in the world economy, we simulated the model to find the effects of various likely shocks over the period: the effects of each such shock are shown in the columns 1–8 of Table 3. We identified the following as in combination producing the best fit (accounting for about 80 per cent of the variation in the relevant fact of the period):

- 0.8 per cent p.a. rise in Southern productivity in manufacturing (the 'trade' or 'emerging market' shock of low-wage competition) – col. 1 effects times 1.6;
- 1.5 per cent fall in the factor share of unskilled labour in all Northern sectors (the 'technology bias' shock of new technology displacing unskilled workers in favour of skilled, mostly through the computer) – col. 2 effects times 1.6;
- 0.8 per cent p.a. rise in general Northern productivity – col. 8 effects times 1.7;
- 1.75 per cent p.a. rise in Northern benefits (and equivalent 'social protection policies, such as practised especially on the European Continent) – col. 3 effects times 1.8;
- 0.62 per cent p.a. fall in Northern unskilled labour supply – due to the spread of higher education in the North – col. 4 effects times 0.6;
- other Southern productivity growth: 0.4 per cent p.a. in primary, 1.5 per cent p.a. in non-traded (due we think to 'leapfrogging' of technology as services like phones, utilities, and infrastructure are installed in the South) and 0.7 per cent p.a. in services – cols. 5, 6, 7 effects, times 0.8, 3.0, and 1.4 per cent p.a. respectively .

The whole thing implies that both trade and technology play a large and significant role in explaining Northern labour market problems. For example, two-fifths of the collapse in Northern unskilled employment is explained by these two factors (with higher education explaining the bulk of the rest). And of that two-fifths just under 60 per cent is due to technology, just over 40 per cent due to trade. If we take the fall in relative unskilled wages, the downward pressure exerted by these two factors is in the same proportion – 60/40. The same is true of unskilled employment, where the rest of the explanation is due to the effect of benefit-equivalent changes, partially offset by higher education in shrinking unskilled supply.

POLICY CONCLUSIONS

Our elaborate calculations show that the emergence of developing countries and their low-wage competition has on its own produced a huge impact on the wages of unskilled workers in the North, both relative to skilled and in absolute terms. An impact of a similar size has come from technological change – again, biased against unskilled workers. But these impacts have been more than offset by other developments: general productivity growth in the North and the expansion of higher education. Looking to the future, we have speculated that, so low is the pool of unskilled labour now, normally rising demand for it in the non-traded sector (the indirect effect of general productivity growth being fastest in the traded sector) may start to provide a powerful offset.

However that may be, the policy implications for a western country are clear. Policies that stimulate productivity growth are helpful. Not only do they raise unskilled real wages, but they also reduce unemployment, both generally and particularly among the unskilled. Such policies are those of free markets, as among much other experience that of the UK shows well.

Also helpful are policies that raise higher education and skill levels. These, by inducing scarcity among unskilled workers, lower their unemployment and raise their real wages, while improving living standards overall.

Policies that raise social protection are damaging. They raise unemployment not merely among unskilled workers but overall. They lower living standards overall, even if they do slightly raise the real wages absolutely of unskilled workers who retain their jobs. These policies have their effect by increasing the inflexibility of the labour market. When we apply these ideas to the policies adopted on the European continent, we find that is no real surprise that in the face of the severe shocks to the world environment of the past two decades, European unemployment has risen so sharply, and that European productivity growth has slowed down. Even though there has been a large rise in higher education, this has been accompanied by policies of heavy state regulation, intervention, taxation, and in particular strong social protection in the labour market.

When we turn to potentially emerging economies, particularly in Africa, we find similarly that policies of heavy regulation, social protection, and unionization, are in many cases blighting the possibilities of rapid employment growth, falling unemployment, and emerging market status. In effect, although explicit wage costs are as yet quite low, there is strong pressure to raise them. In addition the strong power of unions embodies a high implicit cost for inward investors, namely the risk of expropriation by unions through the strike weapon. Yet experience in both rich and poor countries – and other emerging market economies – shows that alternative policies are well within these countries' grasps, once people understand the trade-offs involved. It would be a tragedy if such potentially promising situations were turned into yet more socialist debacles.

FURTHER READING

Athukorala, P., 'Manufactured exports from developing countries and their terms of trade: a reexamination of the Sarkar-Singer results', *World Development*, **21** (1993), pp. 1607–13.

Baker, Colin (1997) 'State of Emergency: crisis in Central Africa, Nyasaland 1959–60', *International Library of African Studies*, no. **7** (1997).

Barrell R., Pain, N., and Young, G., 'Structural differences in European labour markets' (1994), ch. 7, pp. 214–57.

Bean, Charles, and Crafts, Nicholas, 'British economic growth since 1945 – relative decline . . . and renaissance?', *Economic Growth in Europe since 1945*, eds. N. Crafts and G. Toniolo (Cambridge University Press, 1996).

Bernard, A. B., and Jensen, J. B., 'Exporters, skills upgrading and the wage gap', (Center for Economic Studies, Bureau of the Census, Washington DC, research paper 94–13 (1994)).

Crafts, Nicholas, *Britain's relative economic decline 1870–1995* (Social Market Foundation, 1997).

Feenstra, R. C., and Hanson, G., 'Foreign investment, outsourcing and relative wages' [1995], forthcoming in *Political Economy of trade policy: essays in honour of Jagdish Bhagwati* (MIT Press).

Gundlach, E., and Nunnenkampf, P., 'Globalisation and structural unemployment', *Konjunkturpolitik*, **40** (1994), pp. 202–25.

Heckscher, E., 'The effect of foreign trade on the distribution of income' [1919], *Economisk Tidskrift*, pp. 497–512; reprinted as Chapter 13 in *AEA Readings in the theory of International Trade* (Blakiston, Philadelphia 1949), pp. 272–300.

Lawson, N., *The View from No.11* (Bantam Press, 1991).

Lawrence, R. Z., and Slaughter, M. J., 'International trade and American wages in the 1980s: Giant sucking sound or small hiccup?', *Brookings Papers: Microeconomics 2* (1993), pp. 161–226.

Metcalf, D., 'Transformation of British industrial relations?', in Barrell (1994), ch. 4, pp. 126–57.

Minford, P., 'Deregulation and unemployment – the UK experience', *Swedish Economic Policy Review*, **1**(1) (1994), pp. 113–49.

Minford, P., *Markets Not Stakes* (Orion, 1998).

Minford, P., Riley, J., and Nowell, E., 'Trade, technology and labour markets in the world economy, 1970-90: a computable general equilibrium analysis' [1997], forthcoming in *Journal of Development Studies*; earlier version, CEPR working paper (1996) entitled 'The Elixir of development'.

Minford, P., Sprague, A., Matthews, K. G. P., and Marwaha, S., 'The Liverpool Macroeconomic model of the United Kingdom', *Economic Modelling*, **1**, Jan. 1984.

Minford, P., Matthews, K. G. P., and Rastogi, A., 'A quarterly version of the Liverpool model of the UK', Liverpool Research Group in Macroeconomics, working paper 90/06 (University of Liverpool, 1990).

Nickell, S., and Bell, B., 'The collapse of demand for the unskilled and unemployment across the OECD', *Oxford Review of Economic Policy*, **11**(l), Spring 1995, pp. 40–62.

Nickell, S., 'The distribution of wages and unemployment across skill groups', mimeo, Institute of Economics and Statistics, Oxford, December 1995.

Nunnenkamp, P., Gundlach, E., and Agarwal, J. P., *Globalisation of production and markets*, Kieler Studien, Kiel Institute of World Economics (J. C. B. Mohr (Paul Siebeck) Tubingen, 1994).

Ohlin, B., *Interregional and International Trade* (Harvard University Press, 1933).

Rowthorn, R. E., 'A simulation model of North-South trade', *UNCTAD Review 1995* (United Nations, New York and Geneva, 1995).

Rowthorn, R. E., 'Replicating the experience of the NIEs on a large scale', mimeo, Economics Faculty, University of Cambridge, May 1996.

Samuelson, P. A., 'International Trade and the Equalisation of Factor Prices', *Economic Journal*, **58** (1948), pp. 163–84.

Sarkar, P., and Singer, H. W., 'Manufacture – Manufacture Terms of trade deterioration: a reply', *World Development*, **21** (1993), pp. 1617–20.

Stolper, W., and Samuelson, P. A., 'Protection and real wages', *Review of Economic Studies*, (1941), pp. 58–73.

Thatcher, M., *The Downing Street Years* (HarperCollins, 1993).

Wood, A., *North-South Trade, Employment and Inequality – changing fortunes in a skill-driven world* (Clarendon, 1994).

2

WORLD TRADE AND DEVELOPMENT

SANJAYA LALL*

This essay examines whether conventional trade theory can explain how some developing countries grow more effectively than others. Dr Lall's work is a case study of the performance in exported manufactures of various regions and countries. He tests whether conventional trade theories stand up to the empirical evidence of the past few decades. Trade theories begin with the theory of **comparative advantage,** which owes much to the economist David **Ricardo**, and the later **Heckscher-Ohlin factor proportions theory**, as developed by Samuelson and Stolper. Readers who are not familiar with these notions might precede a reading of the essay with a look at the relevant entries.

Dr Lall provides an insight into how the basic theories may be developed to include a role for governments, market failures, and various levels of technology. Or, conversely, how the conventional theories still hold when such factors are allowed for.

We have included the essay particularly because it provides an excellent insight into how economic theory can be subjected to empirical analysis, and because it also represents a good example of the kind of empirical study which is common in today's economics. In fact it originally appeared – in longer and more detailed form – as an economic paper, and we are grateful to the publishers for allowing us to reprint extracts here. It should be read alongside the essay on Asian economics by Jeremy Pink, 'Asia: The Lessons for Economics', and also as a contrast to the empirical analysis and conclusions of Patrick Minford in his essay 'The Supply Side and the Limits to Intervention', parts of which also deal with developing countries in the context of **supply-side economics.**

TRADE AND DEVELOPMENT: A STUDY OF MANUFACTURING EXPORTS BY DEVELOPING COUNTRIES

Developing countries are rapidly increasing their shares of world trade in manufactured products, signifying major changes in the global

* The author is grateful to the World Bank for providing trade data from the UN COMTRADE database and for helping tabulate the figures. All the information presented here has been processed from this data by the author.

location of industrial production. Traditionally, they have been exporters of primary and resource-based products; more recently, they have become large exporters of simple labour-intensive manufactures. Their **comparative advantage** in these activities is not difficult to explain. Natural resources provide it for primary products and processes. For labour-intensive products, their advantage appears to be dealt with adequately by conventional trade theory (*see* **Heckscher-Ohlin factor proportions theory**), where comparative advantage is determined by the relative endowments of labour and capital (plus human capital, i.e. skilled labour, in later versions). Developing countries have relatively more labour than capital, and more unskilled than skilled labour: thus, under assumptions of **perfect competition** and efficient markets, their comparative advantage will lie in activities that use more (unskilled) labour. Despite its simplifying assumptions (such as the absence of **economies of scale**, no product differentiation, equal access between firms and countries to technology, no learning costs, similar tastes, no international factor mobility, and so on), the Heckscher-Ohlin model and its variants appears to capture this particular reality. Whether or not the model is a correct representation of reality is another matter, to which we turn later in this essay.

At first sight, received theory explains less well two aspects of export performance by developing countries: their growing role in exports of complex industrial products, and the enormous differences between them in export growth. On the first, many of the fastest growing exports from the developing world involve large scales and advanced organization of production, high levels of skill and capital-intensity, sophisticated technologies, brand differentiation and close linkages with developed supplier chains. The activities concerned tend to have high entry barriers, fast moving and difficult (often closely guarded) technologies and significant marketing costs. Simple wage cost advantages, especially in unskilled labour, do not count for much here. Such exports are traditionally the preserve of advanced industrialized countries, and trade theory posits that developing countries cannot have a comparative advantage here. Yet this is where they are increasing their market shares fastest.

On the second aspect, export dynamism is highly concentrated and differentiated in the developing world. A handful of countries dominate exports of both simple and complex manufactured products, and there are striking differences in the evolution of the technological 'content' of their export bundles between the successful exporters. Some of these differences in overall export growth may be explained by trade strategies: many countries pursued inward-oriented strategies that fostered inefficient activities and discouraged efficient ones from exporting. However, there still remains a great deal of unexplained inter-country variation in both export success and composition. Trade liberalization (*see* **trade bodies**) over the past decade or more has not led to widespread growth of manufactured exports (labour intensive or other) from low wage countries. Nor have all important exporters changed the structures of their exports at the same pace: in some there has been stagnation, even regression, over time. Differences in the technological composition of exports have been accompanied by different roles for the main actors involved in export activity. Why such variation between countries with roughly similar 'endowments'?

Several explanations are possible. One may be simply statistical: what appear to be complex exports may reflect simple labour-intensive operations undertaken in developing countries in advanced products, with the technology-intensive processes remaining in industrialized countries – the Heckscher-Ohlin model applies. But this would 'explain' only a part of the phenomenon; there are also many advanced processes being used in export activities in the developing world. Important theoretical issues thus remain. On the theoretical front, one answer may be to differentiate between the stages of growth of developing countries (Balassa, 1986), rather than lumping them together, as some analyses do, as an undifferentiated mass. Factor accumulation with rizing incomes within the group then changes comparative advantage towards more capital and skill-intensive products; the most dynamic exporters of complex products will be those with the highest incomes. Another may be to introduce international factor mobility: with capital mobility, relative capital-labour endowments would no longer determine comparative advantage – the main determinants would be other immobile factors needed to complement physical capital: the main one proposed recently is human capital (Wood, 1997), but there is a long tradition in the Heckscher-Ohlin literature of using skills as a variable (Keesing, 1966).

These approaches stay within the broad assumption of 'efficient markets' of traditional trade theory. Others discard this and introduce a variety of factors that lead to increasing returns, externalities and market failures. One set is 'strategic' trade theory and 'new economic geography'. This uses economies of scale, cumulative causation and agglomeration externalities to explain which countries enjoy comparative advantage (Krugman, 1986, 1991, Puga and Venables, 1997, Venables, 1996a, 1996b). Another deals directly with how technology is absorbed and used in developing countries. This argues that having access to technology is not the same as its efficient use (the general assumption of trade theory): there may be costly, prolonged and uncertain learning processes involved, with widespread spillovers (even 'collective learning' between groups of firms), imperfect factor markets and severe coordination problems (Stiglitz, 1996, 1997, Rodrik, 1996, and, as applied to developing countries, Lall, 1992) (*see* 'Technology' by Richard Lander). Thus, comparative advantage can *still* reflect the different abilities of countries to overcome these deficiencies in the realization of scale, agglomeration, learning or coordination economies. These approaches complicate the prediction of comparative advantage, since history plays an important role, as does government policy. In the presence of market failures, appropriate policy to overcome failures can create 'genuine' comparative advantage rather than temporary distortions (that promote exports by subsidies).

This essay argues that 'strategic' trade theory and 'the new economic geography' takes us furthest in understanding the patterns of comparative advantage in the developing world; further than conventional trade theory. The next section reviews recent manufactured export performance by different technological categories and by different developing regions and countries. This is followed by a summary of the findings and a review of the explanations.

PATTERNS OF INDUSTRIAL EXPORT SUCCESS

We start by looking at world exports over 1980–96. Figure 1 shows that manufactures were the main component of trade and the driver of its growth; primary products stagnated through the period. The early 80s saw little growth (2.3 per cent p.a. for manufactures and a slight decline in totals); the next 10 years witnessed a sustained boom (12 per cent p.a. for manufactures), though rates of growth fell in the 1990s.

World trade in manufactures, at least as reported in UN data (which has several missing countries), is almost fully accounted for by industrialized and developing countries; the former socialist countries contributed 1.1 per cent in 1980 and 1.7 per cent in 1996. Developing countries increased their manufactured exports rapidly over this period, from \$102 bn to \$835 bn, their share rizing from 9.8 per cent to 23.0 per cent. Their rates of growth (Fig. 2) were correspondingly higher: 14.0 per cent for developing as compared to 6.6 per cent for the industrial countries. This holds for each sub-period, except for the last year (1995–96) when there was a significant slowdown in world trade and the

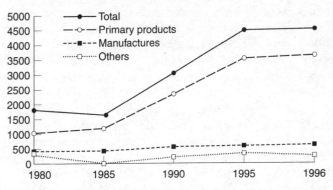

Fig. 1 Values of world exports ($ billion)

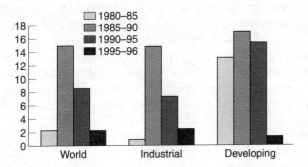

Fig. 2 Growth rates of manufactured exports

developing world fell behind the industrial countries. (As shown below, the brunt of the slowdown was borne by Asia, particularly Thailand, leading to a sudden rise in the trade deficit and precipitating the financial crisis – *see also* 'Asia: The Lessons for Economics' by Jeremy Pink.)

Let us now classify exports by their technological characteristics. This is not a straightforward task. The trade data used can conceal variations in technologies between sub-groups. The technological features of identical product in one country may differ from that in another, depending on the stage and nature of production (e.g. semi-conductors may be a high-technology export from Korea but relatively low-technology in Malaysia, where final assembly and testing take place). Technological characteristics may change over time, and differences between categories may be difficult to define precisely. And so on. Even taking these caveats into account, however, the data can give a reasonably broad picture of technological patterns. Precision is not a major consideration here, and we try to take some of the important qualifications into account.

While many technological classifications are used, there is general agreement on the broad distribution of activities. The OECD (1987) proposes a classification based on resource-intensity, scale-intensity, labour-intensity, differentiation and relationship to the science base (for an application to developing countries see Guerrieri, 1993). Many simply divide products into 'low' and 'high' technology groups according to their R&D spending or use of scientists and engineers. We use a four-fold categorization: resource-based (RB), low technology (LT), medium technology (MT) and high technology (HT) manufactures. RB products include processed foods and tobacco, simple wood products, refined petroleum products, dyes, leather (not leather products), rubber products and organic chemicals. LT products include labour-intensive manufactures like textiles, garments, footwear, toys, simple metal and plastic products, furniture and glassware. MT products are those with complex but not fast-moving technologies (though some entail considerable engineering and design effort): automotive products, chemicals, industrial machinery and simple consumer electronics. HT products include fine chemicals and pharmaceuticals, complex electrical and electronic machinery, aircraft and precision instruments.

Figure 3 shows the distribution of these categories in world manufactured trade and Fig. 4 their rates of growth. In general, the data show a rapid and sustained technological upgrading of the export basket. There are steady declines in the shares of RB and LT products, largely compensated for by a rise in HT products, whose share reaches 27.7 per cent in 1996. From being the smallest category in 1980, HT surpassed RB by 1985 and LT by 1996. The bulk of world manufactured trade is in

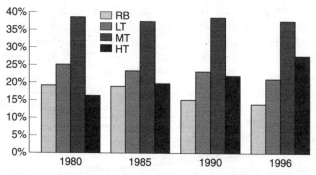

Fig. 3 Shares of technological categories in world manufactured trade

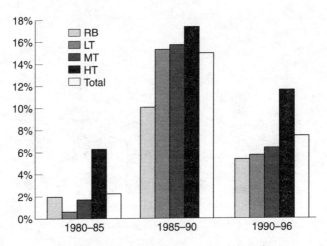

Fig. 4 Rates of growth by technological categories (% p.a.)

MT products, but these slightly lose their share (by 1.4 points) over the period. Under present trends, HT products will soon be larger than MT.

Figure 5 shows export growth rates for industrialized and developing countries. The latter have higher rates of growth in each category, but their lead over the former in growth rates rises with technological complexity (from 2.2 percentage points for RB to 11.3 points for HT products). To some extent these differences may simply reflect initial market shares: if growth were assumed to be equally feasible across all technological categories, a 'catching up' process would lead to relatively faster growth in categories with the smallest initial market share. But this does not hold fully. Take the difference between world and developing country growth rates to control for market conditions: the relative rate of growth for developing countries is highest (9.5 per cent) for HT, which is third by initial market share, and about equal for MT and LT (5.9 per cent and 5.7 per cent), where there are large disparities in initial shares. Catching up is much greater in high rather than medium technology products. In any case, the assumption that catching up is equally feasible across technologies is probably not very persuasive; no trade theory would subscribe to it.

Changes in market shares over the period are shown in Fig. 6. By 1996, the developing world held 23.0 per cent of the world market for manufactured exports, compared to 9.8 per cent in 1980. Its highest share, not surprisingly, was in LT products, but HT's share was only 4 points behind and growing much faster. From the industrialized world's

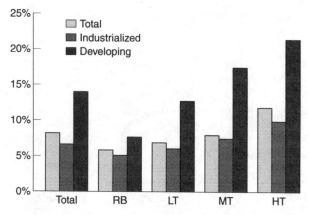

Fig. 5 Growth rates of exports 1980–96 (% p.a.)

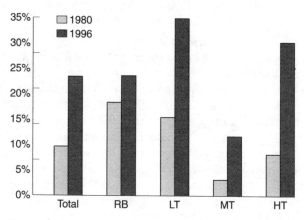

Fig. 6 Shares of developing countries in world exports, 1980–96

perspective, the smallest loss of share was in RB, and the largest in HT, followed by LT. In MT it continued to hold nearly 90 per cent of the world market. The large loss in low technology products is expected; perhaps what is surprising is that advanced countries still retain two-thirds of the market (showing, perhaps, that many LT products are not so 'simple' in all stages of production – e.g. high quality garments require high inputs of skill). Resource based exports aside (where the developed world shows surprising resilience), the main competitive strength of industrial countries appears to lie in medium rather than high technology manufactures.

This is not because 'high' technologies are easier to access or master by developing countries than 'medium' level technologies – this is clearly not the case. It is because the MT category contains several products, such as transport equipment and machinery, which are difficult to relocate economically in developing countries. These products are technologically demanding, linkage-intensive and 'heavy', and reaching world levels of competence in them requires not just technological sophistication (design and development) but also long accumulation of skills and technical knowledge along much of the production chain. Most engineering products also require well-developed supplier and subcontracting links (increasingly so with **just-in-time** production systems) for efficient production, and many have low value-to-weight ratios.

In the HT category, by contrast, while 'core' production processes and product design may be extremely complex, there are many labour-intensive assembly processes that are easily 'separable' from innovation and advanced production. Since many products or components have high value-to-weight ratios, and assembly has low skill needs, they are ideal for relocation in poorer countries despite the weak technological bases of those countries. This has been a prime force behind the recent globalization of their production (Yeats, 1998). The relative performance of MT and HT exports largely reflects this difference: the real edge of advanced countries in innovation is not affected.

The relocation of simple processes does not, however, account for *all* the growth in HT exports from the developing world. An important, and increasing, part of their HT (and MT) exports involves complete manufacturing, backed by local design and development. While this is largely undertaken by local firms, multinational companies' export operations in some countries, starting with simple assembly, are also increasing their local physical and technological inputs.

There are thus two determinants of export success in complex products: genuine advantages, based on the local growth of technological and other capabilities, and globalization, to relocate for cheap labour. The countries with genuine advantages are those that have been able to foster considerable experience-based learning, formal technological activity and inter-industry linkages up to the 'best practice' levels needed for international competition: these are few in number. Those participating in globalization, by contrast, owe their success to low wages combined with a certain level of worker skills and discipline, good infrastructure and a stable and welcoming regime for multinational producers. In addition, privileged market access to major importing countries has been a critical factor for some countries (Yeats, 1998). The distinction between the two groups is not always clear, however, when assembly activities upgrade and integrate backwards (*see* **integration**). But this is still relatively limited, and it is possible to distinguish broadly between the two groups.

In sum, the developed world's underlying competitiveness in technology-intensive products is not eroding at anything like the pace suggested by the export data. What *is* eroding is simple labour-intensive processes across the whole spectrum of manufacturing activity. Nevertheless, this does not mean that the developing world remains confined to the bottom of the technology ladder: some success in complex exports is based on the genuine development of technological knowledge and skills. Let us now analyse this at a more detailed level.

REGIONAL PATTERNS IN DEVELOPING COUNTRIES

Data on regional shares of manufactured exports by technological categories are presented in Table 1 (note again that several countries are not reported in the UN data, but these are not major exporters of manufactured products, so that the aggregates are not too distorted). They show a striking degree of concentration in the developing world. Asia dominates the picture, accounting for nearly 80 per cent of the total manufactured exports in both 1980 and 1996. Latin America (including Mexico) is a distant second, accounting for under a fifth of total developing world manufactured exports. However, it raises its share over the period at the expense of Africa and the Middle East.

SSA1 (shown including and excluding South Africa and Mauritius, both unusual cases in terms of industrialization and export orientation in Sub-Saharan Africa) suffers significant losses of market share in total and in all categories. SSA2, excluding the two regional 'outliers', practically disappears from the map in terms of manufactured exports (except for RB, where it accounts for under 1 per cent). And this is in a context of widespread trade liberalization in the region, with among the lowest wages in the developing world. Simple exposure to world markets, the basis of structural adjustment policies pursued in many African countries, is now widely acknowledged as being insufficient to stimulate industrial or export development there, in the absence of the right policies and factors to manage technological learning (Lall, 1995); but this a different story, not germane to this discussion.

The dominance of Asia persists through all technological categories. It is most marked in HT and LT, and least so in RB and MT categories.

Table 1 Regional shares of developing country manufactured exports

	1980	1990	1996
Total			
Asia	78.1%	76.7%	78.4%
LA1	7.6%	12.3%	16.7%
LA2	N/A	9.0%	7.5%
SSA1	7.0%	2.4%	1.4%
SSA2	2.0%	0.5%	0.1%
ME	7.4%	8.6%	3.5%
Resource based			
Asia	60.4%	57.7%	64.8%
LA1	13.9%	19.4%	27.7%
LA2	N/A	16.0%	22.9%
SSA1	11.0%	5.2%	2.6%
SSA2	4.8%	1.4%	0.8%
ME	14.7%	17.7%	4.9%
Low technology			
Asia	89.2%	81.1%	79.7%
LA1	3.6%	9.0%	12.1%
LA2	N/A	7.5%	6.1%
SSA1	4.9%	2.1%	1.7%
SSA2	0.3%	0.3%	0.0%
ME	2.3%	7.8%	6.5%
Medium technology			
Asia	73.7%	66.6%	66.6%
LA1	8.5%	21.7%	28.1%
LA2	N/A	12.0%	10.6%
SSA1	8.4%	2.6%	2.5%
SSA2	0.8%	0.5%	0.0%
ME	9.4%	9.2%	2.8%
High technology			
Asia	96.6%	94.4%	88.6%
LA1	1.6%	4.1%	10.6%
LA2	N/A	2.6%	1.1%
SSA1	1.1%	0.4%	0.2%
SSA2	0.2%	0.1%	0.0%
ME	0.7%	1.1%	0.5%

Definitions: 'Asia' includes all countries in Asia except for Japan, the Central Asian republics and those included in the Middle East. 'LA1' includes Mexico, 'LA2' excludes it from the Latin American region. 'SSA1' covers all countries in Sub-Saharan Africa including South Africa and Mauritius; 'SSA2' excludes these two. 'ME' stands for the Middle East, and includes all Arab countries in Asia and North Africa, plus Iran and Turkey.

Over the period, however, it loses market share to LA1 in all the categories apart from RB, where both gain at the expense of the other two regions. In LT products, Asia also loses share to the Middle East, where one country, Turkey, emerges as a major exporter of textiles and garments to Europe under special market access provisions (its relatively high wages would probably make it uncompetitive with respect to Asia in open competition). The highest gains in share for LA1 are in MT (19.6 points) and RB (14 points).

Asia's export dominance over the period, and Latin America's relative improvement since 1980, raise intriguing questions. Though these cannot be explored here in detail, let us note some historical background. In Asia, the early export orientation of the East Asian Tigers (Hong Kong, Singapore, Korea and Taiwan) led to their growth of LT exports in the 1960s. In the 1970s and 80s, this was followed by rapid upgrading of the export and manufacturing structure in the latter three economies, largely as a result of deliberate industrial policy and investments in skills and technology. The new Tigers (Indonesia, Malaysia and Thailand) followed after the 1970s, adopting export-oriented policies but based on the offshore-assembly route to growth. This gave them a combination of high technology (led mainly by OECD multi-nationals) and low technology (led by multi-nationals from the mature Tigers) exports, but relatively little indigenous contribution in terms of skills or technology. China then emerged as a 'super exporter' in the 1980s, setting up special economic zones to serve as an assembly base for the Tigers, but accompanied by growing competence in local enterprises and some former import-substituting industries. As the data below show, these countries dominate Asian exports; other Asian countries, including giants like India, count for relatively little.

Figure 7 shows the 1996 structure of exports by each region. Asian exports are dominated by HT products, the only region for which this is so; this is followed by LT products. LA1 is dominated by MT (auto and process industry) products, while LA2 is dominated by RB (only SSA2 has a higher share) and with a very low share of HT products (only SSA2 has lower). SSA1 has strong positions for LT (garments from Mauritius) and MT (machinery and intermediates from South Africa) products; SSA2, by contrast, has an overwhelming share of RB products, the classic pattern of exports by underdeveloped countries. In ME, Turkey (and to a lesser extent other garment exporters like Morocco and Tunisia, also with privileged access to Europe) account for the high share of LT exports.

In terms of growth rates (Fig. 8), the highest total is for Asia (16.9 per

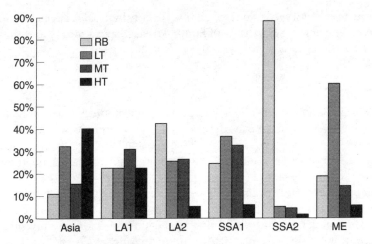

Fig. 7 Export structures, 1996

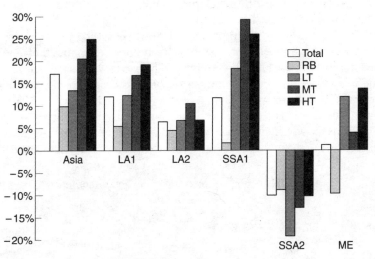

Fig. 8 Export growth by regions, 1985–96 (% p.a.)

cent), followed by LA1 (12.0 per cent) and SSA1 (11.6 per cent). SSA2 shows a fall of –10.2 per cent: this exaggerates the true picture, since there are many missing country export values for 1996. However, even the 1995 figures (when data for most African countries are available) yield a negative figure overall (–4.4 per cent) as well as for each of the categories separately. Asia has the highest growth rates in each category with the exception of SSA1, which records very high rates because of its small base and the expansion of South African exports after the ending of trade sanctions.

COUNTRY-WISE EXPORT PERFORMANCE

Let us look now at the country-level data. For this, we focus on the 12 leading manufactured exporters from the developing world: the four Tigers, the three new Tigers, India and China, and the three largest Latin American economies. Table 2 shows their total manufactured exports over the period (including the very unusual 1995-96) and their annual rates of growth; Annex Table 1 gives some of these data for each technological category. These 12 countries accounted for 92 per cent of total developing country manufactured exports in 1996; the top three accounted for 43 per cent, the top four for 56 per cent, the top five for 65 per cent, and the top ten for 88 per cent, of the developing world total. The analysis of exports by developing countries devolves to explaining what happens to these few leaders.

These countries led the rapid export growth enjoyed by the developing world as a whole. Reflecting the cycles in world trade, they had much faster growth in the latter half of the 1980s than in the period before or since. The 1995–96 slowdown was particularly marked for Hong Kong (whose own exports were stagnating in any case), Thailand and Korea, but all countries in the group suffered. Singapore held up the best of the Tigers, as did Indonesia the new Tigers; Mexico led with nearly 20 per cent growth (a substantial reduction nevertheless from the 1990–95

Table 2 Largest 12 developing exporters of manufactured products

Country	VALUES (US$ M.)					GROWTH RATES (% p.a.)				
	1980	1985	1990	1995	1996	1980–85	1985–90	1990–95	1995–96	1985–96
Hong Kong	12,750	15,476	26,929	27,605	25,211	4.0%	11.7%	0.5%	−8.7%	4.5%
Singapore	14,328	18,492	48,062	107,768	114,528	5.2%	21.0%	17.5%	6.3%	18.0%
Korea	14,890	23,317	57,920	111,236	111,155	9.4%	20.0%	13.9%	−0.1%	15.3%
Taiwan	18,214	28,295	62,211	103,987	108,514	9.2%	17.1%	10.8%	4.4%	13.0%
Indonesia	3,827	3,572	11,091	25,906	28,639	−1.4%	25.4%	18.5%	10.5%	20.8%
Malaysia	5,949	8,317	20,660	63,439	67,140	6.9%	20.0%	25.2%	5.8%	20.9%
Thailand	2,572	3,794	16,563	43,697	42,995	8.1%	34.3%	21.4%	−1.6%	24.7%
China	N/A	13,380(a)	46,513	127,633	130,266	N/A	23.1%(b)	22.4%	2.1%	20.9%(c)
India	4,265	5,409	12,477	22,803	23,396	4.9%	18.2%	12.8%	2.6%	14.2%
Argentina	3,113	3,501	6,342	10,962	11,098	2.4%	12.6%	11.6%	1.2%	11.1%
Brazil	N/A	14,599	19,036	27,935	28,566	N/A	5.5%	8.0%	2.2%	6.3%
Mexico	N/A	8,432	13,533	64,690	77,280	N/A	9.9%	36.7%	19.5%	22.3%
Total	79,905	146,588	341,336	737,657	768,777	12.9%	18.4%	16.7%	4.2%	16.3%
All LDCs	102,347	188,203	408,684	826,079	835,081	13.0%	16.8%	15.1%	1.1%	14.5%

Notes: (a) 1984. Data for total manufactured exports not available for China for 1980–83 or for 1985. (b) Growth 1984–90 (c) Growth 1984–96.

rate). Note that the slowdown in the new Tigers was not, as is thought in the region, due to a sudden intensification of competition from China – China slowed down like the rest.

While the largest developing country exporter is now China, it was not the fastest growing. The leaders in growth were Korea in the early 1980s, Thailand overall and in the late 1980s, and Mexico in the 1990s. In total export values, the three mature Tigers (Singapore, Korea, and Taiwan) come after China.

Korea and Taiwan rely primarily on local firms for exports. Starting with low-technology exports in the 1960s, they used a battery of trade, industrial, financial and technological interventions to deepen the industrial base and move into more advanced activities (Lall, 1996). Korea used infant industry protection, subsidized and directed credit, **research and development** support and other similar selective measures to promote large private conglomerates that would spearhead the growth of heavy industry and enter high technology exports. Taiwan intervened less in the industrial structure, but promoted its small and medium sized enterprises with trade protection, subsidized credit, training and technology support and export marketing.

Over three decades the Tigers built up the most advanced technological bases in the developing world, leading it in terms of R&D expenditures and the creation of technical manpower: all intrinsic parts of industrial policy to establish competitive positions in targeted activities. Korea today has the highest enrolments in the world at the tertiary level in science, mathematics and engineering as a proportion of its population (1.55 per cent), followed by Taiwan (1.09 per cent), compared, say to 0.88 per cent for Germany or 0.70 per cent for the USA (Lall, 1998). The proportion of Korean R&D spending financed by industry as a proportion of its GDP is the highest in the world (2.3 per cent), surpassing Japan (2.0 per cent), USA (1.5 per cent) and leading European countries (1.0 per cent for the UK, 1.4 per cent for Germany and 1.9 per cent for Sweden, see Lall, 1998). This gives the two Tigers unrivalled technological bases in advanced industrial products, putting them in a different category from other developing countries: for instance, the nearest in terms of technical enrolments is Chile (0.67 per cent) and in R&D financed by industry is Singapore (0.69 per cent).

Each of the new Tigers displays a strong growth performance, led by Thailand in the 1980s and Malaysia in the 1990s. While all rely heavily on multinationals for exports, each takes a different path. Malaysia, the earliest to embark on the path of export-oriented growth, caught the semiconductor assembly boom at its peak in the early 1970s (with investment by US firms), then moved into a wide range of electronic and electrical products (with the entry of Japanese multi-nationals). This accounts for its high share of HT exports, higher than for any country except Singapore. However, it remains at a lower technological level than the latter, with a smaller base of technical skills and low technological and other inputs locally; in comparison to Korea and Taiwan, which have lower shares for HT in their exports, Malaysia also has an undeveloped technology base (with industry-financed R&D at 0.17 per cent of GDP). Thailand has a lower proportion of HT activities than Malaysia (but a larger indigenous industrial class in resource-based and low technology products). Indonesia, the latecomer to this group, has the cheapest labour and lowest levels of human capital, and the lowest technology content in its exports.

Table 3 gives the distribution of manufactured exports over the technological categories in 1985 and 1996. Of the mature Tigers, by 1996 Singapore has the highest share of HT products (and one of the highest in the world), Hong Kong the lowest. Taiwan has a slightly higher share for HT, but less for MT, products, where Korea has an edge in automobile and machinery exports. China has the highest share in the group of LT products, but changes cannot be traced before 1990 because of data deficiencies in the early years. Indonesia has high weights of RB and LT products, but with a sharp rise in the share of HT products (China also has a sharply rizing HT share in the 1990s). India has a relatively simple and stagnant structure, with the lowest share in Asia of HT exports. In Latin America, Argentina suffers a slight decline

Table 3 Structure of manufactured exports by leading developing countries

	1985					1996			
	RB	LT	MT	HT		RB	LT	MT	HT
Hong Kong	2.1%	64.3%	14.2%	19.3%	Hong Kong	4.4%	52.7%	14.0%	28.9%
Singapore	42.3%	10.8%	14.6%	32.3%	Singapore	12.7%	7.9%	14.0%	65.4%
Korea	7.8%	59.9%	12.2%	20.1%	Korea	9.4%	28.4%	26.6%	35.7%
Taiwan	8.7%	57.3%	13.3%	20.7%	Taiwan	5.1%	33.9%	20.2%	40.9%
Indonesia	72.2%	19.2%	5.9%	2.8%	Indonesia	34.9%	41.9%	8.5%	14.7%
Malaysia	53.7%	9.7%	5.5%	31.0%	Malaysia	17.8%	13.1%	8.7%	60.4%
Thailand	42.1%	38.2%	6.6%	13.1%	Thailand	14.5%	35.6%	13.5%	36.3%
China (1990)	11.7%	57.1%	21.8%	9.4%	China (1990)	9.8%	56.3%	13.4%	20.6%
India	40.3%	46.1%	10.6%	3.0%	India	31.1%	52.3%	13.1%	4.4%
Argentina	67.5%	15.6%	11.8%	5.1%	Argentina	49.1%	18.8%	28.8%	3.3%
Brazil	32.6%	33.3%	27.1%	7.1%	Brazil	25.6%	31.8%	34.0%	8.6%
Mexico	20.2%	15.0%	29.2%	35.6%	Mexico	7.1%	20.9%	35.2%	36.9%

in the HT share over time, to 3.3 per cent in 1996, the lowest in the group; however, its processing and auto industries give it a strong showing in MT products. Brazil is roughly similar, with a somewhat better showing in HT exports.

SYNTHESIS AND EXPLANATIONS

Let us start with the basic facts emerging from the above analysis.

- World trade in manufactured products displays a steady and significant move up the technology scale, with high technology products gaining at the expense of all others, especially the resource based and low technology groups. Medium technology products continue to retain the largest share of trade, but may soon be overtaken by high technology products.
- The location of export production is changing significantly. Developing countries have had rapid export growth, accompanied by significant diversification away from traditional resource and labour-intensive products. They have higher rates of growth than industrialized countries in all categories, with the fastest relative growth being in medium to high technology products. Because of certain technological features, the erosion of competitiveness in the industrial world has been lowest in medium technology products.
- Exports by developing countries are highly concentrated, and the level of concentration has risen over time. The same handful of countries dominate exports in all technological categories, though with important differences in their export structures. Other developing countries, the vast majority, remain marginal to export activity, despite having adopted more liberal trade and investment policies. Sub-Saharan Africa, excluding South Africa, is losing its already tiny share of manufactured trade. An overwhelming portion of manufactured exports emanates from Asia, in particular from China, three mature Tigers and the three new Tigers.
- The technological upgrading of exports shows three distinct patterns. The first is mainly found in the three mature Asian Tigers: Korea, Singapore and Taiwan. These economies have the most advanced industrial capabilities, and have managed to combine rapid export growth with considerable diversification and deepening of their export bases. Singapore has the most technologically advanced and specialized export structure but its own technological contribution is relatively limited. The other two show more absorptive and

innovative capabilities, with Korea leading in scale and technology intensive activities. While all three possess advanced technical skills, what has driven their technological deepening has been single-mindedly industrial policy by their governments.

- The second pattern involves participation in the globalized production on the basis of low labour costs, with relatively low local technological inputs and weak bases of technical and engineering skills. Among the leading exporters, this pattern is exemplified by the new Tigers and (parts of) China, but much of the developing world's exports of labour-intensive products like shoes, sports goods and garments fall into this category. The countries concerned serve primarily as assembly bases for multinationals or foreign buyers that subcontract to local firms. Their exports have grown rapidly and diversified, but such diversification is largely confined to South East Asian countries, which were able to 'cash in' on the relocation of electronics production, and is not found in other countries, which remain largely concentrated on garment assembly (Sri Lanka, Bangladesh, Mauritius, North Africa or various Caribbean economies). While there has been some upgrading of domestic technological capabilities, the deepening process still lags well behind the mature Tigers.

- The third pattern is exemplified by economies with large industrial bases fostered behind import substitution barriers – the large Latin American countries, India and to some extent China. Ignoring the growth of exports due to special trade privileges accorded to countries like Mexico, these countries display export dynamism in some activities opened up to world markets. This dynamism is far below that of the Tigers, but several instances exist of activities that have taken advantage of their accumulated learning to invest in new facilities. In Latin America this is mainly in the automobile and heavy process industries, while in India and China there are some engineering and light industry exports. However, export growth remains relatively modest (in China much of the growth comes from the globalizing element), and high technology exports are generally absent.

Understanding these trends requires a mixture of the approaches. The growing share of complex products in world trade *per se* lies outside the remit of this essay, and probably does not need much explaining (the sheer pace of technical change may suffice). The fact that the developing world accounts for increasing proportions of complex as well as simple products does raise issues, as does the high level of concentration by origin of exporter and the differing patterns of technological deepening among leading exporters.

A significant part of the growth of high-technology exports by developing countries is, as noted, a statistical artefact, based upon the transfer of simple labour-intensive processes from the advanced to the developing countries. The former retain innovation as well as much of the advanced design and production processes. If export data were available in terms of processes rather than end products (which it is not), much of the recent growth of HT exports from the developing world would show up as low technology. Conventional trade theory would cope quite well with this, especially if capital mobility were permitted. It is when we come to the spread of export activity in the developing world and the 'deepening' of export capabilities in complex products that more questions arise.

Take, for a start, the high degree of export concentration in the developing world, and why so many countries remain 'outside the loop' of growing trade in manufactures. To the extent that trade strategies have been responsible, no particular theoretical insight is required; nor does the rapid growth of exports in response to specific trade privileges require any economic explanation. However, trade policies cannot fully account for export concentration. There is a persistence in export success which suggests that there are cumulative effects arizing from export activity. These may include learning (to enter foreign markets and deal with foreign buyers, Keesing and Lall, 1992), institution building, reputation effects and trust, inflows of information and access to sources of technology, skills and finance. Learning and reputation effects may also spill over across different activities and so stimulate new exports (though this seems to be more prevalent in exporters that have already reached a certain threshold of diversification, and is not evident in countries where exports are confined to a few simple products). Cumulative processes and externalities introduce the possibility of market failure to the extent that they are unanticipated and distort resource allocation, but do not change the basic explanation of comparative advantage.

Cumulative learning effects and externalities arizing from exporting *per se* are not sufficient to explain trade patterns as long as all developing countries are treated as having similar factor endowments. We still have to explain why all developing countries with liberal (or liberalizing) trade regimes are not equally successful in expanding manufactured exports (even taking learning lags into account), and why spillover effects from early exporting have led to very different patterns of upgrading and deepening. All these countries have plentiful unskilled labour, and, in a globalizing world, nearly all have access to capital and technology from advanced countries (and from advanced developing ones). Yet, discounting for trade policies and experience, some reveal much greater ability to take advantage of these flows than others. Taking capital and technology as mobile, which other (immobile) factors can explain differences in export performance?

The main explanation has been in terms of human capital (though others, such as the business environment or physical infrastructure, can be introduced; but trade theory does not treat these, so let us also ignore them). There is certainly a broad correlation between education levels and the sophistication of the export structure. The lag of Africa in getting into even basic export-oriented manufacturing is to a significant extent due to skill, infrastructure and institutional gaps. The most successful exporters, the Asian Tigers, started with high levels of human capital and then upgraded them more rapidly over time than the rest of the developing world. While few would disagree that skills are a crucial element of comparative advantage, two important issues arise for policy: how this endowment is created, and whether having high levels of education is sufficient as well as necessary for export success.

How are skill endowments created? To the extent that human capital is simply a function of incomes, countries invest more in education as they get richer. Comparative advantage changes with accumulation: there is no role for policy here. To the extent, however, that the creation of human capital suffers from market failures arising, say, from the lack of information (people do not appreciate the benefits of education, or educational institutions do not appreciate what sort of education is needed), appropriability problems (individuals who invest in education do not reap its full benefits), short time horizons and risk aversion, or sheer income constraints, free markets cannot provide the optimal amount of human capital. If such market failures exist, government intervention may be needed to realize and improve comparative advantage. Indeed, most governments accept market failures to be pervasive and intervene in education; the case for this in developing countries hardly needs to be argued.

But what *kinds* of interventions are needed? Should they be neutral between activities ('functional'), or targeted to particular needs ('selective')? Evidence suggests that both can be justified, depending on the circumstances and the level of industrial development. In early stages of industrialization, when mainly simple assembly and processing are involved, skill needs are fairly general and the correct policy is to provide functional support for primary and secondary schooling (including basic vocational training). In later stages, with more complex technologies and technological functions, skill needs are more demanding and specific (an electronics engineer cannot design a chemical plant). If the educational sector does not anticipate correctly emerging skill needs, or people are unwilling to invest in longer and costlier courses, governments may have to mount targeted interventions to create the particular skills needed by the evolving industrial structure (or by their own industrial policies).

The experience of the mature Tigers suggests that both functional and selective educational interventions have been important, with the latter gaining precedence with growing industrial complexity. Each Tiger geared its educational interventions to meeting the technical needs of industries, especially those being promoted (this was one of the most important strategic tools used by Singapore; see Selvaratnam, 1994). These interventions were an integral part of overall industrial policy (Lall, 1998), and have to be considered as such rather than as independent strategies for human resource development.

Is skill upgrading, however, a *sufficient* as well as a necessary explanation of export patterns? We suggest that it is not. The augmented H-O-S model with human capital (which takes into account the level of skills in addition to the traditional factors of land, labour, and capital) retains many assumptions of traditional models, and neglects such crucial factors within manufacturing as increasing returns, externalities, linkages, information failures and learning costs. These can affect the location of activity. Where scale and agglomeration economies exist, countries without other advantages can establish competitive leads by being first movers and increasing their lead over time (Krugman, 1986, Venables, 1996a, 1996b). Where there are unpredictable, prolonged, costly and interlinked learning processes, with diffuse externalities and failures in information markets, the realization of comparative advantage can be held back by market failures (Stiglitz, 1996). Agents operating under free market conditions cannot take these effects fully into account in their individual decisions, and countries can improve their locational advantages by, say, policies to promote early entry, overcome learning costs and coordinate interrelated activities. Further, if learning costs rise with the complexity of the technologies involved, interventions may be necessary to promote diversification and deepening over time. Thus, improving human capital *per se* is a necessary but not sufficient condition for changing locational advantages.

Additional factors need to be invoked to show how the other influences on competitiveness work.

There can be significant agglomeration benefits in low technology activities; learning, skill creation and export activity in 'clusters' can have strong spillover effects and affect the development of comparative advantages. The small and medium-sized fashion producers in the industrial districts of 'Third Italy' are the best known example, but there also exist several successful clusters in the developing world (Nadvi and Schmitz, 1994). The capacity to master and deploy simple technologies differs greatly between countries, depending not just on the base of skills but also on policies and institutions that help firms to learn. This suggests that the new approaches to location have much to offer in explaining the evolution of trade patterns.

However, it is in explaining competitiveness in complex activities, where learning is most prolonged and costly, uncertainties greatest and coordination problems most difficult to resolve, that the new approaches have the strongest edge. Conventional factor endowments, even including human capital, cannot fully explain location: using technology efficiently requires building strong local capabilities because of the inherent tacit elements of technology (Lall, 1992). To the extent that the process faces market failures which can be overcome by policy, location comes to depend upon the effectiveness of governments in promoting learning and co-ordination. The experience of the Tigers suggests that coherent interventions across all these markets, including the promotion of infant industries or clusters, played a critical role in their growth and deepening (Lall, 1996). Note that 'picking winners' or promoting national champions was only one form of industrial policy; there were others with lower degrees of targeting (Korea had the greatest technological ambitions, so intervened the most, Singapore and Taiwan intervened at less detailed levels).

Strategic interventions, while present, played a smaller role in the (relatively limited) export deepening of other important exporters. The new Tigers, China and Mexico benefited more from foreign investors using their cheap, literate and disciplined labour than from strategies to upgrade their competitive base. While they did develop pockets of indigenous capabilities, in general their interventions were not as effective as in the three mature Tigers. They were not as clearly directed to creating international competitiveness by overcoming market failures in learning; they pursued other objectives, and their administrations were less flexible, educated, informed and autonomous. Most important, the interventions were designed and implemented in a setting of pervasive inward orientation, with export sectors remaining enclaves. In contrast, the Tigers pursued strong export orientation, involved industry in decision making and made favours to industry conditional on export performance (what the World Bank, 1993, terms creating 'contests'). Thus, the incentive systems under which firms (and policy makers) operated were very different, with different results. While all this may not result in a 'theory' of location or comparative advantage (since government policy cannot be endogenized), it does provide a good explanation of observed trade patterns.

What of the policy implications? While the existence of market failures makes it possible to provide a case for government intervention, there always remains a real and important danger of 'government failure'. Development experience is rife with instances of such failure, and has led many economists to believe that governments *cannot* improve upon deficient markets, that, in other words, the consequences of government failure are invariably worse than those of market failure. This may be too extreme. Government failure is not inevitable, and where industrial policy has worked well, as it has in parts of East Asia, it has accelerated the learning process significantly. The real issues are the conditions under which governments can be more effective, the choice of the right set of interventions in those conditions, and ways of improving government capabilities (Lall and Teubal, forthcoming). The new international rules of the game, which rule out many interventions that worked well in the Tigers, are beneficial in that they constrain developing country governments from inefficient policies; they also rule out some that are justifiable.

To conclude, there are many patterns of comparative advantage evolving in the developing world, and a variety of possible explanations. Conventional trade theory offers some insights, but the newer approaches to trade and location provide more appealing explanations. If market failures in industrial development, and the role of governments in correcting them, were taken into account, we would have a richer, and more realistic, understanding of location in the developing world.

Annex Table 1 Export of leading developing countries by technological categories

Resource based

	Values ($ million)			Growth rates (% p.a.)		
	1985	1990	1996	1985–90	1990–96	1985–96
Hong Kong	326	864	1,109	21.5%	4.3%	11.6%
Singapore	7,823	12,321	14,530	9.5%	2.8%	5.8%
Korea	1,821	3,223	10,451	12.1%	21.7%	17.2%
Taiwan	2,470	3,759	5,517	8.8%	6.6%	7.6%
Indonesia	2,578	5,670	10,008	17.1%	9.9%	13.1%
Malaysia	4,470	6,491	11,959	7.7%	10.7%	9.4%
Thailand	1,596	4,009	6,254	20.2%	7.7%	13.2%
China (a)		5,435	12,726		15.2%	
India	2,179	4,266	7,270	14.4%	9.3%	11.6%
Argentina	2,364	3,638	5,444	9.0%	6.9%	7.9%
Brazil	4,755	4,950	7,320	0.8%	6.7%	4.0%
Mexico	1,703	2,856	5,454	10.9%	11.4%	11.2%

Low technology

	Values ($ million)			Growth rates (% p.a.)		
	1985	1990	1996	1985–90	1990–96	1985–96
Hong Kong	9,956	15,146	13,286	8.8%	-2.2%	2.7%
Singapore	1,990	5,523	9,045	22.7%	8.6%	14.8%
Korea	13,978	29,171	31,519	15.9%	1.3%	7.7%
Taiwan	16,211	28,759	36,756	12.1%	4.2%	7.7%
Indonesia	684	4,500	11,986	45.7%	17.7%	29.7%
Malaysia	811	3,166	8,792	31.3%	18.6%	24.2%
Thailand	1,448	6,821	15,293	36.3%	14.4%	23.9%
China (a)		26,579	73,345		18.4%	
India	2,492	6,251	12,239	20.2%	11.8%	15.6%
Argentina	545	1,449	2,088	21.6%	6.3%	13.0%
Brazil	4,857	6,727	9,093	6.7%	5.2%	5.9%
Mexico	1,266	2,463	16,135	14.2%	36.8%	26.0%

Medium technology

	Values ($ million)			Growth rates (% p.a.)		
	1985	1990	1996	1985–90	1990–96	1985–96
Hong Kong	2,205	4,315	3,541	14.4%	-3.2%	4.4%
Singapore	2,703	7,493	16,091	22.6%	13.6%	17.6%
Korea	2,838	8,886	29,540	25.6%	22.2%	23.7%
Taiwan	3,750	10,911	21,895	23.8%	12.3%	17.4%
Indonesia	211	663	2,430	25.8%	24.2%	24.9%
Malaysia	460	1,336	5,862	23.8%	28.0%	26.0%
Thailand	252	1,606	5,852	44.8%	24.0%	33.0%
China (a)		10,142	17,403		9.4%	
India	574	1,508	3,070	21.3%	12.6%	16.5%
Argentina	413	1,036	3,197	20.2%	20.7%	20.4%
Brazil	3,951	5,566	9,698	7.1%	9.7%	8.5%
Mexico	2,459	6,918	27,170	23.0%	25.6%	24.4%

High technology

	Values ($ million)			Growth rates (% p.a.)		
	1985	1990	1996	1985–90	1990–96	1985–96
Hong Kong	2,992	6,604	7,277	17.2%	1.6%	8.4%
Singapore	5,976	22,725	74,863	30.6%	22.0%	25.8%
Korea	4,680	16,641	39,645	28.9%	15.6%	21.4%
Taiwan	5,864	18,781	44,345	26.2%	15.4%	20.2%
Indonesia	100	257	4,215	20.9%	59.4%	40.6%
Malaysia	2,577	9,667	40,528	30.3%	27.0%	28.5%
Thailand	497	4,127	15,623	52.7%	24.8%	36.8%
China (a)		4,367	26,792		35.4%	
India	165	452	1,019	22.3%	14.5%	18.0%
Argentina	180	219	368	3.9%	9.1%	6.7%
Brazil	1,036	1,793	2,445	11.6%	5.3%	8.1%
Mexico	3,005	1,296	28,521	-15.5%	67.4%	22.7%

Note: (a) Chinese exports in 1984 could not be allocated over the technological categories because of many missing values.

FURTHER READING

Balassa, B., '"Stages Approach" to Comparative Advantage', *The Newly Industrializing Countries in the World Economy* (Johns Hopkins Press, 1986).

Benavente, J. M., Crispi, G., Katz, J. and Stumpo, G., 'New Problems and Opportunities for Industrial Development in Latin America', *Oxford Development Studies*, **25**(3) (1997) pp. 261–78.

Guerrieri, P., 'International Competitiveness, Trade Integration and Technological Interdependence', in C. Bradford (ed.), *The New Paradigm of Systemic Competitiveness: Towards More Integrated Policies in Latin America* (OECD Development Centre, 1993).

Keesing, D. B., 'Labor Skills and Comparative Advantage', *American Economic Review*, **56**(2) (1966), pp. 249–58.

Keesing, D. B., and Lall, S., 'Marketing Manufactured Exports from Developing Countries: Learning Sequences and Public Support', in G. K. Helleiner (ed.), *Trade Policy, Industrialization and Development: New Perspectives* (Clarendon Press, 1992).

Krugman, P. (ed.), *Strategic Trade Theory and the New International Economy* (MIT Press, 1986).

Krugman, P., *Geography and Trade* (MIT Press, 1991).

Lall, S., 'Technological Capabilities and Industrialization', *World Development*, **20**(2) (1992), pp. 165–86.

Lall, S., 'Structural Adjustment and African Industry', *World Development*, **23**(12) (1995), pp. 2019–31.

Lall, S., *Learning from the Asian Tigers* (Macmillan, 1996).

Lall, S., 'Putting Knowledge to Work for Development' (World Bank, Washington DC, background paper for the *World Development Report 1998*).

Lall, S., and Teubal, M., '"Market Stimulating' Technology Policies in Developing Countries: A Framework with Examples from East Asia' (1998), *World Development*, **26**, forthcoming.

Nadvi, K., and Schmitz, H., *Industrial clusters in less developed countries: Review of experience and research agenda* (Institute of Development Studies, Brighton, discussion paper 339 (1994)).

OECD, *Structural Adjustment and Economic Performance* (OECD Development Centre, 1987).

Puga, D., and Venables, A. J., 'Trading Arrangements and Industrial Development' (World Bank, Washington DC, policy research working paper no. 1787 (1997)).

Rodrik, D., 'Co-ordination failures and government policy: A model with applications to East Asia and Eastern Europe', *Journal of International Economics*, **40**(1/2) (1996), pp. 1–22.

Selvaratnam, V., *Innovations in Higher Education: Singapore at the Competitive Edge* (World Bank, Washington DC, technical paper no. 222 (1994)).

Stiglitz, J. E., 'Some Lessons from the East Asian Miracle', *The World Bank Research Observer*, **11**(2) (1996), pp. 151–77.

Stiglitz, J. E., 'Market failures, public goods, and externalities', in E. Malinvaud (ed.), *Development Strategy and the Market Economy* (Oxford University Press, 1997).

Venables, A. J., 'Trade Policy, Cumulative Causation, and Industrial Development', *Journal of Development Economics*, **49**(1) (1996a), pp. 179–98.

Venables, A. J., 'Localization of Industry and Trade Performance', *Oxford Review of Economic Policy*, **12** (1996b), pp. 52–60.

Wood, A., 'Exporting Manufactures: Human Resources, Natural Resources, and Trade Policy', *Journal of Development Studies*, **34**(1) (1997), pp. 35–59.

World Bank, *The East Asian Miracle: Economic Growth and Public Policy* (Oxford University Press, 1993).

Yeats, A. J., 'Just How Big is Global Production Sharing?' (World Bank, Washington DC, policy research working paper no. 1871 (1998)).

This essay appeared in longer form in *The Oxford Review of Economic Policy*, Vol. 14, No. 2, 1998, published by Oxford University Press.

3

THE LIMITS TO
GLOBAL MARKETS

NEIL MACKINNON

A recurring theme of this book is the expansion of global financial (and other) markets over the past couple of decades. This has been driven partly by technology (making it possible to trade anywhere on the globe, 24 hours a day, provided a telephone, modem, and computer are at hand), and partly by deregulation. The old restrictions on capital flows between countries, which used to limit how much currency could be taken abroad, or which institutions could grant certain types of loans, have now largely disappeared. One of the main drivers has been the need for companies, especially multinational companies, to raise funds globally. Another has been the competition among financial centres to capture as much as possible of the global business, forcing banks and stockbrokers to provide a variety of global services rather than concentrating on national pre-occupations. Small wonder then that we read of doomsday scenarios involving global meltdowns, or global capital shortages, or an international banking crisis. During the recent turbulence in Asia and East Europe, much attention was paid to increasingly global markets and their role in facilitating short-term capital flows, which in the case of East Asia, for example, were blamed by some for the catastrophic collapse of currencies (*see* the essay by Jeremy Pink: 'Asia: The Lessons for Economics'). With globalization came the ubiquitous hedge fund, taking bets on currencies, interest rates, share prices, or any other financial instrument, and leveraging its exposure so that its trading could create disproportionate swings in the assets being bought and sold. The implication was that global markets meant greater volatility, and the question was how to deal with the volatility – or even whether to opt out of the global market.

In this essay Neil Mackinnon carefully tracks the development of today's global markets, from the days of the **gold standard** through to the period of **Bretton Woods**. His essay should be looked at alongside the entries on many of the financial institutions such as **banks, bond markets, stock markets**, etc. It also looks at how **exchange rate** theory and such phenomena as **hot money** operate in practice. His conclusion is that governments, far from being powerless to act in global markets, actually still comprise a major and effective power in them. The key, as with most markets, is to ask whether the fundamentals are at odds with the market. If they are not, then governments can go some way, especially if they act in concert, to smooth out some of the erratic day-to-day moves; if they are, there is little that governments can do to try to prevent the markets correcting prices and flows.

For a perspective on why the markets may not always follow the fundamentals, see the essay by Paul Ormerod, 'What Economics is Not'.

GOVERNMENT AND THE GLOBAL FINANCIAL SYSTEM

When we think about international financial markets, it is commonplace to take the notion of 'globalization' very much for granted. But what do we mean by this concept?

It is not entirely true, for example, that globalization of the international financial markets is something that has happened only over the past ten years or so. If we go back to the era of the **Gold Standard**, which lasted from approximately 1870 to 1914, the scale of total capital flows as measured by the average of the absolute values of current account deficits relative to GDP for the major capital-exporting and capital-importing countries was higher during 1870–1914 than in subsequent decades. The main capital exporter over that period, the United Kingdom, saw annual capital outflows averaging almost 5 per cent of GDP, and reaching 9 per cent at its peak.

Significant capital mobility after the First World War only lasted until the advent of the 1930s Depression. The economic slump, together with the 1929 **stock market** crash, severely dented international investors' confidence and resulted in a dramatic shrinkage in international portfolio flows. Many countries, especially the United Kingdom, made a big mistake in trying to return to the pre-war Gold Standard at exchange rate parities which were entirely unsuitable and which only intensified the economic problems of that time. Mass unemployment generated intense political pressures for a change in economic policies and effectively forced the major economies to abandon the Gold Standard as a policy instrument. Those economies which left the system found that they enjoyed a fairly rapid turnaround in their economic situation. For example, sterling was devalued in 1931 and the Roosevelt Administration did the same to the dollar shortly afterwards. By 1935, industrial production in both economies had returned to pre-depression levels. In sharp contrast, economies such as France, which grimly stuck to the exchange rate, paid a price in terms of experiencing a prolonged recession throughout the 1930s.

The main problem which occurred throughout the period was what commentators dubbed 'beggar-thy-neighbour' policies. What this means is that individual economies can devalue their currency, experience a subsequent pick-up in economic activity, and see a drop in unemployment. The problem is that all economies cannot devalue their currencies at the same time. A currency devaluation for one economy is a currency revaluation for another economy. A devaluation increases exports while a revaluation reduces exports. In these circumstances, each individual economy has an incentive to beat its neighbour to the draw by using the **exchange rate** as a **trade** weapon. But there are winners and losers as a result. The winners see their economies outperform the losers. Not surprisingly, the losers are not particularly pleased about the outcome and might impose trade barriers such as import duties as a way of preventing the devaluing economy from enjoying an 'unfair advantage'. To a large degree, this is what actually happened during the 1930s. It created a high degree of infighting amongst the major economies and an almost total breakdown in international cooperation and coordination. It helped spawn the phenomenon of 'isolationism' in the United States and the growth of fascism in Europe.

POST-WAR POLICY

The experience of the 1930s highlighted some key lessons for policy-makers. First, the flow of investment capital had tended to be highly variable, with sharp increases in flows often followed by sharp downturns. Second, downturns or a complete cessation of capital flows often involved a sharp disparity in economic conditions between capital exporters and capital importers. Third, periods of high capital mobility were typically ended by major political and economic crises, such as the First World War and the Great Depression. Fourth, currency devaluation resulted in trade conflict and loss of international cooperation. Losers often responded by imposing trade tariffs or capital controls.

In the aftermath of the Second World War, policy-makers were keen to avoid repeating these mistakes. Also, many policy-makers were greatly influenced by the ideas and theories of the economist John Maynard **Keynes.** The role of governments rather than markets as the main influence for the allocation and distribution of output was in the ascendant. Capital controls remained in place and the **Bretton Woods** system fixed exchange rates in order to avoid a repeat of the 1930s 'beggar-thy-neighbour' policies. The United States played a central role in maintaining the system of exchange rates throughout the 1950s and 1960s, having become the leading creditor nation, with the leading share of world output and trade. The US dollar became the key currency in the world's financial system, with most countries holding their foreign exchange reserves in dollars.

In any system of fixed exchange rates, the role of the so-called 'anchor' currency, such as the US dollar in the Bretton Woods system, is crucial. For the system to work properly the lead nation must pursue monetary and fiscal policies which are not **inflationary.** Otherwise, other economies in the system will object to the lead economy 'exporting' inflation and jeopardizing the exchange rate linkage. Agencies such as the **IMF** and World Bank were created to monitor and promote the stability of the international financial system as well as assisting in post-war reconstruction and development. Governments were expected to adjust their economic policies to maintain the agreed exchange rate parity within balance of payments constraints. Exchange rates could only be adjusted if countries were said to be in 'fundamental disequilibrium', in other words, if there was a persistent current account or trade deficit. This was the situation in which the United Kingdom found itself in the 1960s, which culminated in the **devaluation** of sterling in 1967.

The Bretton Woods system faced increasing strains, not least of which was the inflationary impact of the US financing of the Vietnam War. International investors began to lose confidence in the Federal Reserve's inflation-fighting ability as well as in the US government's ability to maintain the convertibility of the US dollar with gold. Increasing capital mobility, declining trade barriers as successive GATT negotiations broke down tariff barriers, and developments in technology all contributed to an increasing disenchantment with the Bretton Woods system. If the United States was not going to play by the rules, so the argument went, then there was little incentive for other countries to play by the rules either. In the end, the Bretton Woods system broke down in 1973 and resulted in a return to **floating exchange rates**.

Some countries persisted with efforts to stabilize exchange rates. For example, Europe introduced currency arrangements known as the 'snake', in which EC central banks agreed to limit currency fluctuations to a common margin of 2.5 per cent. Eventually, the 'snake' was superseded by the launch of the EMS in 1979. Generally, most policy-makers felt that a system of floating exchange rates allowed them freedom to pursue independent economic policies. Monetarist theories that achieved popularity during the late 1970s emphasized control of money supply growth as a key economic policy instrument. Keynesian policies had fallen into disrepute, as they were seen as having failed during the period of **stagflation** of the early 1970s.

THE 1980S AND 1990S

The capital flows that took place between the first oil crisis of 1973 and 1982 were closely associated with the recycling of oil revenues. After the first oil price shock, many economies failed to tighten **monetary policy** quickly enough to offset inflation risks. After the second oil price shock most countries had learnt their lesson, and raised **interest rates** enough to prevent another outbreak of inflation. The United States led the way with an aggressive tightening of monetary policy in 1979. The subsequent increase in real interest rates made life very difficult, especially for heavily indebted emerging market countries. Net private inflows to the emerging markets fell from a peak of nearly $49 billion in 1981 to a net $5 billion outflow in 1984. In 1981, it was estimated that the exposure of US banks to Latin American debt amounted to 97 per cent of capital. The debt crisis that started in 1982 derived from a combination of unsustainable policies pursued by a lot of emerging market economies. Typically, external borrowing was used to finance large fiscal imbalances, which contributed to a rise in inflation. Also, the recession which afflicted most major economies in the early 1980s sharply cut the demand for the exports from the emerging market countries, making it difficult for them to service their debt. By 1986, the ratio of external debt service payments to exports of goods and services was 44 per cent.

There were also problems facing the major economies as a result of a massive appreciation in the US dollar. A combination of high US interest rates as well as tax cuts implemented by President Reagan made the United States a very attractive place for international investors. A surge of capital inflows pushed the dollar higher on the foreign exchanges, to such an extent that it created what economists called 'misalignment'. For economies such as Germany and Japan , a stronger dollar meant a weaker Deutschmark and Japanese yen. In turn, this increased the risk of inflation in Germany and Japan. The pressure for action intensified, resulting in the Plaza Agreement in 1985 which was designed to bring about an orderly decline in the US dollar. As it happened, the dollar had already peaked in February of that year and had started to depreciate because of market worries concerning the very high US budget and current account deficits. Indeed, the dollar started to fall so much that the G-7 economies had to intervene in the foreign exchange market merely to stabilize the currency; this was formalized in the Louvre Accord of 1987. Since then, a high degree of cooperation amongst the G-7 has been maintained in order to ensure a broad degree of stability in the foreign exchange market.

Differences of opinion between the United States and Germany over the appropriate dollar–Deutschmark exchange rate played a large part in triggering the 1987 stock market crash. This led **central banks** to provide liquidity in order to avoid a repeat of the 1929 experience. Some central banks overdid it, though. For example, the United Kingdom cut interest rates much more than other countries, and along with tax cuts ahead of the 1988 election triggered a consumer boom which ended in the 1990–92 recession. Elsewhere, Japan slashed interest rates, mainly under pressure from the US to stimulate the economy. Unfortunately, very low Japanese borrowing costs led to an explosion in Japanese property and share prices. What goes up normally comes down. The Bank of Japan, worried about inflation, hit the brakes by tightening monetary policy but this punctured the 'bubble' with dramatic effect. The collapse of the Japanese stock market brought about the worst recession Japan had experienced in 50 years. The massive depreciation of the yen since 1995 also contributed to the break of the US dollar peg against most Asian currencies during 1997 which in turn triggered a collapse in the Asian stock markets, followed by recession (*see* Jeremy Pink: 'Asia: The Lessons for Economics'). The downturn also affected other economies, in particular Russia, which was unable to sustain its fixed exchange rate of the rouble against the dollar, despite intervention in the markets. The resulting collapse of the rouble and the Russian stock and bond markets was followed by the government defaulting on its debt, leaving Western banks, hedge funds, and investors exposed and fearful that the turmoil could spread to Western Europe and the United States. There were pressures, too, on Latin American markets. The main central banks, and in particular the US Federal Reserve, loosened interest rates again to maintain liquidity and confidence. Some governments whose economies had been severely affected by the downturn, such as Malaysia, effectively introduced restrictions on capital flows to stop **hot money** from further undermining their currencies. Others followed different interventionist policies: Hong Kong's government intervened in the stock markets. The IMF received extra funding, mainly from the United States, to better equip it to provide support for economies which were under severe pressure.

CONCLUSION

The moral of the story is that economic policy does not take place in isolation from the real world. Everything affects everything else. Some commentators argue that in a world of globalized financial markets, in which money flows outweigh trade flows by a multiple of ten, markets or speculators are too powerful. At the last count, the daily turnover in the foreign exchange market per business day amounts to over $1.2 trillion, of which 25 per cent goes through the London market. However, governments are powerful and carry economic clout. In most OECD economies, governments account for around 40 per cent of spending in their own economies, so economic decisions relating to tax and spending are undoubtedly important. Government economic policies become unstuck when monetary and fiscal policies are regarded as either unsustainable or unbalanced (as, for example, in Russia). Remember that governments which want to spend more sometimes have to borrow more. This is where the markets come in as financial intermediaries. Governments can always borrow, but it depends at what price. Here, the markets will make a judgement based on the government's track record with regard to borrowing and repayment as well as its attitude towards inflation and the exchange rate. The experience of the most recent recession taught the financial community that not all markets enjoy the same rules and regulation: in Asia there were few curbs on borrowing, and accountancy and governance standards were in some cases much looser than in western economies, meaning that the downturn was more severe when it did happen. It is likely that some markets which do not enjoy the same degree of liquidity or stability as those in the United States or Europe may employ short-term restrictions on capital flow to reduce some of the biggest shocks. But this will only work as a short-term measure: it may provide some respite to an economy in which the fundamentals are sound, but will otherwise quickly become unworkable.

The global nature of markets means that central banks may need to devise their monetary policies, and governments their fiscal policies, with a longer-term view in mind: the exposure of their own investors and banks to other markets may be just as important as the state of the domestic economy. Thus, for the United States it may be considered better for long-term price stability at home perhaps to have a stable Latin America; consequently, any shifts by the Federal reserve will have implications, and may be designed to have implications, in an international context. This is the case with all the economic giants:

Japan, and the Euro group, now carry out monetary and fiscal measures which have repercussions far beyond their shores, just as the fortunes of the emerging economies in turn affect the developed world. Policy, as well as capital, has become global.

FURTHER READING

Chossudovsky, Michel, *The Globalisation of Poverty: Impacts of IMF and World Bank Reforms* (Zed, 1997).

Cohen, Daniel, and Lindenfeld, Jacqueline, *The Wealth of the World and the Poverty of Nations* (MIT Press, 1998).

Eichengreen, Barry, *Elusive Stability* (Cambridge University Press, 1993).

Eichengreen, Barry, *Globalizing Capital: A History of the International Monetary System* (Princeton University Press, 1998).

Gray, John, *False Dawns: The Delusions of Global Capitalism* (Granta, 1998).

Hahn, Frank, and Solow, Robert, *A Critical Essay on Modern Macro-Economic Theory* (Blackwell, 1997).

Korten, David, *When Corporations Rule the World* (Berrett Koehler, 1996).

Krugman, Paul, *Currencies and Crises* (MIT Press, 1992).

Olson, Mancur, *The Rise and Decline of Nations: Economic Growth, Stagflation, and Social Rigidities* (Yale University Press, 1984).

Rodrik, Dan, *Has Globalisation Gone Too Far?* (Institute for International Economics, 1997).

Skousen, Mark, *Economics of a Pure Gold Standard* (Foundation for Economic Education, 1998).

Soros, George, *The Crisis of Global Capitalism* (Little, Brown, 1998).

4

WHAT ECONOMICS
IS NOT

PAUL ORMEROD

Economic theory is based on assumptions about behaviour and time. These assumptions are taken into account when the theory is applied in order to explain and predict events. But time and again, economics has stood accused being unable to foresee trends, market changes, and catastrophes. Some question the empirical basis which drives policy: it is full of lags, inaccuracies and inconsistencies, to trip up central bankers, business people and governments. Others question the theory itself, and often succeed in developing new or alternative theories. Thus **Keynes** addressed the issue of global recession, the **monetarists** addressed the problem of **stagflation**, **Heckscher** and Ohlin and Samuelson took us forward from **Ricardo** in analysing world trade. Economists also routinely build in caveats about **neo-Classical economics**, for its static and short-term assumptions. They constantly tell policy-makers and investors that markets can go down as well as up, and that, as Neil Mackinnon indicates in his essay 'The Limits to Global Markets', often we are all powerless to do anything about it. But in the broadest sense we argue that economics will 'get better' at understanding, explaining, and predicting.

Paul Ormerod takes a radically different tack, by suggesting that many of the basic mechanistic assumptions of economics are worse than inadequate or flawed: in effect they simply do not work. He provides devastating evidence of the failure of conventional economic forecasting, and goes on to argue that actual market behaviour is influenced as much by the behaviour of others in the market, or by agents simply changing their minds, as it is by so-called fundamentals. The reality is a complex mathematical pattern of probability which today's computer power allows us to analyse more effectively than economists of previous generations. The essay – and Professor Ormerod's other work – give us an excellent introduction to some of the techniques of the science of **econometrics**, and leaves us grasping at some of the more frightening implications.

Professor Ormerod concludes that economists need to shed what he calls the 'security blanket' of the orthodox approach, and develop new and better ways to explain the market system. We see in several of the other essays how markets are becoming more powerful, global and 'open', with all the dangers inherent in that: good reasons, then, to approach our work and predictions with the Ormerod warnings very much in mind, if we want to avoid being surprised by events.

The market economies of the West represent by far the most successful form of economic organization yet devised. Whilst there are important differences between individual countries, it is their common acceptance of the capitalist mode of production which is the basis for their prosperity.

In the many millennia of human history prior to the Industrial Revolution, economic progress was extremely slow and hesitant. Countries could and did suffer economic setbacks which persisted for centuries. Indeed, it is arguable that the quality of material life of the average citizen of the Roman Empire of the first century AD was superior to that experienced subsequently almost everywhere until the Europe of the eighteenth century.

The past 200 years have seen an explosion in economic growth and living standards which is entirely without precedent. Comparisons over time are fraught with difficulty, but in the UK, for example, where industrialization first began, output per head in real terms has risen at least ten-fold over this period.

During the twentieth century, the potentially competitive form of economic structure offered by the centrally planned economies of the Soviet bloc was eventually shown to be inadequate. Their command systems proved very effective in mobilizing resources for the first stages of industrialization – so much so, that as late as the 1950s many Americans feared that the Soviet Union would overtake them economically by the end of the century. But further progress proved difficult.

The study of the western market economies is therefore extremely important. A better understanding of these instruments of prosperity is not merely an abstract intellectual goal, but one which may bring direct practical benefits.

Conventional economic theory is often described as being the theory of 'free markets'. In everyday English, the western economies are often referred to as the 'market economies'. Partly because of the imprecision of language, and partly encouraged by the bulk of the economics profession, it is easy to draw the conclusion that 'free market' theory is *the* theory of how the 'market' economies actually behave in practice.

But this is exactly what orthodox economics is *not*. It does not give a good account of how the western economies behave at the overall level.

The theory is by no means an empty box, and it does offer a number of important insights. But it is rather like physics before Newton. Certain aspects of the world are understood quite well, but only a distinctly limited amount of reality is illuminated.

This criticism of conventional economics is by no means new. In the 1930s, it was made by two great thinkers, usually perceived as being at opposite ends of the ideological spectrum. Towards the end of his long life, Friedrich von Hayek became the intellectual pin-up of the free market Thatcher and Reagan administrations. But Hayek's theories are far more subtle than politicians appreciate, and as early as 1935 he expressed the view that the actual behaviour of the capitalist economies was quite different to the postulates of free market theory, with the latter relying upon 'unrealistic special assumptions'. At virtually the same time, **Keynes** argued forcefully that the characteristics of the world assumed by orthodox economics 'happen not to be those of the economic society in which we actually live, with the result that its teaching is misleading and disastrous if we attempt to apply it to the facts of experience'.

The names of Keynes and Hayek are prominent in the public domain. That of American economics Nobel prizewinner Kenneth Arrow is far less well known outside the discipline of economics. But Arrow, now approaching his eighties, has been probably the most fertile economic theorist of the second half of the century. His greatest contribution was to place free market economic theory for the first time onto a serious, modern mathematical basis – a formidable intellectual task, a side product of which has been to clarify more rigorously than ever the limitations of the orthodox view of the world.

In short, Arrow has played a major role in the development and refinement of free market theory. Yet in 1994, he concluded that the persistence of high levels of unemployment in the West for long periods of time represented an 'empirical refutation' of such theory. For a scientist, these are strong words indeed. In everyday language, we might say instead 'the theory doesn't fit the facts' or, even more simply, 'it's wrong'. For according to theory, prices should adjust so that eventually supply and demand are brought into balance in every market. And the labour market from this perspective is a market just like any other, in which quantities of labour – people and the hours they want to work – are bought and sold. But throughout the history of the capitalist economies, except for relatively brief periods, the supply of labour has been higher than the demand. More people want to work than there are jobs, and hence the existence of unemployment.

Much of the problem for economics is that economists see the world as a machine. A very complicated one, perhaps, but nevertheless a machine, whose workings can be understood by putting together carefully and meticulously its component parts. The behaviour of the system as a whole can be deduced from a simple aggregation of these components. A lever pulled in a certain part of the machine with a certain strength will have regular and predictable outcomes elsewhere in the machine.

This view dates back to the second half of the nineteenth century, when the foundations of the current orthodoxy were first laid. Economics was greatly influenced by the achievements of the physical sciences, which were visibly transforming the world. Envious of the success and prestige of scientists, economists turned their analysis in this direction. And the intellectual self-confidence of scientists in the Victorian era stemmed precisely from a mechanistic view of the world. The complications and paradoxes posed by, for example, quantum physics did not emerge until the turn of the century, and it is only in the last couple of decades of our own century that the world of chaos has been discovered.

Real scientists are now only too well aware that the view of the world as a complicated but, in essence, straightforward machine gives an inadequate account of many important aspects of reality. But in the physical sciences, the mechanistic perspective does illuminate many problems with great success. Bridges stay up. Aircraft fly. Cars move. And they do so because the mechanical principles on which they operate are well understood.

In contrast, economists cling to the mechanistic view with ever greater fervour, despite the large and growing amount of evidence that it is not appropriate. An important illustration of this is given by economic forecasting, which still dominates the conduct of economic policy in the West. Finance ministers and central banks pronounce from time to time on the future course of factors such as the growth of the economy, **inflation** and unemployment, and their statements are eagerly dissected. Much effort is made by governments to try to make the future better than it would otherwise be by changing policies, on tax rates, interest rates, public expenditure and so on.

But this whole process is based on illusions. The illusion that it is possible, on a consistent basis over time, to make forecasts which have a reasonable degree of accuracy. And on the resulting illusion that governments can use these forecasts to successfully control short-term developments in the economy.

Even a cursory acquaintance with the evidence on the accuracy of macroeconomics forecasts raises doubts as to their value. In the June 1993 OECD *Economic Outlook,* the forecasting record of the G7 governments, the **IMF** and the OECD itself was assessed over the 1987–92 period. The accuracy of one year ahead forecasts for growth and inflation was compared with the very simple rule that next year's growth or inflation would be the same as this year's. That rule itself gave very poor forecasts, with large errors. But it was just as good as the forecasts which were actually made and arguably, in the case of inflation, marginally better.

The problems of forecasting are not confined to official bodies, nor are they particular to any school of thought as to how the economy operates. Over time, all approaches, whether governmental or private, Keynesian or monetarist, have done equally badly. From time to time an institution may appear to perform well, but in the longer run there are no unambiguous rankings of accuracy.

The problems caused by the mechanistic view are also seen in a key aspect of orthodox economic theory, namely the behaviour of individuals. People are postulated to act completely rationally. Enormous amounts of information are assumed to be gathered by each individual and then processed efficiently before deciding how his or her money should be spent or saved. As it happens, it has been demonstrated mathematically that the theory requires everyone to have access to, quite literally, an infinite amount of computing power, but this proof, inconvenient as it is for orthodoxy, is rarely mentioned outside specialized post-graduate courses. And there is an enormous amount of evidence from psychology which suggests that individuals frequently behave in ways quite different to those postulated by orthodox economics.

But there is also a very practical implication of the theory which is quite at odds with reality. In a world of rational consumers, each efficiently processing vast amounts of information, markets cannot make mistakes. The consumer is sovereign. But there are many examples of products which are technologically inferior not just surviving, but driving out of existence competitors with distinctly superior qualities. The free market in practice sometimes chooses not the best, but the worst.

Think of the development of the market for video recorders, which featured the struggle between Betamax and Sony. Betamax machines were easier to operate and had a number of features which even now are not embodied in the standard model of VCR. But Sony drove its technically superior rival out of existence. A longer-lasting illustration, so deeply embedded in our culture that it is scarcely ever noticed, is the design of the QWERTY keyboard. At various times during the last century more efficient designs have been invented and marketed seriously, but all have failed. The inferior technology prevails.

Such phenomena *can* be accounted for by changing an absolutely central assumption of conventional theory. In the standard view, the tastes and preferences of individuals are fixed, and rational choices are made on this basis. But in reality, people are often influenced directly by how others behave, and alter their tastes accordingly. A neighbour buys a new car, a relative gets a video recorder, and suddenly people in the locality or family decide that they, too, want one.

Once this assumption is made, the process by which a product can drive out a rival or, once established, be very difficult to dislodge, can be understood intuitively. If by luck or a smart marketing campaign, a product gains an early lead over its rival, a self-reinforcing process can be set up. The more people who buy it, the more likely it is that those contemplating buying will also make the same choice; the more likely it is that shops will stock it more readily, and so on.

The scholars who established the basis for modern economics in the late Victorian era knew perfectly well that this was an important feature of the real world. But they were obliged to make the simplifying assumption that it did not exist. This was not because of stupidity – far from it – but because the mathematical tools required to analyse such processes did not then exist. For example, a complete analytical under-standing of the principles by which an inferior product can eliminate its superior rival was only achieved in 1983 by the British polymath Brian Arthur, jointly with two Russian mathematicians.

The questions tackled by Arthur and his colleagues can be stated quite simply, but they lead to difficult problems in non-linear probability theory. An urn of infinite capacity is postulated to exist. It contains a mixture of white and black balls. A random sample of balls is removed from the urn, and various rules exist about the collection of balls which is put back in. For example, if more than half the balls removed turn out to be white, the whole sample is returned to the urn, along with an additional white ball. If more than half are black, the sample plus an extra black ball are put back. What, if anything, can we say about the proportion of white to black balls which will emerge in the urn in the long run?

Arthur and his colleagues were able to say a great deal about what would happen under various replacement rules. Their work may seem far removed from the practical question of why one make of VCR drove out another, but it is not. In terms of two rival new products, we can think of each purchase made by an individual consumer as the equivalent of choosing a ball of one colour, and of putting it back along with another ball of the same colour into the urn. Adding the ball shifts, ever so slightly, the probability that the next ball drawn – the choice made by the next consumer about which product to buy – will be of the same kind.

A different set of circumstances in which, and the mechanisms by which, individuals might influence directly the behaviour of others was explored by the British economist Alan Kirman in the early 1990s. This approach relies heavily upon computing power to generate solutions and so, quite literally, was simply not available to previous generations of researchers, regardless of their theoretical powers.

Kirman tackled a question which baffled biologists. Two food sources were set up, equidistant from a nest of ants, and each time an ant removed a grain, another was added. So the two piles were absolutely identical. Ants are known, when returning to the nest, to pass signals to others about which trail to follow for food – the behaviour of an ant directly influences the behaviour of others. The biologists worked out theoretically the proportion of ants which would visit each pile. But the reality of the experiment was quite different to expectations. The proportion was never static, but changed constantly. Periods of relative stability were punctuated by episodes of large and rapid change. Puzzled, the biologists repeated the experiment with different species of ants, which pass messages to each other in different ways. They had one food pile, and observed the proportion of ants passing over two identical bridges to get to it. But the results were the same.

Kirman solved the problem with a model of brilliant simplicity. Each ant, when emerging from the nest, has a probability of repeating its own past behaviour in terms of which pile to visit or which bridge to cross. It has a probability of changing its own mind, and, to complete the picture, it has a probability of being influenced by ants which it meets returning to the nest. This model, straightforward to describe, gives rise to complex patterns of behaviour which are qualitatively identical to those observed in the experiments.

This kind of behaviour is not confined to the humble world of ants. It pervades dealing rooms in financial markets. Traders, like ants, can repeat their own past patterns of behaviour, can decide to change their own minds, or can alter behaviour in response to the bombardment of information they receive about how others are acting. This latter in particular causes important problems for the ability of orthodox theory to account for what happens on the world's foreign exchange and **stock markets**. It is here above all that conventional free market theory ought to give an extremely good account of what goes on. Yet it does not.

The problem is that asset prices – such as the dollar/sterling exchange rate, the price of General Motors shares – are much more volatile than standard free market theory says they should be. They move up and down much more than they ought to according to orthodoxy. And in particular there are too many big changes. Of course, not every day sees a crash such as that of 13 October 1987, when the value of many shares fell by 20 per cent in a single day. But large changes in individual share prices are often seen. And major currencies can, after long periods of comparative stability, change very rapidly in value, by large amounts.

The idealized world of free market theory ought to be closest to reality in exactly these markets. Financial markets operate in an almost completely unrestricted way, largely free of government intervention; information is widely and very rapidly available to all agents in the market – there are a large number of buyers and sellers; markets exist not just to buy and sell today, but contracts can be struck now to trade in a variety of complicated ways at dates in the future.

The individual buyers and sellers ought to process all the information available on an asset efficiently, and set the price accordingly. For share prices, for example, the relevant information is the flow of dividends which is expected to accrue from the ownership of shares in the company. But actual dividend payments fluctuate much less than do the associated share prices.

The fact that asset prices are much more volatile than free market theory suggests may seem a rather esoteric criticism, even though from a purely scientific point of view it is very powerful. But it has a serious practical implication. Recent years have seen spectacular growth in **derivatives** markets. These often extremely complicated financial instruments are widely used by companies around the world to cover themselves against the risks associated with future changes in share prices and exchange rates.

From time to time, scandals such as the Barings débâcle break out, but the real problem goes much deeper than occasional bouts of chicanery or outright criminality. The highly abstruse formulae which are used as the basis for the pricing of derivatives are essentially calculated on the assumption that the degree of asset price volatility is that implied by conventional economic theory. So the whole structure of world derivative markets carries an extra degree of risk which is not reflected in the prices. As yet, no one has been able to solve the problem of how important this is in practice. If we are lucky, it will be small. If not, free market theory could precipitate a major financial crash.

More generally, there is no guarantee that the untrammelled use of the price mechanism will lead to an efficient allocation of resources. The textbooks for Economics 101 spend a long time 'proving' that the price mechanism in a free market does work in this way. At its most elegant, the theory is a dazzling intellectual construct. But the textbooks do not mention that their 'theorems' only hold in a timeless world, in which the future does not exist.

A crucial research task in post-war economics, which attracted some of the finest minds in the profession, was precisely to incorporate the future into the free market theoretical model. But by the end of the 1960s it had been demonstrated conclusively that this was not possible. Once the future is introduced into the core theoretical model of economics, the widely taught propositions on the efficiency of the price mechanism are no longer valid. This does not mean that prices do not matter at all, that individuals and companies do not react to price changes. But it does imply that the whole process is far more subtle than is allowed for by conventional theory.

In many ways, the discipline of economics is more divided than for a very long time. The majority of the profession clings more and more tightly to orthodoxy, almost as a security blanket. The more imaginative, particularly in America, are thinking of new and potentially better ways of understanding the marvellous system of the western market economies. In Europe, North America, Japan and now in Asia, this economic system has freed millions upon millions of people from lives of grinding poverty and unremitting drudgery.

In the new ideas and paradigms which are being explored, some elements of the old orthodoxy will certainly survive. But the first step forward is to dispel the illusion that free market economic theory is an adequate description of the western market economies in practice. Above all else, that is what conventional economics is *not*.

FURTHER READING

Heji, Schumacher, Hanzon (eds), *System Dynamics in Economic and Financial Models* (John Wiley, 1997).

Krugman, Paul, *Peddling Prosperity* (W. W. Norton, 1994).

Mankiw, Romer and Weil (article): 'A Contribution to the Empirics of Economic Growth' (*Quarterly Journal of Economics*, 1992).

Mullineux, A. W., *Business Cycles and Financial Crises* (Harvester Wheatsheaf, 1990).

Ormerod, Paul, *Butterfly Economics* (Faber & Faber, 1997).

Ormerod, Paul, *The Death of Economics* (Faber & Faber, 1994).

Veblen, Thorstein, *The Theory of the Leisure Class* (various paperback editions).

II
THE GLOBAL
CONTEXT

5

ASIA: THE LESSONS FOR ECONOMICS

JEREMY PINK

For 20 years many of the East Asian economies, particularly those that became known as the 'Tigers' (Singapore, Hong Kong, Malaysia, South Korea, Taiwan, Thailand, the Philippines, even Indonesia), were regarded as textbook examples of high-growth, high-productivity, rapidly emerging nations. During much of the same period the Japanese economy was taken as a mighty powerhouse not just for Asia but for the world as a whole, and Japanese products ousted many American ones, even in the US domestic market. China was set to become the home of the new revolution – not a Marxist one, but a highly capitalist version, as western firms prepared to reap the benefits of a market of over a billion consumers.

In 1997 it all appeared to turn upside down. Currency crises forced a series of devaluations which exposed major economic defects – some structural, some due to patronage and corruption in the banking and industrial systems of several of the Tigers. Japan's currency was over-valued: its institutions were in need of reform; its economy was stalled and would later move into recession. Japan's downturn – combined with the devaluations and a flight of capital on an unprecedented scale – turned the Asian Economic Miracle into the Asian Crisis. Stock markets crashed around the world: there were fears that the 'Asian contagion' would spread to Eastern Europe and Latin America, taking the US and Western European economies down too.

The International Monetary Fund moved in to shore up some economies, but its prescriptive policy requirements were too much for others, who chose to go it alone. There were suggestions that China would devalue its currency, adding its own massive economy to the deflationary forces in the region. There was mob violence in Indonesia. And in Japan observers lost count of the number of worthless fiscal stimulus packages which were unveiled to try to tackle recession without addressing Japan's urgent banking and structural problems. Yet at the time that this book is published the outlook for Asia has shifted from the negative to the beginnings of positive. Jeremy Pink examines the lessons for Asia and for economics. He concludes that it is our best measure so far of what we mean by the Global Economy (*see also* essays by Neil Mackinnon and

David Hale), and that it was in a sense the global nature of economies and markets that limited the danger of the 'Asian contagion'.

As with the other two 'regional' essays, this is a way of looking at economic theory in practice across many countries: it can be read along with the entries on **exchange rate theory**, **balance of payments**, **theory of trade** and **trade bodies**.

Asia's Economies Until 1997

In the 20 years to 1997, the International Monetary Fund estimates that Asia's economies (excluding Japan) experienced annual real gross domestic product increases of between 7 and 7.5 per cent per year. That means that Asia's GDP doubled every ten years, and quadrupled in real terms from 1980 to 1997. Compared to western economic growth of less than 3 per cent per annum in real terms during that same time period, it is unsurprising that Asia was regarded as 'an economic miracle'.

Over the same 20 year period, many Asian countries climbed the economic food chain. Countries like Singapore, Korea, Hong Kong and Taiwan made the transition from low-cost manufacturing centres to high value-added service economies. Meanwhile, other Asian countries stepped in as new low-cost manufacturing centres. Countries like Indonesia, China, Thailand and Malaysia emerged as cheap labour sources for western and Japanese companies.

During most of this period, the main economic power in the region was Japan. Japan in its own right had experienced what many described as an economic miracle. After the Second World War, Japanese business and government together systematically built the country into the world's second most powerful economy after the United States. The government essentially closed the domestic market to foreign competition, to allow home-grown enterprises time to develop and prosper. Japanese businesses took the form of a series of *keiretsu*, vertically integrated companies that straddled virtually every facet of the Japanese economy. And the *keiretsu*, such as Mitsubishi, Matsui and others, enjoyed unbridled growth during the post-war period. They promised lifetime employment. They developed and created manufacturing standards that produced goods of a much higher and more consistent quality than their international counterparts. Japanese businesses became experts at enhancing and honing existing technologies and then taking those products to market. By the early 1970s, Japanese car makers were dominating even the once immune US market. The Japanese economic miracle was in full swing.

The Japanese *keiretsu* were to a large extent free of competition within their domestic markets, which were notoriously difficult to penetrate because of government regulations. The banks were a ready source of credit, and because of the special relationship among government, banks, and *keiretsu*, there was little to restrict lending, underpinned by the high savings ratio typical of the region (for Japan, around twice that of the United States). This explains the property and asset boom of the late 1980s and early 1990s.

Slowdowns in the western economies which had become markets for Japanese goods, as well as parking places for financial assets, along with chronic current account surpluses and a strong yen, reduced demand for exports, and tended to bring money 'back home'. The banks continued to lend as the *keiretsu* continued to push for market share in an international market which was either shrinking or barely growing.

The result was the bursting of the asset bubble, and the first signs of recession in Japan. This took place in the context of the smaller economies of Asia expanding, and basing that expansion once again on easy credit, a large market for cheap exports in Japan, and inward investment from both the West and Japan.

The iceberg struck in July 1997. On 2 July, the day after Hong Kong reverted to Chinese rule, Thailand effectively devalued its currency, the baht. One dollar, which used to buy about 25 baht, now bought more than 35. That devaluation led to a downward spiral in many other Asian economies. Thailand called in the IMF. Devaluations and recession became the norm. Malaysia blamed international speculators. Korea watched as some of its *chaebol* (the equivalent of the Japanese *keiretsu*, with the same close relationships with the banks) – and its banks – went bust. Indonesia suffered social unrest, much of it directed at the ethnic Chinese who control a majority of the local economy but make up only about 10 per cent of the population. Markets around the world trembled, investors left not just Asia but all emerging economies, speeding the collapse of Russia and causing anxieties about Latin America. Growth in the United States and Western Europe was said by many to be under threat.

It is worth noting what set off the devaluations in Thailand and some of the Asian economies. Many had linked their currencies to the US dollar. Thailand set its exchange rate at roughly 25 baht to the dollar and Indonesia put its currency at roughly 2,200 rupiah to the dollar, with a planned devaluation of about 5 per cent a year. In a rush to build infrastructure and to grow their economies, countries and companies had borrowed money at these exchange rates to fuel expansion. A company, for example, would borrow money in US dollars and plan to pay it back in its local currency. Or, it would borrow money in Japanese yen – especially as the US dollar appreciated against the Japanese currency – and pay it back in the local currency.

Credit expanded wildly, as foreign investors perceived little or no currency risk. Banks granted loans to borrowers with dubious credit records or for projects with little economic viability. Banks also offered higher and higher returns to investors, which in turn sent interest rates soaring. It was only a matter of time before the markets realized that many of their loans were not viable, and moved to withdraw their investments. By the same token, it was only a matter of time before the lack of return on these investments – financed in dollars or yen – meant that the baht would lose value against the dollar: in simple terms, there weren't enough baht to buy the dollars to pay back the loans. The central bank and the government could not sustain the exchange rate. They let it float, and the roof fell in.

For neighbouring Indonesia, Malaysia, and the Philippines, the same questions were asked. Rightly or wrongly, a massive capital outflow had begun, and exchange rates across the region tumbled.

IMF AND GLOBAL FEARS

The IMF became involved in Thailand, Indonesia, and South Korea, providing loans to help restructure banks and financial institutions. Recipients of IMF funds are generally expected to follow tight fiscal and monetary policies, to maintain exchange rates and government solvency. Double-digit interest rates became the norm, and although the IMF later adopted more lenient policies as a deflationary swing became evident, there has been criticism of its role. Some countries, such as Malaysia, chose to go it alone, with premier Mahathir Mohamad delivering sharp rebukes for western financial speculators, whom he blamed for undermining Asian currencies. In the West, too, there were calls both for the IMF to be granted more funding – at the time, it was awaiting US Congressional approval for a further $18bn worth of funds – and for it to be replaced by a more regionally based Asian Monetary Fund, or AMF. One of the most consistent IMF critics is Jeffrey Sachs, professor of International Trade at Harvard University. He argues that for a region such as Asia, with the highest savings ratios in the world, the anti-inflationary prescription of tight monetary and fiscal policy – which may have worked in other parts of the world like Latin America – was both unnecessary and dangerous.

Certainly the downturn was both sharp and deep. By 1998, countries which had been known as 'tigers', such as South Korea, Malaysia, the Philippines, Thailand, Singapore, and Hong Kong, were looking at negative or flat growth, which in a region accustomed to expansion of 8 per cent or more per annum felt especially harsh. Indonesia had negative growth of around 15 per cent.

Fears in the West of the spread of what became known as the 'Asian contagion' turned out to be largely unfounded. This was partly because the economic fundamentals in the United States and Europe were generally sound, and also because the US Federal Reserve eased its monetary policy not only to provide domestic liquidity but also to provide calming signals to economies closer to home, such as South America. Most of Europe also eased interest rates, a trend probably driven more by the need for convergence ahead of the single currency than fear of recession amongst central bankers on the Continent (*see* essays by Ian Harnett and David Hale). Companies with direct exposure in Asia were affected, but equity markets recovered in late 1998, recovering all or most of the gains made during the boom period up to the summer of that year. The buoyancy of equities markets may have owed something to the change in the pattern of share ownership in Europe, and the development of it in the US (*see* 'New Patterns of Economic Behaviour' by Justin Urquhart Stewart).

THE ASIAN SUPERPOWERS: EXAMPLE OR CAUSE?

Japan could be regarded as the leader of the 'Asian economic miracle', but equally may be seen as a major factor in the extent and duration of Asia's present recession. Japan was a ready market for goods produced in the less mature economies, with their lower labour costs. Japanese companies invested heavily, opening plants in many of the developing countries of the region. The Japanese downturn came before that in East Asia, which it helped precipitate. Creaking or downright fraudulent banking systems which had made too many bad loans were thrown into sharp relief when the enterprises they propped up found themselves in a contracting market. When the collapse came, instead of weaker currencies making goods more competitive in Japan, consumer spending there had all but dried up. The Japanese banking system had imploded under the weight of its own bad loans, and successive governments had failed to tackle the problems. There had been various attempts at fiscal stimulus as well as banking reform, but until late 1998 the markets and most observers had regarded them as 'too little too late'.

China played a different but no less important role. Under Deng Xiao Ping the communist People's Republic had embraced many of the tenets of capitalism. It liberalized its banks and opened its financial markets, ushering in an era of dynamic and unprecedented growth. Citizens abandoned rural areas and flocked to urban centres looking for better jobs and brighter economic fortunes. From 1992 to 1995, China achieved double digit growth in domestic gross domestic product. In 1992 alone, GDP grew at an astounding rate of 14.5 per cent. But, as capitalism took hold, income gaps in the country widened and the inflation rate climbed. China had to take steps to shore up and stabilize its economy.

Under Finance Minister Zhu Rongji, the government tried to steer the economy from the brink of overheating to a relatively soft landing. The difficulty was that if reform were to continue, high levels of growth would be necessary to prevent mass unemployment and possible social unrest. This particularly applied to the state-owned enterprises (SOEs), the groaning monoliths of a Stalinist command economy which still represented the bulk of Chinese manufacturing and infrastructure. Their role was not only to maintain employment, but also to provide for welfare needs such as pensions and housing. Small wonder then that the banks were instructed by the government to continue lending to the SOEs, even though they were inefficient and never had a chance of becoming profitable.

One issue facing the Chinese government was its corrupt and ineffective tax collection system. Any fiscal measures to stimulate growth and provide welfare were extremely hard for the central government to execute, as the system relied largely on local officials – often with their own local agenda and political masters – to collect revenues. The other problem concerned monetary management: as was so common in Asia, the banks were saddled with bad loans, many of them to the SOEs. The fear of a run on the banks dogged financial planners and it was quite common for savers to find their money was 'unreachable' – an attempt to maintain solvency in the banking system. This meant that instruments such as interest rates had less meaning than in a more open economy.

On top of all these conundrums came the recession in the region. The Chinese had pegged their currency, the yuan, to the dollar, like so many of their neighbours. A devaluation of the yuan would have had the effect of making Chinese products cheaper overseas, and stimulating domestic production, but it would also have made imports largely disappear in what was still essentially a third-world economy. This could have choked off the consumer revolution that China's new leaders had pursued with the goal of higher living standards across society.

Of course for the rest of Asia the effect of a yuan devaluation would have been catastrophically deflationary. The real fear in late 1998 was whether the Chinese could 'hold the line' in the face of recession and restructuring. Officially the predictions of around 8 per cent growth in 1998 were maintained, and there was still optimism that rates of between 4 and 5 per cent would continue over the next year or two. At this point it is too early to know whether a recovery across the region would come soon enough to re-expand China's growth without the need for devaluation.

THE LESSONS

Probably the main lesson from the Asian expansion and recession is that rapid growth can be achieved and enjoyed, but that any cyclical downturn will show up weaknesses which may have lain uncovered or ignored in the banking system. In the case of Asia, the banking problems combined with traditionally high savings ratios created major deflationary pressures. The Japanese economy, whose banking sector was paralysed by bad debts, and whose spending was choked by a lack of confidence and a cyclical downturn after over-expansion in the 1980s, played a major role in the duration and severity of the Asian recession. The IMF may have inadvertently exacerbated the downturn. The recession did not become global because the economic conditions were different in Europe and the United States, and because monetary conditions there were eased. Eventually growth should return to most of the Asian economies, but it remains to be seen whether the overhaul of the banking and accountancy sectors will be sufficiently thorough and transparent to avoid difficulties in the next cyclical downturn.

FURTHER READING

Haley, George *et al.*, *The New Asian Emperors* (Butterworth-Heinemann, 1998).

Henderson, Callum, *Asia Falling: Making Sense of the Asian Currency Crisis and its Aftermath* (McGraw Hill, 1998).

Ito, Takatoshi, *The Japanese Economy* (MIT Press, 1992).

Katz, Richard, *Japan – The System that Soured: The Rise and Fall of the Japanese Economic Miracle* (M. E. Sharpe, 1998).

Lardy, Nicholas R., *China's Unfinished Economic Revolution* (Brookings Institution, 1998).

Li, Conghua, *China: the Consumer Revolution* (John Wiley, 1998).

Phongpaichit, Pasuk, and Baker, Chris, *Thailand's Boom and Bust* (University of Washington, 1998).

Sako, Mari, and Sato, Hiroki, *Japanese Labour and Management in Transition* (Routledge, 1997).

Tsuru, Shigeto, and Galbraith, John Kenneth, *Japan's Capitalism* (Cambridge University Press, 1996).

6

THE UNITED STATES
AS GLOBAL LEADER

DAVID HALE

This essay gives us practical testimony of the global markets and the forces moving them. We saw in the essay by Neil Mackinnon how capital markets have grown increasingly international, and the Asian and Russian collapses of 1997–98 carried shockwaves across the globe which sparked major fears even in the world's largest economy. Hale argues that a mixture of monetary and fiscal policy, combined with the buoyancy of the US equities market, limited the extent of the downturn. He outlines the lessons for economics and for policy.

The changing patterns of investment behaviour and demographics – and their lessons for economics – are discussed further in the essay by Justin Urquhart Stewart. And naturally the essay can be read in conjunction with its counterpart on Asia, by Jeremy Pink. As the US economy is a driver for world trade and financial flows, Europe may take heart (especially given the positive outlook for the euro which we see in the essay on Europe by Ian Harnett).

Hale's essay uses some of the concepts outlined in the entries on **theory of trade**, **stock markets**, **inflation** and **money supply**.

It also touches on current thinking in macroeconomic management, where small monetary changes in good time are regarded as preferable to heavy pressure to expand or contract the economy (see, therefore, **monetary policy**, **supply-side economics** and **neo-Keynesian economics**).

CAN AMERICA'S STOCK MARKET BUBBLE PREVENT A GLOBAL DOWNTURN?

One of the great surprises of the US economy during 1998 was its capacity to withstand the economic shocks resulting from the east Asia financial crisis and the Russian default, something in which the stock market played a pivotal role.

At the end of 1997, most economists were revising downward their forecasts of US output growth by 0.5–1.0 per cent to adjust for the impact of the east Asia crisis on both import and exports. As the United

States sends about one third of her exports to Asia and is the major market for the exports of Asian countries which had experienced large currency devaluations, it was widely perceived that the US trade deficit would deteriorate considerably. The concerns about export losses were especially great on the west coast of the United States because the states in that region depend far more heavily upon Asian trade than other regions. In 1995, for example, the Pacific coast states sent about 45 per cent of their exports to Asia, compared to 15 per cent for the southeast and mid-Atlantic states and about 30 per cent for states in the middle west. In the case of California and Washington, the Asian market accounts for over half of exports. America's service sector suffered from the Asian downturn as well. There was a sharp drop in Asian tourism to Hawaii, while Las Vegas casinos reported that their baccarat tables suffered a 25 per cent slump in the first half of 1998 because of the loss of the high rollers from the overseas Chinese communities of southeast Asia.

The Asia crisis had a negative impact on US trade during the first quarter of 1998. During that period the trade deficit widened by an amount equal to 2.0 per cent of real GDP. Exports to the three Asian countries with IMF programmes slumped by 37 per cent during the first two months of 1998, while exports to Japan fell by 7.6 per cent.

But the trade deterioration did not dampen the economy's overall growth momentum because the growth rate of domestic final sales accelerated to 6.1 per cent from 1.9 per cent during the fourth quarter and thus boosted the growth rate of total output to 4.2 per cent from 3.7 per cent during the final quarter of 1997.

The equity market remained resilient, rising to new highs during the first five months of 1998 because of investor optimism about the benign outlook for interest rates as well as confidence that the east Asia crisis had been contained. The poor performance of Asia's economies probably also boosted foreign demand for US financial assets, after two years of unprecedented growth in foreign purchases of US bonds and equities. During 1997, foreign investors purchased $66 billion of US equities and $184 billion of US Treasury securities, compared to $12.5 billion of equity and $232 billion of government securities during 1996. The buoyancy of the US equity market helped to bolster household wealth and encouraged consumer spending to rise at a 5.7 per cent annual rate during the first quarter.

This set the tone for some of the most dramatic mood swings ever in the US equity market, initially starting with Russia's default on its sovereign debt in mid-August 1998. There was a flight to quality in financial markets all over the world which drove up the borrowing costs of developing countries and dramatically increased spreads between various categories of domestic bonds. The widening in domestic bond spreads resulted in high losses for America's largest hedge fund, Long-Term Capital, which then had to turn to the Federal Reserve Bank of New York for help in restructuring its balance sheet. These shocks produced an abrupt tightening of credit conditions throughout the US economy. Banks curtailed credit lines to property developers and other marginal borrowers. The issuance of new bonds and commercial paper plummeted. At the IMF meeting in early October, some senior Federal Reserve officials stated that the world financial system was in the midst of its greatest crisis since the Second World War.

The mood of pessimism did not last long, however. The stock market stabilized during October as the Fed moved to ease interest rates and then rallied to a new high in mid-November in response to both further Fed easing and a wave of merger announcements. How could investor sentiment change so dramatically, when large parts of the world economy were still suffering from recession and the outlook for US corporate profits appeared to be deteriorating?

There were several factors which combined to change investor sentiment. First, the Federal Reserve moved decisively to ease monetary policy. Despite the fact that the US economy had been enjoying robust growth and was probably at full employment, the Federal Reserve Governors recognized that the contagion effects of the Russia crisis were a threat to both the world economy and to US financial stability. If they had procrastinated, there probably would have been a much sharper deterioration of domestic financial asset prices during late September and October.

Secondly, the US Congress responded to the crisis by finally approving the Clinton administration's request for $18 billion of new funding for the IMF. The approval of the US equity contribution permitted the IMF to raise over $90 billion of new capital from all of its members and once again play a more effective role as a global lender of last resort. Prior to September, by contrast, the US Congress had been hostile to the IMF and thus increased market anxiety about its ability to help countries experiencing liquidity crises. Indeed, the Russian default itself had a devastating impact on investor confidence precisely because it called into question the ability of the IMF and the US Treasury to manage risks in the global financial systems. Before August, it had been widely assumed that Russia was 'too nuclear to go bust'.

The third factor which boosted the market during November was the relatively good performance of the Democrats in the mid-term Congressional elections. Before the poll, many investors had feared that a Republican victory would produce a long impeachment trial after the Starr inquiry, crippling the Clinton presidency and undermining the ability of the United States to play an effective leadership role. With the Japanese government deeply unpopular and the new German socialist government a relative unknown, the markets had become concerned about a systemic leadership void in the G-7, not just the United States.

Finally, the G-7 countries, under the leadership of British Chancellor of the Exchequer Gordon Brown, issued a communiqué during late October 1998 outlining an agenda for strengthening the global financial system through boosting the capital of the IMF, improving bank supervision and developing better strategies for crisis management. As with all G-7 statements, the communiqué was stronger on themes than details, but its goal was to assure the markets that the G-7 governments recognized that the crisis environment which followed the Russian default would require structural reforms, not just monetary fine tuning.

The rally in the US equity market in November and December of 1998 was so dramatic that most analysts were convinced that the risk of a 1999 recession had abated, while others were concerned about the possible re-emergence of a bubble economy. The equity market rose to new highs despite the fact that US corporate profits had peaked nearly a year before. There was also a speculative frenzy in Internet-related equities on a scale comparable to the greatest financial manias in recorded history. (*See* 'Technology' essay by Richard Lander.)

The mini-boom on Wall Street was exactly what the world economy needed in order to cope with the contagion effects of the Asia crisis and Russia's debt default on the credit access of developing countries. To avoid a dip in world economic growth to its lowest level since the Second World War, the US economy would need to sustain a growth rate well above 2 per cent in 1999. At the time of the IMF meeting in early October 1998, there was so much pessimism about the credit environment resulting from the Russia default and the Long-Term Capital débâcle that many influential American forecasters predicted the United States would experience an outright recession during the first half of 1999. As there is no clear alternative to the American growth locomotive for sustaining the world economy, such an outcome would have been extremely negative for the already depressed economies of Asia, Latin America, and other regions sensitive to declining commodity prices or volatile capital flows.

There is little doubt that the stock market has become an important growth stimulant in the US economy. The ratio of stock market capitalization to GDP has shot up to 140 per cent, the highest level ever recorded in US history. The previous peak was 82 per cent of GDP, in 1929, while the 60-year moving average is about 49 per cent. The stock market boom lowered the cost of equity capital and thus helped to encourage a large increase in business investment. There was also a dramatic expansion in the number of equity IPOs, with benign consequences for both employment creation and capital spending. The household sector has enjoyed such large wealth gains that consumer spending during 1998 increased more rapidly than income and caused the personal savings rate to become negative for the first time in 60 years. The stock market also helped the United States to finance its current account deficit by attracting an unprecedented flow of foreign capital into the equity market. In the first half of 1998, for example, foreign demand for US equities was $88 billion at annual rates, compared to purchases of only $10–15 billion per annum during the mid-1990s. In fact, the United States is developing a new balance of payments equilibrium in which the household sector is financing both consumption and the current account deficit, by selling overvalued corporate equities to foreign investors. Whereas Japanese purchases of Treasury bonds were the swing element in financing the US current account deficit during the late 1980s, it is now European demand for US equities and other financial assets which is funding the current account deficit. In the first half of 1998, for example, European investors purchased $143 billion of US securities, whereas Asian investors purchased only $6.6 billion.

As the stock market has emerged as a far more important force in the US economy than ever before, it also represents a potential new source of vulnerability. There is little doubt that a large and sustained correction in the equity market would now have a more powerful dampening effect on the US economy than any other stock market correction of the modern era.

There are several potential factors which make a downturn possible. First, the US corporate sector is now experiencing a profit squeeze. There will probably be only a modest profit decline during 1998 and 1999 compared to profit contractions of 20–30 per cent in traditional business cycle adjustments. But with the market selling at a p/e multiple above 25 and analysts still forecasting double-digit profit growth next year, at the time of writing it is unclear how many profit disappointments investors will tolerate as the economy slows. If the Fed approaches a go-slow approach to new monetary easing, negative profit surprises could produce larger price corrections than they did during a period when interest rates were falling.

The profit squeeze has resulted from traditional business cycle factors, such as tight labour markets, and a world economy with so much surplus capacity that it is difficult for goods-producing firms to raise prices. The downturn in profits poses macroeconomic risks for the economy, because capital investment has been one of the economy's major growth locomotives during the past few years, and eroding profit margins could dampen business enthusiasm for new investment. In fact, there is an intense debate underway about whether capital spending could drag the economy into recession. The pessimists point out that capacity utilization rates have already fallen below 80 per cent because of the surge which has occurred in productive capacity growth since 1995. The optimists point out that capital spending has been overwhelmingly concentrated in short life capital equipment which becomes obsolete every two or three years. In 1998, for example, high technology equipment spending was likely to be about $383 billion, compared to only $24 billion for industrial buildings and $134 billion for heavy industrial equipment. In the early 1980s, expenditure on heavy industrial equipment was twice as large as spending on high technology items, whereas high technology goods are now three time more important. If the obsolesence factor were to dominate, capital spending could slow, but not by enough to produce a broad-based downturn.

The most positive factor in the capital spending outlook is the continuing resilience of consumer spending. There was a healthy gain in retail sales after the stock market turbulence of 1998. This helped the corporate sector to finish 1998 with lean inventory and to resume modest growth of industrial production.

The second risk confronting the equity market is the danger of a credit crunch. The financial market shocks clearly produced a shift towards caution in both the banking system and the domestic credit markets. The US economy depends far more upon securitized finance than other industrial countries. The bank share of US credit flows has been declining for several years, while sectors such as asset-backed securities, commercial paper and bonds have been growing steadily. In the first half of 1998, for example, bank lending was about $221 billion compared to $218 billion for commercial paper, $1.4 trillion for bonds and $321 billion for asset-backed securities.

The lending squeeze resulting from the financial shocks will probably reduce credit access for marginal borrowers, such as corporations with low credit ratings and sub-prime household lenders, but it is unlikely to produce an across-the-board contraction of credit availability. The mutual fund industry is not experiencing redemptions. Insurance companies have surplus liquidity. The US banking system has tripled its equity capital during the 1990s. Broad measures of the money supply are still expanding at a double digit pace. The only sector which is experiencing a large and sustained contraction of liquidity is hedge funds. Hedge fund deleveraging will lessen the supply of capital for investment in speculative securities, such as emerging market debt, but it should not have a lasting impact on the domestic debt and equity markets. The recent upsurge of merger announcements also suggests that there will be a fresh supply of liquidity for the equity market from firms purchasing shares or simply eliminating them through mergers.

The third risk for the US equity market is that the large current account deficit now developing could make global investors more apprehensive about dollar securities and reallocate their portfolios into the new European currency. The fact that the United States will have a current account deficit of over $300 billion during 1999, while Europe will still have a surplus exceeding $100 billion suggests that the new European currency should be encouraged to appreciate in order to help Europe play a more supportive role in the global economy. (*See* 'Europe – the Next Five Years', by Ian Harnett.) A scenario which could alarm the domestic financial markets would be one in which the dollar fell so sharply that foreigners abandoned US financial assets, forcing interest rates to rise sharply. Several factors suggest that the dollar will not experience a large depreciation against the new European currency. First, it appears that the growth rate of the US economy will be at least 1.5–2.5 per cent in 1999 and thus match the growth rate of the leading continental European economies. Secondly, the major continental European banks have potentially serious problems developing with emerging market lending. As a result of their experience in Latin America during the 1980s, American banks were cautious about lending to developing countries during the 1990s, whereas European banks were encouraged by their governments to expand in east Asia because of concerns that otherwise, the United States and Japan would dominate the region. The problem of the European banks with loan quality, coupled with the low level of inflation now prevailing in Europe, should encourage the new European central bank to reduce interest rates during the first quarter of 1999. Thirdly, a large dollar depreciation against the euro is the issue which would have the greatest potential to provoke a conflict between the new European Central Bank and European finance ministers.

Most European governments have rejected the proposals from Mr Oskar LaFontaine for greater fiscal stimulus, and some even contend that they favour the so-called Greenspan/Clinton model of an easy monetary policy coupled with a tight fiscal policy in order to promote lower interest rates. They also recognize that such a policy mix would be less likely to promote currency appreciation than a high fiscal deficit policy modelled after the American one during the Volcker/Reagan years. The problem for Europe is that the United States has developed a large external deficit despite a federal budget surplus, because of changes in private savings behaviour. The current account deficit is being financed by foreign demand for US securities, which could now falter because of a stock market correction. Since the European economy is dominated by medium technology industries which are exchange rate sensitive, a sustained dollar depreciation against the euro would provoke strong political demands for a mixture of monetary fine tuning and intervention to stabilize exchange rates. The European Central Bank is very sensitive to these dangers and thus will attempt to restrain appreciation in the value of the euro to a maximum of 10–12 per cent during its first few years.

The fourth risk facing the US equity market is that the global financial environment will continue to be treacherous and could provoke new crises comparable to those which destabilized the markets during 1998. Asian economies such as Korea and Indonesia will continue to be mired in severe recessions, which could strain the tolerance of their populations for orthodox economic policies. It would be difficult for any developing country to produce a shock to the psychology of global investors as severe as the Russian default of August 1997, but concern about political and social stability could continue to inhibit capital flows to emerging market countries and thus limit their potential for rapid recovery.

Finally, there is a risk that America's large and growing trade deficit could provoke new tensions over product dumping by developing countries in the US marketplace. The expansion of the trade deficit will probably also make it difficult for the administration to obtain new fast-track trade negotiating authority. Fears of a trade war would probably encourage heavy selling of the US dollar and could set the stage for a large correction in the equity market as well.

Could the Dow Jones Average Rise to 12,000?

While the risks in the equity market outlook are well known, there is also potential for positive surprises. First, central banks could continue to reduce interest rates because of concern about deflation. Several countries have recently reported outright declines in their consumer price indices (Japan, China, Singapore, Sweden, Brazil). If the Federal Reserve reduces its official funds rate to 4.0 per cent and the new European Central Bank eases by 50 basis points, it would not be difficult to imagine further equity market rallies in both North America and Europe.

The second factor which could help to produce a better than expected environment for US equities would be a recovery in the Japanese economy large enough to set the stage for a gradual improvement in the US trade deficit after 1999. The Japanese government has unveiled so many stimulus packages during recent years that investors have become jaded and cynical about the prospects for a Japanese recovery. But the legislation which is now being implemented goes much further than ever before in attempting to address the problems of the banking system while providing nominal fiscal stimulus equal to 4.8 per cent of GDP in the form of large reductions in marginal income tax rates, new incentives for information technology investment, and other forms of public spending. This package has more potential for success than others because of its microeconomic details. It is essential that Japan should achieve a recovery by the year 2000 in order to provide the global economy with a new growth locomotive. If Japan does not recover, the Asian economies will also suffer and the US trade deficit could expand towards $400 billion, or a level which could generate great political conflict. There is a risk that at some point a Tokyo equity market upturn could divert funds from the New York equity market but the US financial markets would still fare better if there were a more broadly based global recovery than one dependent solely upon further dramatic expansion of the US trade deficit.

The third factor which could help US investor confidence would be more signs of recovery in the emerging market countries. Investors will be searching for signs of recovery both because of the implications for corporate profitability and to reassure themselves that developing countries will not follow the example of Malaysia (exchange controls) or Russia (default). It is important to recognize that most emerging market countries are responding to the crisis in ways which should enhance their future financial stability and thus make their economies even more attractive for foreign investors than they were at the start of the 1990s boom.

The crisis of the past 12 months in emerging markets resulted from microeconomic factors, not global monetary policy shocks, and so the key to restoring growth will depend heavily upon microeconomic reforms. Developing countries have to find new ways to regulate the growth of short maturity dollar borrowing by their corporate sectors when their local interest rates are above dollar interest rates. They have to obtain more foreign capital in order to strengthen their banking systems and lessen their vulnerability to future liquidity shocks. In some countries, there is also a need for changes in the corporate governance process in order to insure that managements focus on profitability, not just growth of sales and output. During the 1990s, many Asian corporations made capital spending decisions without any regard to profitability and set the stage for capacity gluts which then guaranteed that they would lose money. During 1998, there were several examples of policy reform designed to address the microeconomic factors which set the stage for the recent crisis in emerging markets. China has been playing a very constructive role in the east Asia crisis and has promised to maintain a stable exchange rate through 1999 and is boosting infrastructure investment in order to stimulate growth and restrain unemployment as the state enterprises restructure. The fact is that Washington and Beijing have been engaging in unprecedented co-operation to stabilize the east Asia region at a time when Japan's capacity to play a leadership role has been crippled by her economic weakness. Such a development can only enhance the prospects for east Asian political stability and financial recovery in the early years of the new century.

In 1990, the emerging market countries had an aggregate stock market capitalization of $613 billion, compared to $8.8 trillion for the industrial countries. In 1996, this market capitalization peaked at $2.1 trillion, compared to $18.1 trillion for the industrial countries. Today, the emerging markets probably have an aggregate capitalization of only $1.7 trillion, compared to nearly $25 trillion for the industrial countries. But as a result of the reforms now underway in Asia, Latin America, South Africa and other regions, this market capitalization should begin to rebound in the near future and expand significantly again when the world economy recovers in the year 2000. The fact is the emerging market countries now account for only about 6–7 per cent of global stock market capitalization despite the fact they represent 45 per cent of world output, 70 per cent of world's land area, 85 per cent of the world's population, and 99 per cent of the projected growth in the world labour force during the early decades of the twenty-first century.

The final factor which could bolster the US equity market would be a decision by the Clinton administration to promote social security privatization. The administration has long been reluctant to accept the privatization concept, but with the federal government running a budget surplus and the stock market enjoying a healthy rebound, the Republicans are likely to make this issue a priority during the next few years. On current trend lines, the social security system will develop a surplus which is projected to peak at about $3 trillion in 2010–15. If one third of this surplus were to be invested in equities, it would represent a holding equal to about 8 per cent of current stock market capitalization, or an amount equal to about 40 per cent of current mutual fund holdings of US equities. There is growing acceptance of the argument that some portion of the fund should be invested in equities, but there is less consensus about whether individuals should be permitted to make investment decisions about the allocation of assets in their social security funds. In the United Kingdom there were tremendous abuses of private retirement savings accounts when the government gave individuals more control over how the assets were allocated. The insurance industry sold many households products which were not suitable for retirement saving and then had to offer them refunds when the government intervened to correct the abuses. While the mutual fund boom has made the US household sector far more familiar with the security markets than ever before, a large share of the population would not have the sophistication to make investment decisions without special assistance.

A decision by the Clinton administration to pursue social security privatization would also give it more flexibility on the question of a tax cut. At present, the administration is advocating that it should use the budget surplus to create a larger reserve for the social security fund. If it decided to pursue a different strategy for social security, it would be able to consider using the surplus for alternative purposes. The major argument for tax cuts is that they would permit the United States to stimulate consumer spending and bolster the world economy without relying excessively on monetary policy. It could be argued that the current policy mix of a large federal surplus and monetary easing is increasing the risk of a bubble developing in the US equity market.

There are only a few forecasts now available for the year 2000, but the majority suggest that 1999 will be a trough year for the global economy and that global output will then rebound to at least 2.5 per cent or more in the year 2000. It does not appear that the financial contagion resulting from the Russia default will impair credit flows within the financial systems of the United States and Western Europe. As a result, the world is heading for a very imbalanced equilibrium over the next year or two, in which the developing half of the world will experience a recession, while the industrial half will enjoy moderate growth. This imbalance has been temporarily benign for the US economy by restraining interest rates and inflation while encouraging larger capital flows into the US equity market. But as the Russia default illustrates, it contains political risks which can produce dangerous outcomes, while requiring the United States to run such a large trade deficit that not even the internationalist tone of American economic policy can be taken for granted indefinitely. The challenge for policy makers will therefore be to restore balance to the world economy and to lay the groundwork for a broad based global recovery before the American equity market experiences such great speculative excesses that not even Alan Greenspan will be able to fine tune a soft landing for it.

There is little doubt that the financial shocks of 1997–98 re-established America's role as the leading economic superpower. In Asia, the United States played the dominant role in guiding the IMF programmes – for all their controversial implications – and defining the response of the international community to the crisis. One thing is certain: the dynamism of America's economy, and the role of her equities markets, has made her the dominant player in guiding the international financial system. The buoyancy of the US securities sector, combined with responsive monetary policy, limited the global implications of the so-called Asian and Russian contagions. The question now looming over both America and the world is whether Washington will be able to address the political dimensions of the globalization challenge before another great financial accident intrudes upon her prosperity.

FURTHER READING

Djelic, Marie Laure, *Exporting the American Model: The PostWar Transformation of European Business* (Oxford University Press, 1998).

Friedman, Milton, *Monetary History of the United States 1867-1960* (Princeton University Press, 1963).

Haugen, Robert A., *Beast on Wall Street: How Stock Volatility Devours our Wealth* (Prentice Hall, 1998).

Henwood, Doug, *Wall Street: How it Works and for Whom* (Verso, 1997).

Kindleberger, Charles P., *Manias, Panics, and Crashes: A History of Financial Crises* (Wiley, 1996).

Krugman, Paul, *Pop Internationalism* (MIT Press, 1997).

Shilling, A. Gary, *Deflation: Why It's Coming, Whether It's Good or Bad, and How It Will Affect Your Investments, Business, and Personal Affairs* (Lake View, 1998).

7

EUROPE – THE NEXT
FIVE YEARS

IAN HARNETT

The last year of the Millennium will be recorded in history as the year in which Europe experienced one of its most radical changes since the end of the Roman Empire: the introduction of a single currency and a single monetary authority. The experiment is limited initially to 11 countries, but they include the continent's largest economies, with the exception of the United Kingdom. There has been widespread political debate over the long and at times painful journey to this point: economists, however, have mostly agreed about the significance of the event. This essay takes a cool look at the implications, and notes some of the dangers which may lurk for the participants.

The introduction of the euro brought changes in monetary policy which even before 1999 may have played a part in helping to limit the effects of the Asian recession and the Russian default. Lower interest rates calmed markets on both sides of the Atlantic in 1998 (*see also* essays by Jeremy Pink and David Hale). The new bloc which has come into being is a new economic superpower. Europe's prospects, which at the time of writing look as strong as they ever have, will be watched carefully from now on by economists and policymakers everywhere.

This essay should be read along with the entries on **trade cycles** and **currency**, as well as those on economic management, particularly **fiscal**, **monetary**, and **exchange rate policy**. What emerges is a clear insight into the way that economies use various levers to try to protect themselves, with or without success, and what happens when one or more of those levers are taken away or radically altered.

The advent of European economic and monetary union (**EMU**) in 1999 has already produced major changes in European economics and politics which will continue through the next five years. Not only will the members of EMU have a single currency with a single interest rate, but increasingly there will be closer ties in terms of fiscal policy as the European process moves inexorably towards political union.

The EMU bloc more than matches the United States in terms of its size, population and impact on the world economy. However, EMU will not be deemed to have succeeded unless current high levels of unemployment are reduced. The main prospect of this happening comes from lower interest rates and risk premia – assuming that the European Central Bank (ECB) maintains its vigilance against **inflation**, eventually boosting the productive potential of Europe.

National governments will need to recognize that labour market deregulation and lower corporate taxes are the only competitive tools left in a fixed **exchange rate** regime if they want to attract new **capital** – the key to lower unemployment, in the longer-term. In the short-term, however, this will mean that the restructuring of the high-cost Northern European economy will continue, with the share of manufacturing industry in GDP declining significantly.

Europe will also face the challenge of increased pensions provision for an ageing workforce. This (together with the 'stability and growth pact' – see below) implies that **fiscal policy** will remain tight, but also suggests that governments will need to encourage the emergence of an equity culture in Europe. Tight fiscal policy and low inflation should, however, ensure that the euro is not inherently weak. It may even take up a role as a global reserve currency.

In the longer-term, the strength of the euro will be determined by how rapidly Europe adapts to this new economic order. Governments which delay such changes will be left behind, resulting in increased social tensions and political unrest. Europe may well have to face a similar cathartic event to the miners' strike of 1984 in the United Kingdom, in order, finally, to force national governments to embrace the necessary reforms.

If Europe's politicians can rise to the challenge of making the currency bloc competitive, then the benefits of lower capital costs should eventually bring with it lower unemployment and sustainable, non-inflationary growth. This will present the preconditions for the second decade of the twenty-first century focusing on the possibilities of European political, rather than economic, union.

EUROPEAN ECONOMIC AND MONETARY UNION – A NEW PHASE FOR EUROPE

The dream of a United Europe has, in one form or another, been at the heart of most of the economic and political developments of at least the last century (although only since the 1950s has the achievement of this dream been envisaged as occurring through political co-operation, rather than through military domination of the continent).

EMU, commencing on 1 January 1999, signals the beginning of the next phase of that dream, bringing closer the political as well as economic unification of Europe.

THE LONG ROUTE TO A SINGLE CURRENCY

The genesis of EMU dates back to 1951 when the Paris Treaty created a European Coal and Steel Community of six members (Belgium, France, Germany, Italy, Luxembourg and the Netherlands). The Treaty of Rome, in 1957, saw these countries draw closer to create the European Economic Community (EEC) with its broader economic objectives: coordination of economic and monetary policies and an agreement to treat exchange rates as 'a matter of common concern', with a joint monetary committee and agreement to create increased links between the central banks.

As early as 1961 a European Monetary Reserve System for Europe was suggested by Jean Monnet, but it was the report of Pierre Werner in 1970 (at that time Prime Minister of Luxembourg) which first outlined a three-stage plan for economic and monetary union (which was originally targeted for completion by 1980). The eventual move towards a single European currency was seen by many, even from the early days of the EEC, as the inevitable response to the pressures of an increasingly deregulated global economic system.

The eventual collapse of the **Bretton Woods** system of quasi-fixed international exchange rates (between 1967 and 1973), in the wake of the Vietnam War and the first oil price shock, resulted in plans for a single European currency being put on hold. These developments also demonstrated the importance to Europe of an increasingly coordinated response to such global phenomena. One report by the EC Commission (*European economic and monetary union in 1980*), published in 1975, went on explicitly to argue that EMU would imply the need for a 'European political authority'.

Although the Werner plan was put on hold, the nine members of the EEC (Denmark, Ireland and the United Kingdom having joined in 1973) agreed to the creation of the European Monetary System (EMS) in 1979 (although the United Kingdom decided to stay out of the Exchange Rate Mechanism (ERM) of the EMS). The ERM allowed most currencies to trade within a ±2.25 per cent band (the Italian lira had a 6 per cent band). At this time the ECU also came into being, the first real claimant to being a pan-European currency. The ECU was a weighted basket of all member currencies as its own unit of account. In its infancy this system of quasi-fixed rates saw eight realignments before the end of 1984.

The signing of the Single European Act in 1986 finally put Europe firmly on the road towards European economic and monetary union. It is one of the great ironies of British politics that Margaret Thatcher (such an arch Euro-sceptic in later years) was a signatory to this Act, which had at its heart the completion of the European single market by 1992. It committed all EC governments (which by then numbered 12, with the accession of Greece in 1981 and Portugal and Spain in 1986) to early monetary union as a necessary step towards completing the single market.

The final form that monetary union would take was outlined in the Delors Report of 1989. This suggested a three-stage plan for EMU, and was agreed in Madrid in June 1989. This, in turn, led to the revision of the Single European Act agreed at Maastricht in December 1991 where all the EU heads of state signed up to the criteria to be met by individual countries for the creation of a single currency by 1999 at the latest.

All along the route towards European economic and monetary union, the political response to economic issues has driven the process.

THE MAASTRICHT CRITERIA WILL SHAPE EUROPE IN THE NEW MILLENNIUM

The development of Europe's economy over the coming five years will largely have been determined by the Maastricht Treaty. Following agreement at Maastricht of the set of criteria necessary for the creation of a single European currency, Governments across Europe adopted stringent economic convergence measures in an attempt to meet these requirements.

Five central economic criteria had to be met by each member country wishing to sign up to the new European economic order:

- **Inflation**: to be no more than 1.5 per cent above the level of the three best performing member states.
- Sustainability of public finances: defined by a deficit/GDP ratio of 3 per cent or less (unless the deficit is declining and close to 3 per cent, or is 'exceptional and temporary').
- Debt/GDP ratio: this must be below 60 per cent or 'sufficiently diminishing' and approaching the reference value at a satisfactory pace.
- Maintenance of 'normal' currency margins within the ERM for two years before EMU.

- Long-term **interest rates**: The durability of EMU convergence is to be measured by whether the nominal long-term bonds were within 2 per cent of the three member states with the best inflation performance.

The Maastricht Treaty also contained a set of subsidiary criteria relating to broader economic issues. All member countries needed to have created politically independent central banks. Concerns were also expressed about imbalances in real exchange rates, current accounts and unit wage costs.

THE CONVERGENCE IN THE APPROACH TO EMU

At the end of 1991, when the Maastricht treaty was signed, few would have predicted the degree of success in reducing the level of inflation, interest rates, and the size of fiscal deficits across Europe. Indeed, with less than two years to go, there were few expectations of all 11 members qualifying for EMU, especially not countries such as Italy and Spain.

At the beginning of 1992, the average of German and French inflation was over 3.5 per cent: as EMU began, it was around half that level. At the same time the level of bond yields across Europe has fallen for the core countries from close to 8.5 per cent to just under 5 per cent as average deficit/GDP levels decreased from almost 5 per cent to close to 3 per cent.

The improvements in both inflation and interest rates largely resulted from the battle to bring fiscal deficits into line. Since the early 1990s European economic policy has been dominated by tight fiscal policy. Although this has allowed **monetary policy** to remain loose, rates have not been low enough to prevent European unemployment rising to historically high levels – an average of 11 per cent across the EU-15 on the official EU Eurostat definitions (compared to 8.3 per cent in 1991), with German unemployment rising to over 4.5 million at its peak in 1997. There was further pressure with the recession in much of Asia and the collapse of the Russian economy during 1997–98 (*see* 'Asia: the Lessons for Economics' by Jeremy Pink). The ability of the new European structures to reduce these unemployment rates will be the benchmark by which the European electorate will judge EMU in the next five years.

THE GLOBAL IMPACT

While the economy of the largest European nation, Germany, was less than one third that of the United States, the new EMU bloc that is being created boasts a GDP level of just under $6 trillion, compared to $6.6 trillion for the US; the EU-15 GDP total is close to $7.1 trillion. This compares to just $3.6 trillion for Japan, and signals that the integration of the European economies may well lead to a substantial shift in global economic power in the next millennium.

The group of 11 EMU countries have a combined population of almost 290 million people (out of an EU-15 total of about 370 million). This contrasts with the United States population of only 270 million and that of Japan, 127 million.

Although the size of the combined European economies may match that of the United States, there is still a substantial gap in the GDP/capita in the two blocs, with citizens of the United States enjoying close to $30,000 compared to just over $21,000 in both the EU-15 and the EMU-11. It is also worthwhile noting that Japan has a higher GDP per capita in dollar terms than either the United States or Europe, at $34,000, although this declined in 1997–98.

One feature of the new Europe is that there is still a substantial divergence of GDP/capita across the EMU-11 states, from almost $33,000 per head in Luxembourg to just $10,100 per head in Portugal. This disparity in per capita incomes is one of the key challenges facing the governments and the European Central Bank.

One implication for the new European economy is that it will not be significantly 'open'. For the last century Europe has been a series of small open economies, with most countries exporting and importing between 20 per cent to 40 per cent of GDP. If the new EMU bloc is analysed as a large, closed economy, however, only around 10 per cent of European exports are external to the EU-15 bloc (although this is closer to 15 per cent for the EMU-11 bloc).

It was already apparent by the mid-1990s that the convergence of European monetary policy (in terms of fixity of interest rates and broad convergence in economic policy in order to reduce fiscal deficits) would bring with it a greater impact for the intra-European **multipliers.** The pace of economic recovery between 1993 and 1994 within continental Europe surprised nearly all economic commentators at the time. The pick-up in growth seen in late 1997 and early 1998, based on the acceleration in growth in Southern Europe (prompted by the fall in interest rates ahead of EMU) also helped to keep European growth stronger than would otherwise have been expected. These intra-European growth multipliers will also become more significant since fixed exchange rates pass the process of adjusting economic disequilibria from the price mechanism to the real side of the economy.

In the past, if there was excess demand in one region of Europe, this would typically have been adjusted by an increased current account deficit, and a downward pressure on the currency, which would have resulted in a change in relative prices and consequently in volumes of imports and exports. With a fixed exchange rate, however, the most likely route for the disequilibria to be removed is by this excess demand being translated into higher domestic wages and a sharp loss of relative competitiveness, resulting in a sharp slowdown in economic activity.

The facts clearly support this hypothesis. The convergence of inflation in the approach to EMU is one of the most highlighted benefits of the Maastricht process. Indeed, the volatility of inflation across Europe is at its lowest level since 1973. However, the counterpart to this has been much greater economic volatility. This greater volatility in activity rates can be seen clearly in both the GDP data and the industrial production data in previous periods of fixed exchange rates i.e. pre-1973. There was greater variance in activity rates between the members of the EU bloc pre-1973. It was also the case that activity levels were more volatile in each of the major countries within the EMU bloc (notably Germany and France) pre-1973.

The volatility of EU industrial production on a rolling five-year period was almost twice as high pre-1973 as in the subsequent 20 years. However, as the ERM (and latterly the Maastricht criteria) have become more of a binding force on economic activity since 1983, the five-year variance of EU industrial production has started to rise again. This contrasts with behaviour in the United States and the United Kingdom, where the volatility of industrial production has been falling almost continuously since the mid-1980s.

THE NEW INSTITUTIONS

Although the ECU became the euro on 1 January 1999, creating a single currency in Europe, this was seen by many as only having an impact on government and business in the first instance. The true effect, however, will be much wider, since it was with the creation of this paper unit of currency, the euro, that a new institutional order arrived at the heart of European decision-making, particularly in the shape of the European Central Bank (ECB).

Europe was well prepared for the loss of interest rate control that is implied by the move to a single European Central Bank by the stipulation that the central bank of each country joining EMU had to have established political independence. However, the idea of a politically independent national central bank taking actions which are appropriate to control inflation in any given country is an entirely different concept to that of the European Central Bank acting to ensure that European inflation remains subdued across the region as a whole.

While the principal objective of the ECB is to maintain price stability (it is generally assumed that this will mean low positive inflation rates, rather than the total absence of inflation), there is a secondary objective: to support the economic policies within the EU with a view to supporting sustainable growth, employment and economic convergence.

The ECB Governing Council is the decision-making body of the ECB: the Governors of the participating member central banks decide on the stance of monetary policy.

The operational ground rules involve a combination of broad monetary targets along with inflation targets. Monetary targets are notoriously difficult to achieve – especially when measured across Europe as a whole – but inflation as measured in consumer price levels is a lagging indicator. After the victory of a centre-left government in the German elections in late 1998 and the global economic slowdown at the same time, there were demands from politicians in France and Germany that the ECB should also consider activity indicators, such as unemployment, in the policy-setting process. The combination of 11 experienced senior central bankers and the officials of the Bank should be more than enough to take into account all the impacts of any change in monetary policy that is proposed.

It is probable, however, that demands for greater political accountability and transparency of the ECB will require a response. This may be in the form of a more explicit ECB annual report to the European Parliament. This could be similar to the Humphrey Hawkins testimony in the United States in which the chairman of the Federal Reserve Board reports to the Congress on the economy.

It is also clear that although there may be greater volatility in growth rates across the European region and also probably for the region as a whole if beating inflation remains the sole objective of policy.

THE EURO: 'HARD' OR 'SOFT'?

The big question which faced both the financial markets and the new ECB board was whether the euro would become a 'hard' or a 'soft' currency. Two things will determine this over the longer term: the attitude of the European Central Bank and the fiscal attitude of the constituent governments.

Any newly created independent central bank would undoubtedly want to establish its credibility with the financial markets. This was the case with the Banque de France (which kept its policy on rates at least as tough as that of the Bundesbank after it was given its independence, even though the political leaders of the day would have preferred to have seen rates cut in order to reflect domestic economic weakness). The Bank of England raised its rates seven times in almost as many months following its independence in May 1997, after the victory of the Labour Party in the 1997 election.

What is certain is that for at least the first two to three years of the euro's existence, before notes and coins are introduced in January 2002, the tone of the monetary stance is likely to be tougher than that seen in the latter days of the DM, when the Bundesbank adopted an approach of benign neglect to a 25 per cent depreciation in the currency between August 1996 and August 1997 in order to prevent the German (and in consequence the European) economies moving into a tail spin of deflation.

Therefore the risk is that in the early days of EMU, monetary policy will be kept unnaturally tight, limiting the growth potential of the region. The economic downturn in Asia created fears of recession in Europe with too tight a policy. And there is also the argument that an excessively strict monetary policy would fail to secure acceptance of the benefits of the change to the new economic system with the broader populace.

The good news is that with European inflation looking as though it will end the millennium at around 2 per cent or possibly even lower, it is unlikely that interest rates will rise back to the levels seen in early 1990s, when European short-term rates were over 8 per cent.

The second factor that will determine the strength of the euro is the degree to which fiscal policy remains tight. At the heart of the debate on the future of European policy lies the decision to allow national governments quasi-independence over their fiscal stance. Each national government is able to issue bonds (denominated in euros) to finance their national **budget deficits**. In an attempt to ensure that this should not result in a relaxation in the overall fiscal stance, and a weakening in the euro relative to the DM, the German government insisted on a 'stability and growth pact'. This limits individual governments to fiscal deficits no greater than 3 per cent of GDP; for every 1 per cent over the top of the 3 per cent deficit rate, a 'fine' of 0.1 per cent of GDP will be imposed.

There are a number of criticisms of this system. First, some feel that such a small fine is inadequate (there is a maximum of 0.5 per cent of GDP, which would only kick-in after a 6 per cent deficit to GDP ratio. The second criticism is that there are so many exceptions (notably when the deficit GDP ratio is a function of slower growth rather than fiscal imprudence) that such fines are effectively optional. Finally, there is the view that punishing fiscal deficits with fines is like punishing speeding cars with a request to drive faster.

The major constraint, however, is unlikely to come from the 'pact' itself; it is more likely to come from the markets, since in a euro government debt market, excessive issuance by any one country is likely to result in higher issuance costs and increasing yield differentials. A buyers' strike in an offending national debt market would quickly create a strong disincentive for profligacy.

The Euro as a Reserve Currency

It is also possible that, with the size of the euro-bloc being almost equal to that of the United States and exceeding that of Japan, the euro may become a reserve currency. Currently holdings of EMU currencies (mainly DM) outside the EU bloc represent 33 per cent of global reserves compared to 48 per cent for the dollar. However, foreign central banks will need to hold euros for international trade, providing an additional source of demand for euros. The EU as a whole currently has almost twice the share of world trade relative to the United States (at 20 per cent compared to 12 per cent). While it may be some time before the euro is recognized as a true reserve currency, it is already clear that there is an increased demand. It is also the case that with the increased openness of the European financial markets, there will be an increased demand for euros.

The combining of exchange reserves also serves to protect the strength of the euro, since the ECB has at its disposal up to Eu50bn, with each central bank providing contributions in the same proportion as they do to the ECB capital.

Taking all of these considerations together, it appears that the case for the euro to be a weak currency in its early years is somewhat limited. However, this is only on the basis of what has happened to the DM since the mid-1990s. The longer-term outlook will be determined by the ability of Europe to keep inflation and unit wage costs under control and competitive at a global level. If Europe retains unit wage costs above those elsewhere in the world, then it is likely that the currency will have to weaken in the longer term.

THE PENSIONS PROBLEM

Another major risk to the longer-term outlook for the fiscal stance and hence the currency comes from the ageing of the European population. The most recent EC projections suggest that the rapidly ageing population in Europe will impose unsustainable demands on the state provision of pensions in the coming three decades. Assuming that current pension provisions are maintained into the next millennium, the total cost of the ageing population would be equivalent to an extra 3 per cent to 4 per cent on the annual deficit/GDP ratio by 2030 (even on the basis of optimistic assumptions about the growth profile). Already, politicians across Europe are attempting to address such problems, but with mixed success. The two main routes being propounded are: changes to the pension system itself, reducing the level of benefits and increasing the retirement age; and alternatively changing to front-loading state pension payments, which increase the attractiveness of personal pension provisions as well as increasing the incentives for equity investments where long-term returns have been greater (thereby potentially reducing the degree of under-funding).

Even with these changes, however, the implication is that if the stability pact is to hold for the long run, then rather than aiming to keep the deficit at 3 per cent of GDP, politicians will need to aim for balanced budgets and a reform in the pension provision at a national level.

One of the key arguments in favour of retaining national autonomy over fiscal policies is that it will force each member government to tackle the pensions issue. Without this autonomy, if fiscal policy were centralized, there would be the risk that the more frugal countries of Europe would have to pay for the past generosity of some other European nation states.

SPECULATION AGAINST THE EURO

It seems unlikely, therefore, that the early period of EMU will witness, as some have speculated, a dramatic loosening of the fiscal stance which could provide the basis of a speculative attack on the newly created currency. The risk of a true speculative attack on the currency seems limited, for a number of reasons. Besides the fact that neither monetary nor fiscal policy is likely to be conducive to such pressures, the cross-rates set within EMU are unlike those set in the ERM. In EMU the exchange rates set from January 1999 to January 2002 are immutable, i.e. investors will be guaranteed that they can receive the set rate of euros for any national currency unit within EMU.

The only reason for a speculative attack on one currency within the EMU bloc would be the expectation that a national government might withdraw its currency from the bloc for domestic reasons. However, this seems highly unlikely. In the approach to the introduction of notes and coins, the main constraint would be that anyone trying to sell a particular currency will have to take on the combined reserves of the whole of Europe. Also, there will be the practical difficulty that since all outstanding debt and new issuance was converted into euros from 1999, attempting to buy enough of one currency to sell another may prove difficult. Even if investors buy or sell large quantities of any euro currencies, the quantities of euros will remain unchanged. The only real source of currency speculation would be where the markets perceived that there was sufficient underlying economic or political friction to encourage a national government to take back control of the determination of interest rates from its own central bank. It would be unlikely to gain much from withdrawal since the risk premium would undoubtedly rise. After the end of the dual currency period there would also be the practical difficulty that it would take several years to print enough bank notes to start working in a national currency again!

EUROPEAN CURRENCIES OUTSIDE EMU

It is less clear how those currencies whose governments remain in the EU but outside EMU, in what has been dubbed ERM-2, will fare. Those countries that wish eventually to be considered for entry to the EMU bloc will have to have served a time in the ERM-2, making the currency susceptible to attack. However, unlike the original ERM, new members cannot dictate what level each country will enter at. The ECB will have a role in determining that rate, and in consequence the sum of Europe's foreign exchange reserves will be at the disposal of the proposed member country should a currency attack emerge. Also the commitment to the fiscal stability measures and the presumed convergence of ERM-2 member rate to ECB central rates should also limit the scope for economically justifiable attacks.

THE LONGER TERM

Institutional arrangements within Europe look set to change dramatically during the first decade of the new millennium, with the creation of a new single currency zone. But the introduction of the euro, with its associated uniform interest rate and continued tough fiscal stance, suggest that the pattern of low inflation and slow growth seen in the last five years of the twentieth century is likely to persist for much of Europe in the first five years of the twenty-first century.

Much of the debate within the Anglo-Saxon economies has been about the benefits from a single currency of reduced exchange costs. Although these might amount to some 0.5 per cent of GDP at most, there are costs associated with the introduction of the euro (notably an estimate of some $50bn for Europe's 300 largest companies alone, according to a KPMG report, with the total cost world-wide being some $150bn). The largest gains for Europe as a whole will probably come from a reduction in the risk premium associated with capital investment if inflation is seen as being institutionally beaten, thus reducing bond yields and boosting the longer-term productive potential of the region.

The winners in both the short and the long run from the imposition of a single exchange rate and single interest rate will be those industries and countries where there is a sustainable competitive advantage.

One of the features of the fixed exchange rate zone will be that there will be a high degree of price visibility as companies are no longer able to disguise differential pricing behind currency fluctuations. This exposes the cost structures underlying business. Success in Europe in the new millennium will come from being the lowest-cost producer. This will be as relevant at a national level as at an individual corporate level.

For those industries where there is no significant cost or non-cost competitive advantage, then the single European currency will expose the weakness of Europe's cost structures, with its overly regulated labour markets. This implies that Europe's manufacturing industry will come under increasing pressure in the next decade to continue the trend towards restructuring. As Asia emerges from recession it will be more competitive, and there are also likely to be increased shareholder demands for improving returns on capital (*see* 'Changing Trends in Management' by Robert Beynon). Manufacturing companies across Europe continue to provide returns to shareholders well below those in both the financial sector and the more consumer-related areas such as pharmaceuticals.

The experience of the United Kingdom in the 1980s, more often than not, was that restructuring turns out to be a euphemism for downsizing. The manufacturing sector's share of GDP fell from close to 30 per cent to under 20 per cent in a little over ten years. What this highlights is that there will be countries which will be winners and those that will be losers. With the increased focus on costs, the relatively high unit wage costs in Germany will remain a burden to the manufacturing sector in that economy. While companies such as VW and BMW will continue to compete, they will increasingly do so through non-EU investments, placing considerable pressure on German manufacturing employment. The pressures that are likely to be witnessed in Germany from this direction are likely to be replicated throughout the northern parts of the EMU bloc. In contrast, Italy and Spain will benefit from considerably lower interest rates than in the past, as a reward for the tangible gains that have been made in holding down inflation and containing their budget deficits. This will have the further effect of reducing the cost of capital in these economies and boosting the rate of growth that should be sustainable over the next decade. These economies will also benefit from their lower labour costs. Spain has already gone some way to restructuring its labour markets so as to make inward direct investment more attractive.

This leads to one of the most important conclusions about the future shape of Europe. Within a fixed exchange rate regime, where the domestic political focuses remains on reducing unemployment, securing inward direct investment (the only way of boosting relative employment) becomes each national government's primary objective. Governments across Europe will be forced down two parallel paths, of labour market liberalization and corporate tax reduction. The latter course has already been shown to be highly effective in the case of Ireland, where corporate tax rates were cut to 10 per cent for companies creating jobs in the region.

National governments will have a stark choice: reform, or watch other countries within the EMU bloc grow considerably faster, with unemployment falling. It is clear that Northern Europe, currently more prosperous but with higher costs, needs to embrace such a philosophy earliest.

One implication of this is the likelihood of major political upheaval and social disturbance across Europe in the next decade. In the United Kingdom such labour market and taxation reforms only came after the union movement was effectively broken in the miners' strike of 1984. Europe is likely to have to suffer a similar cathartic experience if change is to be made rapidly.

The only alternative to such moves will be a long-run decline in the value of the euro. This too has its problems. In the United Kingdom through the 1980s, despite the pace of industrial restructuring, the nominal value of sterling fell from DM5 to just below DM3. This resulted in inflation and interest rates which were above those of major trading partners. Despite the weakening nominal exchange rate, the real effective rate remained uncompetitive, resulting in continued upward pressure on unemployment. Only once the restructuring of the labour market and of corporate taxation had been fully implemented, and sterling allowed to float to a new lower level, did the change in culture begin to produce real changes in the economy.

The Equity Culture

A change in the industrial culture of Europe is likely to take place rapidly because of the pensions issue. The need to encourage the development of an equity culture in order to help ease the pension burden is paramount. Further measures will be introduced across Europe giving tax breaks to companies raising equity capital, which will encourage a greater focus on more effective corporate management and government. Increased equity awareness will also lead to greater focus on the returns that European companies make on behalf of investors, prompting an increasing adoption of economic value added (EVA) as a measure of competitiveness, both across regions in Europe and within companies and sectors. The equity culture will be aided by governments privatizing and deregulating industry as a means both of reducing national deficit levels and keeping domestically determined prices under control by non-monetary policy means. (*See* essay on 'New Patterns of Economic Behaviour' by Justin Urquhart Stewart.)

Although governments may wish to encourage equity investment, the underlying economic environment will continue to support bond investment. Low inflation and volatile activity rates more naturally lend themselves to investors moving into bonds. With debt levels contracting as some countries move into primary surplus, bonds will become scarcer, pushing up bond prices and depressing yields.

The implication of low bond yields, together with the corporate restructuring that we are envisaging and the increased demand for equities from the changing attitudes to pensions, suggests that the demand for European financial assets will remain strong and that the gains seen in European markets in the second half of the 1990s are likely to be continued in the first decade of the new millennium. The structure of European equity markets is likely to change, with shares in major European companies likely to be quoted in euros on a single European bourse, with smaller companies quoted on the remnants of today's national bourses.

Conclusions

The adoption of a single currency in Europe will produce one of the most dramatic changes in economic structure since the breakdown of the Bretton Woods system almost 30 years ago.

While there will be some benefits from lower transaction costs, the main positive impact from EMU should come from lower interest rates and reduced risk premia as a relatively tough European Central Bank keeps inflation subdued. These lower costs of capital should boost the long-run productive potential of Europe as a whole.

The pressure of an increasing pensions burden will be two-edged. While it will mean that fiscal policy remains tight, limiting the pace of economic growth, it will also lead European governments to encourage the emergence of a broader equity culture. The commercial discipline that comes from an increased emphasis on the use of equity capital should also improve the efficiency and returns of European industry.

The downside from this will be a continuation of the restructuring seen during the 1990s. The political pressures from continued high levels of unemployment will result in labour market deregulation and lower corporate tax rates across Europe, as governments recognize that these are the last two competitive tools open to them. Governments which try to delay such change will be left behind, resulting in increasing social tensions within Europe as those countries that do change increase shares in economic prosperity.

Coping with these social pressures will be the toughest challenge for the next generation of European economic policy-makers, realizing the dream of Werner and Delors. The final step in this process will not be European economic union, but European political union.

FURTHER READING

Artis, M. J., Lee. N. *et al.*, *The Economics of the European Union* (Oxford University Press, 1997).

Barro, Robert J., and Grilli, Vittorio, *European Macro-Economics* (Macmillan, 1994).

Burda, Michael, and Wyplosz, Charles, *Macro-Economics: A European Text* (Oxford University Press, 1997).

Frieden, Jeffry, Gros, Daniel, and Jones, Erik, *The New Political Economy of EMU (Governance in Europe)* (Rowman and Littlefield, 1998).

Gros, Daniel, and Thygesen, Niels, *European Monetary Integration* (Longman, 1998).

Molle, Willem, *The Economics of European Integration* (Ashgate, 1998).

Munchau, Wolfgang, *The Birth of the Euro* (Penguin, 1998).

Temperton, Paul, *The Euro* (John Wiley, 1998).

III
THE WORLD
TOMORROW

8

NEW PATTERNS OF ECONOMIC BEHAVIOUR

JUSTIN URQUHART STEWART

What are the macroeconomic implications of an exploding base of equity investment, an ageing population in many of the developed economies, a revolution in technology at least as great as that of the Industrial Revolution, and new ways of approaching management and the oldest economic activity of all, buying and selling?

Of course, nobody knows for sure. This section of essays tries to set out some of the issues, and the current thinking about them.

The first essay is perhaps the most clearly grounded in finance and economics, and in some ways serves as an introduction for our attempts to sketch out the future. Justin Urquhart Stewart describes the investment revolution, and one of its key drivers: the population, political, regulatory and technological changes responsible for the shift of social welfare from the corporate and public sectors to the private.

We have already seen in the previous section, in the essay on the US economy, how a highly buoyant US equities sector has helped limit the effects of downturns in Asia and the collapse of Russia. The following essay will catalogue the implications for microeconomic behaviour, and what they mean for future growth and stability.

The essay may be read in the context of the broad macroeconomic entries (especially **Keynes**, **monetarism** and **inflation**), but also alongside such entries as **stock markets**, **bonds**, and of course with the other essays in this section – those on technology, management and the new marketing.

The collapse of communism, together with demographic and technological changes over the past couple of decades, have confronted the fields of economics, management and politics in developed countries with major questions which are diverse and complex, but which combine under the general heading of new patterns of economic behaviour.

The essays which follow on technology, management and relationship marketing, cover some of these areas in more detail. Here, we examine in the broadest sense the questions facing companies, policymakers and individuals over the next 20 years, and their implications for the science of economics.

AGEING POPULATIONS

Demographic changes which have occurred in most developed economies, of greater life expectancy combined with lower rates of childbirth, have created ageing populations. These pose problems of social welfare funding, particularly of pensions, for the next generation. The bulge of the high birth-rate baby-boomer age group, which will reach retirement age over the next couple of decades, the trend towards lower retirement ages, and the fact that health care has become more expensive with technological development, all combine to create the so-called 'demographic timebomb'. In Germany, where 10 per cent of the workforce is unemployed, social security contributions are reckoned to cost 20 per cent of an employee's gross income (half of that paid by the employer), rising to 30 per cent as the baby-boomers move into retirement. Labour force participation of men aged 60–64 was around 80 per cent in 1960 in most OECD countries. This has now declined to 50 per cent in the US and is below 35 per cent in Germany, Italy and France, at the end of the 1990s.

All of this is creating growing pressure on funding. Most pension and social security spending has traditionally been funded by central governments on a 'pay as you go' basis, where today's contributions are used immediately to pay for today's social security and pension provision – today's working population paying for today's retired, sick, or unemployed individuals. Retaining this form of payment from the tax system over the next few decades will create impossible strains on fiscal policy, requiring either budget deficits and their attendant implications for monetary policy, or much higher taxes, with attendant problems for production costs.

For this reason, many western governments are now experimenting with 'funded' systems of social security, which may be, but are not necessarily, operated by the private sector. Under these systems, individuals set aside some of their current earnings to pay for their own social welfare in the future, and most of these savings can be invested in the financial markets.

THE EQUITIES EXPLOSION

In the United States initiatives to encourage individuals to fund their own retirement provision, such as the '401-k' system (where employees agree to voluntary deductions of their pay, which are topped up by their employers) have led to a massive inflow of funds to the equities markets, largely through mutual funds. The industry estimates that some $21bn per month is flowing into US mutual funds, and currently around 90 per cent of this is invested in equities.

Other countries are likely to develop similar systems. It is important to note that instances exist of schemes which are run to a greater extent by the state, e.g. the Singapore Provident Fund, into which the workforce must pay 20 per cent of its earnings.

Much of this funding of social welfare so far relates to pension provision, although some politicians believe health and unemployment benefits could be similarly funded. That debate is beyond the scope of this essay. What is important for economists is the implication of the upsurge in private funds for investment in financial markets. The essay by David Hale, 'The United States as Global Leader', examines the extent to which a relatively buoyant stock market helped to dampen the effects of the Asian recession. The positive implications are that a ready source of funds for investment help to encourage a relatively loose monetary policy, while allowing fiscal policy to remain tight (the so-called Clinton–Greenspan coalition).

The implications of serious deflation within the developed economies have yet to be tested. If equities are overpriced relatively to the performance of the companies they represent, the danger is of an 'asset bubble' bursting, severely cutting the value of individuals' investments for their retirement and welfare funding. This did not occur after the Asian crisis and the Russian default in 1997–98, because in general the fundamentals remained strong in most western economies. It may not always be so.

The Role of the Markets

Clearly, the more global and liquid the financial markets, the easier it is for funds to flow to where the best returns may be had. Such international investment may not be appropriate for most individual investors, and there have already been grave concerns about the sophistication of the 'new investors' as prey to salesmen of financial products. (Indeed, there was a foretaste of this problem when the UK pensions industry was forced to pay many millions of pounds in compensation to investors who were encouraged to opt out of their employer-provided pensions schemes into private products, when many would have been better off staying put.)

But provided that most individuals continue to channel their savings into professionally managed schemes, the argument goes, the dangers are reduced. This argument, however, does not tackle the issue of global recession. There exists in theory the possibility of a global lack of confidence bringing about deflation which would make the Asian crisis look like a small correction, and in the new investment climate this would lead not just to the standard recessionary devil of unemployment, but serious poverty for a population which may be least able to fend for itself.

THE ROLE OF GOVERNMENTS, BANKS, REGULATORS, AND TECHNOLOGY

Certainly governments have a role in becoming the providers 'of last resort', using fiscal means to underwrite catastrophic market failure. This should have a calming effect on the markets similar to that of the monetary easing by the Fed and some of the other Western central banks during the Asian recession. There is always the spectre of a collapse of confidence so great that short-term fiscal stimulus and funding will be unable to hold the deflationary waters.

The role of the regulators in keeping a watch for banking adequacy and over-leveraged hedge funds is also important. Funds unwinding highly leveraged positions did not create the Asian crisis, but it certainly added to its severity. Banks making bad loans for questionable projects made matters very much worse. Stricter regulation both within economies and internationally is likely to follow, and is likely to make the global economy somewhat safer, at least until the lessons are forgotten and new banking products are developed.

Technology is important because it can help to provide information in more detail and with more precision than ever before. This is helpful not just to the fund managers who control vast sums in international markets; it also helps the consumer to 'shop around' to find the best combination of risk and return.

CONCLUSION

The current changes are likely to lead to a wealthier but more volatile world economy. Economists will need to provide quantitative analysis of the connections between trade, markets, liquidity, and credit. Governments will need to understand that securitization of their social welfare commitments does not mean 'opting out', and certainly will need to take on a role of last resort. Regulators need to be more sophisticated, and more powerful.

The three essays which now follow should be read in the context of the new challenges facing economics and the global economy.

FURTHER READING

Bootle, Roger, *The Death of Inflation* (Nicholas Brealey, 1997).

Clarke, Thomas, and Pitelis, Christos, *The Political Economy of Privatisation* (Routledge, 1995).

Galbraith, John Kenneth, *Money: Whence It Came, Where It Went* (Penguin, 1995).

Giddens, Anthony, *The Third Way* (Polity Press, 1998).

Hansmann, Henry, *The Ownership of Enterprises* (Harvard University Press, 1996).

Hirschman, Albert O., *Rival Views of Market Society and Other Recent Essays* (Harvard University Press, 1992).

Krauskopf, Jack, *The Privatisation of Human Services* (Brookings Institution, 1995).

Moran, Michael, and Prosser, Tony, *Privatisation and Regulatory Change in Europe* (Open University Press, 1994).

Saunders, Peter, and Harris, Colin, *Privatisation and Popular Capitalism* (Open University Press, 1994).

Solomon, Michael, Barnossy, Gary, and Askegaard, Soren, *Consumer Behaviour* (Prentice Hall, 1998).

Strange, Susan, *Casino Capitalism* (Manchester University Press (reprint), 1997).

Strange, Susan, *Mad Money* (Manchester University Press, 1998).

Tittenbrun, Jacek, *Private vs. Public Enterprise* (Janus, 1996).

Yergin, Daniel, and Stanislaw, Joseph, *The Commanding Heights: The Battle Between Government and the Market Place that is Remaking the Modern World* (Simon and Schuster, 1998).

9

TECHNOLOGY

RICHARD LANDER

A world in which information is without boundaries, both within companies and within societies; a world in which routine machine-minding can be eliminated from manufacturing; a world in which the power grows exponentially to test, model and connect hypotheses and empirical research: this is the scene for the new economic age. Unlike other phenomena such as the investment revolution (see previous essay), technology acts primarily on the supply side, implying that it is both more exogenous and less cyclical than other economic drivers. This essay should therefore be examined in the context of the entries on **supply-side** measures and the **Harrod-Domar** and **Solow economic growth models**. It should also be seen as powerfully related to **employment**, trade theory and the essays of both Sanjaya Lall and Patrick Minford.

In one sense it is the least complete of all our essays: not because the pace of change is creating new technologies by the day, but because we are still in the process of refining and developing the models which can analyse its impact – models which in themselves will rely increasingly on tomorrow's information technology for their accuracy and insight.

See also Paul Ormerod, 'What Economics is Not'.

The role of the information revolution on economic activity cannot be under-estimated. In some respects it has challenged our assumptions about micro- and macroeconomics in a way that the early aspects of industrialization sent the **Classical economists** reaching for a body of theory which could provide some context to the real-world changes that were then taking place at what appeared (at the time) to be a mind-boggling pace. Industrialization required the development of theories about pricing, specialization, trade, profit, and markets. The current revolution requires new thinking about the value of ideas, economic development, **investment, employment,** and **infrastructure.**

The greatest problem for social scientists during all periods of rapid change is to separate the fashionable irrelevant from the real switch-points. Since the Victorian era a fascination with the future has fostered a predictive industry which in general has tended to bear little relationship to what has actually come to pass. Its implications for economics often have been at most tangential; occasionally they have been critical. Look at travel as an instance. The dream of rapid travel became a reality when the speed and technology of steam locomotion, linked to an increased demand for freight and passenger transportation to service the industrialization process, justified the considerable capital expenditure required to build and operate the railways. Private travel became a reality for increasing numbers of individuals when mass production techniques allowed the manufacture of motor cars at a low enough unit cost to justify the capital expenditure required to design and build the cars. The dream of commercial air travel only became viable after the technological development of aircraft as war machines. Space travel – so far – has not become a viable means of mass transportation – not because the rockets have failed to work, but because the cost/demand/investment reward has never added up.

With the information revolution, we see a dream (every book in the world, every movie and TV show, every newspaper, every shop, every **stock market**, every office, available to anyone who wants them when they want them at minimal cost), a very real **demand** (which economy does not require all or most of the above, and what a blessing for those which traditionally have not had the wherewithal to purchase and distribute them, what a disadvantage for those who choose not to take advantage of such information), an investment requirement (which, compared with capital projects such as building railways, is minute), and much confusion.

Digital technology allows the dream to become a reality: quite simply, it provides a way of capturing information and transmitting it at a fraction of the cost previously. The main impediment to the free flow of information – the cost of storing and disseminating it – has disappeared at a stroke. The reason that billions of people daily travelled to process information in offices in cities no longer applies. The reason that people travelled to a place of transaction (the shop, the bank, the post office) no longer applies. The reason that entertainment was based on a 'shared real-time experience' no longer applies. Add to all of that the information-processing power of modern computers, and you have the makings of a revolution. What nobody yet fully understands is how to turn it into business, what the social implications may be, and when the process will reach its limits to growth, if they exist.

This essay cannot examine the full range of economic implications of the information revolution. Instead we will concentrate upon some of the microeconomic specifics, the macroeconomic implications, and the control of the revolution and its regulation.

We begin with the main blood supply of the information revolution. If the computer is the heart, the Internet is its veins and arteries. Already the Internet has changed the world we live in and the economic rules and systems that govern that world. The legacy of a communications system that was developed for the Pentagon and pioneered in the universities of the Western world barely existed in the public mindset at all, five years ago. Today it has bought wholesale change to industries ranging from the newspapers to computers, from flower deliveries to books to compact discs.

On the one hand, the Internet has enabled companies to communicate at large with their key stakeholders – employees, stockholders, competitors, suppliers, customers – with an efficiency of speed, accuracy and cost never seen before. On the other, it is regarded as the niche medium to end all niche media for targeting small groups of people brought together by a need or interest, ranging from mountain climbing to drug dependency to the same home town.

Entire chains of commerce are threatened by the Internet's ability to disintermediate the relationship between manufacturer and end user. Yet at the same time, new Internet-based services to advise and guide the technologically bewildered are springing up daily to replace the ranks of brokers, agents and wholesalers whose very existence is threatened.

Trying to measure the effectiveness and potential of the Internet as a tool for economic change is a thankless task. Until the global downturn in 1998, many firms had enjoyed a bull market in which few prospects of any profits in a three year horizon allowed them to trade at 20 times annual revenues and more – ratios which caused one group of rational analysts to proclaim the stock prices as being far too low, and another group (equally rational) to warn of a bubble and a downturn which could shake the world. It remains to be seen whether the earnings ratios can be achieved again and maintained, and that will depend on the overall direction of the financial markets. One certainty is that in the words of Nicholas Negroponte of the MIT Media Lab, we are moving from an atom-oriented world in which goods and services are physically transported across the world, to a bit-oriented economic sphere in which anything that can be digitized and squirted down a telecommunications pipe probably will be; the obvious examples being information, software, and entertainment.

How fast this happens depends on a number of factors.

- Infrastructure, which means the extent to which an entity or city or country is 'wired' and able to receive and transmit messages from the Internet. For example, the United States is generally regarded as being three or four years ahead of Europe in 'on-line' terms; it also explains how some developing countries with little in the way of old-style telecoms networks are now benefiting from new fibre-optic links which allow vastly greater dissemination of digital information than in countries where established phone networks or cable systems will struggle to cope with the demands of the Internet.
- Substitutes: for example, in the United Kingdom there is an eclectic mixture of national newspapers which form a primary information source for much of the population; France has its own analogue version of the Internet, MiniTel (set up in the 1980s and heavily funded by the French government), which may discourage 'trading up' to full on-line services; on the other hand totalitarian nations which have little freedom of information and access to international media have tended to embrace the Internet despite their governments' usually ineffective attempts to restrict its distribution and content.
- Consumer culture: in its broadest sense, this is the level of acceptance of the Internet and its on-line products, and can be driven by the marketing investment of the software companies, the amount of hardware penetration within companies and households, and related consumer issues such as the penetration of cable and the existence of digital TV.
- The regulatory environment: how much convergence is there between, say, phone, TV, and computer companies; who can provide the information 'software' and who the distribution hardware; how open is the market to international competition? All of these issues have an impact on the spread of the information revolution. (At the end of this essay we examine further the role of regulators – national or supra-national – as the industry develops.)

It is in the physical world of goods delivered to the homes of consumers and the goods yards of business customers that the economic disruptions of the Internet are being felt with most force. At its most basic level, the Internet lays down a communications infrastructure that is universal and inexpensive to access.

Just-in-time manufacturing, for example, was not invented by the Internet but has been hugely accelerated by the network's development. Previously, suppliers and customers in a just-in-time process needed to develop expensive proprietary messaging systems along with applications to access each other's databases. Today, those systems and applications can be developed on top of the Internet's standard protocols. The same developments are occurring in consumer industries where a browser (free) an Internet connection (several are free, others may cost around $20 a month, plus the cost of a local-rate telephone call) and a basic PC gives consumers access to a physically unlimited choice of goods and services, and often the ability to specify exactly what they want from a supplier. A prime example is Dell Computers which sells millions of dollars' worth of PCs a day on-line to customers who can specify almost every variable of the computer they choose. As marketing guru Regis McKenna points out, Dell has succeeded not because it is a technological leader – its PCs are pretty much the same as everyone else's – but because its logistics of receiving, building and despatching its products are better than any of its competitors. Dell has become a logistics company, building on demand in response to a virtually costless sales motion.

That is fine for Dell, whose brand reputation has become a product and a reflection of its presence as an on-line supplier of goods. For those companies whose branding and reputation has been built up over decades in bricks and mortar, the Internet poses as many problems as opportunities. Take for example, the European grocery business, where supermarkets have been tiptoeing into the seas of Internet ordering. The Tesco chain, for example, has developed a software program which allows customers to order and pay across the Internet and to specify delivery dates, all for a nominal fixed fee. In general the policy is one of defensive caution – eager not to lose face with the technically savvy public who want to shop this way (and who are prepared to master the rather clumsy software provided). Once the order has been placed, fulfilment reverts to the analogue era through a series of faxes, expert shoppers and small delivery vans, whose costs far exceed the on-line fee. Where next for these companies? Do they assume that a mass market for on-line shopping will emerge, making it worthwhile to develop the necessary software, centralized warehouses and transport fleets that will enable it to deliver a profitable service at a price consumers are prepared to pay? And if it does, what does it do with existing and planned superstores and adjacent car parks and petrol stations, dry cleaners, crèches and cafés that have built their brands as retailers and, in the case of Tesco and others, providers of financial services?

To make matters worse, two vital factors that cushion the merchandiser in the physical world scarcely exist in virtual space. The first is that the profit advantage of the first player to enter a market is much shorter than in the 'real' world. The consumer's access to information is virtually perfect on the Internet, as is the competition's ability to respond literally from scratch, in the absence of the defence mechanisms afforded to a leading player by property availability, building time, recruitment cycles and so on.

The second factor is the diminishing and changing relationship with the consumer as this near-perfect market for goods and services erodes the concept of brand loyalty. As firms try to translate their brand values from the real to the virtual world, they are faced with an online audience for whom price is a far more important concept.

This again is a hugely uneven process but one in which technology is beginning to operate in consumers' favour. 'Agents' – software mechanisms that search the Internet to provide details and comparisons of similar goods and services – are growing in sophistication. So too is the appetite for auctions, in which suppliers and consumers get together online to clear goods and services at near-perfect prices. Already the travel and car markets are beginning to feel the pinch of this new sales channel. One travel site has even produced 'reverse auctions' for air flights, in which a would-be traveller, rather than bidding for a given flight, specifies preferences for route and price and bids are invited to fill the order from airlines.

The possibility of immediate on-line transactions has revolutionized the stockbroking industry, which is rapidly dividing into the 'advice and face' style of the older established houses, and the 'execution only' stockbrokers which have exploded with the growth of individual equity holdings in North America, East Asia, and Europe. (*See* essays by Justin Urquhart Stewart and David Hale.)

The distinctions between telecoms (point-to-point), broadcasting (point to multi-point), and the Internet (point-to-point or point to multi-point) are eroding with the onset of digital multi-channel TV and e-mail. For advertisers the challenge is to target a niche or even an individual, while at the same time coming to terms with the fact that mass real-time audiences are evaporating (US network market shares have been falling for more than a decade, as have those of most terrestrial broadcasters in western Europe). For programmers, the challenge is to use interactive varieties of the product to add value, but particularly to create revenues, which do not 'cannibalize' the basic product. Thus *The Wall Street Journal Interactive Edition* – owned by Dow Jones – the first newspaper on-line site to become profitable, developed a business model based on subscription rather than advertising revenues (unlike the paper-and-ink version). The company found that far from cannibalizing the base readership, they had reached a new on-line audience, in many ways broader and with more growth potential than their traditional newspaper subscribers. Not only that, they found that once the initial investment was made, the costs of distribution on-line were minimal compared with operating a global network of printing and distribution chains. The key, however, was in the pricing. In the case of the *WSJIE*, the starting price ($49) was lower than that of the 'ink-and-paper' subscription (with incentives for existing newspaper subscribers). But unlike many other publications which have tried and failed to charge for their on-line versions, the strength of the existing brand and its 'upscale' (and therefore generally more 'wired') readership ensured sufficient take-up. For most on-line publications the investment will take longer to pay off. But what is important is that compared with investment in, say, conventional television, the Internet provides a highly effective distribution structure at a fraction of the cost.

Clearly, then, a revolution is occurring at a microeconomic level, and decisions about product development, pricing, ownership and investment are key to its future. The effects at the macroeconomic level divide into the pure mechanics of how government **monetary** and **fiscal policies** are being affected, and will be affected, and the broader societal changes, with their implications for infrastructure, trade, and employment.

Monetary policy has already felt the effect of the information revolution. Just as globally deregulated capital markets could not exist without a high level of information technology (so that it is possible to trade **currencies**, or **bonds**, or equities, across the world, within seconds), so the same technology helped create the deregulation and international flow of capital: any economy which closed its capital markets would quickly find itself in a backwater of economic growth, whereby international companies would simply locate elsewhere rather than be restricted in their operations. There is still not complete freedom of capital: countries such as China, eager to retain some of the benefits of economic development within their borders rather than see them paid to shareholders in New York or Frankfurt, have opened up to foreign enterprise through a system of joint ventures with local entities. Nonetheless an examination of the **balance of payments** of most industrialized countries indicates how large a proportion is now taken up by international flows of capital. Monetary policy must therefore use the markets, rather than defining them: gone are the days when a central bank could simply decree the **interest** rate or the asset ratio of its commercial banking sector.

Fiscally, the issues are just beginning to be addressed. **Taxation** of goods is already occupying the minds of special advisers and policy-makers as digital delivery of software, information and entertainment becomes a multi-billion dollar business. There is still no definitive answer on how to levy a point-of-sale tax on a piece of software written in China and downloaded by a user in Spain from a server located in California.

The American doctrine, as espoused by White House adviser Ira Magaziner, is that it is impossible to tax bits and bytes, unlike atoms, and that in the interest of expanding the overall level of trade and commerce, the Internet should be declared a tax-free zone. The rationale may be sound but the doctrine is more than a little cute from a country with virtually no federal sales tax and where state and local politicians have made attempts to tax interstate electronic commerce on the grounds that the telephone wires carrying the transaction run under their soil!

European governments can afford to be less sanguine but have little room for manoeuvre. While popular pressure over the past decade has seen many countries shift from direct taxes to sales taxes and VAT – often at rates of 15 per cent or more – the tides of monetary union are blowing their economies towards cross-border fiscal transparency, even without the guiding hand of the Internet.

Perhaps the Internet will trigger another quantum change in the way governments raise their taxes. Perhaps, as Negroponte believes, taxes will become a largely voluntary affair, because governments will be unable to enforce them. At the societal and infrastructure levels, most governments are only starting to wake up to the changes. The first awareness is that to be 'wired' is not just desirable; it is essential for business, for education, and for trade. There has not been a chance yet to measure the success of the early 'wired city' projects in countries such as Malaysia and Singapore, given the recent economic problems of South East Asia (*see* essays by Sanjaya Lall and Jeremy Pink). What is evident is that countries with old-fashioned or virtually non-existent communications networks, which are therefore simpler to replace *in toto*, are already winning aspects of the investment race. It is currently easier to make a phone call in former East Germany than in the western part of the country, while China's universities (and their armies of Java programmers) will soon run their Internet network along a brand-new fibre ring, while western countries struggle to upgrade and prolong existing infrastructure. Most governments in western Europe are following the United States in emphasizing the importance of connectivity for education. Often the major problems are less the actual investment than the regulation or deregulation that is necessary to make it happen (see below).

As for **employment** patterns, the market place has already made the running. Airlines have moved their entire reservations and bookings systems to English-speaking low labour-cost economies such as India. Even within regional economies, there is no longer a need to site labour-intensive operations where labour is most expensive – i.e. large cities. In the United Kingdom, Sky Television runs its entire subscriber management system out of Scotland; many UK insurance and travel agencies run their telephone sales and fulfilment out of the Irish Republic. The development of sophisticated voice-recognition computers will soon make the human element less relevant anyway.

The implications for office and manufacturing culture are far-reaching. Given that it is already cheaper to provide a computer, modem, and telecoms link than it is to (through the going wage) finance the cost of commuting to city offices, the skyscraper office full of staff executing what is currently, but perhaps not for much longer, the labour-intensive side to commerce, must be on its way to the history books. With international tele-conferencing and exchange of information allowing identical manufacturing and quality control processes to exist from Seattle to Shenzen, the implications are clear and already being felt. Most computer chips are manufactured in low-wage economies; much basic manufacturing has already moved to the same places. For governments the implications for transport, for education, and for trade, will lag behind the micro-reality, but will be inescapable within a few years. It is not the role of this book to probe the sociological consequences of such changes, but it is worth pausing to speculate about the 'wired' citizen in a predominantly 'wired' economy, and the marginal citizens and the marginal economies for whom the information revolution is not yet within grasp.

All of that may mean tough decisions ahead for governments. But in their traditional role of economic police officers, surely the policy-makers can feel secure? Needless to say, like the mercantilists faced with free trade, or the turnpike authorities faced with the railways, the national government **regulators** are under overwhelming pressure. Take the question of financial regulation. Just when the major western economies felt they had nailed down the threat from untaxed and unregulated investment markets in tax havens, along came the Internet, operating not only from traditional havens in the micro-states of the world but also from infant states such as Belarus or Azerbaijan, where farms of Internet servers offer new opportunities for the investment-wealthy of the world. Even in countries where today capital flows and interest rates have been deregulated, governments are finding that investment and marketing rules can be largely flouted by companies working across borders. Regulators in the United Kingdom – in many ways the most open major financial centre in the world – have railed against on-line stockbrokers from the United States whose web sites are deemed to be advertising without regulatory approval because they can be seen by web surfers in the British Isles.

Most important is the 'gatekeeper' problem. If it takes the US federal government several years to challenge Microsoft about open access to the Internet, one could be forgiven for wondering whether smaller national governments will have any effective role in regulating the information revolution. The importance for economists is not the political and cultural elements, but the safeguards against **monopoly** or **oligopoly** control. If the revolution is not to be derailed by anti-competitive mergers, sub-technology (e.g. TV digital decoder boxes), and anti-entry pricing, the need is for supranational regulators along the lines of the supranational **trade bodies** such as the WTO. That requires a leap of faith on the part of those governments which ardently protect their own utility-based telecos and broadcasters, and an acceptance of the power of a regulatory body whose powers may exceed those of national laws. It is a recipe for litigation, interest groups, and patronage. But there have been few economic revolutions which were not full of lawyers and lobbyists. The difference is that this one will be even faster – and there is more at stake.

FURTHER READING

Downes, Larry, *Unleashing the Killer App: Digital Strategies for Market Dominance* (Harvard Business School Press, 1999).

Dreyfus, Hubert L., *What Computers Still Can't Do: A Critique of Artificial Reason* (MIT Press, 1992).

Kelly, Kevin, *New Rules for the Economy: 10 Ways the Network Economy is Changing Everything* (Fourth Estate, 1999).

Knight, Lee W., and Bailey, Joseph P., *Internet Economics* (MIT Press, 1998).

Lander, Richard, and Shircore, Ian, *Mastering the Internet* (Orion, 1999).

Negroponte, Nicholas, *Being Digital* (Hodder and Stoughton, 1995).

Schwartz, Evan, *Webonomics* (Penguin, 1999).

Seybold, Patricia, and Marshak, Ronni, *Customers.com* (Century/Arrow, 1998).

Shapiro, Carl, and Varian, Hal R., *Information Rules: A Strategic Guide to the Network Economy* (Harvard Business School Press, 1998).

Tapscott, Don, *Growing Up Digital: The Rise of the Net Generation* (McGraw Hill, 1999).

Tapscott, Don, and Caston, Art, *Paradigm Shift: The New Promise of Information Technology* (McGraw Hill, 1992).

UK Dept. of Trade and Industry (and Spectrum Consultants), *Development of the Information Society* (HMSO, 1996).

Various, *Economics of Technology* (North-Holland, 1994).

10

CHANGING TRENDS
IN MANAGEMENT

ROBERT BEYNON

The changes described in the previous two essays, involving patterns of
spending, saving, welfare provision, and the technological revolution,
have also affected the way companies and economic entities are managed.

This essay tracks the developments in management, and their
relationship with theories of the firm. Beynon analyses the moves toward
greater globalization, the implications of just-in-time production, and the
increasing concentration on shareholder value. He argues that they have
encouraged firms and employees to adopt more contractual relationships, rather than the traditional notions of lifelong employment, with
the company as parent.

Many of these themes also appear in the next essay, on relationship
marketing. The implication is that – certainly in the developed economies – companies are moving out of the machine age and into the
technology age. That affects the way that most of us will work in the
future, and just as importantly for this book, the way that we view microeconomics.

The essay therefore refers back to many of the entries in this area, and
can be seen as a modern update of some of the neo-Classical ideas.
Perhaps more than any other area of business and economics, management theory tends to follow the practical world of production, employment, and organization, and of course broad economic trends. So it is
hardly surprising that management theory has never experienced such
rapid change as it has over the past decade, or indeed such popularity as
a subject of study.

Compared to economics, management theory is a relatively new
discipline. The question of why firms exist and what they set out to
achieve did not attract serious study until the turn of the twentieth
century. Although the nature of firms and management has changed
considerably (especially in the last 30 years, as this essay will show),
some of the earliest theories about a firm's *raison d'être* have proved
quite resilient. The two which underpin much of later management
theory – and practice – are:

- the **neo-Classical** argument that a firm's goal is profit maximization ;
- the transaction costs theory of the firm, put forward originally by the economist and management theorist Ronald Coase.

Neo-Classical theory defines what it is that a company does, or needs to do, for survival. It tells us that firms will seek to produce at a level which maximizes their short-term profits (*see* **theory of production costs, theory of consumer demand**). This theory has been criticized as unrealistic: its assumptions about perfect competition and relatively static time frames in particular are rarely seen as being valid in the 'real' world. Nonetheless it is useful in providing a definitional framework for the firm or any other economic entity, and by this definition the profit motive cannot be in doubt.

But taking neo-Classical theory as a starting point, management ideas need to take into account its various practical shortcomings. First, it assumes that it is the firm as an entity taking decisions, where clearly, a firm is a complex structure made up of individuals who may have their own agendas. Due to the fact that the owners of the firm – the shareholders – are not the same people as those who run the firm – the managers – they may not necessarily share the same profit maximization goal (the principal–agent problem). Managers, it has been suggested, may be more interested in maximizing sales or in growing the **assets** of the firm, rather than in pursuing short-term **profits**. In addition, managers may be aiming to achieve no more than a satisfactory level of profits, the owners being unaware that more profit could be achieved. This is known as the problem of asymmetric information – the managers know more than the owners. These difficulties are often demonstrated in the growth and development of real companies, but there are limits which are a function of the working of market forces. For example, a company which has grown too large and whose assets are therefore worth more than its current profitability may fall prey to a takeover bid or **asset stripping**. The time element has been used to justify managers pursuing a sales growth or diversification strategy: they are hoping to realize future profits from their activities. Efforts to align the goals of shareholders and managers have led to managerial and employee incentive schemes and a focus on the need for all parts of the organization to be able to sing from the same hymn sheet or visualize the same goal. The time factor may be seen as a refinement of the static neo-Classical thinking: clearly, companies need to invest to ensure the flow of future profits to the shareholders. This is seen most clearly in firms which need to concentrate heavily on **research and development**:

pharmaceutical, high-tech, and many of today's global manufacturing companies.

Ronald Coase started out from the premise of the neo-Classicals, but developed a more behavioural approach, and in that sense can be seen as the father of comprehensive management theory ('comprehensive' because it takes an overall, rather than a partial approach). Writing in the 1930s, he argued that firms are created when an activity can take place more efficiently within an organization rather than buying that activity in the open market place. Say, for instance, a baker delivers his bread to local customers. He wants to ensure his bread will be delivered. He can hire a local firm to deliver his bread for him, but he faces two problems. First, he can't be sure about the reliability of the firm, and secondly he is dependent on the guarantees the firm offers. The first problem is known as bounded rationality. The second, which we met in the case of managers knowing more than owners, is asymmetric information. By using his own van and employing a person to drive it, the baker has greater control of the resource and can be more sure that his bread will reach his customers, as he can more easily direct the operations of his employee. Transaction cost theory has formed the basis of more recent economic explanations about a firm's activities and can equally be applied to multinational firms as to our local baker. If a resource is in scarce supply in the open market, it can be cheaper for an organization to develop those competencies necessary to provide that resource in house. Thus, firms grow because the organization can more effectively conduct some types of transactions. From this have followed resource-based theories, which see firms as bundles of resources – both physical machinery and employee skills. These resource bundles are allocated in certain ways, depending on the mix of resources open to the firm. As firms mature and grow, they develop their own unique sets of resource bundles. Different bundles of resources donate the development of different strategies and can help explain why similar firms develop in different directions over time.

If neo-Classical and transaction costs provided the early framework, much of the development of modern management theory has grown from the changing business environment. The rate of change over the past decade or so has, as we will see, brought something of a revolution to the body of thought.

The industrial age made mass-production possible. In the so-called machine age, work was largely repetitive and routine. Employees were often tied to a production line which dictated the pace at which they worked and the functions they performed. Managers were there to ensure tasks were performed correctly; they commanded and controlled the processes. Decisions were taken at the top of the organization and workers did as they were told. Because of the mechanistic nature of the work, tasks and processes could be easily quantified and measured: management was treated as a science. The best known of these management scientists was the American theorist F. W. Taylor. He argued that in a factory, there was a best way to perform a task. By watching employees perform, and timing their actions, any unnecessary moves could be eliminated and the task could be carried out more efficiently. Other workers could then be trained in the new technique. The message was clear: stick to the rules. Employee initiative was not encouraged.

Taylor's work influenced Max Weber, who was interested in the structure of an organization. If a 'best way' of carrying out a task could be found, then logic suggested there could be a 'best way' of structuring an organization. Weber concluded that a bureaucracy was the most efficient ways of running a firm, as against the unpredictability of a firm run by a charismatic manager, or the supposedly unprofessional manner of a family-run firm.

The effects of Taylor and Weber's work was long-lived: some would argue too long-lived. All their focus is on the internal operations of an organization. And that was also the focus of the management. Customers would get what they were given. Or as Henry Ford famously remarked: 'You can have any colour of car you like, as long as it's black.' The ways of working, the managerial roles and the organizational theories of the machine age only fit a slow moving or static competitive environment. World recession during the 1930s, and the collapse in world trade which followed it, meant that companies tended to concentrate on the national market. There was little labour mobility: a job, if you were lucky enough to have one, was often regarded as being for life.

The business climate and management theory developed over the decades, but it was the 1970s which finally saw the end of the machine age. Just as the oil shock and the **stagflation** which followed it put into question the **Keynesian** orthodoxy in economics, so a combination of deregulation, technology, and trade changed the way companies operated.

- The liberalization of trade through organizations such as GATT made it possible for western companies to export their goods to new markets. But conversely, it also allowed lower-cost developing economies to export their cheaper products. The cars that were made so efficiently on the Henry Ford production line with the help of Taylorism, now had to respond to the challenge of cheap foreign makes.

- The process of deregulation, partially driven by the new appeal of **supply-side** measures for policy-makers, accelerated the break-up of private-sector monopolies and the privatization of state enterprises.
- The same process of deregulation opened up global capital markets and the banking system. This gave companies access to a wider pool of both equity and debt financing. In some cases this encouraged over-expansion, such as during the **junk-bond** heyday of the 1980s in the United States.
- The pace of technological change increased exponentially (see Richard Lander's essay, 'Technology'), enabling computers to take over many of the mundane tasks previously performed by the workforce, and creating the information superhighway.

All these factors meant that it was necessary for organizations to change not just how they worked, but in some cases the actual work they did, in order to survive. Organizations and managers now had to look externally, to understand the potential threats within the competitive environment and how the structure of their industry might change and develop. It became critical for organizations to be able to respond quickly to the changing environment. Not understanding change could mean the organization didn't survive.

A case study in slow responsiveness was the Swiss watch industry. One of the country's major industries, it dismissed the development of electronic watches as a minor threat. The industry paid dear. While Swiss watches are highly regarded, the mass market has gone to the Japanese and only recently have the Swiss made a comeback with Swatch and Swatch-style products. And with the growth of low-cost Asian and Latin American markets stealing much of the traditional manufacturing market in western economies, there has been a shift from a manufacturing base to a service economy which required the development of different skills.

In order to be able to respond quickly to changes in the market place and to meet the demands of the greater competitive environment, organizations have developed new ways of working. **Just-in-time** manufacturing, for example, developed in Japan, involves making goods to order in response to the demand from customers. This pull-led system – where the customer dictates the production schedule – is very different to the organization in the machine age, where production schedules would dictate what the customer could buy. If red boxes, rather than blue boxes, are suddenly selling well, the just-in-time manufacturing system will quickly supply red boxes at little cost to itself. With no, or extremely little, stock on the shelves, production of red boxes is not just quick to effect, it also means less of the company's hard-earned revenue is tied up in stocks of the now slow-selling blue boxes. New information technology has greatly helped the development of stock-control methods such as just-in-time.

This focus on the end-user of the product gave companies and managers indications about how they might change the goods or services they produced to better meet consumer demand. But it also requires a shift in organizing the resources within the firm. Henry Minzberg, writing in the late 1970s, built on the work of Weber to show how different organizational structures could be developed to meet different needs. He concluded that flatter structures and more amorphous structures where there is less focus on rigid job structures were more suited for success in environments which required quick decision-making or the need to change to survive in the competitive market place. 'Adhocracy' had replaced the bureaucracy.

The role of managers needed to change. Command and control structures have given way to devolving power down the organization to facilitate quick responses. (The M-Form structure is a way of devolving power into operating divisions, whilst capital allocation is decided at head office, often by senior managers who have an equity stake in the company. This allows the divisions to operate independently under the scrutiny of the centre, which will judge their efficiency and if necessary modify or close them. This compares with the U-Form organization, more common in small and medium-sized companies, where the centralized power structure looks after all the products on an operational level.) In modern companies managers are often seen as coaches and facilitators, helping employees grow and develop. The idea of the right way to do things has gone. Now the focus is on unlocking the potential of the organization through the unique skills that it has which are a sum of the people within it and the processes it uses. With the need to respond to external factors has come the need to manage change within the organization to allow an effective response. In the 1970s and 1980s the impact of technology, coupled with world recession, meant thousands of jobs were lost. For many employees and managers, therefore, change has become synonymous with job cuts and is viewed with suspicion. Much of the focus of management theory in recent years has been on how to get the entire organization to 'buy in' to the need for change and development. Rather than being merely resources to be exploited, as was the case in the machine age, people are now regarded as an organization's greatest asset and much attention has been given to ways in which managers can encourage all members of staff to develop. The demise of the machine age has produced a new kind of contract between workers and the organization. Jobs are not for life; workers are rewarded for the skills they have and promotion is not automatic. The notion of the firm as 'parent' no longer exists.

New deregulated markets, a willingness to embrace change, and better information technology have also spawned an explosion in multi-business companies. Suddenly the transaction costs as outlined by Coase have shifted, and it is possible for a company to realize economies not just of scale but of scope, realizing synergies in accounting systems, IT, transportation, and marketing. There is also the advantage of spreading risk in global markets which are faster to develop and in some ways harder to predict than a more static local environment.

In general the biggest and most successful companies are spread across a wider geographical base. Michael Porter argued that there are industry globalization drivers which determine the potential and need for developing a global strategy. These factors, fuelled by economic, political, technological and social trends, include the convergence of consumer tastes, the possibility of gaining a cost advantage by siting activities in lower-cost countries, the lifting of trading restrictions and the harmonization of standards. The emergence of multinational and transnational companies increases the complexity of business decisions. Where do they source their activities? How should they organize themselves for success? What markets do they seek to compete in? Do they diversify?

With the shift to multi-business and multinational companies has come a reassertion of the need to give owners what they want: a good return on investment. The key question managers must ask themselves is: will their decision increase value for shareholders? The focus on shareholder value has been fuelled by the growing share ownership base. Personal savings and investment instruments run by equity fund managers holding large share portfolios are under pressure to out-perform the stock market average, or, at the very least, to provide a better return to the fundholders than a savings account. Financial institutions are therefore increasingly powerful shareholders, demanding that a company's activities do pay dividends. Managers are therefore required more than before to answer for their activities and persuade the shareholders that if they don't see jam today, the strategy the company is pursuing will pay large dividends in the medium term. There is hardly an annual report in the United States or the United Kingdom that doesn't include the phrase 'delivering shareholder value'. For multi-business companies this puts pressure on the corporate centre to add value. Zeneca split from ICI, and Hanson added value until it simply didn't work anymore. This by no means implies that the period of mergers and acquisitions is over; rather, that management in the post-machine age requires an acceptance of change, which might as easily be demerger as merger. If anything, the market is more aggressive than ever at addressing the issue of the divorce of ownership from control which can be an obstacle to the neo-Classical goal of profit maximization.

Together with their very real consciousness of the markets, companies have also learned that one way to deliver value is to have good relationships with all their stakeholders, not just the shareholders. Keeping hold of the customer base, building good relationships with clients so that they don't choose alternatives, is a sound way of locking in value, as it costs much more to attract a new customer than to service an existing one. Similarly, building relationships with key suppliers, and involving them in the decisions of the organization, ensures their skills are not so readily available to others. This notion is described more fully in 'Relationship Marketing' by Adrian Payne and Sue Holt.

The modern manager therefore has to do many more things than his or her predecessor. Mangers need to be continually scanning the external environment for opportunities or threats; they need, more than ever before, to be able to justify their decisions to shareholders, staff, customers, suppliers. They need to be effective communicators, coaches and strategists. The tool-kit modern managers need is much greater than ever before. Little wonder then, that management education is becoming increasingly popular and management consultancy is having a boom time.

If anything, all the post-machine age trends will be even stronger in the next decade. The competitive environment will become ever faster-changing, spurred on by developing technology, demanding customers and the need for firms to innovate to survive. The product life cycle in consumer electronics, for example, is contracting by the year if not the month, with many products becoming obsolete in less than 12 months. To keep innovating, firms need to be able to cope with constant flux and ambiguity. The ease of communication, coupled with the move into service-based activities has eroded the traditional notion of 'work' taking place in a single location, by the same, fixed team of people. The notion of the virtual organization where individuals who may be scattered round the globe come together to work on projects is being seen increasingly as the way forward. Coupled with the increasing integration of suppliers into a business, it may gradually become difficult to see where one organization stops and another begins. This is truly the successor to the machine age, which we might call the technology age. And because technology frees the most important asset of any company – its people – literally from the machines, management will need to be adaptable, but it will also develop a more holistic approach. Jobs may not be for life, nor companies for single products in single markets. But in general the workplace, at least in the developed economies, will become a more pleasant place, if indeed it exists as a workplace at all.

FURTHER READING

Ansoff, Igor, *Corporate Strategy* (Penguin, 1988 [first published 1965]).

Bartlett, C.A., and Ghoshal, S., *Managing Across Borders: the transnational solution* (Harvard Business School Press, 1989).

Doz, Y., *Strategic Management in Multinational Companies* (Pergamon, 1986).

Johnson, Gerry and Scholes, Kevan, *Exploring Corporate Strategy* (Prentice Hall, 1993).

Mintzberg, Henry, *Structuring of Organisations* (Prentice Hall, 1979).

Mintzberg, Henry, and Quinn, James Brian (eds.), *The Strategy Process* (Prentice Hall, 1991).

Porter, M.E., *Competitive Advantage: Sustaining Superior Performance* (Free Press, 1985).

Yip, George S., *Total Global Strategy* (Prentice Hall, 1995).

11

RELATIONSHIP MARKETING

ADRIAN PAYNE AND SUE HOLT

We have seen in the previous essays in this section how new circumstances in population patterns, technology, and the way that firms are managed are changing the way we describe and participate in economic activity. This essay goes to the very heart of such activity, introducing new ways of looking at pricing, marketing, and the firm itself. Relationship marketing concentrates on the development of loyalty and service, rather than purely transactional approaches to selling goods and services. The essay introduces the notion of time into economic transactions, at a period when companies are increasingly aware that keeping a customer is a great deal less costly, and potentially a great deal more rewarding, than acquiring a new one. It is particularly important in today's markets for services, and increasingly possible with Internet technology, where each product can be tailor-made for an individual customer, and where distinctions between customers and suppliers are becoming much more blurred.

As noted for the previous essay, the theory of management is going through rapid changes which feed into economics. Nowhere is this more the case than in the area of marketing. If the most basic economic relationship (seller, buyer, price) is being transplanted by something more complex (dealing with such issues as fulfilment, bespoke production, and a level of customer information made possible by today's technologies), we are facing some bracing challenges to our traditional notions about how markets operate.

Like the management essay, this work can also be seen in the context of **management theories of the firm**, as well as some of the neo-Classical basics of supply and demand (**theory of production costs** and **theory of consumer demand**) and their associated entries.

THE TRADITIONAL APPROACH TO MARKETING

In recent years the traditional approach to marketing has increasingly been questioned. Doubt has been cast on the relevance of traditional marketing theory, especially when applied to international, industrial and services marketing, where establishing longer-term relationships with customers is critical to organizational success.

The traditional 'marketing mix' or 'Four Ps' approach to marketing was formulated in the 1950s and 1960s in a competitive environment (primarily the North American consumer goods market) that contrasts starkly with the global market place of the late 1990s.

The origins of the term 'marketing mix', to describe the important elements or ingredients that make up a marketing programme, lie in the work done by Michael Borden at the Harvard Business School in the 1960s. He suggested that the following 12 elements should be considered in formulating a marketing programme:

- Product planning
- Pricing
- Branding
- Channels of distribution
- Personal selling
- Advertising
- Promotions
- Packaging
- Display
- Servicing
- Physical handling
- Fact finding and analysis.

Over time, the list of marketing mix decisions was simplified under four headings which became known as the 'Four Ps' (product, price, promotion and place), which are now enshrined in marketing theory. This approach, with its focus on consumer marketing, was very much a product of thinking based on the economic theories of supply and demand. As Theodore Levitt pointed out in 1983, these presume 'that the work of the economic system is time-discrete and bare of human interaction – that an instantaneous disembodied sales transaction clears the market at the intersection of supply and demand'. It also ignores 'time' as a factor in marketing. Increasingly this very transactional view of marketing, with its short-term focus on the 'sale' and the 'acquisition' of customers, is being challenged as products and services become more complex and bespoke, as interdependencies between customers and suppliers intensify and as the competitive environment becomes increasingly global.

THE CHANGING FOCUS OF MARKETING

Since the 1950s the formal study of marketing has focused on an evolving range of marketing sectors, as shown in Fig. 1. In the 1950s, marketing interest was primarily focused on consumer goods. In the 1960s increased attention started to be directed towards industrial markets. In the 1970s, considerable academic effort was placed on the area of non-profit or societal marketing. In the 1980s attention started to be directed at the services sector, an area of marketing that had received remarkably little consideration in view of its importance to the overall economy. At the same time a new emphasis on marketing started to emerge – that of relationship marketing.

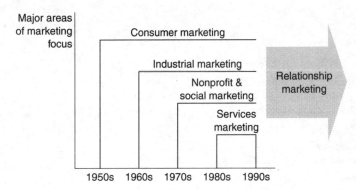

Fig. 1 The changing focus of marketing (based on Christopher, Payne and Ballantyne, 1991)

RELATIONSHIP MARKETING

What is relationship marketing? The term first started to be used during the 1980s, and it is still a relatively new and evolving concept. The basis of the relationship marketing philosophy is that the attraction of new customers is merely the first step in the marketing process. The key is *retaining* that customer. Marketing should not begin and end with clinching the deal – it must also concern itself with keeping, and improving the relationship with the customer. It is this focus on customer retention that makes relationship marketing a different paradigm to traditional marketing approaches, which are concentrated on customer acquisition.

The work of early proponents of the approach, Berry (1983), Levitt (1983) and Bund Jackson (1985) has been built on by others, including

Grönroos (1990) and Christopher, Payne and Ballantyne (1991). Grönroos formulated a relationship-focused definition of marketing where 'the purpose of marketing is to establish, maintain, enhance and commercialise customer relationships (often, but not necessarily always, long term relationships) so that the objectives of the parties involved are met. This is done by mutual exchange and fulfilment of promises'. Christopher, Payne and Ballantyne suggest a theory of relationship marketing that is broader in its approach. The key elements of this view are:

- The emphasis in the interaction between suppliers and customers is shifting from a transaction to a relationship focus (Fig. 2).
- The relationship marketing approach focuses on maximizing the lifetime value of desirable customers and customer segments.
- Relationship marketing strategies are concerned with the development and enhancement of relationships with a number of 'key markets' (Fig. 3). It is concerned with the 'internal market' within the organization, as well as building substantial external relationships with customers, suppliers, referral sources, influence markets and recruitment markets.
- Functionally based marketing within the company is replaced by cross-functionally based marketing focused on customer needs.
- Quality, customer service and marketing are closely related. However, frequently they are managed separately. A relationship marketing approach brings these elements into a much closer coherence.

Instead of a narrow, transactional, one-sale-at-a-time viewpoint, marketing should emphasize relationships between the organization and its markets more strongly. Understanding the dynamics of these markets and identifying the critical features which not only influence

Transaction focus	Relationship focus
Orientation to single sales	Orientation to customer retention
Discontinuous customer contact	Continuous customer contact
Focus on product features	Focus on customer value
Short time scale	Long time scale
Little emphasis on customer service	High customer service emphasis
Limited commitment to meeting customer expectations	High commitment to meeting customer relations
Quality is the concern of production staff	Quality is the concern of all staff

Fig. 2 Transaction versus relationship marketing

Fig. 3 The relationship marketing six markets model (based on Payne, 1995)

and drive a company's strategy but also affect its competitive position are fundamental to managers in the 1990s. The six markets model (Fig. 3) illustrates the markets to which companies need to direct their marketing activity and on which they should formulate strategic marketing plans. It is helpful to look at these six markets in more detail.

CUSTOMER MARKETS

There is no doubt that the primary focus of marketing was, and remains, the customer. However, more emphasis needs to be placed on marketing activities designed for and directed towards existing customers. By placing too much focus on marketing activities directed at new customers, companies often experience the 'leaking bucket' effect, where customers are lost because insufficient marketing activity generally, and customer service specifically, is directed to them. Too many companies, having secured a customer's order, then turn their attention to seeking new customers without understanding the importance of maintaining and enhancing the relationships with their existing customers. This is not meant to suggest that new customers are not important, indeed they are vital to most businesses' futures, but rather a balance needs to be struck between the effort directed towards existing customers and new customers. The relationship marketing 'ladder of customer loyalty' at Fig. 4 illustrates this point. It is apparent

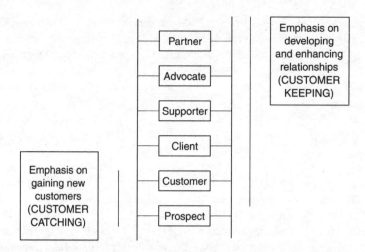

Fig. 4 The relationship marketing ladder of customer loyalty (based on Payne, 1995)

that many organizations put their main emphasis on the lower rungs by identifying prospects and attempting to turn them into customers, rather than on the higher and ultimately more rewarding rungs of turning them into regular clients and subsequently into strong supporters and active advocates. However, it is appropriate to sound a warning shot at this point. There will be customers within a company's customer base that are either unprofitable or expensive to service, which would be inappropriate targets of a relationship marketing approach. While you want to move customers up the ladder, not every customer is created equal. There are some important economic metrics related to customer retention, which will be discussed later.

REFERRAL MARKETS

It has been said that the best form of marketing is to get your customers to do your marketing for you. This is behind the concept of the customer loyalty ladder and is the reason why the creation of advocates is so important. But existing customers are not the only sources of referral. Take banking as an example. Referral sources for a bank would include insurance companies, estate agents, accountancy and law firms as well as existing private and business clients. Companies need to start by recognizing their key referral sources. The present and likely future importance of these sources should be identified and a specific plan developed to determine the appropriate levels of marketing resources that should be devoted to each of them. However, it should be emphasized that the development of these relationships takes time, and the benefits of such marketing activity may take some time to come to fruition.

SUPPLIER/ALLIANCE MARKETS

There is mounting evidence that organizations' relationships with their suppliers are undergoing fundamental changes. The old adversarial relationship, where a company tried to squeeze its suppliers to its own advantage, is giving way to one based more on partnership and collaboration. This emphasizes a long-term very close relationship and a win-win philosophy rather than the win–lose philosophy inherent in adversarial relationships. In the past, firms concentrated on trying to extract the best price from suppliers, but the 'hidden' cost of this was often variability in supply or quality, or both. There is good commercial sense in moving towards partnership and collaboration for most organizations. Relatively few organizations in either the public or private sectors spend less than about 20 or 30 per cent of their total budget on goods and services from outside suppliers. For manufacturers in the United States the average is over 60 per cent of total revenue. Where there is a long-term commitment to a supplier, based upon a mutually profitable relationship, the result will often be:

- enhanced product and service quality;
- a focus on continuous improvement;
- a greater likelihood of supplier-driven product and process innovation;
- lower total costs through supply chain integration;
- higher levels of responsiveness.

Companies like the Rover Group now talk of the 'extended enterprise', in which very close relationships are developed with a much reduced supplier base, the result of which is greater competitiveness in the market place. As companies build these closer relationships and alliances, taking advantage of the greater competitiveness that this may bring, the concept of companies competing is being replaced by the concept of 'supply chains' competing.

RECRUITMENT MARKETS

A number of studies have highlighted the importance that recruitment practices can have upon company performance. Many companies are today learning that the limiting factor on their success is the availability of skilled people, rather than the availability of other resources such as capital or raw materials. Organizations need to market themselves in a way that attracts the calibre of person that matches the profile which the organization seeks to sustain in the eyes of its customers. More and more companies are now identifying the psychometric profile of the type of person most likely to be successful in achieving customer-driven goals. The recruitment process itself is also an opportunity for the company to build a positive image with recruits that they carry forward into employment.

INFLUENCE MARKETS

There has been a tendency to view the management of public relations as a separate activity from mainstream marketing. Under the relationship marketing paradigm, however, the influence market is seen as an integral component of the customer relationship-building process. Influences come in many forms. Government departments and agencies, the media, consultants and advisers, the stock market; the list of potential sources of influence is endless. Every organization can either benefit or suffer from the influence that may be exerted from these sources. A massive industry has grown up worldwide in the management of public relations and corporate communications and its impact has been considerable. As a component of a relationship marketing strategy, the management of influences is vital.

INTERNAL MARKETS

Development of customer relationships can be severely hampered by the structure of the organization. Traditional vertical organizations which are hierarchically structured (Fig. 5) and functionally oriented often optimize individual functions at the expense of the whole business and the customer. Relationship marketing with its emphasis on cross-functional marketing (Fig. 6) focuses on the processes that deliver for the customer. These processes run across functions and in customer-facing organizations, key players are drawn together in multi-disciplinary teams or groups that seek to marshal resources to achieve

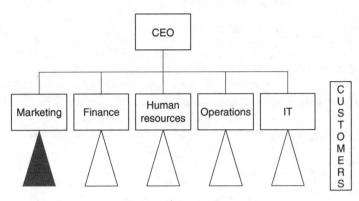

Fig. 5 Marketing as a functional activity

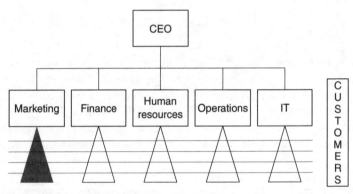

Fig. 6 Marketing as a cross-functional activity

customer-based objectives. Managing the organization that is focused on the customer, requires internal marketing to take place.

There are two key aspects to this. One involves the notion of the internal customer; that is every person working within an organization has both a customer and a supplier. Employees need to recognise that both individuals and departments have customers and then determine what can be done to improve levels of customer service and quality within the organization. The second aspect is concerned with making certain that all employees work together in a way that is attuned to the company's mission, strategy and goals. The importance of this has become particularly transparent in service firms where there is a close interface with the customer. The idea of internal marketing, in this context, is to ensure that all employees provide the best representation of the company to the customer whether by telephone, mail, electronic or personal interactions. The fundamental aims of internal marketing are to develop internal and external customer awareness and remove functional barriers to organizational effectiveness.

Relationship marketing implies, therefore, not just the consideration of better relationships with customer markets, but also the development and enhancement of relationships with the other markets outlined above. Not all these markets necessarily require formal marketing plans, but companies will need to have some form of strategy to address each market, and these strategies need to be deeply ingrained and understood by all staff within an organization. Members of supply markets, referral markets, employee markets, internal markets and influence markets need to be served in the same way that customer markets are and high levels of service quality are essential in establishing and maintaining relationships with all these key markets. Not all the markets require equal levels of attention and resources, so determination of these levels can be achieved through the following steps:

- identify key participants in each of the markets;
- undertake research to identify expectations and requirements of key participants;
- review current and proposed level of emphasis in each market;
- formulate desired relationship strategy and determine if a formal market plan is necessary.

Customers need to be divided into new and existing categories in order to avoid, as noted earlier, companies placing all their emphasis on getting new customers at the expense of existing ones.

So, relationship marketing is emerging as an actionable framework for developing enduring, longer-term (and hence more profitable) relationships with customers.

The six markets model provides a framework for managers to manage and plan their marketing activity. But what impact does this view of marketing have on our traditional views about the economic measures of marketing?

RELATIONSHIP MARKETING AND CUSTOMER RETENTION ECONOMICS

As we have already discussed, relationship marketing is concerned more with customer retention than with customer acquisition. There are sound economic reasons for this. Improvements in customer retention of just a few percentage points can have a dramatic impact on improvements in profitability. According to Bain & Company, the US strategy consulting firm, there is a high correlation between customer retention and company profitability. Its research showed that a 5 per cent increase in customer retention leads to a considerable rise in net present value profits (see Fig. 7). This increase can be as much as 125 per cent for a credit card company and 50 per cent for an insurance broker. While it is not easy to obtain a 5 per cent increase in customer retention, even a 1 per cent increase could yield a considerable improvement in profitability. Research has also shown that it can cost as much as ten times more to find a new customer than it does to maintain a current one. The costs of customer defection to a company are therefore very high.

The key reasons why retaining customers is so profitable are:

- sales and marketing and set-up costs are amortised over a longer customer lifetime;
- customer expenditure increases over time;
- repeat customers often cost less to service;
- satisfied customers provide referrals;
- satisfied customers may be prepared to pay a price premium.

In measuring customer retention, Bain & Company calculated the profitability of the customer based on the notion of customer lifetime value (CLV). This is the expected cash flow over a customer's lifetime;

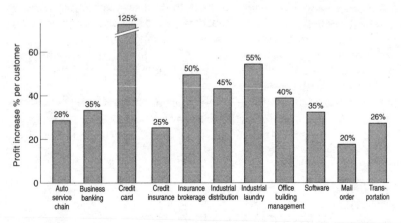

Fig. 7 Profit impact of a 5 percentage points increase in customer retention for selected businesses (source, Bain & Company)

the longer they stay, the more profits they bring to the company. For example, a credit card company may spend approximately £20.00 to recruit a customer and to set up a new account. The newly acquired customer will use the card slowly to begin with, until they become familiar with its convenience. If the customer stays a second year, then the economics of profitability to the company greatly improve. As purchases increase, the operating costs of managing the account decrease. In such cases, a service company's major outlay is at the beginning of the relationship. To calculate a customer's real worth a company must look at the projected profit over the life of the account. A credit card company will probably lose money should the account defect within the first year. If a customer stays with the company for more than three years, when the costs of administration are low, then the profits start to accrue.

It is worth pointing out that marketing that is directed at retaining customers can be expensive, and needs to be closely evaluated against results. As we have already said, not all customers are profitable. It is therefore important to understand the relative profitability of different customer segments. The greatest retention efforts should be directed to those segments that are presently or potentially the most profitable. It should be recognized, however, that even unprofitable customers may be valuable in their contribution towards fixed costs, and considerable caution is needed in the allocation of fixed and variable costs, to ensure that customers who make a contribution are not simply discarded.

The relationship approach to marketing is moving its economic focus away from using the traditional measures of marketing success such as market share and product volumes to measures such as share of customer, customer profitability and customer lifetime value: from market measures to customer measures (see Fig. 8).

Old marketing metrics	New marketing metrics
Market share	Share of customer
Customer acquisition rates	Customer retention measures
Product profitability	Customer profitability
Product based pricing	Customer based pricing
Mass pricing	Individual and bespoke pricing
Transaction based accounting	Customer lifetime value

Fig. 8 The changing metrics of marketing

THE NEW ECONOMICS OF MARKETING

How is a relationship approach to marketing supported by current economic theory? As we have noted above, traditional 'economic' or 'theory of the firm' approaches to marketing such as the theories of supply and demand would appear to have increasingly little relevance to today's complex and turbulent business environment, or to the concept of relationship marketing. The whole question of pricing is an interesting example of this. Price is virtually the only influence whose impact on demand has been modelled by economists and this is assuming that prices are market based. With pricing now being geared to individual customers or to customer lifetime value calculations or to the premium that customers will pay for a bespoke service, and not to the market, it is difficult to see the direct effect and correlation between price and demand that has been taken for granted by economists.

Philip Kotler (1997) has pointed out that economists have failed to address many of the questions of practical interest to businesses and have made little progress in understanding demand. This view is supported by Stanley Slater (1997) who suggests that there is widespread rejection of the neo-Classical view of the firm and that other more recent theories still do not properly address the demand side of marketing. These more recent theories such as the 'behavioural theory of the firm', 'transaction cost theory' and 'resource-based' and resource-dependency theory' all have some relevance, depending on, for example, which aspect of the six markets model you are looking at, but all fall short of a full explanation.

Slater argues that perhaps a customer value-based theory of the firm should be developed: 'a customer value-based theory of the firm would say that superior performance accrues to firms that have a customer-value based organizational culture (i.e, a market orientation), complemented by being skilled at learning about customers and their changing needs and at managing the innovation process, and that organise themselves around customer value delivery processes'. This would arguably be a more relevant proposition for looking at relationship marketing, as there is a problem with taking a wholly economics-based view of marketing and customer-supplier relationships. Research has shown that there are a lot of elements to building longer-term relationships with customers that have little to do with economics and which economic theory can do little to explain. For example, trust, commitment, personal relationships, congruency of objectives between parties, have all been shown to have a significant impact on business relationships. The challenge for economists then is to come up with a theory of the firm that somehow takes account of these aspects of interfirm relationships. Indeed, some of these aspects of marketing owe more to organization theory and behaviour than to any economics-based theory.

And what of the future? One interesting point to note is that in the future it is unlikely that it will be just individual firms that are competing. As companies build relationships such as partnerships, networks, joint ventures, and even virtual organizations, boundaries between companies will become increasingly blurred. Companies which are part of a 'supply chain' built on these types of relationship with all the benefits such as sharing of customer and market information, cost reduction and flexibility, may well have a competitive advantage over those still operating as individual companies.

What other questions should marketers be addressing now? Some examples include: how will the emerging technologies and media, such as the Internet, affect marketing and marketing theories? How should companies approach marketing from a global perspective? What different approaches might need to be taken by virtual companies and corporations? If building relationships matters, how can this be done remotely or by virtual means? What marketing metrics will emerge to measure these new ways of marketing? What impact will all these changes have on our views of marketing theory and economic theory? These are all questions that remain to be answered.

SUMMARY

Relationship marketing focuses on retaining customers and building a relationship with them. It has emerged out of a dissatisfaction with more traditional approaches to marketing (based on mass consumer marketing), especially when applied to service and business-to-business markets. The move from a transaction to a relationship approach requires management to take a cross-functional view of their organizations, so that processes are focused on the customer in order to build in responsiveness and excellent customer service. In addition, management needs to focus on all of the six markets discussed, and not just on customer markets, if they are to manage their relationship marketing successfully.

The focus on customer retention instead of acquisition has a number of advantages, particularly economic advantages in terms of long-term customer profitability and customer lifetime value. The argument for improving retention rates of customers is a compelling one. It is of particular importance in mature markets and is taking over from the more traditional strategies of increasing market share. Equally, there has been a shift in the metrics applied to marketing. These have become more customer-focused and less market-focused.

Finally, the traditional economic theories that have been applied to marketing have less and less relevance as this new marketing paradigm emerges. There are aspects of relationship marketing that cannot be explained by current economic theories which fall short of explaining the less tangible aspects of customer supplier relationships. The challenge for economists is to develop a theory of marketing (or a theory of the firm which applies to marketing) which not only addresses these aspects, but which also takes into account the fast-emerging changes in technology and communications which will fundamentally change the company and the way it reaches its markets and customers in the future.

(*See also* Robert Beynon's essay, 'Changing Trends in Management'.)

FURTHER READING

Berry, L. L., 'Relationship Marketing', in Berry, L. L., Shostack G. L., and Upah, G. D., (eds), *Emerging Perspectives on Services Marketing* (American Marketing Association, 1983), pp. 25–8.

Bund Jackson, B., 'Build Customer Relationships That Last', *Harvard Business Review*, Nov–Dec 1985, pp. 120–28.

Christopher, M., Payne, A. F. T., and Ballantyne, D., *Relationship Marketing: Bringing Quality, Customer Service and Marketing Together* (Butterworth-Heinemann, 1991).

Grönroos, C., 'Relationship approach to marketing in service contexts: the marketing and organisational behaviour interface', *Journal of Business Research*, **20**, 1 (1990), pp. 3–11.

Kotler, P., in Shaw, R., and Mazur L. (eds), *Marketing Accountability: Improving Business Performance* (FT Retail and Consumer Publishing, 1997) pp. 6–9.

Levitt, T., 'After the sales is over . . .', *Harvard Business Review*, Mar–Apr 1983, pp. 117–24.

Payne, A. F. T., *Advances in Relationship Marketing* (Kogan Page, 1995).

Slater, S. F., 'Developing a Customer Value-Based Theory of the Firm', *Journal of the Academy of Marketing Science*, **25**, 2 (1997), pp. 162–67.

SELECT BIBLIOGRAPHY

These relatively recent books are suggested in addition to the standard classics such as Keynes' *General Theory* or Smith's *Wealth of Nations*, and also to standard microeconomics texts. They are intended to supplement the source and additional reading lists at the end of each essay, and in general deal with the broad range of macroeconomics.

Aghion, Philippe, and Howitt, Peter, *Endogenous Growth Theory* (MIT Press, 1998).

Galbraith, John Kenneth, *Money: Whence It Came, Where It Went* (Penguin, 1995).

Hahn, Frank, and Solow, Robert, *A Critical Essay on Modern Macro-Economic Theory* (Blackwell, 1997).

Hoover, Kevin D., *The New Classical Macro-Economics* (Blackwell, 1990)

Minford, Patrick, *Markets Not Stakes* (Orion, 1998).

Obstfeld, Maurice, and Rogoff, Kenneth, *Foundations of International Macro-Economics* (MIT Press, 1996).

Romer, David, *Advanced Macro-Economics* (McGraw Hill, 1995).

IV
A–Z OF
KEY THEMES AND
MAJOR FIGURES

GROUPED LIST
OF A–Z ENTRIES

To make the A–Z section easier to use, we include below a grouped list of all the entries. The asterisked entries are definitions of the broader topics covered in this dictionary. Entries with an asterisk at the head of individual lists are intended as subject headings for that particular grouping.

MICROECONOMICS

*Theory of production costs
*Theory of consumer demand
Supply curve
Demand curve
Revenue (total, marginal, average)
Engel's law
Utility
Opportunity cost
Upward sloping demand curve
    (Veblen effect)
Kinked demand curve
Giffen good
Price effect/wealth effect
Diminishing marginal returns
Elasticities
Economies of scale

*Factors of production
Production function
Wages (labour theory of value)
Value added
Cobweb theorem
Scarcity
Surplus

*Perfect competition
*Monopoly
X-inefficiency
Nationalization
*Oligopoly

*Pricing practice
Revenue (company)
Turnover
Consumer
Money

*Management theories of the firm

*Business strategy (mergers and
    acquisitions)
Williamson trade-off model
Integration
Capital intensive
Market structure
Product
Research and development
Just in time
Product life cycle

149

*Shares/share capital
Dividends

*Asset
Asset stripping

*Debt
Gearing
Credit
Junk bonds

*Accounts
Off balance-sheet financing
Profit
Profit sharing
Valuation
Risk capital

*Governance

*Regulation

MACROECONOMICS

*Keynes
*Monetarism
IS/LM
Inflation
Quantity theory of money
Cambridge equation
Interest rate
Bonds
Keynes – money demand
Money supply
Bank credit multiplier
Money supply/aggregate demand
    linkages

*Circular flow of national income
GDP/GNP
Accelerator
Multiplier
Automatic stabilizers
Leakages

Taxation
Savings
Paradox of thrift
Investment
Consumption function

*Business cycles
Endogenous growth theory
Kondratieff cycle
Harrod-Domar growth model
Solow growth model

Normative/positive/welfare
    economics
Infrastructure/social costs

Long/short-run

*Employment
Stagflation
Wage–price spiral
Structural unemployment
Minimum wage
Phillips curve
Expectations-adjusted Phillips curve

*Fiscal policy
Transfer payments
Budget deficit
Public debt
Laffer Curve
PSBR/PSDR
Black economy

*Monetary policy

*Supply-side economics

*Theory (benefits) of trade
Comparative advantage/gains from
    trade
Heckscher-Ohlin factor proportions
    theory
Balance of payments

Exchange rate policy
Fixed/floating exchange rates
Currency
Gold standard
Edgeworth Box
Technological gap theory
Devaluation/revaluation
Marshall-Lerner Condition
J-curve
Most favoured nation
Bretton Woods system
IMF
Trade bodies
Hot money
EMU
PPP

*Stock market
Bulls
Bears
Share price index
Securities
New issue market
Insider trading
Institutional investors
Tap issue
Underwriting
Unit trust/mutual fund

*Bank
Building society/thrift
Clearing bank
Central bank
Merchant bank
Venture capital
LIBOR

*Derivatives
Futures
Options/calls/puts
Swaps
LIFFE
Commodities markets

*Econometrics
Game theory
Regression
Probability
Concentration measures
Gini coefficient
Pareto
Lorenz Curve
*Classical economics
*Neo-Classical economics
*Neo-Keynesian economics

Gresham's Law
Walras's Law
Galbraith
Malthus
Marshall
Marx
Mercantilism
Mill
Pigou
Ricardo
Say
Schumpeter
Smith
Modigliani
Hicks
Cambridge school
Austrian school

A

ACCELERATOR The accelerator is the principle that **investment** varies in direct proportion to output, or **GDP**, but that it is more volatile to changes. And since investment is an input to the **circular flow of income**, it works with the **multiplier** to cause further increases in output.

The accelerator's operation can be expressed as:

Change in $I = a$(change in output),

where I is the level of investment, and a is the accelerator.

The accelerator principle that the level of investment is more volatile than the actual change in demand can be explained in the following simple example.

Suppose a firm uses 20 machines to produce 100 units each, selling 2,000 units each year. It replaces two of the machines each year. Now suppose demand rises by 500, to 2,500 units. That's an increase of 25 per cent. The firm is going to need another five machines in the year in question, an increase from two to seven. That's an increase of 250 per cent. That will feed through into the machine-making sector, and in turn bring about greater increases in output via the multiplier.

Now suppose that the same firm believed that instead of increasing, demand was liable to fall by 200 units in the following year, from 2,000 units to 1,800. The firm would simply not replace two of its old machines that year, which would mean that its requirement for new machines would be zero, even though demand for its own product had fallen only a little. Again, this will have a feed-through effect on the circular flow via the multiplier.

Keynes argued that the working of the multiplier and the accelerator together could explain the fluctuations of national income which are characteristic of the **business cycle**. In particular, for the accelerator there is a tendency at the bottom of the cycle for demand to be stimulated simply by the most basic replacement of worn-out capital. In our example the firm which reduced its spending on new machines to zero in one year would (assuming there was *some* demand for its products) eventually have to replace some of its machines.

There is a similar accelerator effect on stock inventories, which are increased or decreased depending on expectations of future demand (our firm which expected a reduction in demand might simply run down its stocks, not ordering anything more from suppliers, whilst during an anticipated boom it would want to build up its stocks, increasing the demand from suppliers at a greater level than the initial increase in demand).

ACCOUNTS Accounts are the financial statements of a business, prepared from a system of recorded financial transactions. They provide essential information such as liquidity, **profit** margins, **revenues** and costs, as well as **assets** and liabilities. Governments require that the accounts of public limited companies be published so that all shareholders, auditors and creditors may be able to assess their financial position. Accountancy rules vary considerably in different countries; as business activities become increasingly global in extent, there is growing pressure for all firms to conform to a standard procedure.

The most general financial statements submitted by both public and private corporations are the profit and loss account (also known as p&l) and the balance sheet. The profit and loss account is a financial statement showing revenues, costs, as well as the profit and loss resulting from operations in a given period. It is a flow representation of the performance of the company from one period to the next. The profit and loss account should reveal information about the company's profit margins and costs, as a percentage of revenues, as well as providing an insight to budgeting.

In contrast to the p&l account, the balance sheet reveals a company's net worth. It distinguishes between those items owed by the corporation and those owed to it. The items and property owned by the corporation are referred to as assets, and are reported on the left-hand side or top of the balance sheet. Usually they are organised in terms of liquidity, with the most liquid assets or the current assets appearing first, followed by less liquid, or fixed assets. The items of **debt** owed by the company are listed on the right-hand side or on the bottom of the balance sheet, as liabilities. The difference between the total assets and the total debt is the shareholders' equity, and represents the net wealth of the company. Often this value will differ from the market value of the company, which relies on investor expectations and the stockmarket economics of demand and supply.

Another element in the accounts is the cash flow statement, which measures the inflows and outflows of money. Whereas p&l statements are concerned with the generation of revenues and influences of costs, the cash flow statement focuses on the flow of a specific type of income – money. In this way shareholders, auditors and creditor may ascertain the firm's ability to cover day-to-day expenses, as well as the stability of cash inflows. If a firm's working capital (a measure of a firm's liquidity, subtracting its current liabilities from its current assets) does not sufficiently cover its debts, it is said to be 'overtrading'.

In order to ensure that firms' accounts are consistent with government standards, companies are required to submit their accounts for **auditing**. Audits are legal requirements for a company's balance sheet and p&l, as well as the underlying accounting system and records, examined by a qualified accountant (auditor).

(*See also* **governance**, **management theories of the firm**.)

ASSET For the economist and the investor, one of the most difficult processes is estimating what a company is worth. A reasonable guide is to look at its net assets: i.e. what it owns (assets), minus what it owes (liabilities).

For an understanding of the different kinds of assets and what they represent, it is necessary to look at the firm's balance sheet. Here, the items or properties that are owned by the business and which have **money** value are recorded as the assets of the company. Generally there are three types of assets that a firm can record:

1. Physical assets: these include plant and equipment, land, as well as **consumer** durable goods.
2. Financial assets: including **currency**, bank deposits, **shares** and other types of **securities**.
3. Intangible assets: these are not actually items or pieces of property in the tangible sense, but include the value of the firm's brand name or its goodwill. Goodwill is an accounting measure of the market value of a firm less its other net assets.

Some manufacturing firms also hold assets in the form of raw materials, work in progress and finished goods (which are their inventories). These assets are the stock of the firm and have been accumulated to keep up with **demand** for their finished goods, as well as smoothing the production process by having raw materials and work in progress available for completion.

Assets are also organized on the balance sheet according to their liquidity. The more liquid assets appear first on the asset side of the balance sheet, with less liquid assets appearing near the end. The collection of liquid assets such as securities, money owed by debtors, as well as cash, which are held for short-term conversion within a firm are termed current assets. The current assets of a firm are used for numerous accounting ratios and generally indicate the ability of the firm to pay off its debts. Fixed assets, however, are items such as buildings and machinery bought for long-term use rather than resale. They are recorded at their historical costs less depreciation accumulated.

Depreciation is the fall in the value of an asset resulting over years of wear and tear, which is the gradual deterioration in the efficiency (and value) of a productive asset through constant use. Depreciation is an important concept in accounting simply because the condition of plant and equipment used in production deteriorates over time and these items will eventually have to be replaced. But until they are replaced, a firm cannot simply record them at their historical cost, for with time the value of the item is likely to have fallen.

The accounting treatment for depreciation is to divide the historic cost of the fixed asset over a number of accounting periods (its estimated life). The depreciation expense incurred in every successive accounting period is then deducted from the profit and loss accounts in order to spread the original cost of the asset. It should be noted that often the net value of a fixed asset may contrast with its market value simply because the manner in which depreciation was estimated did not accurately take into account the useful life of the asset. In this circumstance, a firm could become a victim of **asset stripping** when its market value is well below its value in terms of its net assets because management has not taken the proper measures to record its assets appropriately, thus misleading its shareholders.

Some items depreciate but are not owned by the company: they have been leased or rented, and do not appear on the balance sheet. This is known as **off balance-sheet financing**. It frees the firm's long-term capital for other things. And it also improves the firm's return on capital employed. The return on capital employed is an accounting measure of the firm's profitability.

One measure of what a company is 'worth' relative to its ownership structure is its asset value per share. This is calculated by taking the total value of the firm's assets (including goodwill), minus its liabilities, divided by the number of ordinary shares. This gives a guide to what each share would represent of the company, if it were wound up or sold.

This rough assessment of a firm's worth has given rise to the concept of 'asset growth maximization' in the theory of the firm. The basic principle of the traditional company is that it aims for profit maximization. This provides maximum benefits to shareholders. Some economists have suggested that in large public companies operating in conditions of imperfect competition (*see* **oligopoly**), the managers will aim to improve their own rewards, rather than those of the shareholders. Typically salaries, bonuses, status, etc., will increase as the firm becomes larger, so that senior management will aim for the maximum growth of net assets instead of maximum profits. The downside is that this can depress share prices, because too high a proportion of profits will be held back to finance continued growth. And below a certain share value, the company, based on its asset value per share, will become ripe for a takeover (i.e. the company based on its asset value per share is worth more than its current market capitalization). We can observe this in the valuation curve below, which relates the share value to the growth rate of the firm.

The rise in the valuation curve from increasing asset growth increases the share value. But beyond point X, share values decrease because dividends are cut to finance further growth. Y represents the share price below which the company becomes a takeover target (net asset value exceeds market capitalization). Therefore, according to the theory of asset growth maximization, management will tend to operate around, or slightly below, X^*.

(*See also* **governance**.)

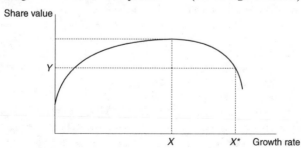

Asset growth maximization

ASSET STRIPPING Asset stripping means the acquisition of a firm for a price well below its total asset value, and the subsequent sale of those **assets**. It is a hostile transaction, where the asset stripper is a predator which takes over another firm with a view of selling off that firm's assets wholly or in part, for financial gain rather than to continue operations. Thus, after acquisition, the assets of the firm are sold to other parties for significantly more than the purchase price of the company.

This generally occurs when the realizable market value of the firm's assets are much greater than what it would cost the predator to buy the firm. The way to assess the value of assets in terms of a firm's ownership is by net asset value per share (total assets including goodwill minus liabilities, divided by the total number of shares issued). So when a discrepancy exists between the 'true' asset value per share of the firm being targeted and the price per share required to take over the firm by the predator, it is likely that a takeover, and maybe asset stripping, will occur. This discrepancy between the share price and the asset price per share can arise in two ways. First, it is possible that the management of the targeted firm has valued particular assets well below their market price. Thus, if an asset's depreciation is not taking circumstances in the market into consideration (such as inflation or changes in expectations increasing the market price of an asset), then asset prices may be out of line with their respective market prices. Secondly, a poorly managed firm or one that has had 'unlucky' experiences could create a situation in the market where a low share price based on investor expectations does not accurately reflect the true value of the firm.

An asset-stripping takeover is generally viewed critically simply because it takes no interest in its effects on stakeholders such as employees, suppliers and customers. It does little to increase economic growth or maintain employment. Nonetheless it could be argued that it is a way for the market to correct an inaccurate perception about a firm's real value, and that in many cases the assets sold are put to use elsewhere.

AUSTRIAN SCHOOL A group of economists in the University of Vienna active from the late nineteenth century. The school is unusual in being somewhere between the **Classical** and **neo-Classical** areas of thought, and also (in later years) being neither **Keynesian** nor **monetarist** in its approach. The school is associated with the work of Menger, which led to a theory of value based on marginal utility (thus embracing elements of Classical and neo-Classical traditions). Menger's work was continued by the economists von Wieser, who also developed the notion of **opportunity cost**, and Bohm-Bawerk, who examined the role of **capital** and the **interest rate**. Modern economists of the Austrian school look closely at market processes and prices, while accepting some elements of Keynesian theory. Some parts of the work of J. R. **Hicks** are close to the beliefs of the Austrian school.

AUTOMATIC STABILIZERS A way of smoothing out the ups and downs of the business cycle without governments using specific fiscal policy.

A built-in (or automatic) stabilizer effect operates counter-cyclically within the **circular flow of national income**.

A rise in national income (and aggregate demand) will mean: (a) fewer people are claiming unemployment and welfare benefits, reducing these payments which are injections into the circular flow, tending to damp down national income; (b) more people will pay more tax as their personal incomes increase, increasing withdrawals, again tending to put the brakes on spending and income. The reverse is true in periods of economic downturn.

Sometimes the 'stepped' nature of tax brackets causes 'fiscal drag', which is a specific form of built-in stabilizer. As real or money incomes rise, people move into higher tax brackets and the total withdrawal becomes greater. Conversely, the opposite occurs in periods of economic contraction (although wages are often 'stickier' in a downward direction).

The theories of Keynes suggest that built-in stabilizers are an insufficient 'levelling' force on the business cycle, and argue that reflation requires more positive measures such as public works. The monetarists, on the other hand, look to monetary policy, and in many cases to supply-side measures, these being more likely to allow demand to find its own level, partly through the action of built-in stabilizers.

B

BALANCE OF PAYMENTS This is the statistical presentation of a country's trading relationship with the rest of the world. In other words, the total of all imports and exports, including capital or investment flows. The balance of payments can be seen as a conventional balance sheet, and since it also records changes in official reserves which will be necessary to finance any **surplus** or deficit, the balance in that sense always balances.

Different countries record their balance of payments in different ways. Most have the following elements.

- The current account, which is divided into (a) visible trade, and (b) invisible trade. Visible trade is simply the import of goods and services over a given period. Invisible trade will include payments for such items as shipping, tourism, insurance, and banking. It also includes payments received from investments and loans (including profits for companies which have, say, set up factories overseas) and government spending and receipts for defence.
- The capital account, which measures the change in total assets and liabilities of a country. This category includes investment overseas (note that the investement by a firm to set up a factory overseas will be recorded here as a capital outflow,

whilst the profits from it are 'invisibles' on the current account). It also includes international bank loans and capital flows, which have greatly increased in many countries with the globalization and liberalization of international financial markets. Changes in official reserves are also recorded here.

- The balancing item, which is simply a statistical device to mark any inflows or outflows which have not been recorded, but which are known to have taken place because the government or central bank will have recorded all flows of foreign currency.

Adding all of these together gives the balance of payments for official financing. If outflows exceed inflows, we have a deficit, and if inflows exceed outflows, there is a surplus (corresponding to the notion of exports as an injection and imports as a leakage in the circular flow of national income). To balance the books, a government can either borrow, or allow its gold and foreign currency reserves to run down, in the case of a deficit; or repay borrowing and/or increase reserves in the case of a surplus.

Clearly, a country's balance of payments will normally show a surplus or a deficit: it is highly unlikely that outflows and inflows will be exactly equal year to year. Assuming that the variations are relatively small and can be easily financed, there is no economic policy implication. However, a chronic deficit or surplus does bring problems which most governments seek to rectify. There is in any case a self-correcting tendency if exchange rates are allowed to move freely: a deficit will tend to devalue the currency, whilst a surplus will revalue it, and this, by changing the relative prices of imports and exports, will tend to level out the imbalance (*see* **exchange rate policy**, **J-curve**, **Marshall-Lerner Condition**). Governments which are committed to fixed exchange rates (such as the **Bretton Woods** System) will need permission to change the value of their currencies, and sometimes world trade/currency bodies such as the **IMF** will require them to adopt certain domestic monetary or fiscal policies to underpin any devaluation or revaluation.

BANK A bank is a financial intermediary whose primary functions are borrowing and lending money. A bank borrows money, paying a return on it to the depositor, creating a liability. It can then loan money to borrowers, whose borrowing forms the **assets** of the bank. Banks have an important role in the creation of money (see below); they are also involved in the mechanics of transferring funds, guaranteeing creditworthiness and exchanging money.

Generally speaking, banks are organized as corporations and are either privately owned or state run, or some combination of both. Although some countries may not formally require banks to be incorporated, all banks are subject to government regulation and supervision (usually through the **central bank** of the country) in the interest of the safekeeping of their clients' deposits.

Banking dates back to antiquity, but the earliest model of contemporary banking can be traced back to seventeenth century English goldsmiths. At that time the main form of payment for goods and services was gold. Carrying around gold involved obvious risks and inconvenience; as a consequence, people would 'deposit' this gold with the local goldsmith in exchange for a receipt. These receipts were the basis for the system of paper **money** as we know it today. Goldsmiths found that the actual gold called upon to be removed by depositors usually represented only a small fraction of the amount stored, and so they were able to lend out gold, to be repaid at some time in the future with principal and **interest**.

Banks can influence the **money supply** through the action of the **bank credit multiplier**. In essence this operates because the money loaned by the banking system against customers' deposits will typically find its way back into the banking system. Money borrowed is used to pay for goods and services whose vendors place it in their own bank accounts. It then forms another deposit against which the banks can lend further money, and so the process continues. Thus a single deposit can create a several-fold increase in the amount of money, because of the actions of the banks.

Banks can help growth in an economy by lending for investment. Here the effect of another kind of multiplier, the **Keynesian** multiplier, will create an increase in the national income which is greater than the amount of the money loaned on the initial investment. Banks are often cited as having been important catalysts for the expansion of industry and trade in the eighteenth and nineteenth centuries in Europe and North America.

Banks therefore have a major role in macroeconomics, and governments often use the banking system to control the economy through **monetary policy**. This may include changing the ratio of reserves to borowing, or it may involve the operation of **interest rates**.

Bank classifications include commercial banks, central banks, **building societies** (thrifts), and **merchant banks** (investment banks). These distinctions depend on the type of clients the banks serve (whether they are the general consumer, private businesses, or the government) as well as the range of products and services they provide. The evolution of banking around the globe has blurred these distinctions somewhat, so that many functions overlap. Although there are many different types of bank, two common features are as follows.

1. The monetary liabilities exceed the reserves. The monetary liabilities, which consist of clients' deposits, exceed reserves because banks hope that at any given time not all clients are going to come to the bank to withdraw their total deposit, and therefore the bank can lend out a large portion of this money. Banks finance their operations through the interest differential. Essentially this implies that the interest they charge on loans is higher than the interest they pay on clients' deposits.

2. Liabilities of banks are more liquid than assets. Since the bulk of liabilities is client deposits of money, this will tend to be more liquid (easily converted to money) than assets consisting of loans to clients as well as investments. This is because the terms on loans are fixed for some time in the future.

In terms of the balance sheet of banks, while clients' deposits obviously represent the largest portion of liabilities, investments in the form of purchases of government and private **securities** represent a large portion of assets. Similarly, in terms of the income statement, interest is a major source of income for banks. The short-term rate that they charge their most creditworthy clients is referred to as the 'prime rate'.

The majority of the clientele of commercial banks tend to be in the business sectors while thrifts or savings and loan institutions supply funds and take deposits from the general public. Although these represent the bulk of the clientele, in most cases the clients of various forms of banks are quite broad. There are other financial institutions that cater to a specific niche in the market and supply funds solely to this form of clientele. For example, **venture capital** is the term for funds that are supplied to entrepreneurs with innovative products. They generally have higher rates of interest because of the greater risk associated with their operations. Although the different classifications of banks do indeed cater to different segments of the market, the general trend seems to indicate that these distinctions are gradually fading.

BANK CREDIT MULTIPLIER This is the means by which banks use deposits to 'create' money. Suppose person A deposits £100 into the bank (we will assume for the purposes of this example that there is only one commercial bank, which represents all the banks in the commercial sector). The bank has a cash reserve ratio (usually defined by law or by the **central bank**) of 20 per cent (i.e. 20 per cent of its deposits need to be held in cash) That means it can then lend £80 to person B, who will buy goods worth £80 from person C, who will place the money in the bank. The bank can then lend £64 to person D, who will buy goods worth £64 from person E, who will deposit £64 in the bank. The bank can lend £52 to person F. And so on. Eventually the bank will have deposits of £500 from the initial deposit of £100.

In this simple instance we can say that the credit multiplier is 5. That is,

$$\frac{1}{\text{cash reserve ratio}} \quad (1/5).$$

Clearly this is a powerful multiplier effect, and since the bulk of the **money supply** is made up of bank deposits, controlling it will be a powerful tool of **monetary policy**. Generally speaking, the government uses 'open market operations' to take money out of the economy. It sells £100 worth of **bonds** to, say, person A, who then withdraws that amount from the bank, thus stopping the whole multiplying process of credit creation.

If the government wished to expand aggregate demand in the economy, perhaps by running a **budget deficit**, it would use the money from the sale of bonds on public spending. Person G, who works for the government, then deposits £100 with the bank and the whole process starts again – except that with the effect of the Keynesian demand **multiplier** the total amount of income will increase by several times the initial £100 injection, causing a corresponding multiplied increase in credit creation, and significantly increasing the money supply. That, say the **monetarists**, is likely to be highly **inflationary**, although **Keynesians** will argue that inflation will be less the further the economy is from full employment.

BEARS Bears, in **stock market** terminology, are investors who sell shares (**securities**) in the belief that prices will fall. Similarly, a bear market is a stock market in which prices are falling. Such a market is predominantly comprised of sellers.

The main purpose of selling shares when prices are expected to fall is to realize a profit by buying back the shares at a later date for a lower price. If an investor already holds shares and sells them, his position is referred to as a 'protected bear'. He can then buy back the same number shares at a later date so that his position in the market has not changed. But if the price of the share has dropped, the investor will have realized a profit. Another bearish position can be obtained even if shares are not held by an investor. These positions are referred to as 'selling short'. An investor who sells a share that he does not hold with the intention of buying the share at some time in the future is said to be 'selling short'. As this strategy is only profitable when prices are falling it is normally associated with bearish investors.

To entice investors to buy, rather than sell, in a bear market, prices must be reduced. Thus, buyers in the market have greater bargaining power. These circumstances arise when investors' expectations of the market or economy are pessimistic, or when other investment opportunities such as less risky government **bonds** and treasury bills seem more attractive.

BLACK ECONOMY The 'black economy' refers to economic activity which is not declared for tax purposes. It also includes economic activity in goods and services which are rationed or price-controlled (a 'black market'). The predominant activities of the black economy are personal services and repair work carried out by self-employed individuals, including those who are moonlighting from paid employment. Payments are usually made in cash, so that there is no record of the transactions.

A black market can be regarded as a sub-section of the black economy, because those involved in black market activities will almost never declare them. They will usually make their profits by buying and selling of goods at a price higher than those set by the government. Sometimes the goods traded in black markets are not even classified as legal by the government.

These markets tend to develop in developing economies with centralized governments and in developed economies during times of emergency such as wars. The reason for the higher prices is a simple result of the equilibrium law of **demand** and **supply**. Because governments ration the output of certain commodities, markets are not able to clear in terms of demand and supply. In most cases it may be that at the rationed level of output more quantity is demanded than supplied. This gives rise to a secondary market, referred to as the black market, which can accommodate this excess demand by charging a higher price for the rationed good. The fact that trading in these markets is not legal gives another opportunity for sellers to charge higher prices for bearing the risk of being caught.

Since income in the black economy as a whole is not declared for taxation purposes, it is nearly impossible to measure in terms of its size. For accounting purposes this poses a serious problem in accurately measuring the other important factors such as the growth rate, income levels, and unemployment in the economy.

BONDS A bond is a debt asset, i.e. a financial instrument in which the issuer (borrower or debtor) promises to repay to the lender (investor) the amount borrowed plus interest over the period of time. The issuer of the bond may be a central or a local government, a company, or a supra-national organization (such as the World Bank). Trading in bonds and trading in **securities** are the two key activities in the international financial markets. The important difference between a bond and a security is that the bond does not confer ownership, only debt. Bond markets themselves fall into various categories, including the national bond market, the international bond market, and also the primary and secondary markets (the primary dealing with **new issues**, the secondary trading already existing bonds).

A bond will have both nominal and market characteristics. The nominal characteristics are the maturity, the face value, and the coupon. The majority of the bonds are term bonds, which run for a given period (the maturity) and after that become due and payable. We refer to term bonds as 'bullet-maturity' or 'balloon' bonds. Bonds with a maturity between one and five years are considered short-term, while those between five and 12 are intermediate term. Bonds with maturity exceeding 12 years are viewed as long-term bonds. All obligations whose maturity is less than one year are commonly referred to as money market instruments. There are cases that allow the issuer or the investor to modify the maturity of a bond. The 'face value', also called the 'principal' of the bond, is the starting price of the bond in the financial market. A bond's 'coupon' is the interest rate paid periodically during the life of the bond. Typically, the coupon payment is delivered biannually in the US, while for Eurobonds the payment is made annually. Zero-coupon bonds offer the investor the opportunity to buy a bond below its principal (starting or face value) and to benefit from its appreciation as it approaches the maturity date. In this way it ensures for the investor a certain return if held until maturity. The coupon rate may be modified periodically according to some pre-agreed standard reference. For example, the benchmark might be the London Interbank Offered Rate (**LIBOR**). Institutional

investors may find floating-rate instruments attractive in periods of exchange and interest rate volatility. Floating-rate bonds usually have a minimum coupon rate (called the title's 'floor') and/or a maximum return (called a 'cap'). If a title has both it is said to be 'collared'.

All bonds also have their market attributes. These are the market price, the market return and the market interest rate. All these may be radically different from the asset's nominal characteristics: they are subject to the financial market forces of supply and demand. The market price of an asset and its effective interest rate (= yield) are inversely related. In other words, the bond with a face value of £100 and a coupon rate of 10 per cent will yield 20 per cent if its price in the market falls to £50 (the 10 per cent is paid on the face value rather than the market price). In aggregate, the speculative demand for money will also be inversely proportional to the movements of the market interest rates.

Another feature of bonds is their various levels of security. Real property (e.g. in the form of a mortgage) or personal property may be used to increase the security of a title beyond the issuer's general credit standing. If it involves personal property it is called a 'collateral trust bond'. If it entails claims on the issuer's assets, the bond is called a 'debenture bond'. A bond may also be guaranteed by another entity, as is the case of government-owned institutions (utilities, in some countries) issuing bonds guaranteed by the government. High-interest low-security bonds issued by companies, sometime to finance a leveraged buy-out, are known as **junk bonds**.

One other issue is the convertibility of the bond. Some bonds are 'exchangeable', that is they allow their conversion to another asset (usually the common stock of the issuing firm). Other bonds permit conversion into gold or another precious metal.

A set of bonds that grant their owner the right to enter into another financial negotiation or transaction with the issuer are said to have a 'warrant'. Bonds with attached warrants are very common in the Eurobond market. There are many kinds of warrants. An equity warrant allows the holder to buy common stocks of the issuer at a specified price. A debt warrant permits the purchase of more bonds at the same price and yield as the host bond. The currency warrant enables the owner to exchange one currency for another at a fixed exchange rate. Finally, there is the gold warrant, which allows the owner to purchase gold from the issuer of the title.

A bond indenture might contain a 'call' option, which enables the owner of the bond to retire the debt fully or partially before the maturity date. In this way it permits the investor to diversify his/her portfolio (and risk) when market conditions are unfavourable. The indenture may also contain a requirement that the owner should retire a prearranged portion of the issue each year. This title then is referred to as a 'sinking-fund requirement'. Another provision the indenture may have is the 'put' feature. This enables the owner to sell back the title to the issuer at par value on designated dates. Again, this last provision increases the flexibility of the investor.

All of a bond's features are crucial for its valuation. Just as important is the role which bonds themselves play in the financial markets. The issuance of government debt is an important part of **fiscal policy**, especially to fund a **budget deficit**. But it is also part of **monetary policy**, because government debt has a direct bearing on **interest rates**. (*See also* **monetarism**, **Keynes**.)

BRETTON WOODS SYSTEM (BWS)
This is the international monetary system which came into effect at the end of the Second World War. It was named after the conference held in 1944 at Bretton Woods, New Hampshire, USA – the same conference which established the International Monetary Fund (**IMF**).

The interwar period had been characterised on the one hand by close cooperation among central banks under the **gold standard**, and on the other by the hegemonic influence of the Bank of England. Governments restored the gold standard during the 1920s, but did so in a somewhat arbitrary way, unilaterally setting gold values for their currencies. John Maynard **Keynes** pointed out (in 1925) that these actions never took into account the exchange rates that were implicitly determined by them. In addition, fiscal deficits and international debts accumulated from the First World War exacerbated the problem. The result was not surprising. Efforts to contain disturbances failed, the more so during the worldwide recession of the 1930s, and led to the collapse of the new gold standard in less than ten years. This gave rise to various floating exchange rate regimes characterized by international intervention. During the late 1930s the central banks started once again to approach the idea of mutual cooperation, but the outbreak of the Second World War put an end to this.

Floating exchange rates were deemed detrimental for three reasons. First, fluctuations in the exchange rate can induce via the balance of payments unfavourable displacements of productive resources from the domestic sector to the export sector. This is a costly procedure and in many cases unwarranted, for it might be temporary in nature. Secondly, floating rates increase risk and discourage international trade. Thirdly, future expectations are heavily influenced by this kind of volatility. Market instability is one of the immediate consequences.

Individual governments, moreover, were not in a position to coordinate the international monetary system. Therefore, a need for policy coordination to induce stability, promote national sovereignty and protect the international community from unpleasant developments was regarded as essential. It would take the form of a new international monetary system. The proposals came from two sides: the American, headed by Harry Dexter White, and the British, led by John Maynard Keynes. Of the two plans Keynes's was the most radical, but was not adopted finally. Keynes worried about balance-of-payments problems for post-war Britain and a depression in the US in the long run. To prevent those repercussions he suggested the creation of a new international currency issued by a new international institution to be founded. White's plan was less ambitious. It would provide the new institution with a stock of gold and national currencies instead of a new currency. In the end the adopted plan resembled White's proposal, with some Keynesian concerns addressed as well. The established new international institution was the IMF. Every participant country had to peg its exchange rate to gold or to the US dollar. The US in turn would peg the dollar to gold, at the rate of $35 per ounce. Furthermore, all countries were required to make their currency convertible, while every subsequent change in their **fixed exchange rate** regime should be subject to the approval of the IMF. The pegging of exchange rates lasted until the end of the 1960s without any substantial changes, although a major realignment occurred in 1949 when sterling was devalued. The pound was again devalued in 1967, while the French franc was devalued in 1969. On the issue of true convertibility, most European countries did not for many decades lift their capital controls to allow the free flow of funds, at the pegged exchange rates. In fact some countries had limits to the movement of capital as late as the 1990s.

An IMF member country with a balance-of-payments problem could also utilize its 'subscription quota', freeing up funds to keep the exchange rate intact but reducing the country's voting rights inside the IMF.

BWS established a supposedly uniform treatment of all countries, but did not function symmetrically in terms of the condition of a country's balance of payments. Although deficits were thought unacceptable, surpluses were tolerated. The impact of a deficit was the exhaustion of a country's reserves, which increased pressures for a devaluation of its currency. Deficit countries were prone to devalue frequently, leading to a revaluation of the US dollar (against whose value all the other currencies were pegged). This in turn gradually weakened the competitiveness of the US economy.

The domination of the US dollar gave important privileges to the US government but restricted its policy potential. It became impossible for the US to conduct independent policy moves without affecting the gold price of the dollar. The role of the dollar was underestimated in the beginning. It gradually became the currency in which most of the IMF countries expressed their reserves. In order to keep its dollar rate at $35 per ounce, the US was required to keep the requisite quantities of gold reserves: the more valuable the dollar, the more gold would be needed. But because the dollar was a reserve currency, the US could persuade other countries to accept dollars instead of gold for their exports, making it easier to finance a trade deficit without losing gold. Gradually the dollar became the standard means of payments under the Bretton Woods System.

The system collapsed in 1971, under the influence of a large US deficit and rumours of a Deutschemark revaluation, as well as a major purchase of gold by the Bank of England. The Nixon administration froze prices and wages to combat inflation, imposed a 10 per cent tax on imports and closed the Treasury's gold window. A new realignment of the pegged exchanged rates was the aim of these policy moves. This proved futile, however, and after a transition period the BWS came to an end in 1973. Since then exchange rates have mostly floated, and the IMF has abolished the obligation of a country's member to peg its currency to gold. However, the IMF supervises closely the economic performance of its member countries closely and intervenes whenever a country asks for assistance to combat persistent and threatening problems. Examples are the various Latin American countries and more recently some of the Asian 'tiger' economies.

The imminent arrival of a single currency for Europe (*see* **EMU**) in one sense spells the return of fixed rates in that region, although as the euro will be one currency which will take over from those of individual countries, currency and trading activity between Europe and the rest of the world will not change qualitatively. The interesting question of the next few years will be whether the euro will take over from the dollar as the main transaction, or reserve, currency.

BUDGET DEFICIT As part of their **fiscal policy**, governments may use a budget deficit to stimulate a sluggish economy (or a budget surplus to cool down an overheated one). A budget deficit occurs where the receipts (usually from taxation, but also from the sale of government holdings or assets) are lower than government spending. The important point is that the deficit has to be financed (i.e. paid for by borrowing).

It was **Keynes** who first argued for

the use of fiscal policy to regulate the economy, and in particular to allow governments to 'spend their way out of recession' through budget deficits. This set the tone for much of the demand-led style of economic management for western governments until the 1970s, when **monetarists** started developing the arguments for a balanced budget.

If taxes and sales of assets do not provide a level of revenue that matches government spending, the deficit can be financed by selling government **bonds**, which are (usually long-term) IOUs underwritten by the state. Since the government has to go into the market and offer these bonds at competitive rates of interest, there will be a tendency for interest rates to rise. Critics of long-term budget deficits argue that this will make it more difficult for the private sector to borrow money, both because of the higher interest rates and because the available capital will tend to flow toward the public sector. The phenomenon is known as 'crowding out'. With higher interest rates there is a tendency for the currency to increase in value, making exports less competitive and possibly causing problems for the **balance of payments**.

If the government then spends the money, however, it will eventually flow back into the banking system, and allow **banks** to make further loans against it. Therefore in terms of **money supply**, financing a budget deficit by selling bonds (or other instruments like savings certificates) to the public will be broadly neutral.

On the other hand, if the government borrows from the banks themselves, there will be an initial reduction in the cash assets of the banks, reducing their ability to lend. If we again assume that the government spends the money it has borrowed, this finds its way into the banking system exactly as above. But this time there has been a net increase in the total amount of bank deposits (whereas in the case of borrowing from the public the net amount remained constant). Because of a mechanism known as the **bank credit multiplier**, this increase in deposits has a many-fold effect on the money supply.

The examples given above allow governments to use the same mechanisms they employ to fund a budget deficit as a tool of **monetary policy**. By raising more money from individuals and the banks than they need to spend, they can reduce money supply. This is known as 'overfunding'.

Budget deficits tend to occur counter-cyclically regardless of government policy, and as such are a form of built-in stabilizer. When incomes are rising and unemployment is falling, tax receipts will tend to rise and welfare payments will tend to fall, moving the budget away from deficit. When incomes are falling and unemployment is rising, the budget deficit will increase for the opposite reasons. Therefore there is a braking tendency at the top of the cycle (reducing injections relative to withdrawals) and a corresponding pump-priming tendency at the bottom.

(*See also* **PSBR** (Public Sector Borrowing Requirement).)

BUILDING SOCIETY/THRIFT Financial institutions that accept deposits upon which they pay interest while making loans by arranging mortgages on property are referred to as building societies in the UK. Their US counterparts are usually referred to as savings and loans, or thrift institutions.

Building societies in the UK grew out of the friendly society movement of the late seventeenth century, designed to encourage thrift and self-help among people of modest means. These non-profit organizations were established after the Building Societies Act of 1874, the purpose of which was to register these institutions formally. Subsequent Acts such as the Building Societies Act of 1986 have tightened the controls over the societies' financial management. They have also broadened the scope of the services that a building society may provide to its clients.

Building societies generally accept deposits, which may be withdrawn on demand up to a certain limit, or on a month's notice for larger amounts. Alternatively, investors may also deposit funds into shares of societies. Building society shares should not be confused with the common terminology of shares as representing a percentage of ownership of a corporation. Building society shares tend to have more restrictive conditions on withdrawal of funds, but compensate for these restrictions by offering a higher rate of interest. In addition to the retail market of individual investors, societies also raise funds through the money market or wholesale market.

Building societies provide loans for individuals purchasing homes and do so by arranging mortgages. Most of these mortgages may be repaid with an assurance policy, so that the amount of the loan remains outstanding until the policy matures. Generally the rate of interest on loans is close to rates offered by similar institutions.

Through legislation, building societies have been able to expand the range of their services to include money transmission on foreign exchange, personal financial planning, as well as estate agency and valuation. Recently in the UK many of the building societies have changed their status into ordinary companies, and many millions of savers and borrowers became shareholders in the process, known as demutualization. This further extends the range of services the societies can offer, and effectively turns them into retail banks.

In the United States there were severe problems during the 1980s for the thrifts, many of which became bankrupt. One reason for some of their difficulties was that they were lending at a fixed rate of interest while having to pay savers a variable rate, which during periods of high interest rates wiped out their margins. The US government rescued many of the Savings and Loans, while ordering a tightening of the regulatory conditions.

BULLS Bulls, in stock market terminology, refer to investors who buy shares for a short term in the hope of selling them at a future date for a higher price. Bulls are the opposite of **bears**, and tend to be associated with more aggressive investors. Thus, a bull market refers to a market with increasing **security** prices. The market is predominantly made up of investors who are more likely to buy shares than to sell them.

A share price may actually rise if a sufficient number of bullish strategies create an artificial **demand**. By buying a significant number of shares, bullish investors may create the illusion that these shares provide an attractive investment opportunity in the market, as a result of which more investors would be willing to hold these shares. With this illusion of demand, sellers have greater bargaining power and can charge a higher price in the market, thus fulfilling the expectations of the bulls.

The more aggressive investing strategies associated with bullish investors implies that they tend to be more tolerant towards risk. Thus, bad news circulating about a specific firm will not necessarily drive these investors out of the market. In fact, these investors may even purchase more shares in the hopes that when the bad news passes, the firm's share price will rise once again. Bullish investors tend to be optimistic and can reduce the chances of a large drop in share prices by creating artificial demand. On the other hand, bullish investors may also push the price of a share up to an unreasonably higher level, thus inflating the price. When the price of the share is out of line with shareholders' perception of its true value, then the share may be susceptible to a fall in price.

BUSINESS CYCLES This is the tendency for an economy to expand or contract, reflecting what are known as 'cyclical' changes rather than the fundamentals for economic growth. An economy which may be growing at, say, 2 per cent over a 30-year period, will exhibit significant moves up and down relative to that line over, say, a five- or six-year period.

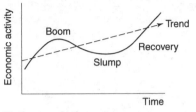

Business cycle

The traditional stages of the trade cycle are as follows.

● Depression, which is the lowest level, characterized by spare capacity, weak **demand**, and unemployment. In most economies there is a self-righting mechanism which leads to the next stage.

● Recovery, although economists disagree about how long the self-righting takes, and whether it is always strong enough to bring about a full recovery. One element that most agree on is that as capital wears out and requires replacement, the recovery will be sparked by an injection of investment, which will then feed through to the circular flow of national income via both an **accelerator** and a **multiplier** effect, causing a larger increase in aggregate demand and output than the nominal investment. Others argue that as real **wages** fall with the reduced demand for labour, the cost of production will eventually become low enough to persuade companies to start increasing output once more. So the recovery will be characterized by growing demand and output, falling stock inventories, and higher levels of employment.

- Boom, the top of the cycle. By now the increased confidence may lead to increased demand and labour shortages, leading to rising prices and nominal wages, causing inflation. This will eventually erode confidence, as businesses and workers see their profits and wages eroded by higher prices. There may then be a natural reduction in demand, or demand may push up imports, causing a trade deficit and further eroding the value of the currency. Sometimes governments will try to curb wage demands, perhaps using an incomes policy to attempt (usually unsuccessfully) to halt the **wage–price spiral**. Because capital replacement works on a longer-term basis than consumer spending, the investment accelerator may work in reverse (new machinery ordered during recovery and early boom will mean that productive capacity is at maximum levels, with no need yet to replace old equipment). The economy then moves into the next stage.
- Recession, whose symptoms are falling demand, falling employment, and an easing of inflationary pressures on prices. Sometimes the recession may be very steep, and may be driven by a fall-off in confidence in the equity and other financial markets (as in the Great Crash of 1929). Eventually the bottom of the cycle is reached, and the whole process starts anew.

There is little dispute about the reality of the trade cycle; what divides economists is what, if anything, can be done about it. Classical economics argues that if real wages are allowed to fall and markets are allowed to operate freely, the negative effects of recession, slump, or depression will right themselves naturally. **Keynesians** argue that it is possible for an economy to become 'stuck' at a low point in the cycle, and that various forms of demand management are required to stimulate activity. At the same time, they believe it is possible to 'fine tune' demand, to stop recovery leading to inflation. The period of 'stagflation' (high unemployment and high inflation) in the 1970s brought the policies of **monetarism** and **supply-side economics** to the fore. The monetarists argued that the money supply was the variable which most affected prices in the 'real economy', and that 'sound money' (with the money supply not being allowed to grow faster than real output) would prevent inflation at the top, or even throughout, the cycle. Supply-siders argued that liberalization of markets, especially labour markets, would increase productivity and allow steady growth without inflation.

One of the issues which has been a common thread is how reliably we can measure certain key variables such as the money supply or demand. A current issue is the increased globalization of capital markets, along with a greater tendency for large, regional economic blocs to dominate activities (e.g. the EU or NAFTA). This has tended to mean that trade cycles become more global, or at least regional. A final factor which will dominate economic thinking in the next decade is the technological revolution and its impact on productivity and employment levels, perhaps ultimately leading us to rethink the notion of the conventional trade cycle altogether.

BUSINESS STRATEGY (MERGERS AND ACQUISITIONS) Most companies aim for profit maximization and growth (although the two may not always be compatible – *see* **management theories of the firm**), and to achieve growth over time they need either to expand internally, or look outside. The former is known as 'organic growth', in which a company seeks to increase its market share or to diversify into new products. Sometimes it will expand vertically up or down the production chain (a self-generated form of **integration**), so that, for instance, a car manufacturer might start to make its own tyres, or open its own retail outlets. Organic growth has the advantage of building upon the firm's existing skills and knowledge, and of course maintaining control within the existing management and shareholding.

Frequently, though, the best path to growth involves an external strategy, through mergers or acquisitions. These are the amalgamation of two or more firms either through mutual agreement or in the form of a 'hostile takeover'. The combination of two or more firms through mutual agreement is referred to as a merger, whereas acquisitions or takeovers usually involve one firm mounting a hostile takeover bid for another without the consent of the victim firm's management. This occurs when the acting firm is able to gain control of more than 50 per cent of the shares of the victim firm.

Generally, mergers and acquisitions (M&As) can be classified into three types:

1. A *horizontal* M&A is an amalgamation of direct competitors. The purpose of a horizontal M&A is to enable the combined firms to make use of **economies of scale** in an effort to reduce costs.
2. A *vertical* M&A is a combination of firms which are in a supplier–customer relationship. Vertical M&As allow firms to coordinate production plans more efficiently to smooth production and reduce inventory costs (*see* **just in time**).
3. A *conglomerate* M&A is typically carried out by a firm whose strategy is one of diversification. Here the combination of firms serves the purpose of reducing industry-specific risks, by spreading activities among several sectors. It can allow synergies in management and operations, so that for example a conglomerate which includes a financial services division and a strongly marketing-led division can bring the two skill sets together, creating efficiencies (economies of scope) for the whole company. (In this instance these may be smarter accountancy for the marketing-oriented division, and better marketing for the financial services.)

M&As should allow firms to maximize economies of scale, and increase market power. If this puts them into a potentially price-controlling **monopoly** or **oligopoly** position, the merger is likely to require the prior approval of one or more **regulators**.

Sometimes the outcome of a merger results in a clash between different management styles causing a demerger. Demergers often come about when the original firm carries on as a separate department even after a merger, causing internal conflicts in management. Usually, after a de-merger the existing shareholders are given shares in both companies. Similar to a demerger is the break-up of a company. This may be part of an **asset-stripping** strategy, or it may be a divestment (sale or closure) of parts of the firm in an attempt to reduce diseconomies of scale, or to focus production in the most profitable areas. Divestment, if it involves a sale, can be seen as the opposite of an acquisition or merger.

A popular extension of the M&A, which began in the 1980s, was the purchase of firms or divisions of a firm by its own management. These acquisitions, which are known as management buy-outs (MBOs), are a means of divestment by the parent firm from a particular line of business. One way to finance an MBO is the issue of high-yield debt paper, commonly known as **junk bonds**. In the case where firms are purchased by the existing management, shareholders of the firm may be prepared to accept management's financial terms of purchase because they see it as better than an hostile outside take-over, which may disrupt the organization. In the interest of shareholders all the specific financial details must be covered before MBOs take place.

Generally speaking, the tactics for acquisitions are more complex than those for mergers, simply the acquisition is not a mutual agreement between both (or in some cases, all three or four) parties involved. Most of the tactics of acquisitions, and their colourful nomenclature, relate to aggressive or defensive strategies. A 'black knight' is the term for a firm that launches an unwelcome takeover bid for another, whilst a 'white knight' refers to an intervening firm rescuing another from a hostile bid. In defensive strategies, the 'pac-man defence' involves the firm being bid for, itself making a bid for the acquiring firm. The 'poison pill' involves the victim firm merging with or acquiring other firms in order to make itself structurally less attractive to the bidder. A 'shark repellent' is any measure specifically designed to discourage takeover bidders. An example could be increasing the proportion of shareholder votes needed to approve the bid above the usual 50 per cent level.

Some acquisitions are known as 'reverse takeovers', typically when a smaller but dynamic firm wishing to expand rapidly takes over a larger but less progressive company. Again, sometimes junk bonds are used to finance the activity, or else the assets of the firm being taken over are used as security for the debt.

Through its life a company may embrace both organic growth policies and M&A activity, sometimes at the same time. Different countries, and different corporate cultures, may favour one more than the other. **Bullish** stock markets are generally viewed as favourable to M&As (shareholders may be less risk-averse, anticipating strong results from the amalgamation). Similarly all growth, including M&As, will tend to be stronger, and for the company easier, during the recovery and boom phases of the business cycle.

C

CAMBRIDGE EQUATION This is an approach to the Classical **quantity theory of money** which looks at **money supply** and **demand**, prices, and transactions in an economy from a rather different perpective to that developed by the economist Fisher. It was the work of Cambridge economists **Pigou** and **Marshall**. Fisher's main concern was with the volume of transactions that a specific quantity of money is able to accommodate. The Cambridge School economists paid more attention to the amount of money an individual demands in order to accomplish his/her transactions. The emphasis in the Pigou/Marshall analysis was on the microeconomic underpinnings of aggregate behaviour, while the Fisherian approach is characterized by a concern for the macroeconomic aspects. The functional form of the Cambridge equation is

$$Md = kPY$$

where P is the general price level, Md is the nominal money demand, k the proportion of the nominal income a person is using for transactions and Y the national income. In this case the inverse of the income velocity of circulation is equal to k.

Fisher's macroeconomic approach aims to attract attention to the importance of the institutional framework, whereas Marshall and Pigou made a priority of their concerns about the term structure of interest rates and their future expected values. The Cambridge equation above may be interpreted as saying that the nominal money demand is a fixed proportion of the value of the nominal national income. The component k is assumed fixed with respect to time, especially in the **long run**. In this way the Cambridge equation respects the Classical dichotomy between real and nominal variables and thus preserves one more tenet of the Classical tradition: the neutrality of money. That is, that the working of the money supply does not affect the 'real' working of employment and output in the economy. The Cambridge equation and its variants formed the starting point for the development of modern monetarism, which went on to refine how monetary variables could provide an explanation for the working of the whole economy.

CAMBRIDGE SCHOOL The term is applied to the followers of **Keynesian** economic thought, and to some extent **Classical** theory, at Cambridge University. The school's followers argue that **neo-Classical** analysis is wrong to project microeconomic behaviour into the aggregate of the macroeconomy. They argue, for example, that there is no direct relationship between the rate of **profit**

and the capital intensity of the economy as a whole. They have questioned the idea of **production functions** such as Cobb Douglas, again arguing that in aggregate it is not compatible with its micro-level origins. The Cambridge school also advanced Keynesian theories (*see* **neo-Keynesian**) to embrace the idea of a full employment equilibrium and an examination of wages and profits. The main recent Cambridge economists have been Joan Robinson (1903–83) and Nicky Kaldor (1908–86), with some of the earlier inspiration coming from **Marshall** and **Pigou**, as well of course as Keynes himself.

CAPITAL INTENSIVE A firm which produces its output of goods and services using a large proportion of capital equipment as inputs and a relatively small proportion of labour is said to be capital intensive. For capital intensive firms, issues such as **investment**, inventory, and cost-benefit analysis are crucial, because a large portion of the firm's operations depend on capital.

One measure of the proportions of capital and labour used in the production of outputs is the capital–labour ratio. Specifically, this is the total number of capital hours divided by the total number of labour hours employed for production. The proportions of capital and labour which a firm uses in production depend mainly on the relative prices of labour and capital inputs and their respective productivity. Thus, in capital intensive firms the cost of capital in relation to labour is relatively low, while capital tends to have greater

productive value. This is because the relative productivity of these **factors of production** depends on the degree of 'standardization' of the product. Where standardized products are sold in large quantities it is possible to employ large-scale capital intensive production methods which facilitate **economies of scale**.

An industry comprized of many firms employing a greater portion of capital than labour is referred to as a 'capital intensive industry'. These types of firms tend to mass-produce, and make use of economies of scale to provide a large quantity at a relatively low price. By employing capital in terms of heavy machinery and equipment, capital intensive firms invest in assets that generate income with minimal labour. Examples of such industries include oil refining and modern steelmaking, as well as many other mass produced manufacturing processes.

(*See* **theory of production costs**, **diminishing marginal returns**.)

CENTRAL BANK The central bank is the body which acts as banker to a country's commercial (**clearing**) **banks** and the government, and is responsible for the operation of **monetary policy**. It is often, although not necessarily, also the body which issues the **currency**.

Often the central bank is known as the 'lender of last resort', because it will generally underpin the commercial banking sector. There have, however, been occasions when central banks have allowed commercial banks to go bust, in order to send a realistic message to the markets.

Some central banks operate

monetary policy entirely independently of government. Examples are the Bundesbank in Germany, recently the Bank of England, the Federal Reserve Bank in the US, and the European Central Bank. (*See* essay on Europe by Ian Harnett.) Constitutionally, central banks have requirements to pursue stable prices, through **interest rates** or the **money supply**. This leaves governments to manage the economy through **fiscal policy**. The idea is that politicians will, if they are allowed to, make monetary policy decisions for short-term political gain; this may be more difficult with longer-term fiscal decisions.

The actual management of monetary policy is part of the operational role of a central bank. By buying and selling **bonds** on the open market, they can affect interest rates or the money supply. They can also execute policy by buying and selling financial instruments to the banking sector. In the days before global capital markets, central banks were able to use simple directives to control credit (such as ordering changes in the reserve ratio), or they could demand that the commercial banks hold special deposits at the central bank, thus reducing their ability to create money (*see* **bank credit multiplier**). With the possibility of borrowing from other lenders in other markets, the central bank needs to operate within the markets. And there are limits to how far it can 'stand against' the markets, especially the currency markets. Despite open market operations costing many billions of dollars, the European central banks failed to stop the markets selling sterling and forcing it out of the Exchange Rate Mechanism in 1992.

CIRCULAR FLOW OF NATIONAL INCOME The circular flow of national income is perhaps the most fundamental conceptual tool in macroeconomics. Before describing it, we should outline some of its basic premises.

- National income is also national expenditure which is also national output (*see* **GDP/GNP**): what is earned is spent, and goes to pay for production of goods and services.
- Within the circular flow there are certain **leakages**, where money (or goods and services) flows out of the system, and certain injections, where it flows in.
- Two kinds of flow exist: monetary, and 'real', meaning goods and services, flowing in opposite directions.

The economy of any country is shaped roughly by four distinct entities:

- households;
- firms;
- the government;
- the international sector.

The first two compose the private sector. The third is the public sector and the fourth the external sector (which represents imports and exports). We shall try to describe the diagram on the following page. The households are either employed or unemployed. In the first case they sell their labour power to the firms in the private sector or the government in the public sector. They get in return wages (W) from the firms and from the government the wage bill part of the public expenditure (G). In the case of

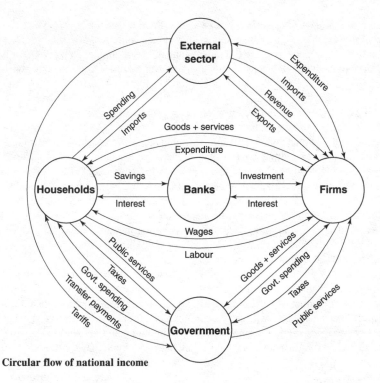

Circular flow of national income

households that are unemployed, they collect **transfer payments** (*Tr*) in the form of either unemployment wages or welfare benefits from the state.

The private sector pays taxes (*T*), which become a revenue to the government for the provision of public services such as national defence, national security, health services, education, etc. Furthermore, the government along with the households buy from the firms goods and services produced in the private sector, and their expenditure contributes to the total revenue collected by the firms.

Households do not spend all of their income, some of it being saved. The financial markets (shown for simplicity in our diagram as '**banks**') pay interest on these **savings**. This

allows firms to borrow to pay for capital **investment**, and they pay interest to the banks on these loans.

Goods and services from the private sector are also sold abroad, as exports (*X*), and their pecuniary return accounts for a part of the firms' total revenue. Households, firms and the government also buy goods and services from abroad, called imports (*M*), paying in return the corresponding expenditure. Imports also generate revenue for the government, in the form of tariffs collected. The total national income in the economy is:

$$Y = C + I + G + (X - M)$$

where *C* is the total consumption, *I* is the total investment, *G* the total

177

government spending and $X - M$ the total net exports – i.e. exports minus imports $(X - M)$ or the trade balance. The disposable income is

$$Yd = Y - T + Tr.$$

Here Tr is the total net transfers to the economy. (Yd here is then divided into C and S, which is savings.)

Because the 'real flows' correspond one-to-one with the monetary flows, in the opposite direction, in reality we have two circular flows: a circular flow of income and a circular flow of **factors of production** and goods and services.

The leakages (sometimes known as withdrawals) are taxes, savings, and imports; and the injections are government spending, investment and exports.

The following markets deal with all flows involved in this set-up:

1. the product market (goods and services);
2. the factors market (labour, capital and land);
3. the money market (savings and investment);
4. the international market (imports and exports).

(*See also* **GDP/GNP, fiscal policy**.)

CLASSICAL ECONOMICS The bodies of economic theory which prevailed during the eighteenth to the middle of the nineteenth centuries. Classical economics saw the start of the industrial revolution, and was much concerned with its implications: on population (**Malthus**), on economic growth, and on labour (**Ricardo, Marx, Mill, Say**). Classical economics identified the **factors of production**, and con-

centrated on ascribing values to them to create some form of pricing mechanism. *The Labour Theory of Value*, for example, attempted to value goods on the basis of the units of labour and accumulated labour, which was represented by capital.

In essence, Classical economists believed in the efficiency of competitive markets. The next broad school, **neo-Classical economics**, developed the specifics of pricing and resource allocation and in general took a more microeconomic stance. (*See* **theory of consumer demand, theory of production costs**.)

CLEARING BANK Clearing banks are financial institutions which settle mutual indebtedness between a number of organizations and in the UK are members of the London Bankers' Clearing House. The functions of clearing banks are very similar to those of commercial or retail banks. However, the two terms should not be used interchangeably, as not all retail banks are licensed members of the clearing house.

Prior to 1984, a clearing house would set all claims among its members against one another and each day balance the accounts, any differences in the total indebtedness being paid by cheques drawn from the Bank of England. The process essentially reduced unnecessary costs associated with matching and paying of each individual transaction by balancing member accounts of the clearing house at the end of each business day. This process was made more efficient in 1968 by the introduction of BACS, the Bankers Automated Clearing Service.

Generally, a clearing bank operates current accounts by receiving deposits as well as taking in and paying notes and coins, and issuing debt in the form of loans. Although these are the basic services that most clearing banks provide, some have also begun to compete with the **merchant banks** by trading more extensively in foreign currency and **securities** as well as providing trustee and executor facilities.

COBWEB THEOREM The cobweb theorem is one of the first examples of a dynamic, as opposed to a static, model in economics. It looks at changes in price, **supply**, and **demand** over a period of time. Its name is derived from the 'cobweb' pattern which results from these movements, as we shall see below.

The cobweb theorem takes demand as a decreasing function of current price, but supply as an increasing function of the previous period's price. The best example might be farmers, whose decision about how much of a crop they plant will be determined by today's price, but the crop itself will not be harvested until next year. By then its price may have changed, although the amount supplied will have been predetermined. The agricultural application of the cobweb theorem is sometimes known as the 'hog cycle', based on the number of pigs which are raised for market.

The key point, as we shall see below, is whether demand is more or less inelastic than supply. One leads to a convergence toward a market-clearing price, the other to increasing levels of instability.

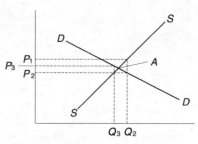

Cobweb theorem, *Fig. 1*

Figure 1 shows what happens when demand is more elastic than supply, i.e. the absolute slope of the supply curve SS is greater that of the demand curve DD. This year the price is P_1, leading to a quantity supplied in the following year of Q_2. This level of supply will correspond to a new price, P_2, in the same year. The next year a quantity of Q_3 will be supplied, based on the price of P_2. That will correspond to a price of P_3 on demand curve DD. At that price, the quantity supplied will be lower in the following year, corresponding to a slightly higher price. But the oscillations are becoming smaller and the price and quantity will eventually settle at point A.

Contrast this to what is going on in Figure 2, where demand is more inelastic than supply. The oscillations

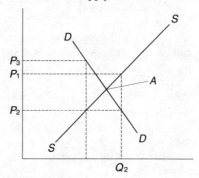

Cobweb theorem, *Fig. 2*

become greater in each time period, resulting in price and quantity moving further and further away from A.

The cobweb theorem teaches us to concentrate on time lags in production, in the context of price elasticities. In reality, producers will anticipate what is going on, so that a farmer might anticipate what is likely to happen to price in the forthcoming period and plant according to expectations rather than purely to the current price.

(*See also* **theory of production costs, theory of consumer demand**.)

COMMODITIES MARKETS A commodity is any product, good or service, but in investment it refers to any type of raw material that trades on a commodity market. Commodities come in two forms: hard and soft. Hard commodities are metals and solid raw materials, whereas soft commodities are items such as grain, coffee, cocoa, wool and cotton. A commodities market is a market where these commodities are traded. It is how they are traded that is of interest to economists. The significant point about commodities markets is their function in hedging and arbitrage.

In a global economy, it is not possible for a manufacturer simply to turn up at a farm or mine, inspect the commodity, and buy enough of it to make the chocolate bars, or shirts, or tin cans, that will meet demand in the shops. The crop might fail or the mine may become exhausted. The commodities exchange allows the end-producer to enter into a contract whereby a certain amount of the commodity is delivered in the future. An intermediary will take some of the

risk by selling **futures** contracts. This trader will usually hedge exposure by obtaining access to commodities from several different sources. In this way a single change in conditions for the raw materials can be 'smoothed out' for the eventual consumer: a crop failure in Brazil may not necessarily mean we pay more for a cup of coffee in London, New York, or Sydney. (Of course, the more reliant a commodity is on one particular area or supplier, the more these price fluctuations will pass through the system.) So commodities markets can trade both futures (which is a piece of paper guaranteeing a certain quantity of something at a given date, and of a certain quality), as well as 'actuals', which are typically traded in auctions where each lot can be physically examined for its quality. Both types of commodities markets need an accepted system of adjudication to make the final judgement in the inevitable disputes that result from trading physical products or the rights to them.

Naturally with any type of futures trading there is the possibility of arbitrage. If I think that this year's coffee harvest will be a bumper one, I might well commit to delivering certain amounts of coffee to the end-company at a higher price than I think will prevail in six months, allowing me to buy more cheaply and realize a healthy profit. Of course, I might be wrong, and lose out on the deal.

One problem for the producing countries is that this kind of trading allows speculators to buy or sell large proportions of the commodity being produced, and push its price higher or lower, often having a significant direct impact on farmers and miners.

This is often used as an argument against free trade, with producing countries forming cartels to try to control the price of the commodity worldwide (e.g. OPEC for oil prices). Free trade advocates argue against cartels, by pointing out that they are a disincentive to greater efficiency in the production of commodities.

The big global commodities markets are in London, Chicago, New York, Amsterdam, Sydney and Singapore, whilst some markets in the producing centres such as Calcutta are referred to as 'terminal markets'.

COMPARATIVE ADVANTAGE/GAINS FROM TRADE This is the theory that underpins all of international trade. According to the theory, countries which specialize in making the goods and services which they are best equipped to produce will be better off if they trade with other countries which are better suited to making other products. Suppose one country, A, is better at making cars than computers. Another country, B, is better at making computers than cars. It's clear that both will be better off if A specializes in cars and B specializes in computers. But David **Ricardo** was the first economist to illustrate how the principle of comparative advantage works even if country A could produce both cars and computers more cheaply than country B. He did this by comparing comparative costs, specifically the input of the **factors of production** (land, labour, capital) required to produce the goods and services in question.

If we take countries A and B and measure the number of person-hours required in each case to make one

computer and one car, we arrive at the table below:

Country	Cars	Computers
A	90	100
B	120	110

(person-hours of output required to make each unit)

Country B is less efficient at making both cars and computers than country A. Nevertheless, they can still benefit from specialization and trade. Suppose A specializes in cars, which it can make with fewer person-hours than it takes to produce a computer. To make an extra car instead of a computer (the **opportunity cost**), 100 person-hours would be available – and that would make 100/90 car units – in other words, more than one extra car.

Now let B specialize in the product it makes comparatively more cheaply – computers (even though one computer requires more person hours than it does in A). The 120 hours freed by switching from car making will produce 120/110 computer units. At what rate do they trade? A computer costs 100/90 car units in A, and a car costs 120/110 computer units in B. Therefore any exchange rate which has A paying less than 100/90 cars per computer and B paying less than 120/110 computers per car will leave both better off. For the sake of simplicity, suppose they trade at one car for one computer. So A sells one car to B, leaving it with 100/90 car units, while B sells one computer to A, leaving it with 120/110 computers. Both have more than the one car and one computer they started with.

Ricardo's law was later developed into the **Heckscher-Ohlin** principle which states that a country will specialize in the goods that call on the factors of production it has most of: in other words, a country which has a large cheap workforce will export labour-intensive goods, whereas a country which has abundant efficient machinery will export capital-intensive products. The principle only deals with supply, and ignores differences in demand in different countries. When we look more closely at the car trade, for example, we might find that although a car produced in country A is cheaper than one produced in B, people in B might be highly attached to their home-produced marque and prefer to pay a little more than would the people in A. And in a highly complex multi-product world economy, it is much harder to quantify the gains from trade. Nonetheless, it is the broad principle that underlies both GATT and the World Trade Organization.

(*See also* **Edgeworth Box, Pareto**.)

CONCENTRATION MEASURES The extent to which economic activity is concentrated among a large or small number of firms or economic entities can affect **pricing**, output, **employment**, efficiency, and competitive behaviour. So various measures of concentration have been developed to help provide a snapshot for economists, entrepreneurs, and regulators. Clearly, a **monopoly** will be one extreme of concentration, with **perfect competition** the other.

One way to measure concentration is the 'concentration ratio', which calculates how much output, or capital, or employment of an industry is concentrated in the top handful of companies (in the US this is usually

the top four; in the UK it is the top three to five). The disadvantage of this measure is that it takes no account of the relative sizes of the top handful of firms (one may be enormous while the other two or four may be relative minnows); nor does it take account of the relative sizes of the remainder.

The Herfindahl Index works by measuring the sum of the squares of the market share of all the firms in the industry as a whole. A value near to zero implies that the market is spread across a large number of firms; a value near 1 implies a near-monopoly.

Concentration can be viewed graphically in the **Lorenz Curve**, which plots the relative contribution to the market for a given set of the largest firms. The **gini coefficient** is directly linked to the Lorenz curve and quantifies the degree of concentration.

Obvious difficulties in defining concentration include the perameters of an industry (mass media companies may not appear to control a high proportion of the newspaper industry, but if they also control television and radio and telecoms, a different picture can emerge); and also the role of multinationals which may control a high proportion of one part of an industry – say, the production of raw materials – while not appearing heavily concentrated in the consumer sales of that industry in certain countries.

(*See also* **theory of production costs**.)

CONSUMER The consumer is the key to microeconomic **theory of consumer demand**. He or she is generally assumed to be 'rational', which in economic terms means able to make choices in a consistent way, and in a way that creates the maximum level of **utility**. Economists analyse utility in terms of a basket of goods with prices varying for one of the goods (direct utility) or in terms of goods which may be purchased taking into account the real income level, which will vary as prices rise or fall (indirect utility). (*See* **price effect**.)

Consumer theory is by definition based on the behaviour of individuals. In more general terms, the consumer may be regarded as the end-user in a chain of economic activity.

CONSUMPTION FUNCTION An important element in the theories of **Keynes** and subsequent economists. The consumption function is a way of expressing the amount of household income which is consumed, as opposed to saved. For an economy as a whole, the consumption function determines total consumption spending as a proportion of total household disposable income (i.e. income after tax withdrawals have been subtracted).

Keynes believed that the most important determinant of economic performance was aggregate demand (the total of all the spending in the economy). By far the highest pro-

portion of this is from consumer expenditure, so understanding how it operates at various levels of income is fundamental in managing the economy. Keynes argued that with increasing income, the tendency increased to save proportionately more and consume proportionately less. To make this clear he introduced the concepts of 'marginal propensity to consume' and 'marginal propensity to save'.

If consumer spending (C) is related to the level of disposable income, we can say

$$C = f(Yd).$$

The marginal propensity to consume is the percentage of any extra unit of disposable income which will be consumed, rather than saved,

$$\text{so MPC} = \frac{\% \text{ change in } C}{\% \text{ change in } Yd}$$

and the marginal propensity to save, where savings are S,

$$\text{MPS} = \frac{\% \text{ change in } S}{\% \text{ change in } Yd}.$$

Since all of disposable income must be either spent or saved,

$$\text{MPC} + \text{MPS} = 1.$$

We can now express this as a diagram.

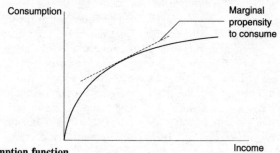

The consumption function

In this example, we have shown that as income increases, consumption also increases, but at a decreasing rate (MPC falls as MPS increases). The consumption function is the unbroken line in the diagram, and its slope at any point (the tangent) is the MPC at that level of income. When the MPC is close to 0 (the slope of the consumption function is relatively flat), this means that a large portion of extra income is saved. Conversely, when the MPC is close to 1 then the household spends a large portion of any extra income on consumption.

Keynes used the consumption function to help plot the equilibrium level of national income. Later economists have questioned whether consumption is simply a function of current disposable income. Milton Friedman argued that people will tend to base their consumption on what he called 'permanent' incomes. In this way short-term changes due to, say, sudden price hikes of certain goods such as oil, or changes in taxation, both of which will affect disposable income, will be 'smoothed out' by people using up their savings, indicating that consumption may be kept constant by variations in the MPC (and of course the MPS). Work by **Modigliani** – and empirical studies – also suggest that different age groups have markedly different consumption functions (for example, young people may spend more and save less in the hope they will earn more later on, whereas middle aged families at the same income level may try to save more for their own old age and their children's futures). This *life cycle hypothesis* implies that age (or time) can be as much of a determinant of the level of MPC as disposable income.

(*See also* **inflation**.)

CREDIT Credit refers to the granting of goods, services, or cash in return for a promise of future payment, usually accompanied by an **interest** charge. It is a transaction involving the transfer of these goods, services, and cash where the one issuing the transfer is the creditor, and the one receiving is the debtor. It is a form of **money**.

The basic purpose of credit in an economy is to transfer from those who own to those who wish to use capital, thus actively using the capital in an economy that would otherwise be idle. Credit facilitates the movement of goods and services in a more sophisticated way than notes and coins or the barter system, and reduces friction in the market.

The credit operation is generally carried out through documents known as credit instruments, which include bills of exchange, money orders, cheques, drafts, as well as **bonds**. Credit can be used by households, firms or governments to smooth out consumption (for households), operations (for firms) and the overall level of activity in the economy.

Households use money orders, cheques, credit cards, bank loans and instalment credit to satisfy their consumption needs. Consumer credit permits the purchase of retail goods and services with little or no downpayment in cash. In instalment buying and selling, the consumer agrees to make payments at specific intervals in set amounts. Credit cards are issued by local and national retailers and by banks. Cardholders usually pay an annual fee and a monthly interest charge on any unpaid balance. The major bank cards also provide short-term personal loans. Issuance of credit to consumers rests on their credit history, which is essentially the record of the consumer's honesty in fulfilling financial obligations (sometimes requiring a guarantor to secure the loan).

Firms primarily use credit to help finance operations, either for expansion or for greater efficiencies (perhaps to purchase new and better plant). The chief function of business credit is the transfer of capital from those who own it to those who can use it, in the expectation that the profit from its use will exceed the interest payable on the loan (*see* **debt**). Issuance of credit to firms occurs through the distribution of debentures, which use corporate assets as a form of security on the loan. Should the firm default on its payments, the debt holders are the first claimants on the property of the firm, with preferred shareholders and ordinary shareholders following (*see* **shares**).

Governments rely on credit to finance government expenditure as well as the operation of the economy. The issuance of government debt does not have any specified claim on government assets, but depends on the confidence and good faith of the general public, as well as political stability in the government. Governments often try to manage the availability and cost of credit to companies and individuals through monetary or fiscal policy.

Occasionally a government will need to look for emergency credit from outside its economy. Sometimes this can be achieved through the global capital markets or the **banks**; sometimes it will turn to bodies such as the **IMF** for a loan, which will normally come with strict conditions about economic policies in the future.

CURRENCY This is the most common form of money, and the most liquid component of the money supply. Any commodity used as a medium of exchange, a store of value and a unit of account may qualify as currency. Nowadays, currency represents only a small portion of the total liquidity in all modern western economies (in the case of the US only 5 per cent of the total liquidity (L) is circulating as currency). The historical development of the concept was not uniform across the world, and far from universal. Precious metals were preferred first in the historical development of money and currency, due to their relative scarcity, their indestructibility and their divisibility. Silver, copper, gold and bimetal standards were used in transactions and trade in all ancient civilizations from Babylon and Egypt to Greece. Roman and Byzantine emperors issued currencies to celebrate their enthronement. Medieval rulers would circulate new currency to finance their spending. This action in modern economics is called 'seignorage' (after the French term for a feudal lord – *mon seigneur*). But after the rise of sovereign nation states a decline is observed in the use of commodity money, which was replaced by paper money (fiat money). It is remarkable, however, that the exchange ratio of silver to gold (13 to 1) remained stable for almost 800 years, until the establishment of the gold standard, given that the supply of both metals was quite volatile. The fixity of the currency's ratio, rather than its intrinsic value, is the major guarantee for its potential to serve as a means of exchange. Therefore, 'bad' state money used to drive out the 'good' (*see* **Gresham's Law**). Silver gradually disappeared from circulation and gold followed, serving only as a store of value for a country's central bank. The emergence of the US dollar in the post-war era as world currency facilitated this trend. However, the deregulation of the gold market in 1971 effectively remonetized gold. Until we reach a point where a world government can establish a common paper currency, gold will remain in circulation as a counterpoint to the volatility of the world economy.

Other forms of money have developed in this century, following the information technology revolution. Credit cards and 'plastic' money threaten the dominance of paper currency. Computer-aided technologies have revolutionized transactions, making payments faster and easier, minimizing transaction costs at the same time. It is certain that this area will continue to change in the near future, given the rapid advances in information technology and the need to make money universally available in a global market.

(*See* 'Technology' essay by Richard Lander.)

D

DEBT The amount of money owed by a person, firm, or government (debtor) to a lender (creditor) is referred to as debt. Debt occurs when **consumption** is greater than income generated for a given period. Put another way, it occurs when a person or an institution chooses to borrow money to purchase goods and services, to increase production by investment, or – in the case of governments – to manage the economy. Debt requires **credit** to be available in the economy and is issued through debt contracts, which require the debtor to pay back the initial sum borrowed plus any interest charges for the duration of the loan.

Companies use a wide array of debt, depending on their specific needs. Loan capital refers to interest-bearing borrowed funds of debt capital. (In the US the various instruments of loan capital issued by companies are known as corporate bonds.) Those who provide loan capital to the firm do not receive a portion of profits like those who buy **shares**; neither do they have any ownership rights. They do, however, receive regular interest payments on the initial sum provided. The interest rate charged may be fixed, floating or subordinated. Fixed interest rates set out a prespecified rate of interest that is applied to the debt, whereas floating rates may fluctuate according to some indicator (usually the prime rate of interest charged by banks). Subordinated loans are much more uncertain; they occur typically when the creditworthiness of the company is not particularly reliable, or sometimes when they have been issued against the company's assets to finance a takeover or leveraged buyout. For this reason most subordinated loans are referred to as '**junk bonds**' and normally have much higher interest rates associated with them. Interest is not paid on subordinated loans until all the payments are made on the other types of debt (sometimes known as 'senior loans' or (US) 'senior bonds').

One of the most common forms of debt used by companies is the debenture. These are fixed-interest securities issued by limited companies in return for long term loans. They are normally dated for redemption within ten to 14 years and are secured against specific assets of the corporation. Interest payments must be made regardless of the firm's profit or loss. In the event of a default on payment, debenture holders may force the liquidation of the company, and rank ahead of shareholders in the claims on the company's assets.

The combination of loan capital and share capital comprises the capital structure of the firm; its ratio is known as the firm's **gearing** (US =

leverage). The higher the level of debt versus equity capital, the more 'highly geared' the firm is said to be.

Companies also try to protect themselves, both from market movements which could turn against them as borrowers, but also against fluctuations which affect them as creditors. They can use 'hedging' to reduce risk from changes in interest rates or currencies. This usually involves the purchase of **derivatives**. Broadly, the company is doing one of two things: it is either 'guessing ahead' about what the market might do (for example, the forward purchase of foreign currency so that the company's inflows or outflows in that currency are not adversely affected by market moves); or else it is **swapping** one kind of debt exposure for another (maybe fixed interest for floating, if it expects market rates to fall; or a back-to-back loan where two companies who have debts in each other's currencies swap them, allowing each to borrow in its own currency).

The nature and size of a company's debt should be accurately reflected in its balance sheet. In evaluating the value of the company, the **stock market** will usually take into account future profit expectations, the performance and indebtedness of other companies in the same sector, and the general outlook for the economy as a whole.

DEMAND CURVE Demand is one of the keys to understanding the behaviour of individuals and firms in an economy (microeconomics) and is the cornerstone of the **theory of demand**.

At its simplest, it is the desire for an economic resource, supported by the possession of the necessary means of exchange to own that resource. The demand curve, one of the most common symbols in economics, measures the quantity of a product which will be demanded at various prices. It is important to understand that a single demand curve refers to a given level of demand, and that it is the quantity demanded that is changing in response to price. For example, if price falls from P_1 to P_2 the quantity demanded on demand curve D_1 will rise from Q_1 to Q_2. An increase in demand is indicated by a shift to demand curve D_2, often a sign that the market for a particular product has increased in size. It means that for each price a greater quantity will be

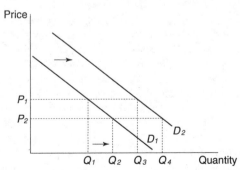

The demand curve

demanded (i.e. sold). Other factors which shift the whole demand curve may be changes in real incomes, or the arrival of substitute products to the market place. On a given demand curve, the measure of how much a change in price will affect the quantity demanded is calculated as the **elasticity** of demand.

DERIVATIVES Derivatives are financial instruments which derive their value from an underlying **asset**. Simple derivatives are known as **options** and **futures.** They give the holder the right, but not always the obligation, to buy **securities, bonds** and **commodities**, at given prices on given dates. Derivatives also include **swaps** on interest rates and currencies, which are a way of swapping debt payments between two parties in a way that suits both: in this case it is the debt that is the underlying asset.

Simple derivatives work like this: suppose I believe that the price of a share will rise to, say, 200p, over the next six months, I might buy some call options at 175p which will allow me to buy the share at 25p below its market price in six months. If I'm right and the share goes to 200p, I will make 25p for each call option. If the share price is only 150p I won't want to buy the share, as I'd make a 25p loss on every call option. So I would not exercise my right to buy the underlying asset – the share – and my exposure would be the value of the call options. Because of the risk I take, the price of the call option will usually be below the price of the share itself. Put options work the other way round, giving the holder the right but not the obligation to sell at a given price in the future: obviously if my put option is above the market price, I will make money by selling, because I can 'buy back' the share for less than I have just sold it.

The attractions of options trading include the ability to hedge: for example, by offsetting the risk of holding a large number of the actual share, by betting on its moving in the opposite direction by holding options. In international trade, the hedging function is an essential method of reducing exposure to currency movements, and most large international companies have their own treasury departments whose aim is to smooth out the effects of fluctuations. In this way a stronger or weaker currency often affects imports or exports less than economic fundamentals would suggest.

There is also the possibility of arbitrage, especially because of the leveraged nature of derivatives profits: the price of a derivative is usually less than the price of the underlying asset. The risks, however, are also greater. And they become greater still with the development of what have become known as 'exotic' derivatives.

Generally speaking, simple derivatives are traded in markets such as **LIFFE** (the London International Financial Futures Exchange). These markets may also trade options based on expectations of **share price indices** or **interest rates**. Exotic derivatives are more likely to be custom-designed, frequently by investment banks, with the customer's particular needs or trading strengths in mind. In one celebrated case in the 1980s several UK local authorities bought derivatives – in this case interest rate swaps – which were based on the gap between the (at the time) very high short-term market interest rates, and their own ability to raise money at long-term low interest rates (because of their relatively low risk for investors). Unfortunately for the local authorities (and, the courts decided, the banks who had sold the derivatives), the short-term interest rates turned down, and many millions of pounds were lost. Similarly, several blue-chip companies lost millions in exotic derivatives (Kodak, Procter and Gamble and Metallgesellschaft all being hit especially hard). With the explosion in global capital markets, and the increased use of sophisticated computer technology to design more and more exotic forms of derivatives, there were fears of a chronic undercapitalization and stock market collapses. Derivatives, and the 'rocket scientists' (financial engineers, who were often highly qualified mathematicians or physicists) who designed them, entered business demonology.

Behind the headlines was an awareness that although markets were more sophisticated, the same basic rules of risk and caution applied. A 1993 report by the Group of 30 (a think tank comprised of 30 individuals from central banks, commercial banks, as well as economic and finance ministers of developed and developing economies) suggested some guidelines for proper practice in buying and selling derivatives. Significantly, however, the G30 found that no further regulation was necessary.

There can be little doubt that trade in derivatives will continue to expand faster than the volumes in general financial markets. It remains to be seen whether their higher degree of risk poses any qualitatively different dangers from any other trade in money or financial instruments.

DEVALUATION/REVALUATION A policy tool which can be used by governments to tackle a chronic **balance of payments** surplus or deficit. Simply, by making the currency worth less against other currencies (devaluing), exports (paid for by buyers overseas eventually in the exporting country's currency) will become cheaper, and imports (which will be paid for eventually in the overseas countries' currencies) will be more expensive. Hence a devaluation will tend to reduce imports and boost exports. The process works in the opposite way for a revaluation.

Such devaluation or revaluation would normally work in a **fixed exchange rate** system, such as **Bretton Woods**, which tied most of the world's major currencies together at defined rates until the 1970s. Various countries were permitted by the 'system' (administered by the **IMF**) to devalue or revalue, to reflect underlying trends in their trade balances with the rest of the world.

In a floating exchange rate system, a self-righting mechanism will tend to take place in the international financial markets. If country A is a net exporter and country B a net importer, there will be a movement into the currency of country A (to pay for all its exports) and a movement out of the currency of country B (it will need to acquire more of country A's currency to pay for all those imports), causing country A's currency to increase in value (effectively a revaluation) whilst country B's currency will effectively devalue. Then the process of country A's exports becoming more expensive relative to country B's products will tend to move the trade closer to balance.

The practice is, as ever, more complex. A major factor is the price **elasticities** of exports and imports. Clearly, the devaluation or revaluation will only work if real changes occur to purchasing habits. The **Marshall-Lerner Condition** states that if the total of the elasticities is greater than unity, then the devaluation/revaluation will work; if not, it will not. There are also time lags, so that a devaluation will immediately be followed by an increase in the value of imports (this is the **J-curve** effect), with the decrease taking some months to become effective.

Furthermore, exchange rate policies should be seen in the context of overall macroeconomic management. In a country where an overheated economy is sucking in too many imports, a policy of domestic deflation may be preferable to devaluation; similarly, a loosening of monetary or **fiscal policy** may have the benefit of increasing imports while at the same time expanding domestic demand, instead of a revaluation, which will only work on external trade.

Monetarists argue that international trade imbalances can be viewed through their impact on **money supply**. A country with a trade deficit will experience a reduction in domestic money supply, as money flows out to the countries from which it is purchasing imports. This will reduce inflation, and the fall-off in demand from a contraction in the money supply will tend to reduce the deficit. Similarly a trade surplus country will tend to suck in funds, raising money supply, adding to inflation. If the government tries to curb this by selling bonds to the public, the tendency will be for interest rates to rise (*see* **monetary policy**), attracting further funds into the country (sometimes known as **hot money**), and adding to the inflationary pressures which will eventually raise export prices, tending to reduce the surplus.

(*See also* **theory of trade**, **Heckscher-Ohlin factor proportions theory**, essay by Sanjaya Lall.)

DIMINISHING MARGINAL RETURNS
The concept of diminishing margins is central to most topics in economics. The basic assumption is that returns to a factor of production increase at a decreasing rate. This notion is applied to the **theory of production costs**, **utility**, **profit** functions and **revenue**.

Diminishing marginal returns is diminishing margins applied to production. In general, a producer employs factors of production, such as labour, land and capital, to generate output (or returns on the factors). By making assumptions about the relative productivity of these factors of production, economists attempt to find the optimal number of factors to employ.

For a given amount of land, we can increase output by adding more factors of production (labourers or fertilizer, say) – but there are only so many factors that can be supported by the fixed amount of land. One extra labourer or bag of fertilizer increases the factor output (i.e. what the plot of land can grow) up to the point where the land yields its maximum extra output for one more additional labourer or fertilizer bag – the point of maximum marginal returns. Beyond this point, the addition of one extra variable factor may still increase total output, but by a progressively smaller amount. The land is being overworked, so that the output from each extra – or marginal – factor is diminishing. Eventually the average factor return will diminish too (i.e. the average production attributable to each labourer or fertilizer bag will fall).

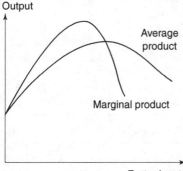

Diminishing marginal returns

The main implication of the concept of diminishing marginal returns to a producer is the need to discover the appropriate level of factors of production to maximize profits. So the main question a producer should be concerned with is the optimal level of labour and capital that will use the fixed resources of the firm to their best use.

DIVIDENDS Dividends are the profits of a company that are paid out to its shareholders.

They are usually expressed as a percentage of the coupon or nominal value of the **share**, so that a share with a nominal price of £1 which pays out a dividend of 5p will be paying a dividend of 5 per cent. If the market price of the share is £2, the dividend yield will be lower: in this case 2.5 per cent. Clearly, when companies are deciding how much to pay out in dividends, they need to take into account the dividend yield as much as the nominal payment.

The decision about how much to pay is taken by the board of directors. Their dividend policy is important, because a company must strike a balance between providing an attractive investment opportunity and as retaining sufficient profits to increase growth.

Another important measure of dividend policy is the dividend cover (US = payout ratio), which is the number of times a company's dividends to ordinary shares could be paid out of its net profits after taxes and interest payments. So if a company issues a dividend of £500,000 on net profits of £1.5 million, then its dividend cover is 3. The dividend can give two types of useful information to the investor. First, it can be an indication of future dividends (a low cover meaning that there will be less retained earnings to pay out the same level in less prosperous years). Secondly, it suggests how committed the company is to investment and growth (a high cover indicating that the company is retaining much of its earnings to be put back into the business for investment purposes).

Sometimes an investor will buy into a share just after the announcement of a dividend. Under this circumstance, or any other defined by the company as ex-dividend, an investor is no longer entitled to receive the company's current dividend: that right stays with the vendor of the share for a period specified by the company.

(*See also* **gearing**.)

E

ECONOMETRICS The development of this branch of economics stems back to the 1930s and the journal *Econometrica*. Oddly enough, the growing popularity of econometrics has made the purpose and definition of this 'applied economics' more ambiguous. Generally, however, it is accepted that econometrics uses applied and theoretical statistics combined with economic theory to analyse economic phenomena.

Econometric theory is concerned with developing appropriate statistical techniques to encounter empirical problems characterizing the science of economics. Models are formulated with some general assumptions with respect to properties of the parameters in the model, and are related to economic theory. One of the more basic models in econometric theory is the classical linear **regression** model (CLRM) in which five assumptions are associated with the form of the model and its properties. More often that not, however, these assumptions are violated, and the aim of the econometrician is to find methods around such violations by employing various statistical techniques.

Econometric theory also attempts to establish certain criteria for the parameter estimators in the economic model. These include the correlation coefficient of multiple determination, but there are many

other techniques and perameters, all designed to help quantify the impact of multiple variables in the economy or economic activity. The most basic estimator applied to parameters of an economic model is ordinary least squares (OLS). More complex parameter estimates include maximum likelihood and Monte Carlo simulations.

A key aspect of econometric theory is specification. Specification refers to the parameters that econometricians choose to include in their models. Sound econometric theory requires that parameters be chosen solely from economic theory. This is what separates statistics from econometrics. Specification errors can occur through using the wrong variables or the wrong relationships between them.

Much of the controversy in econometrics is related to its applications. Applied econometrics attempts to explain theories ranging from macroeconomic studies of unemployment and **inflation**, to microeconomic issues of consumer theory using sophisticated statistical tools. The basis of these tools is regression analysis, which attempts to relate a certain output parameter to a number of relevant input parameters. Once the output and input parameters are entered, regression analysis then estimates the relative significance of the input parameters to explain the output parameter. The difference between the actual and the estimate is referred to as a disturbance term. In addition to the assumptions based on the properties of the model in general, econometricians must also make assumptions on the data to test the degree of accuracy. Hypothesis testing is the primary statistical tool employed to determine the level of accuracy of the parameter estimates. A researcher can choose a subjective degree of accuracy and test the model for robustness within the appropriate interval.

Generally, these economic models can express static or dynamic relationships. Static analysis is primarily concerned with equilibrium notions and employs cross-sectional data from a single period. Dynamic analysis, however, attempts to describe the changes of certain parameters in a model by changes in other parameters in the model. These usually incorporate time series analysis, which charts the parameter of interest (a security, for example) with other parameters that can explain its growth or decay (interest rates, security index, and dividends for example) over a specified period of time. Forecasting techniques have also been developed in time-series analysis, which attempt to determine the future value of a specific parameter, such as growth or the price of a security.

(*See* essay by Paul Ormerod: 'What Economics is Not', which examines some econometric assumptions to question our ability to predict economic behaviour.)

Economies of Scale Economies

of scale occur when the size of production by a firm or economic entity is such that unit costs reduce. They have the effect of reducing the long-run average cost curve, which may continue 'flat', or at a certain level rise as a result of diseconomies of scale. Improved technology on the other hand may continue to lower the cost curve as production increases.

Economies of scale may be internal or external:

- *Internal economies* These may include the more efficient training of a specialist labour force, better bulk deals from suppliers, more effective marketing, and the benefits of using capital at full capacity. Often there will be technological advantages associated with **research and development**, and the large company will usually be more able to raise capital either from **banks** or through the issue of equity. Companies which conduct their business in many currencies can benefit from hedging their foreign exchange exposure. 'Economies of scope' are a form of economy of scale associated with a firm which has undergone some level of vertical **integration** so that it controls more layers of the production process. This allows it to enjoy benefits in terms of stock control, transport, accounting, and perhaps legal services. If the firm grows from horizontal or vertical integration to become an **oligopoly** or **monopoly**, the price control it can exert, as well as the barriers it can impose to new entrants, can also be viewed as an economy of scale.

● *External economies* These arise outside the firm itself but may be of equal benefit. For example, the presence of large firms in a particular country or region can attract better public **infrastructure** (roads, schools, etc.), as well as encouraging the formation of specialist companies which cater for their needs (e.g. specialist suppliers, builders, repair staff, etc.). In some cases governments may provide special tax breaks or other incentives to keep the firm within a country. (*See* the essay by Lall: 'World Trade and Development'.)

There are, however, offsetting diseconomies of scale. These are often associated with the management structure of the company itself, which may become too cumbersome, and less able to react to changes in the market (*see* **management theories of the firm, x-inefficiency**). The company may also become the target of the regulators if it has gained or threatens to gain a monopoly position. It may have greater problems managing its labour force. All of these factors can cause the average cost of production to start rising again, and in some cases the company may choose to break itself up into discrete operating units, to try to keep the benefits of specialization without suffering from overall diseconomies.

In a global economy many firms seek to enjoy the benefits of scale through strategic alliances. These may provide ways to enter markets which may have been previously closed to them (for example by using a local partner in a developing country), or to tie up the market with partners to deter new entrants. Many multinational companies enter into joint ventures or full mergers in some markets, while remaining independent in others.

EDGEWORTH BOX This is a way of expressing possible trading relationships between two individuals or countries by a comparison of their preferences between goods (indifference curves).

The Edgeworth Box consists of outward-marching indifference curves for, say, person A, for two products, say X and Y, and at the same time outward-marching indifference curves for the same two products for person B (*see* Fig. 1). Each indifference curve represents higher or lower levels of satisfaction: the further from the origin (for A the origin is O_A and for B, it's O_B), the greater the satisfaction. The point where A's and B's curves are tangential is the point at which both experience the same marginal rate of substitution for goods X and Y (although not necessarily the same levels of satisfaction, as we shall see).

Take indifference curve A_1. It touches curve B_3 at position C_1. If we move along A_1 to, say, position M, person A is in possession of a large

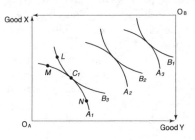

Edgeworth Box, *Fig. 1*

amount of product X and little of product Y. He or she would be happy to forgo plenty of X in order to acquire a little more of Y (a move to position N on indifference curve A_1). Person B, on the other hand (on indifference curve B_3) would be happy to forgo plenty of product Y in order to acquire a little of product X, shown in a move to position L. (This reflects the notion that indifference curves are flatter at either end, because people will value something they have little of relatively higher than something they have plenty of.) So A can trade some of his not-so-highly valued X for B's plentiful Y. In this way they will tend to move toward C_1. This represents the point at which they both experience the same marginal rate of substitution – each has balanced their desire to substitute X for Y at the same level.

Of course, what C_1 does not represent is an equal level of satisfaction. B has more of both X and Y, implying that he or she has made a better trade. Moving along the indifference curves, say, A_2 and A_3 or B_2 and B_1, we can plot the various tangential positions where the curves have the same gradient (C_2 and C_3). Joining these together gives us the 'contract curve' or offer curve (*see*

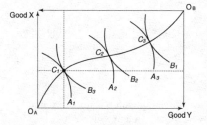

The contract curve, *Fig. 2*

Fig. 2), and where we are on it represents the relative strength of person A or B in the trading marketplace.

(*See* **Pareto**.)

ELASTICITIES Elasticity is a way of expressing the relative sensitivity of demand and supply to price and other variables such as income, or the price of another product. As such it is an important tool in the **theory of consumer demand** and the **theory of production costs**.

Mathematically, the elasticity between two variables is the percentage change in the dependent variable (say, quantity demanded) that comes about as a result of the percentage change in the independent variable (say, price). Thus, in general if we have two points from a graph describing the relationship between X and Y, say the points (X_1, Y_1) and (X_2, Y_2) then the formula for elasticity becomes:

Elasticity between variables X and Y

$$= \frac{\text{Percentage change in } X}{\text{Percentage change in } Y}$$

$$= \frac{(X_2 - X_1)/X_1}{(Y_2 - Y_1)Y_1}$$

This formula is usually referred to as the arc elasticity, because it measures the elasticity between two points on, say, a demand curve. If, however, we are interested in the responsiveness of X at a particular point (referred to as point elasticity), then it becomes necessary to incorporate calculus to determine the elasticity between X and Y at that particular point (the formula for point elasticity is simply the derivative of the logarithm of X divided by the derivative of the logarithm of Y).

The relationship between the two variables is said to be elastic when a small change in Y yields a large change in X (the number is above 1). Conversely, the relationship between the two variables is said to be inelastic when a large change in Y yields a small change in X (the number is between zero and 1). Unit elasticity as the term implies is an elasticity of 1, which indicates that a percentage change in Y yields the same percentage change in X.

We can use the general formula to express price elasticity of demand and supply. If on a standard demand curve we take a price p for product x, which results in a quantity demanded (or sold) of q, then examine a rise in price to p_1, with q_1 demanded, we can examine the price elasticity of product X for the range of prices p to p_1.

So elasticity =

$$\frac{\% \text{ change in quantity}}{\% \text{ change in price}} \quad \frac{[(q_1 - q)/q]}{[(p_1 - p)/p]}$$

and if this number is higher than 1, demand is said to be elastic, whereas below 1 it is inelastic.

Suppose that p were £5 and p_1 were £10, and suppose that q were 10,000 units, and q_1 is 3,000 units, we would see that

$$\text{elasticity} = \frac{233\% \text{ fall in quantity}}{100\% \text{ rise in price}}$$

giving us an elasticity of minus 2.3. In other words, product X is highly price-elastic – at that range in the demand curve. (Note that elasticity

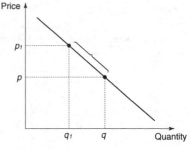

Elastic/inelastic demand

can vary at various points in a demand curve.)

As we saw from the example, a normal backward-sloping demand curve will give a price elasticity which is a negative number. For a supply curve, which slopes forward, the number is positive. So at price p, say £5, suppose 10,000 units of X were supplied to the market, with price p_1 (£10) supplying 15,000 units.

Elasticity of supply =

$$\frac{50\% \text{ rise in quantity}}{100\% \text{ rise in price}}$$

giving us an elasticity of plus 0.5. In other words, the supply of product X is relatively price inelastic at that range in the supply curve.

It will be seen that it is possible to calculate income elasticity of demand, which is

$$\frac{\% \text{ change in quantity demanded}}{\% \text{ change in income}}$$

or cross-elasticity of demand, which is

$$\frac{\% \text{ change in quantity demanded}}{\% \text{ change in price of product X.}}$$
$$\text{of product Y}$$

Cross price elasticity of demand is important when looking at the behaviour of goods which are substitutes (say, air travel and intercity rail travel), or which are complementary (say, computers and floppy disks).

Clearly a knowledge of elasticities is essential not just for the economist in understanding supply and demand theory, but also for the manager or entrepreneur who will need to calculate the effect on revenues of changes in price and other variables. (*See also* **perfect competition**, **monopoly**, **oligopoly**.)

EMPLOYMENT Having as much of the labour force as can work, in work, is one of the two great problems in modern macroeconomics, the other being the control of **inflation**. As we shall see, both issues overlap, and various schools of thought provide differing analysis and solutions to each.

Employment is the level of utilization of the available labour resources in an economy. The under-utilization of labour in the existing production structure results in unemployment, which we classify according to its cause. Thus, we may consider unemployment as:

1. frictional;
2. **structural**;
3. cyclical;
4. seasonal;
5. involuntary–voluntary.

Frictional unemployment relates to that part of the labour force which is in between jobs. Structural unemployment stems from the dysfunctionality, or inadequacy, of aggregate demand to stimulate production in specific sectors of the economy. Furthermore, cyclicality and seasonality of business or trade activities may account for a systematic deviation of employment from its 'natural rate' (*see* **Phillips Curve**). Finally, involuntary unemployment is the idle part of the labour force that is actively seeking jobs. Although these workers are willing to accept the prevailing nominal wages on the job market for which they are qualified, their search is unsuccessful. On the other hand, the voluntary unemployed are those people who choose to put themselves out of the labour force by not accepting the going wage in the market.

Employment theorists have tried to address all five types of unemployment and at the same time to provide remedies. Two basic opposing views prevail:

1. the **Classical** approach, which considers that unemployment is caused by real and nominal wage rates being higher than their market-clearing level, usually because of the activities of governments;
2. the **Keynesian** approach, which treats unemployment as an innate characteristic (or inefficiency) of the market system and attributes it to the insufficiency of total demand to stimulate a full usage of the available labour.

The Classical approach (including **neo-Classical** and **monetarist** variants) treats the employment problem as an issue of market efficiency, while the Keynesian schools approach it as a problem of distributive justice, as well as one of correcting an intrinsic market inefficiency.

For the Classical orthodoxy (*see*, for example, the works of **Marshall**, **Pigou** and **Hicks**), the elasticity of labour demand is influenced by factors such as the elasticity of the product demand, the substitution between labour and capital, the elasticity of the supply of capital, the relative importance of labour in production and the presence of 'distortions' in the labour market (e.g. **minimum wage** laws). Unemployment results also from the inappropriate use of demand stimulus (either **fiscal** or **monetary**), which may also exacerbate the problem of inflation.

The neo-Classical Synthesis **(IS/LM)** emphasizes the role of the 'money illusion' (in which people respond to changes in money prices and wages, as opposed to real, or inflation-adjusted, changes). Neo-Classical economists argue that this tends to raise interest rates and discourage private investment. It also, they say, affects expectations by increasing uncertainty.

The rational expectations hypothesis, as introduced by the neo-Classical school, makes costly information a material part of labour market decisions. If people (or firms) are deprived of the information with which they can make rational decisions, or because certain kinds of **monopoly** power exist over labour, the market will not operate efficiently. This process, along with the presence of unanticipated inflation, will lead to deviations from the competitive general equilibrium solution. In the view of the neo-Classicals, all measures attempting to remove

market imperfections are appropriate since they affect the frictional as well as the structural element of unemployment (see **supply-side economics**). By improving the quality of available information to everyone in the economy, we make the competitive equilibrium more probable.

The Keynesian tradition favours intervention in the form of demand-management. Fine-tuning will reduce the significance of wage and price rigidities, which are thought to prevail in the short run.

Okun's Law empirically identifies a positive relationship between deviations from the potential level of national income, and unemployment levels. This, according to Keynesian analysis, provides a basis for income policies. A careful adoption of labour-saving technical progress with the subsidized training of the labour force to meet the emerging needs is prescribed. The marginal efficiency of the **factors of production**, the propensity to save, liquidity constraints and the volatility of consumption, investment and money demand functions are emphasized in this tradition. The distinction between 'notional' and 'actual' demand in the work of post-Keynesian economists (e.g. Clower, and Leijonhufrund) is central to their 'disequilibrium' approach to unemployment.

The **neo-Keynesians**, without totally discarding neo-Classical recommendations, introduced costly adjustments in the labour market and coordination failures. They also allowed for efficiency wages, implicit contracts and multiple equilibria solutions in order to refine the Keynesian explanation of unemployment.

The common denominator of all Keynesian regimes is the attempt to correct the demand deficiencies. An appropriately coordinated expansionary policy will correct the deflationary gap, preventing detrimental **wage-price spiral** effects and enabling the economy to return to its full employment natural rate position (*see* **fiscal policy**).

It should be remembered that the Keynesian approach to unemployment appealed first to governments which were in some desperation at the mass unemployment of the Great Depression. This solution, which gave governments a tool with which to try to restart the economy, was enthusiastically embraced and remained the general approach to the business cycle until the **stagflation** of the 1970s. It was then that the presence of both high unemployment *and* inflation sent the policymakers looking to other solutions. Perhaps more than with any other area of economics, employment theory has tended to develop with changes in the 'real' world. Over the next decade or so, global capital markets and changes in technology will bring great change to the workings of the labour market. Cyclical changes will become regional or global, and labour mobility will increase in these new markets. Furthermore, the *type* of labour will be a greater determinant in the factor endowments of various economies. (For an example of how this is already feeding into **theories of trade** and development, see 'World Trade and Development' essay by Dr Sanjaya Lall.)

EMU European integration in its historical process has taken various forms, each one with distinct characteristics. First, there was the establishment of a uniform free trade area among member states. Then, a customs union, with the abolition of all customs barriers. The formation of a 'common market' followed in the next phase, which resulted in the creation of a single market for the European Union (EU) countries. Finally, all EU states agreed to progress towards complete monetary unification, including the introduction of a single currency (the euro), at the start of 1999. The framework was laid down in the Maastricht Treaty of December 1991. It established the European Central Bank (ECB), independent of national governments, to control monetary policy and oversee price stability. The single currency means a common structure of interest rates and one inflation rate.

The first 11 states wanting to join the euro zone (the UK's 'opt out' clause in the Maastricht Treaty meant it could stay out of the zone while staying in the EU) had to pass the following 'convergence criteria':

- The inflation rate had to be within 1.5 per cent of the three lowest rates of the admitted countries.
- The long-run interest rates should be within 2.0 per cent of the three lowest rates of the admitted countries.
- The country's national currency for two years prior to admission to EMU had to have remained within the limits set by the Exchange Rate Mechanism (ERM) – i.e. within 15 per cent of the target parity – and not been devalued.

- The government's budget deficit to GDP ratio did not exceed 3 per cent.
- The national debt to GDP ratio was less than 60 per cent.

The goals of the European Monetary System (EMS) were to reduce uncertainty especially regarding exchange rates; to achieve disinflation through policy discipline and credibility gains; to avoid uncoordinated exchange rate policies and to pave the way for a full EMU.

European monetary union has the following anticipated advantages:

- efficient allocation of saving internationally;
- lower foreign-exchange transaction costs;
- reduced uncertainty, hence smaller risk premiums and easier external financing;
- an elimination of the need for foreign exchange interventions among European countries;
- the removal of the threat of balance of payments crises sparked by speculative attacks on currencies.

Some of the key potential problem areas can be identified as:

- The need for high mobility of financial assets and factors of production within the euro zone, to avoid, say, persistent high unemployment in certain areas.
- Related to the above, the question of individual countries continuing to be at different stages of the business cycle, and the inability to deal with that via currency exchange rates or national monetary policy.

- The question of how much fiscal flexibility is available to euro zone governments. Budget deficits will continue to fall under the Maastricht convergence criteria, but outside of the limiting level the question of funding deficits would fall to the ECB, which therefore may come under pressure from individual countries rather than acting for the group as a whole. This could affect the credibility of the ECB.

The supporters of the euro are confident that the system in itself contains the solutions for all these potential difficulties.

(For a fuller discussion of the future issues, see the essay by Dr Ian Harnett: 'Europe – the Next Five Years'.)

ENDOGENOUS GROWTH THEORY The question of what makes economies grow, and whether the rate of growth can be influenced, stimulated, or extended, is one of the subject's biggest challenges. Neo-Classical theories argued that growth is exogenously determined by, say, a certain level of technology or population increase (*see* **Solow growth model**). In the short term it might be possible to increase growth by increasing savings and investment, but the exogenous factors will still define the long-term growth path. By contrast, endogenous growth theory suggests that increases in investment, or research, can bring about long-term changes in growth. Thus growth is determined from 'inside the system' (i.e. endogenously).

A key factor in determining growth

is the nature of technological – or technical – progress. This may be 'Harrod-neutral', where the progress makes labour more efficient relative to other factors, or it may be **'Hicks-neutral'**, where the output of all the factors increases in the same proportion. Clearly the two will have different implications for employment and investment. (*See* **Harrod-Domar growth model** for a discussion of how long-term growth may or may not achieve a full-employment equilibrium.)

Modern computing power and **econometric** techniques have assisted the development of endogenous growth theory, by allowing mathematical testing of various inputs within the system. (*See also* essay by Paul Ormerod – 'What Economics is Not', for a discussion of the limits to forecasting variables such as growth.)

ENGEL'S LAW Ernst Engel's studies of household spending in the last century led to his statement that as incomes rise, people will tend to devote more of their incomes to luxury goods, and less to staples or necessities such as food. In macro-

economic terms, Engel argued that the percentage of its income that a country spends on food is a good measure of its overall economic welfare: the lower the percentage, the higher its welfare.

Engel also contributed to consumer theory, with the Engel Curve, which is a way of examining consumption of a product against income: it's therefore sometimes called an income consumption curve. The shape and slope of the curve tell us about the demand for various products at different income levels. An inferior good, such as poor-quality margarine, shows an absolute reduction as income increases, a staple such as butter shows a relative reduction, and luxury goods such as champagne will be more highly consumed as incomes increase (Fig. 1).

Another way of expressing the Engel Curve is to plot outward-marching indifference curves for two goods, say food and computers (Fig. 2). We represent different income levels as straight lines, sometimes known as budget lines, so that where the income level is tangential to the indifference curve, we have achieved

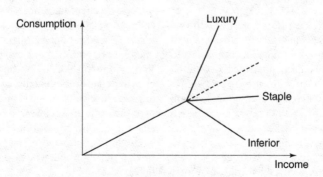

Engel Curve – consumption of various goods at different income levels, *Fig. 1*

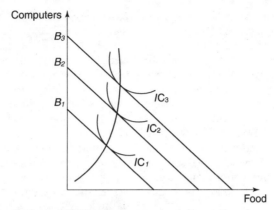

Engel Curve – outward marching indifference curves, *Fig. 2*

the highest possible level of satisfaction (at constant prices) for a level of income (parts of the indifference curve which do not touch the income line cannot be sustained at that income level). This 'consumer equilibrium' will reflect progressively lower relative consumption of staples, like food, as income rises, so that the resulting Engel Curve slopes more steeply. On the other hand the demand for computers increases more strongly as income rises.

(*See also* **Giffen good, theory of consumer demand**.)

EXCHANGE RATE POLICY The exchange rate is the rate at which one **currency** can trade for another, and reflects the relative supply and demand characteristics of each of the currencies. If country A is a net exporter to country B, country B will need to buy enough of country A's currency to pay for the net imbalance. The price of country A's currency will rise and country B's currency will fall. This will tend to make country B's exports cheaper and A's more expensive, thus moving their **balance of payments** back towards equilibrium.

In practice, the exchange rate will either be **fixed** or floating, or some variant in between the two. This means either that the government, through the **central bank**, commits to keeping the currency at a certain value (usually in association with other central banks, who together operate a 'club', such as the **Bretton Woods system**), or that the currency is allowed to float according to market forces. Various arguments can be made for both systems. Fixed rates provide more stability, whilst floating rates allow the currency to react to changes in market forces without the need for relatively costly intervention by governments which may prove ineffective against the currency markets anyhow. The middle way, which is a certain amount of intervention to smooth out the uneven fluctuations, but no attempt to fix the currency at a certain level, is known as a 'dirty float'.

Exchange rate policy should be

seen as part of **monetary policy**. **Monetarist** economists make a point of analysing the relationship of the domestic **money supply** to the exchange rate, since the overall supply of money, they argue, will determine its relative price and therefore the exchange rate, rather than just international net flows. Also important is the effect of the **interest rate**: raising it in order to choke off domestic **inflation** may attract speculative **hot money**, which raises the exchange rate, thereby making exports more expensive and encouraging companies to produce more for the domestic market, leading to increased demand and inflation. By the same token, a falling interest rate for devaluation purposes will make imports more expensive, increasing domestic spending, causing inflation rather than a net rise in exports.

The effect of devaluing or revaluing the currency depends to a large extent on the relative elasticities of demand for exports and imports, a phenomenon elaborated in the **Marshall-Lerner Condition**. There are also time-lags, which give rise to the **J-curve** effect. Another important factor, for international investors, is expectations about future exchange rates: if, for example, the market envisages a 10 per cent devaluation of currency A against currency B, then it will require a 10 per cent premium on any currency A-denominated financial instruments such as **bonds**. This phenomenon, known as the 'International Fisher Effect', after the economist Irving Fisher (1867–1947), means that it should cost the same to borrow in any currency: this is important for the operation of today's

global capital markets, as well as for **derivatives** and hedging activities, where instruments in several currencies may be held to offset the risks of a devaluation or revaluation of one of them.

If a currency is sufficiently powerful or universal for other currencies to denote their value as a multiple of it, it is said to be a reserve currency. Typically, the dollar is regarded as a reserve currency, and there is a possibility that the new euro will eventually become a reserve too. The effect for exchange rate policy is that the demand for the reserve currency will in general be higher (because it will also be used as a third-party trading medium between, for example, two countries whose currencies are both pegged to it), meaning that a balance of payments deficit will reduce its value less (or that payments deficits can be maintained without devaluation), and that a fiscal **budget deficit** can be financed without the same need to raise domestic interest rates.

EXPECTATIONS-ADJUSTED (AUGMENTED) PHILLIPS CURVE This is a long-term refinement of the **Phillips Curve** which addressed the problem that inflationary expectations can undo government attempts to manage **unemployment**. In the classic Phillips Curve a government which tries to reduce unemployment by increasing demand will succeed in doing so at the expense of higher **money** wages and therefore **inflation**. (A move from U to U_1 will cause a move up Phillips Curve P to take inflation from I to I_1.) This is because increased demand will tend to take up excess capacity in the labour market, allowing employees to demand higher wages.

Governments in the 1970s found that they were experiencing higher inflation and higher unemployment – **stagflation**. This called for the redrawing of a longer-term Phillips Curve, which was vertical or almost vertical. It corresponded to the so-called 'natural' rate of unemployment or NAIRU (the non-accelerating inflationary rate of unemployment), which is the level at which wage pressures tend neither to increase nor decrease the current inflation rate, because expectations are in line with that rate.

The diagram shows the steps toward the expectations-augmented Phillips Curve, which is really a series of several short-term curves corresponding to various levels of inflationary expectations. The higher money wages associated with the move along Phillips Curve P will cause higher unemployment (back from U_1 to U) as jobs are 'priced out'

of the market. But with expectations of inflation now at I_1 we are on a second Phillips Curve P_1. Attempts by governments to bring unemployment back down to U_1 will lead to even greater inflation (I_1 to I_2) on the higher curve. In turn higher money wages (assuming the same productivity) mean that more jobs are 'squeezed out', bringing unemployment stubbornly back to U on another Phillips Curve P_2 which corresponds to the even higher inflationary expectations; not a pleasant dilemma for governments.

There are two possible solutions. One is to push unemployment higher – to U_2 on curve P_2, by fiscal or monetary methods. This will move inflation down from I_2 to I_1. But eventually the lower level of money wages which follows from lower inflationary expectations will reduce unemployment as jobs are 'priced into' the market. Hence unemployment falls to U, which is the NAIRU. It can be seen that almost any level of inflation is possible at the given

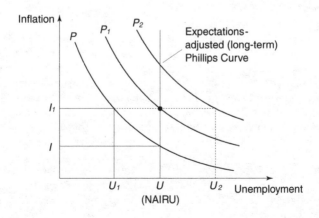

Expectations-adjusted Phillips Curve

NAIRU on this augmented long-term curve, but that short-term moves in unemployment will correspond to higher or lower inflation.

The second solution is to reduce the level of NAIRU, for example by **supply-side** changes which will tend to increase productivity, effectively flattening out the short-term curves as money wages can rise without causing inflation.

The two policies were embraced most notably by the Thatcher and Reagan administration of the 1980s. Many of the European economies currently face consistently high levels of NAIRU. In the case of those in the euro zone, a strong independent European Central Bank will not allow higher inflation. If higher unemployment is politically unacceptable, their only route may be to use supply-side measures to shift the NAIRU lower.

(*See* Patrick Minford essay: 'The Supply Side and the Limits to Intervention'.)

F

FACTORS OF PRODUCTION These are the inputs which, added together, create output, either from a firm or from a whole economy.

Traditionally there are four factors, and each has a reward which represents its cost:

- land, for which the cost is rent;
- capital, which includes machinery and raw materials, and for which the reward is interest on the initial investment, since all capital represents deferred consumption;
- labour, which includes skilled and unskilled human effort, for which the reward is wages; and
- entrepreneurship, for which the reward is profit.

The important point about the factors of production is not their textbook definitions and rewards, but the way in which they are brought together. In microeconomic terms this will define the nature of production and its costs, as well as how much is produced (*see* **production function**, **diminishing marginal returns**, and **theory of production costs**). In macroeconomics and trade theory, the endowment of the factors of production for a given country or trading bloc will define the gains it will achieve from various kinds of specialisation (*see* **comparative advantage**, **Heckscher-Ohlin factor proportions theory**, essays by Sanjaya Lall and Patrick Minford).

Clearly the combination of factors can and will vary over time in an economy. Highly developed industrialised economies will usually rely more heavily on skilled labour to create new products, whilst land and raw materials may be more important in developing economies. Furthermore, the way that individual businesses are organised will make the rewards to the various factors somewhat less clear. (In a large public company, for example, who provides the entrepreneurship – the managers or the shareholders? (*See* **management theories of the firm**.)

FISCAL POLICY Fiscal policy is one of the key macroeconomic tools of government. It uses the tax system and government spending to change levels of aggregate **demand**, and is at the heart of the methods outlined by **Keynes** to smooth out the extremes of the business cycle. (Keynesians and **monetarists** also recognize the role of **monetary policy** as a means of controlling aspects of the economy. The two other broad tools are **supply-side** measures and **exchange rate policy**.)

All governments raise taxes to pay for defence, economic infrastructure, education, welfare, etc. As such, taxation is a **leakage**, or withdrawal, from the circular flow of national income, which corresponds to an injection in the form of the actual spending. Fiscal policy seeks to use the difference between the two either to stimulate the economy in periods of recession or slump, or to cool it in periods of expansion or inflation.

Keynes identified a **multiplier** effect, which ensures that injections to the **circular flow** (increases in aggregate demand) cause a greater eventual increase in the national income. In simple concrete terms, if the government builds a new road, the extra wages for the construction workers will be spent on consumer goods, providing money for the retailers who may buy more from the manufacturers, who may choose to open a new factory, by paying a landlord and the builders who erected it, not to mention the producers of machinery to put in it, and so on.

The multiplier can be defined in this way:

Multiplier =

$$\frac{\text{change in aggregate demand}}{\text{change in national income}} \text{(size of injection)}$$

It is clear that reductions in demand in the form of withdrawals will also have a reverse multiplier effect on national income, and the multiplier works in the same way for other withdrawals such as savings and imports, and for injections such as investment and exports.

During the period of deep recession in the 1930s when Keynes was writing, his views came as a revolutionary change to the **Classical** and **neo-Classical** economics which then prevailed. They suggested the possibility for governments to 'spend their way out of' recession, rather than waiting for the price mechanism to operate on wages and money such that the economy would eventually stimulate itself. This dichotomy is still relevant today in the debates between those who broadly follow Keynesian theory (often called **neo-Keynesians**), and the monetarists whose views largely stem from the Classical schools.

Keynes argued that demand could be increased by spending on public works such as schools, roads, and hospitals. As well as central government, there could also be more spending by local authorities. This would be achieved through a budget deficit, whereby the amount of withdrawals from the economy (tax) was smaller than the amount of injections (public works or any other government spending). Obviously an idea of the size of the multiplier was important to avoid under or overshooting. This kind of fiscal policy formed the backbone of macroeconomic policy for many western governments from the 1930s through to the end of the 1970s. Dramatically it underpinned the New Deal policies of President Franklin Roosevelt in the US (*see* **Galbraith**).

During the 1970s economists noticed that some countries were suffering from both high inflation and relative stagnation in economic growth (a phenomenon known as **stagflation**). This obviously led to problems with standard Keynesian fiscal policy, which assumed the existence of a 'deflationary gap' which could be closed by increased government spending, moving the economy to an equilibrium level around full

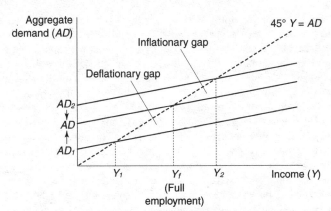

Deflationary gap closed by boosting AD_1 to AD through increase in government spending

Inflationary gap closed by reducing AD_2 to AD through decrease in government spending

Fiscal policy and aggregate demand

employment. Alternatively if there was an 'inflationary gap', a reduction in government spending would bring inflation down to the equilibrium level.

This phenomenon led to a reassessment of fiscal policy as the main tool of economic management. There was concern at the same time about the tendency for fiscal policy to result in a long-term **budget deficit**. Some argued that governments relying on fiscal policy would always tend to spend more than they necessarily needed to. This was partly for the political reason that it is difficult to cancel public works once they are begun; partly because government spending itself has a habit of increasing once commissioned; and partly because at the time, high unemployment was regarded as a greater evil than inflation. There was also an examination of the means used to fund (= pay for) the budget

deficit, and whether it could itself over-stimulate the economy through the **bank credit multiplier** (*see* **PSBR**). Furthermore, it became more politically 'mainstream' to question the whole concept of governments intervening in the economy.

All of this helped bring about a redefinition of fiscal policy to include the aim of moving toward a balanced budget. It should be noted that a balanced budget, where the total of taxation is equal to the total of government spending, is different from a fiscally neutral budget, whose impact on economic output will be neither expansionary nor recessionary. In brief this is because whilst both taxation and government spending have a multiplier effect on national income (output), the effect of higher taxation is often to reduce other leakages such as savings or spending on imports (*see* **taxation**). This means that a bigger increase in taxation is required to match completely the increase in spending – or that neutral budgets have a tendency to be in deficit, other things being equal.

At the same time, the effectiveness of macroeconomic management via fiscal measures was questioned for technical reasons. Many of the measures (output, employment, etc.), are generally lagging indicators, allowing for the possibility that the very issues tackled by fiscal measures may no longer apply. Furthermore, the Lucas critique noted that individuals' behaviour was based on circumstances which exist now, and once these circumstances change (by, for example, fiscal measures), behaviour may change in different, unexpected ways, rendering the policy irrelevant at best, and potentially damaging at worst.

Many governments today use fiscal policy in a more refined form, often taking advantage of better computer modelling techniques (*see* **econometrics**). This allows them to anticipate the business cycle, so that large changes in spending and taxation are avoided. There is also a greater reliance on monetary and supply-side measures. In some countries monetary policy is separate from fiscal policy, and may be run by the **central bank** independently of the government. This is a trend which is set to develop in Europe with the introduction of the single currency and a European Central Bank which will manage monetary policy. Individual national governments will then be left with fiscal policy as their main weapon of macroeconomic management – if indeed they choose to embrace such management.

FIXED/FLOATING EXCHANGE RATES

Exchange rates vary from day to day, often from minute to minute. The movements reflect changes in 'real' trade between countries, as well as arbitrage, hedging, and speculation (*see* **hot money**). A fixed exchange rate guarantees that a currency will trade at a given parity against one or more other currencies. That guarantee comes from the central bank, and usually the central banks of all the countries in the fixed rate 'club'. They use open market intervention to ensure that the currencies trade within a very narrow band of the parity value, buying a currency if its value is falling, and selling if it is rising. The idea is to make it easier for companies to plan their trading activities without having to worry about currency risks. The best example of a long-term fixed currency arrangement was the **Bretton Woods system**, which lasted for almost 30 years and fixed the currencies of its participants against the US dollar and therefore against each other.

The problem with a fixed rate system is that it is not usually possible to maintain a fixed parity through intervention if the economic fundamentals have changed. A country whose trade moved into a chronic **balance of payments** deficit should in most cases devalue to make its exports more competitive. Although this was allowed under Bretton Woods, it required a decision by the **IMF**, and in order to avert pressure for 'competitive' devaluations (with other countries calling to devalue to maintain their exports' competitive edge) it was a rare event. Today's open capital markets are characterized by huge speculative and hedging flows, so it is now even harder for governments to maintain fixed currency values. An illustration of this difficulty was Britain's exit from the European Exchange Rate Mechanism in 1992, when billions of pounds, spent in intervention and a series of interest rate hikes, failed to stop the speculative selling of sterling in the markets.

As a consequence, most currencies are now allowed to float more or less freely. In practice this is a process sometimes known as 'dirty floating', where central banks will try to iron out the biggest fluctuations on a day-to-day basis, but will not attempt to maintain a long-term rate.

European Monetary Union (**EMU**), in which some of the world's most powerful economies have come together to create a currency entity almost as large as the USA, should be seen not as a system of fixed exchange rates, but as a single (new) currency, the euro, replacing eleven, while still floating against the rest of the world, as the mark, franc, lira, etc., all did. Some practical instances of recently failed attempts at fixed parities (of some of the East Asian currencies against the US dollar) can be found in the Jeremy Pink essay, 'Asia: The Lessons for Economics'. (*See also* Neil Mackinnon's essay 'The Limits to Global Markets'.)

FUTURES A futures contract is an agreement to buy or sell the underlying asset for a given price at a specific time in the future. The definition of a futures contract is very similar to that of a forward contract. These forms of **derivatives** essentially lock in an investor for the length of the contract. Theoretically futures are priced in a similar way to forwards; in practice, however, they differ in some respects.

Whereas futures are traded over the counter (OTC) or in organized markets such as the New York Mercantile Exchange, forward contracts tend to be tailor-made to meet the specific needs of the parties involved. Because futures are traded in the OTC market, they are standardized. Being standardized, the contracts specifically state the underlying **asset**, the quantity being bought or sold, the date of shipment, as well as the terms of the shipment. We can broadly divide futures contracts into three categories: commodity futures (say, metals), financial futures (like Treasury bills), and futures on indices (for example, S&P 500).

An investor initiates a futures contract by opening an account with a clearing house. In order to open an account the investor is required to deposit an initial margin into the account to cover the number of contracts bought. Volatility in the price of the futures contract is applied to the investor's account so that net gains and losses are incurred on days of active trade. An investor's account has a lower limit and when the balance reaches this limit (referred to as the maintenance margin), the investor receives a margin call indicating that additional funds must be deposited into the account. With forward contracts, however, net gains or losses are only realized at maturity. For this reason futures are generally used for speculative purposes while forwards are generally used for hedging.

It should be noted that at maturity, the purchaser of a futures contract does not actually acquire the underlying asset, as it will be rolled over to a new contract. Speculation in futures serves to protect both the developers and the users of the commodities from unfavourable and unpredictable price fluctuations.

Financial futures are a method of speculating or hedging on interest rates, currencies, or stock prices or indices. Their use has greatly increased over the past few decades, expanding the size of markets such as the London International Financial Futures Exchange (**LIFFE**). There has been some criticism of the impact that hedge funds and individual speculators may have on real economies through trading in financial futures, but in a global economy where capital markets have become more deregulated, financial futures are regarded as an important way to protect against volatility.

G

GALBRAITH, JOHN KENNETH (1908–)
Canadian economist with radical views about big business and the modern capitalist state. Galbraith has served in several government as well as academic roles; his books have been read more widely than those of most professional economists. His best-known works are *The Affluent Society* (1958) and *The New Industrial State* (1967).

Galbraith could best be described as a 'liberal **Keynesian**', but he is as much a social commentator as a formal economist. He argues that modern industrial society, particularly in the United States, has diverged widely from the traditional norm of the free market. He argues that large companies use advertising to create the demand for many of the goods and services in society, creating waste and a neglect of real needs and equality. He argues that large modern companies have created what he calls a 'technostructure' whose main goals are their own continued survival and growth, rather than simple profit-maximisation (*see* **management theories of the firm**). They use government and workers to perpetuate their aims, hence creating a society of private wealth but public poverty. He borrows from Adam **Smith** the notion of the 'countervailing power'. Smith used this to explain competition between sellers in the market; Galbraith uses it to define the pressure by trade unions for wages. He argues for the countervailing power of the consumer against large firms. Galbraith is not wholly condemning of business, which he says has brought great benefits from technology, but he calls for greater controls by government.

GAME THEORY Game theory is the branch of economics concerned with the study of interacting decision makers. It is a mathematical study of conflict situations. Although one might be tempted to liken it to probability, the emphasis in game theory is the strategic aspect, which is controlled by the participants. Game theorists are concerned with the actions players pursue in a specific game, when all other players are doing as well as possible.

A game consists of a set of players, rules, and strategies with payoffs. Games can be examined in strategic form (sometimes referred to as normal form) or extensive form. The extensive form is a tree diagram representation of a game with each branch illustrating alternate strategies. The strategic form is the tabular representation of the extensive form. This tabular form is referred to as the pay off matrix and displays the payoff of a given player under different strategies.

214

The two forms of games studied in game theory are cooperative and non-cooperative. In general a cooperative game is one where there is a binding pre-game contract between the players, which a non-cooperative game does not have. Thus, non-cooperative games restrict pre-play communication such as sharing payoffs. Solutions concepts in non-cooperative games are related to nash equilibrium, which states that each agent chooses that strategy that maximizes expected pay-off given the strategy of the other agent. Generally, nash equilibrium can be thought of as a rest point in games. Co-operative games permit complete freedom of pre-play communication. Solution concepts in cooperative games are referred to as the core, which can be viewed as an extension of nash equilibrium.

Zero sum games are the simplest games to analyse in games theory, because the interests of the agents are diametrical. Thus the game consists of strategies whose cost to one agent equals the benefit to the other agent. A particularly noteworthy feature of game theory is that solution concepts are not always consistent with intuition. A simple example of this can be observed by examining the payoff matrix of the 'prisoner's dilemma'.

	B Cooperates	B Defects
A Cooperates	1,1	4,0
A Defects	0,4	3,3

Assume we have two players, A and B, and their interests are only partially in conflict. Their strategies are to cooperate or to defect. In the original story, A and B were two prisoners

who were jointly involved in a crime. They could cooperate with each other and refuse to give evidence, or one could defect and implicate the other. The first entry in each cell is the prison term for agent A and the second entry is the prison term for agent B. Since the players cannot collude, they must maximize their strategy given the strategy of the other player. By applying an iterative process to the decision making process it becomes evident that under these circumstances both players will always choose to defect. Intuitively we would like to argue that both players cooperating would be the only reasonable strategy, but upon careful examination it is evident that this is not the case. Agent A is aware that agent B will always choose to defect (this is referred to as a dominant strategy), because under either of A's strategies, B's choice of defection will always lead to a lighter term. Knowing that B will always defect, the optimal strategy for A is also to defect. As a result the solution to this game is for both players to defect. This is often used to illustrate how individual behaviour can lead to an overall solution which is less beneficial for the mass. The optimum solution would have been possible only with collusion.

Applications of game theory are used in many branches of economics, in particular for the study of market conditions such as **oligopoly**, where issues such as collusion, pricing strategy, and pay-off in terms of market share are crucial. It can also help in understanding resource allocation in areas such as welfare economics.

215

GDP/GNP Gross national product and gross domestic product are the thumbnail sketch measures of 'how a country is doing' – the flow of wealth, but not the absolute wealth, of an economy. They are the measures usually used for comparison of different economies, or for comparison of the same economy from one year to another. Measured on a per capita basis, they give a rough guide to living standards within the country.

Strictly defined, gross national product (GNP) is the expenditure necessary to purchase the total output of a country's nationals regardless of the location of their activity. In theory that should be the same as the income of *all* nationals, even though they may have earned it abroad. This is measured in the income method of calculating GNP (see below). What is subtracted is the income of foreigners earned within the country.

The gross domestic product (GDP) accounts for all production, income or expenditure of a country's residents. The criterion upon which GDP is based is residence, while in the case of the GNP it is nationality. So, in GDP we count the income earned by foreigners domestically, but not any income that is earned abroad.

The structure of GNP/GDP is the subject of national accounting. If we subtract the total depreciation of the economy's capital stock from GNP/GDP, we get the net national/domestic product. The depreciation accounts for both wear-and-tear as well as for any devaluation of the economy's capital stock. If, furthermore, we subtract the total indirect business taxes (Ti) we arrive at an aggregate called national income (Y)

which is composed of the disposable income (Yd) and total direct taxation (T). The components of the disposable income are:

- consumption;
- investment;
- government expenditure (i.e. government consumption plus government investment);
- net exports (i.e. exports minus imports, called also balance of trade).

The aggregate measures above may be reported either at current prices, or at constant prices with respect to a base year of reference. To fend off the inflationary effects on the measurement of GNP/GDP, statisticians have devised an index called the 'GNP/GDP deflator'. Its use will turn GNP/GDP from a nominal to a real measure of the country's total economic activity.

In the measurement of GNP/GDP, only the value of all final products is included. Final products are those that cross the ridgeline of production – i.e. they are oriented towards (private or public) consumption or investment, either domestically or abroad. All other goods and services that remain inside the borders of production are called intermediate products, and do not count in the estimation of the country's GNP/GDP. In this way it is possible to avoid double-counting, because a product which is an output by one firm or entity (say, steel in the car-making process) will be an input into the next (actual car assembly). The price of the final car is said to reflect the total **value added** throughout the production process.

Whilst the GNP/GDP may be considered a rough aggregate measure of a country's wealth and welfare, we should note some important reservations. First, GNP/GDP cannot include any reference to the total quality of a country's environment and of course it does not account for the deterioration of it. It does not include the informal sector or even any illegal business activities (collectively known also as the **black economy**). Nor does it include certain payments which are termed 'socially implicit', e.g. the work of parents, carers, etc.

In theory the GNP/GDP numbers can be derived by measuring output, income, or expenditure, since according to the **circular flow of national income**, they will all be equal. In practice there will usually be some level of deviation, and the measurement of output is generally regarded as the most accurate.

GEARING (US = leveraging) Gearing is the relationship of a company's **share** or equity **capital** to its long-term **debt** or loan capital. Companies can raise funds by issuing shares or by creating debentures, which represent long-term debt. The shareholder owns part of the company, and has to take a risk on whether a **dividend** will be paid on the shares. A debenture holder will be a creditor, with no ownership rights, receiving a fixed rate of **interest**. (In general, companies prefer to use share issues or debentures than bank loans or overdrafts to raise long-term capital, as the interest payments are lower.)

There are various possible definitions: one is the market value of fixed-interest debt divided by the market value of share capital. A company with more debt to equity is highly geared (highly leveraged), while one with more equity is low-geared. Neither is necessarily better, and much depends on the prevailing trading conditions and interest rates. The important point about debt interest is that it must be paid before any dividends are distributed. Clearly, if trading conditions are good, and the interest on the loans is relatively low, there could be plenty left over for dividends. But if trading conditions turn down, financing the debt could rule out the possibility of any dividends and may even send the company into liquidation. In general, companies in sectors where profits tend to be predictable and reliable over a number of years can afford to be more highly geared than those in more volatile sectors.

What makes a company choose higher or lower gearing? Partly it is the cost, and economists are divided about the most efficient capital structure. Some believe that when a firm is small, high gearing reduces the risk to investors (interest is paid first), making it easier (cheaper) to raise funds by issuing loan stock. As the firm gets larger it will not want to be burdened by excessive debt payments, and may want to reduce its gearing. This view was challenged by two American economists, Franco **Modigliani** and Merton Miller, who argued that the gearing of companies in the same sort of business with the same sort of risk will tend to reach equilibrium because investors will seek out the best return. The truth is that gearing is not simply a matter of cost and accountancy. The difference between debentures and shares is that the latter represents a dilution of the ownership and control of a company. Some firms – even publicly quoted ones – are more reluctant than others to allow control and ownership to spread to the widest base.

(*See also* **junk bonds**.)

GIFFEN GOOD   A Giffen good can be described as an extreme type of inferior good, which behaves in the opposite way from a normal good, in that a fall in its price will mean that less is consumed. In technical terms this is because the negative income effect more than outweighs the substitution effect.

Suppose that the price of a normal good X fell relative to another good, Y. Two things are happening: a substitution effect and an income effect. The substitution effect is that the consumer will now move to favour his purchases of X rather than Y, by moving along his indifference curve from C to C_1. His budget line will have shifted its gradient to reflect the difference in relative prices.

But the consumer now has more income – or income left over: he can,

if he wants to, buy more of both X and Y, because his total bill for the two has fallen. We reflect this income effect by a shift in the budget line to the right, still showing the new relative prices. The consumer moves to C_2. Suppose X were an inferior good. This means that as its price falls (or as incomes rise) its consumption will rise only slightly as people switch to better substitutes. The income effect is negative: although we have moved to another budget line and indifference curve, C_3, and the consumer will end up buying less of X than he would do if X were a normal good (which took us to C_2). But in this case the substitution effect (the change in relative prices between X and Y) means that the consumer is still buying slightly more of the inferior good than before the price fell. But if X were a Giffen good, the negative income effect (i.e. the move to C_4) after the price cut would be greater than the substitution effect (the shift from C to C_1), meaning that consumption of Giffen X would fall.

Does this bizarre phenomenon happen in real life? The Giffen good is named after Sir Robert Giffen,

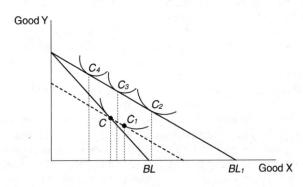

Giffen good

218

an economist who studied potato consumption in nineteenth century Ireland. He argued that a big fall in potato prices actually encouraged people to rely on them less as a staple of their diets, because more money was freed up to buy better substitutes.

GINI COEFFICIENT Mathematically the gini coefficient is a measure showing the degree of inequality in a frequency distribution: in other words, it is a way of characterizing inequality. Frequently it is used to show the **concentration** of companies or economic entities involved in certain aspects of production. It works alongside the **Lorenz Curve** to provide a mathematical way to define concentration by looking at key variables such as the number of people employed, or the output, of certain firms in certain industries as a measure of how concentrated the economic activity is. It provides a summary measure of the extent to which the Lorenz Curve for a particular market deviates from the linear diagonal.

Gini coefficient =

$$\frac{\text{area between Lorenz Curve and } 45° \text{ line}}{\text{area above the } 45° \text{ line}}$$

Alternatively,

gini coefficient =

$$\frac{\Omega \text{ expected absolute difference in a given parameter from two agents}}{\text{Mean value of given parameter}}$$

The first equation can be used directly with the Lorenz Curve to measure the degree of concentration in a given market. The diagram below illustrates how this can be done. The 45° line represents perfect equality. So in the example given, the top 10 per cent of firms supply 10 per cent of employment and the top 20 per cent of firms supply 20 per cent of employment. This linear relationship between the proportion of firms and proportion of employment represents perfect equality. The actual data observed from a census supply the information for the Lorenz Curve. Here we may

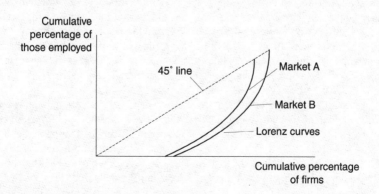

The gini coefficient

actually observe that a large number of small firms supply a little amount of labour, while a small number of large firms supply an ample amount of employment. The degree of this concentration in large firms is measured by the curvature, and the disparity between this concentration and perfect equality is captured in the gini coefficient.

The greater the curvature in the Lorenz Curve, the greater the inequality. This in turn implies that a lower gini coefficient indicates a tendency towards an equal structure, while a larger gini coefficient indicates inequality in the sense of a greater degree of concentration in the market. Thus, in the diagram, market A is more equally spread than market B: the degree of concentration is less and hence market A has a lower gini coefficient. The graphical interpretation is that the curve for market A has less curvature than the curve for market B.

The gini coefficient can also be applied to measure the degree of concentration in other variables. For example, if X represents the consumption of an individual, then the gini coefficient can be computed as half the expected absolute difference in the consumption of any two random individuals in the economy, measured as a proportion of the mean consumption in the economy. Here again, the lower the value of the gini coefficient, the more equal the distribution in the market.

GOLD STANDARD This is the system where countries pegged their currencies – and their **money supply** – to the stocks of gold they held. Gold was the international means of denominating monetary flows from trade between countries. The system was in operation from the nineteenth century to the early 1930s. If a country ran a **balance of payments** deficit – more imports than exports – gold flowed out of the country to pay for the imports, requiring the government to issue fewer coins and notes. This reduction in the money supply theoretically forced prices down. The lower costs of production made the country's exports cheaper; it also made imports seem more expensive, thus tending to even out the deficit. The same process worked in the opposite way for a balance of payments surplus.

The difficulty was that domestic **monetary policy** was subsumed to international trading movements, although governments still had flexibility over **fiscal policy**. But the role of fiscal policy and demand management was not recognised until the works of **Keynes**, after the gold standard had been abandoned. The gold standard was in one sense an early form of international **monetarism**.

After some years of confusion, the world adopted a fixed exchange rate regime known as the **Bretton Woods system**, which has now been replaced by mostly **floating exchange rates**. (*See* **exchange rate policy**.)

GOVERNANCE Governance refers to the act or manner of governing a company. Many of the processes of governance are stipulated by law, although a large portion of them are conventions developed for those with an interest in the company. The usual elements comprising the governance of a company include the governing body of the board of directors, an annual general meeting where interested parties (including the shareholders) attend to receive the annual report, and the chairman's address.

The board of directors, which is effectively the management of a limited company, is comprised of members elected by the shareholders to serve their interests in making decisions regarding strategy and appointments in the company. In practice it is not unusual for the board in some companies to become something of a self-elected oligarchy. Vacancies are filled as they arise by people chosen primarily by the board, and under most circumstances it is unusual for there to be an upset in electing a particular individual to the board. The only instance where changes occur would be a major revolt among the members of the board of directors.

Holding an annual general meeting is common practice, even when a company is not legally obliged to hold one. It is the responsibility of those running the organization to give an account of management's activities and dealings since the previous meeting. Other topics discussed are the annual report, appointments and **dividends**. Limited companies are required by law to hold an annual general meeting within 15 months (no more than 18 months for newly appointed limited companies). They must notify shareholders in advance and specify the meeting as an annual general meeting. Shareholders may attend or send individuals as proxies to vote on relevant issues concerning the firm.

The annual report, which is distributed at the annual general meeting, is a report which contains relevant accounting documents relating to the affairs of the company. These include the company's balance sheet, profit and loss account, as well as cash flow statement. The annual report also includes the chairman's report, which gives an account of the general position of the firm and its future prospects.

One of the problems of modern large companies is what is the 'principal–agent problem', sometimes known as the divorce of ownership from control. The principal (owner or shareholder) will generally want to maximize profits; his or her agent (the management) may have other additional, or perhaps contradictory, aims, such as maximisation of assets, sales, or benefits. (For a fuller discussion, *see* **management theories of the firm**.) The proper exercise of corporate governance should provide some safeguards and checks for this divergence, especially via the AGM and annual report.

Ideally, corporate governance should also take into account the many different classes of individuals with an interest in the company: the stakeholders. Stakeholders are anyone with an interest or stake in the operations and performance of a firm. This goes further than just the shareholders. It would include the managers, but would also take in employees, customers and the community. Employees have an interest in the firm as it provides them with a job and an income. Customers rely on the firm to provide a stable product while the community depends on the firm to do its part as a 'responsible citizen' in the community. There may be quite tangible benefits for companies which are seen to have systems for reporting to and taking account of their stakeholders: today's management theories and emphasis on relationship marketing underscore the advantages, in PR as well as customer and employee loyalties. (*See* essays by Robert Beynon and Adrian Payne/Sue Holt.)

GRESHAM'S LAW Gresham's Law is that 'bad money drives out the good' in an economy. It applies to economies where the medium of exchange has a value in its own right – for example, it might contain precious metals like gold or silver. The law observes that if two coins are in circulation and their face value or redemption value differ from their relative bullion content, the more 'valuable' coin will cease circulating in the economy. In other words, people will 'hoard' the coin with more intrinsic value.

To illustrate Gresham's Law it's worth examining the development of **money**. Before paper money was introduced, governments used precious metals such as gold and silver as a means of exchange. Generally, these metals were a more efficient means of trade, in comparison to the barter system (which required a matching of the goods being traded). The face value or redemption value of these precious tokens was equivalent to their metal content, so they had an intrinsic value. With the expansion of economies and increased trade, the demand for precious metals increased. In order to accommodate this increased demand, governments debased the tokens of exchange. This was done by keeping the face value of the coins unchanged, but reducing their metal content. Essentially, the coins had the same value in the economy, yet their lower metal content meant that more of the coins could circulate. People tended to collect the 'good' old money with the higher metal content, leaving the bad, debased metals to circulate in the system. This was a form of insurance: if consumer confidence in the monetary system failed, the debased coins could easily drop in value (*see* **inflation**). People who saved the good money could protect themselves because the face value of the undebased coins was equivalent to their metal content.

Sir Thomas Gresham (1519–79), who first articulated the law, was a leading businessman and financial advisor to Queen Elizabeth I. His theorem applies also to any other medium of exchange where the relative market value of one outweighs the other, whatever their official rates. So the currency of a very poor country may be officially 'fixed' at a certain rate to, say, the US dollar, but the market (usually the illegal black market) will value the US dollar much more highly. Dollars will therefore be hoarded because they have a value which exceeds their official, or 'face', value against the local currency.

H

HARROD-DOMAR GROWTH MODEL
A theory of economic growth which
suggests that there is no reason why
an economy should grow at a stable
rate with full employment. In a sense
it is therefore similar to the notion –
put forward by **Keynes** that there is no
reason why an economy should find
an equilibrium level of output at full
employment. The Harrod-Domar
growth model was introduced by the
British economists Harrod and
Domar, working largely independently. The model introduces three
separate concepts for growth in an
economy:

- natural growth is the rate at which
  an economy will need to grow to
  ensure full employment, and is a
  function of the growth in the
  working population and technological progress which brings about
  higher productivity;
- warranted growth is the rate at
  which investment will grow, and
  that will depend on the rate of
  savings and the capital–output
  ratio (both dependent on the level
  of output itself);
- actual growth is the growth level
  which happens in reality.

Let's take a closer look at what goes
into creating warranted growth. We
are defining the warranted growth
rate as the level at which savings are
equal to investment (Keynesian theory
arguing that the size of the withdrawal – savings – would equal the
injection – investment). To simplify
matters, let us assume a constant rate
of capital investment and a constant
propensity to save. The warranted
growth rate will therefore be the one
at which the capital–output ratio
creates a level of growth which in turn
provides a level of savings which
equals the investment called for (or
warranted) by the capital output ratio.
So if the warranted growth rate is w,
propensity to save = capital output
ratio $\times w$

$$\text{or } w = \frac{\text{propensity to save}}{\text{capital output ratio}}$$

Clearly this might coincide with the
natural rate of growth – full employment is maintained, and actual
growth, warranted growth and
natural growth will be the same. But
there's no reason in the model to
assume that it will coincide in this
way. If the natural growth rate is
higher than the warranted level,
fewer of the labour force will be employed, and the economy will move
into a recession. If the warranted rate
is higher than the natural rate,
resources, particularly labour, will be
quickly exhausted, with **inflationary**
results.

Note that the model has natural

growth as a function of two exogenous variables, population and technology, and the two factors which can vary warranted growth – the capital–output ratio and the propensity to save – are assumed to be constant. The result will be varying business cycles.

The model has been criticized for assuming that the exogenous variables do not change with changes in output: technology and productivity might expand more quickly in a steadily growing economy; alternatively the cost of labour may well fall in a recessionary period, allowing the natural rate of growth to be reduced. Similarly, the capital–output ratio for investment assumes a that capital investment will always be a fixed proportion of output, and that savings will also always be fixed as a proportion of income: either ratio could change due to changes in expectations, tastes, etc., which would directly affect warranted growth. In particular, if the cost of labour is allowed to vary, it will vary relative to the cost of capital, which could have a major impact on capital spending.

The Harrod-Domar growth model is worth contrasting with the **Solow growth model**, in which technological changes are seen as a major factor in maintaining full-employment growth.

HECKSCHER-OHLIN FACTOR PROPORTIONS THEORY This is a development of the theory of **comparative advantage** in international trade, proposed by two Swedish economists, from whom it derives its name. It examines the nature of advantage based on differences in endowments of **factors of production**, and suggests that countries where one factor (say labour) is relatively cheaper will benefit from trade with another country where another factor (say capital) is relatively cheaper.

In other words, a country (A) which can cheaply make simple labour-intensive goods (e.g. bicycles) will benefit from trading with another country (B) which is better endowed with capital, and may be better at making complex computers. The theory can be developed to show that in conditions of free trade, the inequalities in the cost of the different factors will be levelled by the action of supply and demand. So the extra demand from trade of bicycle exports will tend to raise the price of labour in A, whilst the extra demand for computers from B will inflate its capital prices.

The difficulty is that the theory is too simplistic, not taking into account, for example, different rates of technology, education, **infrastructure**, and macroeconomic conditions. There are also issues which affect **demand** for specific goods in trading countries, such as product differentiation, taste, fashion, etc. Empirical tests were carried out by the economist Leontief. His studies of US trade in the 1950s found that exports from the (generally capital-intensive) United States were in fact labour intensive, and that imports were the opposite. This became known as the 'Leontief paradox'.

The factor proportions theory may not be wrong, but it is important to understand that it is only one element in the reality of international trade.

HICKS, JOHN RICHARD (1904–89) British economist who contributed significantly to both micro- and macroeconomic theory. He developed the theory of indifference curves as a measure of ordinal (i.e. comparable) utility, using it to refine the **neo-Classical theory of consumer demand**. But he is best known for his **IS/LM** model, in which he tried to reconcile the workings of the 'real' economy as expounded by **Keynes**, and the 'money' economy of the neo-Classicals and later the **monetarists**. The aim of non-Keynesians was to achieve the so-called 'neo-Classical synthesis', in which Keynesian non full-employment equilibrium could be argued to be an anomaly created by wage stickiness, or a liquidity trap. Hicks's model did not succeed in the synthesis (arguably because it merely boils down to a question of definitions), but his IS/LM model is still used as a primary tool for understanding the workings of the macroeconomy.

HOT MONEY This is the generic term for short-term flows of money around the international capital markets, particularly in foreign currency. Usually it reflects money flows for arbitrage, or for hedging against foreign currency or **interest rate** exposure. The financial markets exist to find profitable opportunities caused by short-term imperfections in the markets (arbitrage), as well as to manage risk for their clients. The highly sophisticated guessing games they operate involve expectations not just about future currency levels, but about interest rates and many other economic fundamentals (growth, **inflation**, productivity, etc.). Frequently they will buy forward as well as spot, and they might use complex **derivatives** to spread risk and in some cases turn a good profit.

The volume of short-term money flows across the international exchanges has never been greater, because of the process of deregulation over the past few decades. It is many times greater than the flows required for purchasing foreign exchange to buy goods and services. This can make the operation of any **exchange rate policy** difficult, and it is why most governments now opt for 'managed floating' rates (known as a dirty float). This allows **central banks** to go some way to smoothing out the daily fluctuations from hot money flows, whilst allowing the markets to determine the longer-term rates.

I

IMF The International Monetary Fund was born out of the international conference at **Bretton Woods** in New Hampshire in 1944 which established fixed currency exchange rates, based on the US dollar and US gold reserves. Its role was to maintain currency stability and develop world trade. With the collapse of fixed exchange rates in the 1970s, and the economic troubles of several developing economies over the past few decades, the IMF, with its sister organization the World Bank, has developed into a more broad-based global economic entity, part policeman and part counsellor.

The IMF is a United Nations organization whose aims include the promotion of international monetary cooperation, to stabilize currencies, and to balance the expansion of world trade. It also has extensive funds which can be made available, especially to big-debtor countries, mainly through the operation of special drawing rights. These are supported by the creditor countries according to various criteria including the relative size of their exports. The IMF has also provided various kinds of ad-hoc support and advice to countries with specific difficulties. Its support is often conditional on its economic reform strictures being followed. This has discouraged certain governments from approaching the IMF.

The IMF also provides an international forum for regular discussions on development and the international economic scene. In this its aim is to establish some level of consistency in global economic policymaking.

(*See* **fixed/floating exchange rates**, essays by Neil Mackinnon and Jeremy Pink.)

INFLATION Inflation is a continuous increase in the price level, or a continuous fall in the value of money. Economists measure inflation using statistical indices such as the Consumer Price Index (CPI), the Producer Price Index (PPI), or the GNP deflator. Each of them refers to a standard basket of goods representative of the whole economy.

In general and social terms inflation is one of the great economic 'evils' – sometimes counterpointed against the other economic evil of unemployment, and sometimes occurring simultaneously (see below). The implications for a nation of its money becoming worth less over time are easy to see; it is not hard either to extrapolate that beyond a certain level of (hyper) inflation a country will become almost impossible to govern, and indeed there are many empirical historical examples of this. The fact that many of the poorest in society are on fixed incomes – often retirement dividends or pensions – implies that inflation is also regressive in its consequences, a fact that has led many governments routinely to index welfare benefits and pensions. That in itself has important implications for **fiscal policy**, especially if, as is the case with many of today's industrialized economies, the population is ageing.

Inflation as a monetary phenomenon has occurred in many historical periods. Alexander the Great's conquest of Persia (330 BC) is known to have triggered inflation. Under the Emperor Diocletian (c. AD 300) the Roman Empire experienced explosive inflation.

In modern times, some prime examples of extreme rates of inflation are:

- the Great Depression of the 1930s;
- the hyperinflation which affected some of the European economies during the interwar and post-war years (hardest hit were Germany, Italy and Greece); and in China after the fall of the Nationalist regime (1948–49);
- persistent hyperinflation in most of the Latin American countries and Israel during 1970s and 1980s;
- the double-digit inflation rates accompanied by stagnation that hit almost all industrialized countries following the two oil crises of the 1970s. This was called **stagflation**;
- the Eastern European countries during the post-1989 era with their economies in transition towards a market system suffered from significant and in many cases rampant inflation rates.

The causes and effects of inflation have always been the subject of major debate in the literature of economic theory. A distinction can be drawn between *expected* or *anticipated* inflation, and *unexpected* inflation. The two have significantly different sources and effects.

For expected inflation, there are few disagreements about the effects on the nominal variables of wage rates and market interest rates: they will increase by the same proportion as the price level. At the same time there will be greater pressure for the domestic currency to depreciate. There is disagreement, however, about the impact on the rate of growth of the economy as a whole.

One school of thought, which is associated with the work of Mundell and Tobin (1963–65), suggests that expected inflation will stimulate growth. A higher rate of inflation increases the **opportunity cost** of holding money (the value of which will be reduced), which in turn prompts a higher demand for capital goods and a lower demand for money. Companies increase their physical holdings of capital, so increasing the capital–labour ratio (making industry more **capital intensive**), and leading to a higher level of output. An increase in the expected inflation rate therefore, would stimulate growth for the economy. The mechanism is known as the Mundell-Tobin effect.

Another approach is known as the 'overlapping generations model', which argues that expected inflation will reduce growth in the economy. This model is the work of both Samuelson (1958) and Clower (1967). Economic analysis based on the concept of overlapping generations points to the fact that new households are continuously entering economic activity, while others are 'dying'. In this case, an increase in inflation leads to a decrease in the demand for money holdings (just as we saw in Mundell-Tobin). This prompts people to decrease their savings and trade at a lower level with the following generation (i.e. new households). Clower's model has an implication that all transaction costs increase due to expected inflation (i.e. prices will be raised purely in anticipation of higher inflation) – so again there is a lower level of activity. So clearly output will decrease and growth will decelerate if inflation increases the **money supply**.

The third possibility, advanced by the economist Sidrauski among others, is that inflation has no real impact on growth. (this is sometimes referred to as money being 'superneutral'). Fundamentally, the argument is that inflation will not necessarily impact on **interest rates**, so capital and therefore output remain unaffected by what happens to the rate of inflation. A variation of the super-neutrality position is the 'natural rate hypothesis'. This was advocated by the famous **monetarists** Milton Friedman and E. Phelps (1968). Their position is that there is a level of unemployment which is independent of the rate of anticipated inflation. (*See* **Phillips Curve, Expectations-adjusted Phillips Curve**.)

Broadly, the empirical evidence tends to favour the view that expected inflation either negatively affects growth, or else that money is super-neutral and that it may have no direct impact.

Turning to unexpected inflation, it is in some ways easier to identify what causes various economic effects. Empirical studies of business cycles indicate that unexpected inflation will tend to increase real incomes. Furthermore, as incomes rise, money growth increases, and/or the velocity with which money circulates in the economy will rise. The difficulties lie with working out how changes on the monetary side of the economy (say, a growth in **money supply** or an increase in the velocity of circulation) affect the 'real' economy (i.e. output, income and spending). (*See* **IS/LM**.)

This problem is at the root of the debate among economists about unexpected inflation, and in particular about when boom turn to slump, or when does recovery begin at the end of recession. What's known is that a business cycle exists in most developed countries: the question is what drives the inflation associated with it.

Perhaps the best-known body of theory comes from **Keynes**. The Keynesian approach to business cycles and inflation emphasizes the importance of demand, arguing that fluctuations in investment demand, government spending and private consumption will cause output variations and smaller price level effects. But Keynesians go on to argue that eventually wages and prices will adjust fully to the changes in demand. Output may deviate from its full-employment level and will be positively correlated with inflation (demand-pull inflation).

Movements of the price level due to changes in the cost of resources bring about the phenomenon of cost-push inflation (often at times of industrial and social unrest). Cost increases may push the prevailing wage rate, which may be perceived as a 'safety' mechanism by workers (i.e. with an expectation of inflation, there will be increasing demands for higher wages). This phenomenon was observed during the 1970s period of stagflation when growth levels were low. In general, the Keynesian tradition explicity recognizes inflation as being related to the demand side of the economy. It argues that crises (either inflationary or recessionary) are a common feature of the market system and that governments should first and foremost try to address and smooth their consequences.

Another perspective is that of the **neo-Classical** school, which grew out of the monetarist tradition. The neo-Classicals eschew the idea of Keynesian demand management. They argue that if people hold 'rational expectations', the economy will settle at an equilibrium level which relates to the natural rate of unemployment. Inflation occurs because people suffer from a lack of information about prices, and the confusion which occurs will often add to inflation in the short term. Nonetheless, any attempt by the government or **central bank** to manage **monetary policy** will add to the confusion. (In this regard they differ from the mainstream monetarists such as Friedman.) For the neo-Classicals, productive efficiency (i.e. elimination of inflation) should be the primary concern of any policy maker.

The third school of thought is embraced by those who look exclusively to **supply-side** influences, and is known as the theory of real business cycles. Technological shocks are seen as affecting aggregate production, or even specific sectors of the economy (thus the moves and pressures originate from the 'real', rather than the monetary side of the economy – hence the name). These shocks tend to lower prices but also produce a rise in the overall quantity of money and **credit**. Empirical evidence to support the real business cycles theory has been limited, although the technique of 'calibration' (which is widely used in **econometrics**) has been used to examine the effect of some of the variables.

The problem of inflation, from the perspective of an 'open' or internationally trading economy, raises a host of separate issues. Inflation has a direct effect on international capital market transactions and the international trade balance. The prevailing foreign **exchange rate** regime also has an important influence on a country's inflation performance. Fixed exchange rates underscore the limited power of domestic monetary policy. Therefore, an increase in the rate of growth of money supply, which might be expected to devalue the currency, might under fixed rates require tighter monetary policy, or else cause strains within the system as a whole – which may be only temporarily offset by intervention from central banks. Some argue that it was inflation that eventually brought about the collapse of the **Bretton Woods** fixed exchange rate system.

Under flexible or floating exchange rates, however, the problem of inflation becomes even more acute and complex. The forecasting of price levels, or future movements of the exchange rate is a stern task under such a regime. (For a fuller analysis, *see* **exchange rate policy**.)

The most commonly suggested policies to combat inflation have been restrictive **monetary policy** and increased control of **wages** and **prices**. Income policies were suggested as well by the Keynesian side. For extreme cases of hyperinflation a coordination of monetary and fiscal policy can bring an end to the crisis.

Furthermore, post-Keynesians and neo-Classicals emphasize changes in institutional arrangements (supply-side changes, or changes in the way that financial markets operate) – although of course they don't agree on which institutional changes are a priority.

Whilst the problem of inflation continues to challenge economists, improved mathematical modelling techniques, coupled with a gradual improvement in statistical reliability, can be expected to advance the debate considerably during the next decade. Nothing underpins the urgency of such research more than the severe social and political problems which are associated with inflation, although recently a 'golden scenario' has emerged in which inflation in many of the major capitalist economies has become less of a problem than, say, unemployment. It is an open question whether this will continue, and what its implications are to economic theory.

INFRASTRUCTURE / SOCIAL COSTS
Infrastructure (sometimes referred to as social capital or social overhead capital) is the public or social accumulation of capital in an economy. Specifically, it refers to roads, rail-ways, housing, hospitals, schools and other stocks of social capital accumulated from **investment** usually by government, either currently or from earlier periods. Infrastructure also includes intangible items such as an educated or trained labour force, created by investment in 'human capital'. Economically speaking, human capital is the body of human knowledge that contributes the 'know how' to productive activity.

Government spending on infrastructure represents an injection into the **circular flow of national income**, and as such would have a **multiplier** effect, helping to reflate the economy during a period of recession according to the rules of **Keynesian** demand management. Therefore, like other injections, it can be **inflationary** during certain periods in the **business cycle**. Such infrastructure spending was a key part of the New Deal policies to expand the US economy during the Depression of the 1930s, where it was known as spending on 'public works'. Sometimes governments seek to acquire private sector partners in the development of infrastructure, or even to hand over entire projects to companies. (The period of railway building during the nineteenth century was very largely privately financed.) For governments this can be a means to reduce a **budget deficit** while at the same time improving the stock of social capital. Private sector spending on infrastructure is still an injection into the circular flow, and private projects would therefore carry the same multiplier and inflationary or pump-priming potential as would government spending.

Infrastructure is a basic ingredient of economic development, as improvements in the social capital can help attract industry to disadvantaged areas of the economy. Furthermore, a certain basic level of infrastructure will ususally be required for a country as a whole to be attractive for inward invetsment. For this reason, much of development loans and grants (*see* **IMF**) will be directed toward the improvement of infrastructure in less developed economies.

INSIDER TRADING   Insider trading is the buying and selling of **securities** (or any other financial instrument) on the basis of non-public information about the strategies and activities of a corporation (or economy or commodity). Although in theory the price of a security is defined as the present value of all its future income streams, in practice the driving force behind security prices is investor expectations. Thus, fluctuations in investors' expectations of the performance of a corporation are the primary cause of fluctuations in the corporation's security prices. Consequently, having advance knowledge of strategies or events that are likely to affect investors' expectations in the market can be used for profit.

Because such information is necessarily restricted, its use represents an unfair advantage and therefore, any trading based on such privileged information is illegal in regulated exchanges. If accused of insider trading and found guilty, investors are fined heavily and under certain conditions may be imprisoned.

Under the UK Companies Act of 1980 it is illegal for anybody to deal in shares if he or she has access to confidential price sensitive information not available to the other side of the bargain. What is confidential, and how it is to be proved, however, is quite a significant dilemma. Auditors and company brokers are already precluded by their organizations from dealing in transactions that involve client company shares.

To give an example of the difficulty of the scale of insider trading, one simply can observe the large jumps in share prices days before the announcement of a merger or takeover. The jumps in share prices indicate that there are people with privileged information taking advantage of the situation before the announcement is made public. Even with this indication of the existence of insider trading, it is rarely possible to prove that an investor is trading on inside information. The investor may simply be following the market, or the rumours in the market. Although proving that an investor has been involved in insider trading is not a simple task, most exchanges have regulators to monitor unusual transactions, who often use complex computer programs to investigate insider trading.

It is of course very harmful to a **stock market**, or any financial market, to have a reputation of being less than tough about such a corrupt practice. And with the greater deregulation of financial markets internationally, the need for careful monitoring will increase. There were days when the regulator virtually knew everyone in the market: today's minimal restrictions on global capital flows mean that knowing who is in the market, and where they receive their information, is almost impossible. So the modern technology of tracking how prices move is the best way to start the detective work.

INSTITUTIONAL INVESTORS Institutional investors are the large groups of investors who own approximately three-quarters of all quoted **securities** on the world's **stock markets**. They are primarily organizations, as opposed to individual investors, and invest their funds for the clients they represent. The most typical institutional investors include insurance companies, investment and **unit trusts**, and pension funds.

The defining characteristic among these different companies is that they have access to large sources of funds that have been entrusted by a broad base of individual clients. Some of these clients want to save for some time in the future (pension funds), while others may be protecting themselves from uncertain events that may arise in the future (insurance companies). Essentially the moneys deposited cannot be withdrawn easily (usually a penalty is incurred for early withdrawal), so the institutions can put the money to more active use by investing in securities.

Historically, institutional investors sought investment advice from stockbrokers or **merchant (investment) banks**. Many companies now employ their own analysts. Because of the size of their holdings, institutional investors can influence both stock market sentiment and corporate policy. Their purchases of securities may dramatically effect share prices as particular stocks increase in attractiveness to

other less informed investors in the stock market. In this way market sentiment is influenced by the behaviour of institutional investors, rather than the actual performance of the company. Similarly, because institutional investors can build up significant holdings in a company, they are able to affect corporate policy by expressing their concerns at shareholder meetings, in some cases even taking over effective control of a company. Some critics argue that this has tended to encourage a short-term approach, with institutions seeking to maximize their immediate gains at the expense of longer-term strategies. On the other hand, the requirement for institutions to improve shareholder value has in some cases encouraged them to adopt a more rigorous approach to the performance of existing management than might be the case with private shareholders. The process may be helped by their use of their own in-house market experts. (*See* **management theories of the firm**, and the essay 'Changing Trends in Management' by Robert Beynon.)

INTEGRATION Integration refers to strategies by companies to add either economies of scope or **economies of scale** to production capabilities. This is achieved by taking over a number of successive stages in the supply of a product, or by merging with a number of similar firms in a particular stage of production.

Vertical integration creates economies of scope through the control of a number of stages in the production process. The company will be able to reduce its long-term average costs by coordinating and sharing some of the inputs to production. For example, the firm can run its inventories for various stages of production in the most efficient way, not being required to wait for suppliers, and perhaps operating a **just in time** system of production. It can coordinate the design and packaging so that an input can more easily become an output in the next stage of production (so that, for example, a car manufacturer which also owns a steelmaking business would ensure that its steel outputs would be produced in exactly the right size, shape and other technical specifications to become the inputs to the process of making car bodies). Often vertical integration will allow economies of scale, for example through large-scale buying. By centralizing the purchase of, say, electricity, transport, or warehousing, the firm will probably be able to pay a lower unit cost than if it were only concerned with one level of the production and needed much smaller quantities.

'Backward integration' is vertical integration with the firm producing raw materials which were previously supplied to it. An example of backward integration would be our example of the car manufacturer purchasing a steel plant. 'Forward integration' would be the car manufacturer buying retail dealerships or garages. 'Horizontal integration' comes from one firm taking over more of the same stage of production: the car manufacturer merging with another, or taking it over, so as to control a greater slice of the car market. Here, there will usually be economies of scale from larger-scale production, distribution and market-

ing. More importantly, this may allow the firm to have a greater control over price, effectively putting it into an **oligopolistic** or even **monopolistic** position. Companies with a high degree of both vertical and horizontal integration are often able to protect these positions through barriers to entry: for example, by controlling the production of necessary raw materials, or by predatory pricing. Such anti-competitive behaviour might erode any benefits from economies of scope or scale which might otherwise have been passed on to the consumer. (*See* **regulation**.)

INTEREST RATE At its simplest, the interest rate is the price of money. The demand for money and the **money supply** operate together to define the rate at which it is possible to borrow funds. An increase in the money supply, say MS to MS_1, will reduce the rate, and an increase in demand, say from MD to MD_1, will increase the rate. The importance of the interest rate in macroeconomics stems from its use as an instrument of **monetary policy**, to control output, demand, **investment**, and **inflation** in an economy. And it is here, as with so many macroeconomic tools, that there is widespread disagreement about its operation and its effectiveness.

According to **neo-Classical** and **monetarist** thinking, the rate of interest has a strong impact on investment and on consumer spending. It defines the cost of capital for investment, so that high rates of interest may make businesses delay investment whose rate of return does not exceed the cost of borrowing. Its relationship to demand works directly because people regard money (on which they can earn interest) as a substitute for other financial assets or consumer spending. Therefore a low interest rate means people will be inclined to spend more. (Another way to look at this from the monetarist perspective is that an increase in the money supply – and hence a lower rate of interest – will increase people's cash balances, which again will encourage them to spend more). The secondary effect is to make borrowing to finance consumer spending cheaper, again encouraging demand. So for monetarists, interest rates are an important feature of economic behaviour.

Not so, say the followers of **Keynes**. Keynes used the notion of 'liquidity preference' to explain the demand for money. People hold money, he argued, for three reasons: to allow them to buy goods and services (the transactions motive), to have in reserve (the precautionary motive), and to transfer into financial assets such as bonds (the speculative motive). The first two, he argued, are related to the level of income, and therefore are not sensitive to interest rates. The third is based on expectations about **bond** prices, which move inversely to the rate of interest. Therefore a low rate of interest would mean high bond prices, and people would not trouble to hold money to buy bonds in the hope of making a capital gain. A high rate would mean that people would hope bond prices would soon rise, and would hold money. (Keynes also noted the existence of a 'liquidity trap', at which bond prices may be so high that nobody expected them to go any higher, so

that below a certain level of the interest rate no more money would be held.) This all indicates that the demand for money (and therefore the amount supplied) will be highly elastic to the rate of interest, but that general consumer spending will not be (*see* **Keynes – money demand**). Turning to investment, Keynes argued that the rate of interest was much less important than expectations about future demand and income. Thus for Keynes the interest rate was not a powerful macroeconomic tool.

The interest rate is also of importance in **exchange rate policy**, especially now that international capital markets are largely deregulated and money can flow to where the best return exists. Raising or lowering the interest rate can significantly change the rate at which the currency trades against others, and that can be an important element in dealing with a **balance of payments** surplus or deficit. This means that policymakers now have to be aware of both the domestic and the international implications of interest rate changes.

INVESTMENT In economic terms, investment is real capital formation to produce a stream of goods and services for future consumption. (Sometimes 'investment' is taken to mean expenditure on the acquisition of financial **assets**, such as stocks or **bonds**: in general this represents a shift of savings which, though potentially significant in other areas such as **monetary policy**, is a separate discussion from capital formation.) Capital is a **factor of production** which enhances the productivity of other factors (e.g. machines increase the output of labour, or combine harvesters the output of land). The return on capital is sometimes defined as **profit**: the normal profit from any business enterprise, which pays for the risk taken by the entrepreneur by buying (or investing in) capital.

Investment is an injection into the **circular flow of national income**, as opposed to withdrawal in the form of **savings**. Savings provide the means for entrepeneurs to borrow to finance investment, the **interest rate** representing the price of such borrowing. A similar process goes on in the government sector, where **taxation** provides the funding for government spending, some of which is government investment, traditionally in **infrastructure** such as roads, hospitals, or schools. (Some, but not all: governments also consume and make **transfer payments**.) Like all injections, investment carries a **multiplier** effect, each unit of investment increasing the level of output by more than that single unit. Separate from the multiplier is the capital–output ratio, which defines how many units of new capital investment are required to produce one extra unit of national output. (This ratio and its variability are important for predictions of economic growth – see **Harrod-Domar** and **Solow growth models**.)

Investment is also associated with a property that is unique to it in the mechanics of the circular flow: the **accelerator**. The accelerator explains why investment fluctuates more extremely than the general business cycle. Essentially this is because the demand for capital goods will rise or fall in large 'steps', while the firm

using them can increase or decrease its own output more gradually. This accelerator then feeds into the multiplier, so that changes in investment can cause major moves in overall output.

What are the factors which go into the decision about how much investment will be made? This is where we turn to a concept known as the marginal efficiency of investment (sometimes known as the marginal efficiency of capital). It describes the rate of return expected on a given level of investment. If we assume that all investment will be financed by borrowing, or alternatively financed by profits which could earn interest if they were saved (*see* **opportunity cost**), then the cost of capital or investment is defined by the prevailing interest rate. This represents the minimum rate of return that a company will need in order to go ahead with an investment. That said, a company's expectations about future demand will be a major factor in deciding what level to invest at a given rate of interest. If we look at curve II in the diagram, we can see that at a prevailing interest rate of 10 per cent, the firm will invest at X_1, expecting a rate of return of at least 10 per cent. If the interest rate drops to 5 per cent, investment will rise to X_2, which represents a move along curve II. Note that the lowest levels of investment will tend to correspond to higher returns, and higher levels will mean lower percentage profits. This is because a firm will tend to turn first to its most high-yielding – or perhaps most certain – investment projects, only moving to the less certain ones with the lower rates of return once the certain winners have been used up. Thus as interest rates rise, the tendency is for firms to hold back on riskier or least profitable investment projects first. The other important factor is expectations. Suppose that at 10 per cent rate of interest/return, a company was confident that it could sell as much as it made – and more, because it was optimistic about the prospects for the economy. It would now increase its level of investment to X_3, and would make a higher level of investment at any rate of interest/return. So we have shifted to the right from curve II to II_2. Thus the position of the curve shows the level of expectations. Its slope tells us something about the disagreements between **monetarists** and **Keynesians**. Monetarists argue that the rate of interest has a major impact on investment decisions, so their curve will be relatively flat. Keynesians on the other hand argue that expectations are much more significant, so the slope of each of the marginal efficiency of investment curves will be very steep.

Throughout this entry we have taken investment to refer to the acquisition of capital. Stocks and work in progress (inventory investment) are counted in national income accounts as investment, and behave in many respects in a similar way. They represent a stream of goods or services for future consumption, and they have the same accelerator affect as physical capital (all companies tend to run down their stocks in times when they expect sales to be good, while increasing their stocks if they think they will be unable to sell them. Like the accelerator we saw with physical capital, companies can in this case alter their stocks by smaller amounts than they can their production. So aggregate changes in stocks are an important way of gauging future output and demand in the economy, often bringing larger or accelerated changes which then feed into the multiplier).

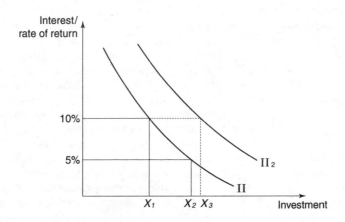

Marginal efficiency of investment

IS/LM This is the theoretical framework devised by the economists **Hicks** and Hansen to bring together the monetary and 'real' parts of the economy, and in a sense to achieve a synthesis of **Keynesian** demand-led 'real' economics with the more **monetarist** approaches of the **neo-Classical** school. It helps provide an elegant tool for understanding the macroeconomy, and is perhaps more effective than the notion of the circular flow at illustrating monetary concepts.

The model plots the rate of interest on the y axis and the national income on the x axis. The *IS* curve shows all the points at which injections and withdrawals are equal. (For the moment, assume a closed economy, with only taxes/government spending and savings/investment. Since taxation and government spending can be exogenous, as they are determined by the government, it is investment and savings which are the key variables, hence the name *IS* curve.) The important point is that this curve shows what needs to happen to the interest rate at various levels of income in order to keep *I* and *S* equal, which is a requirement for the economy to be in equilibrium. It slopes downwards, because at low levels of income, savings will be low, and at high rates of interest, investment will be low too (see **saving**, **investment**, **consumption function**). At higher levels of income, savings increase, and in order to increase investment, interest rates will need to be low.

So anywhere on the *IS* curve could be a point where the 'real' economy is in equilibrium. Anywhere that is not on it will mean that injections and withdrawals are out of step with each other, which will result in either an increase or a decrease in national income.

The other curve, the *LM* curve, (liquidity/money supply), shows the various rates of interest at which the money supply is equal to the demand for money. Since money supply is taken to be an exogenous, government-determined, variable, the curve shows the amount of money which the government will need to supply in order to match the demand for it at various rates of interest. To understand why it slopes upwards let us briefly look at what defines the demand for money. Keynes said that people have three motives for holding money. The first two are transactional, which is the need to have money 'in the pocket' or bank account simply to buy goods and services; and precautionary, which is basically money held 'for a rainy day'. Both of these motives will tend to be stronger as income increases, indicating that the more people are earning, the more money they will be able to keep for transactional and precautionary motives. The third motive operates differently: it is the speculative motive, and represents the money people hold which they might otherwise use to buy financial assets and in particular, bonds. The price to bonds moves inversely with interest rates, so low interest rates mean high prices for bonds. At this point Keynes believed people would hold speculative money because their expectation would be that bond prices would soon fall. Therefore they would not want their money tied up in bonds, but might

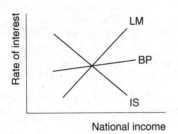

IS/LM model

want to buy bonds when they became cheaper. Similarly, if the price of bonds is low, and interest rates are high, Keynes believed that people would stay in bonds and out of speculative money, on the basis that they could expect a capital gain. So the speculative demand for money moves directly with the interest rates – low rates, low demand, high rates, high demand, whilst the transactional and precautionary demand moves directly with income. Hence the *LM* curve slopes upwards. (We shall examine in a moment the differences between Keynesians and monetarists which essentially hinge on the gradients of the two curves) The *LM* curve therefore shows all the points at which the money supplied is equal to the money demanded, and its curve is defined by the rate of interest and the level of income.

So putting the two together, we can see that the point at which they intersect is the equilibrium point for both the real and the money economies. Some forms of the model also have the *BP* curve added on. This represents all the points of income and interest rate which tends to keep the **balance of payments** in equilibrium, i.e. not in deficit or surplus. In general, at higher levels of income the

tendency is for spending to increase on imports (moving toward a deficit); while a high rate of interest will tend to encourage a surplus on the capital account (hot money and speculative inflows are attracted). Hence the curve slopes upward, with higher interest rates needed to keep the balance at higher levels of income. Note too that in today's deregulated international capital markets, the *BP* curve is highly elastic to the rate of interest. In times of strict capital controls, it could be seen as steeper than the IS curve, for changes in interest rates would not be the only factor in determining the international flow of money. Clearly where all three curves cross, the real domestic and real trading economies are in balance with the money economy.

We should now use this framework for a brief exploration of some of the important differences between the Keynesians and the monetarists. The *IS* curve, according to the Keynesians, is relatively steep, indicating that the level of investment is not very interest-rate sensitive, because future expectations about demand are also a major factor. Thus at higher levels of income, when savings are high, interest rates will need to fall very significantly in order to keep investment at the same level. Keynesians also believe that savings are not very interest rate sensitive, being primarily determined by the level of income. Monetarists, on the other hand, believe that the rate of interest is a major determinant of investment, and that high rates of interest can attract savings. So their *IS* curve is more interest-rate elastic, and therefore flatter.

Turning to the *LM* curve, the Keynesians believe that this is relatively interest-rate sensitive because of the speculative demand for money. Monetarists, on the other hand, believe that the holding of money balances for other than transactional and precautionary motives is abnormal, and that therefore the rate of interest has little effect on the amount of money demanded. (For Keynesians, **bonds** were the only effective substitute for money, and their prices are totally interest-rate determined, whereas monetarists believe that people spend their money balances on a range of financial and physical assets, which can all be seen as substitutes for money. Although their 'return' will tend eventually to equal the rate of interest, the linkage is less strong and direct.) Hence the monetarist *LM* curve is much steeper than the Keynesian one.

What does all this mean for government policy? Clearly, as far as the real economy is concerned, Keynesians have little faith in the rate of interest in a way to stimulate investment. Thus they are more like to resort to fiscal measures which effectively shift the *IS* curve to the right, and therefore the equilibrium point to a higher level of income. (Keynesians are apt to call interest rates a 'blunt instrument'). Monetarists on the other hand believe that lower interest rates can encourage investment. Typically they might increase the money supply (shifting the *LM* curve to the right), causing interest rates to fall and for the new equilibrium to settle at a higher level of income. (For a fuller description of how money supply and interest rates operate together, *see* **monetary policy**, **Keynes**, **monetarism**.)

Clearly, then, the *IS/LM* model can be of considerable analytical benefit. It failed to tackle perhaps the key point of difference between Keynesians and neo-Classical economists. Keynes believed that an equilibrium could exist at less than full employment; the neo-Classicals argued that this could only be for special reasons such as wage rigidities. The *IS/LM* model does not address the issue of the cost and efficiency of the inputs to production (*see* **supply-side economics**).

J

J-Curve If a country devalues its currency to deal with a **balance of payments** deficit (*see* **exchange rate policy**), the tendency will be for the balance initially to worsen (the downward section of the letter J), before improving again. This is because the demand for exports and imports will take longer to adjust than their prices: to begin with, imports become more expensive and exports cheaper, so more money flows out than flows in. After a lag, customers abroad buy fewer of the country's exports, switching to cheaper alternatives, while imports at home will be shunned for cheaper domestically-produced goods. Unlike the **Marshall-Lerner Condition**, the J-curve effect will not define whether or not a devaluation can succeed; it is purely an expression of a time lag.

The same thing applies in reverse for a revaluation (the inverted J-curve effect).

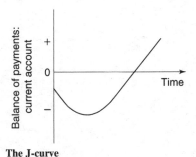

The J-curve

Junk Bonds These are **bonds** (or loan stock) with a very poor credit rating, implying that their risk of default is high. Because of this credit risk, junk bonds are a form of **debt**; and like other bonds, they are **securities**. Junk bonds tend to sell at relatively low prices. The necessary inverse relationship that exists between the price of a bond and its interest rate implies that these junk bonds tend to carry a higher coupon rate (providing a higher rate of interest to the investor).

Junk bonds are typically issued by companies lacking an established earnings history, or having a questionable credit history.

The use of junk bonds became extremely popular in the early 1980s to finance takeovers of large companies. By issuing junk bonds against the smaller company and the larger takeover target, the bidders were able to increase the capital **gearing** of the company, raising the proportion of debt (junk bonds) to ordinary share capital. Junk bonds carry a fixed rate of interest, so that when profits are rising, ordinary shareholders will tend to do well, with a higher proportion of operating profits translating to dividends. In periods of falling profits, however, the cost of servicing the debt will be proportionately higher relative to less indebted (less highly geared) companies, and there will be less to distribute to shareholders. The high risks of junk bonds and the high level of gearing associated with them led to several corporate collapses in the US, although some level of junk bond financing is still present in many takeovers.

JUST IN TIME Just in time, or JIT, is an inventory management technique that was first introduced into car plants in Japan, and later developed in the United States and other economies. The massive improvements brought about by this process have led to the use of the techniques throughout the business environment. Specifically, it is an inventory system in which **products** are delivered to customers, and where materials and components are purchased for the next stage of production at the exact time they are needed – hence the name. The motivating force behind this inventory management system is to reduce costs associated with keeping large inventories of various materials needed at different stages of production.

JIT seeks to economize on finished product stocks by matching the final production of goods with the rate of customers' orders. In this way, management attempts to minimize inventories and to economize on 'work in progress' stocks by synchronizing the flow of materials between the various production processes.

Operation of JIT systems requires a higher degree of cooperation between suppliers and customers. This is because management must always be aware of output demanded, so that it does not have problems associated with backlogs or bottlenecks in production. By keeping an open channel of communication with the customer, the supplier is able to take advantage of the benefits of vertical integration, while remaining independent in its trading in the markets. Such changes in the approach to management are discussed more fully in the essays by Robert Beynon and Adrian Payne/ Sue Holt. Clearly, sophisticated JIT systems require a high level of information technology. The real efficiencies provided by today's computers are analysed in the essay by Richard Lander.

K

KEYNES – MONEY DEMAND The Wall Street Crash of 1929, followed by the Depression of the 1930s, produced scepticism regarding about what was then the received economic wisdom – the **neo-Classical** orthodoxy. Aspects of the **quantity theory of money** were questioned in particular, as it was the guide for monetary policy. **Keynes** published his *General Theory of Employment, Interest and Money* in 1936, offering an alternative interpretation of economic fluctuations in general and the Depression in particular. (The entry on Keynes contains an overview; here we concentrate on the demand for money.) Keynes emphasized on the one hand the role of expenditure on **investment**, and on the other the instability of the **consumption function**. Both were affected by the level of income or the expected level of income/expenditure.

Traditional quantity theorists emphasized the stock of money and the stability of total money demand. The moral of the Keynesian approach was that 'money does not matter'. He did not deny the quantity theory equation ($MV = PT$) in a descriptive sense, but he stated his money demand theory (termed the 'liquidity preference function') in a different way, so that under conditions of unemployment the velocity of money would be highly unstable in the short-run. He also regarded such conditions as prevailing most of the time. In addition, contrary to the **Classical** and neo-Classical schools, he considered that the usual state of the economy in aggregate terms is not characterized by full employment of the available resources, even if prices are thought to be flexible. Thus unemployment in particular, and disequilibriums in general, are not transitory phenomena due to rigidities of the demand components (i.e. wages and prices) or disturbances stemming from the aggregate supply. They are an innate characteristic of the market system.

The Keynesian money demand function has the following three components, which stem from what he believed were the three motives for holding money:

1. transactional (Mt);
2. precautionary (Mpr);
3. speculative (Msp).

The first motive accounts for the fraction of income dedicated to transactions. In a functional form the real money demand for transaction purposes is

$$Mt / p = k*Y$$

Where p is the general price level, and $k*Y$ is a constant proportion of income.

The second component stems from the willingness to avoid risk or risk-related factors in terms of the individual's future income and wealth position. Today we tend to call this motive 'prudence', which is affected by risk aversion. Keynes thought that precautionary savings depend on the disposable income, so that

$$Mpr / p = a *Yd,$$

where $a*Yd$ is a proportion of disposable income.

Finally, the speculative demand arises from the uncertainty as to the future course of the rate of interest. The amount demanded depends on the relation between current rates and rates expected to prevail in the future, i.e.

$$Msp = f(r - r^*),$$

where r is the present rate of interest and r^* the expected rate. An important feature of the total money demand, according to Keynes, is the 'liquidity trap'. This is a specific rate of interest characteristic for any particular economy at which the speculative component of the money demand becomes the dominant one. This occurs when people believe that the prevailing price level of bonds (or other financial assets) is high enough (and liable to fall), so that they massively sell their assets. The potential liquidity problem for the economy is attached to this level of the interest rate *(rmin)*.

The analytical clarity of the Keynesian framework has attracted the interest of modern theorists. Problems such as the connection of money, welfare and wealth and questions relating to the feasibility and efficiency of **monetary policy** have benefited from the Keynesian analysis.

It is important to note that, for Keynes, the substitute for holding money balances was to hold bonds or other financial assets. Compare this with the position of the modern **monetarists** (whose starting point was the Quantity theory): they believe that the substitute for holding money is to hold financial and any other assets. Hence the rate of interest affects spending directly (if the return on other assets or the benefits of buying things is greater than the benefit of holding money, spending will rise), and indirectly through affecting the cost of financing some types of consumption, e.g. credit loans.

Hence, for the monetarists, the demand for money is very much more central; in fact it is the desire to hold 'real balances' which defines the real money supply.

(*See* **monetarism** for a full comparison of the Keynesian and monetarist approaches; *see also* **IS/LM**.)

KEYNES, JOHN MAYNARD (1883–1946) It is no exaggeration to say that the work of Keynes, and in particular his book *The General Theory of Employment, Interest and Money* (1936) revolutionized economics. It challenged the assumptions of the current **neo-Classical** and earlier **Classical** schools, by arguing for the first time that macroeconomic systems were without an equilibrium-creating market-clearing full employment tendency. Radically for the time, he instead suggested that the free enterprise system had a propensity toward instability, and could reach an equilibrium at a level of under-employment. He proposed a new range of vigorous government action to remedy it. It is impossible to assess the impact of his work without a glance at the economic landscape of the time. Most of the industrialised world was deep in recession, stuck there apparently, with mass unemployment creating great poverty and desperation. Economists and policymakers waited for markets to clear, and for activity to pick up again. They trusted in **Say's** Law, according to which prices determine that supply creates its own demand, so that there can never be recession, with demand stalled, in the long term. They urged cuts in interest rates to encourage more investment, and cuts in wages to make labour cheaper and more employable again.

Keynes famously noted, 'in the long run we are all dead'. He believed that cuts in interest rates would not necessarily lead to greater investment, because investment, especially in a recession, is more responsive to expectations than to the cost of capital. He believed that wage cuts would further reduce demand, by reducing disposable incomes. Keynes argued that the levels of income and employment in an economy are largely defined by demand-side factors such as the level of consumption (and that the marginal propensity to consume, rather than save, was itself largely dependent on the level of income) and the level of investment, which was reflected in the marginal efficiency of capital, based very much on expecta-

tions by companies of where demand would be in the future. Clearly, in a period of deep recession, with low and falling incomes and great pessimism about the future, the conditions were not good for demand to pick up by itself. Keynes noted that in the circular low of income, governments could themselves increase demand by spending more on capital projects such as roads, houses, or what came in the US to be known as 'public works'. This, via a process identified by Keynes as the **multiplier**, would feed through an increase in demand which would eventually be several times the level of the original spending. As for how to finance such spending, Keynes argued that a **budget deficit** was appropriate at a time of recession to kick-start economic activity. In other words, classic fiscal policy.

One way to characterize the Keynesian approach to employment and demand is to look at the idea of inflationary or deflationary gaps. By plotting income, or output, on the x axis, and aggregate demand on the y axis, we draw a 45 degree line from the origin, representing all the possible equilibrium positions of the economy, since, according to Keynes and the circular flow principle, there is stability when income/output is equal to demand. Now add the consumption function, which is the line which indicates spending (aggregate demand, which is consumer spending plus government spending plus investment plus the net of exports over imports $(C+G+I+(X-M))$. Many of those elements are exogenous, but consumption spending, which makes up the greatest part of it, rises with income. So our *AD* curve is usually drawn at a gradient which is less than 45 degrees. It intersects the 45 degree line (the aggregate supply curve) at any point. If that point corresponds to a level of income below *yf*, full employment, then a deflationary gap exists. Above *yf* there is an inflationary gap, with upward pressure on prices. For Keynes the trick was going to be shifting the *AD* curve so that it crossed the supply line at *yf*. And that was precisely what the fiscal measures were designed to do – boost aggregate demand through government spending, especially on investment projects, so that *AD* moved upward.

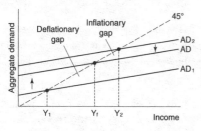

Keynesian economics

On the monetary side, Keynes moved attention away from the neo-Classical **quantity theory of money** statement $MV = PT$ (the product of the money supply and its velocity of circulation is equal to – or the same as – the product of prices and the volume of transactions). He concentrated instead on the demand for money, or liquidity preference. He noted that people hold money as a precaution or for transactions, both of which tend to be a direct function of income, and also for speculative motives. Speculative motives meant people would hold money in the hope that they could use it to buy financial assets, in particular **bonds**. Their price is an inverse of interest rates. Therefore if interest rates are high, people hold money in order to buy bonds in the expectation that their price will rise. If rates are low, people will want to hold less money, not wanting to buy expensive bonds whose price might fall. The money supply could be used to move interest rates up or down through the liquidity preference process. Increase the money supply and people are holding extra money balances, which they will use to buy financial assets – bonds. The bond price rises, and interest rates fall. Importantly, Keynes identified the existence of a liquidity trap, where the elasticity of demand for money becomes infinite. In this circumstance people do not react to an increase in money supply by buying bonds. They believe that their prices are too high, and will come down (interest rates are too low and will rise). People therefore increase their holding of idle balances, and the interest rate remains unchanged.

The importance of the liquidity theory of money is that it allowed Keynes to demonstrate that decisions about investment and decisions about saving are separate, and that both will be affected more by the level of income or future expectations than by the interest rate as such. This – together with the benefits of 'real' demand management – explains why fiscal measures were the preferred method of economic management for the Keynesian school. Keynes regarded interest rates as a 'blunt instrument'.

Later economists have tried to highlight the areas of overlap or agreement between the Keynesians and the neo-Classical and later **monetarist** schools. **Hicks** and Hansen used the **IS/LM** model to help present what was described as the neo-Classical synthesis. Essentially this was the portrayal of Keynes' unemployment equilibrium not as an equilibrium but as an abnormality generated by a phenomenon noted by Keynes himself – the 'stickiness' of wages, which will rise but not fall. Add to that the notion of the liquidity trap and it was possible to argue that if interest rates and wages were not behaving 'abnormally', a full employment equilibrium would always exist. Later Keynesians, known as neo-Keynesians, have refuted this synthesis and placed emphasis on the basic free enterprise instabilities at the heart of the *General Theory*.

Keynes held sway over economic policy-makers from 1936 to the 1970s. At that time a stubbornly high level of inflation, combined with high unemployment (**stagflation**, which Keynesian theory would not have regarded as feasible), plus a change in the political climate in many countries, sent some governments on a search for alternative theories. Many went back to the neo-Classical quantity theorists, who by now had developed their theories and were called monetarists. Also popular were the supply-siders. It is probably accurate to say that today's economic policy-makers have been influenced both by monetarists and **supply-side economics**, but it is also true that the broad theories underpinning economic policy are basically Keynesian.

KINKED DEMAND CURVE The kinked demand curve is used to explain the tendency in **oligopoly** (where a few firms dominate the market) for price and quantity produced by a single firm to reach a level at which they 'stick'.

If one firm raises its price, the others in the market are reluctant to follow suit, hoping instead to gain extra sales as customers move away from the higher-priced producer. On the other hand, if one firm cuts its price, the others in the market are likely to cut as well, this time for fear of losing their own customers to the cheaper firm.

Suppose the prevailing price is P_1. (See Fig. 1.) For one company a

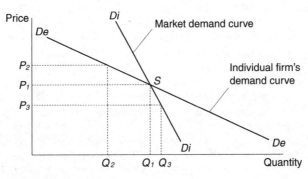

Oligopolistic demand curve, *Fig. 1*

246

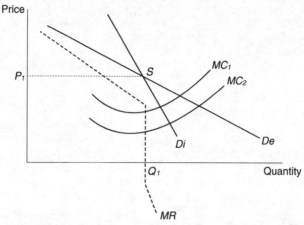

Oligopolistic demand curve, *Fig. 2*

higher price, P_2, results in a move along demand curve *De*, causing a significant reduction in sales (from Q_1 to Q_2) as customers switch to competitor firms. A lower price, however, say P_3, causes a move along demand curve *Di*, bringing about only a small increase in sales because the others in the market have matched the price cut. So the demand curve which exists for the oligopolistic firm is *De* above P_1, and *Di* below it, more elastic for price rises and more inelastic for price cuts. The point at which its gradient kinks, *S*, represents an equilibrium point.

Interestingly we see evidence of 'stickiness', too, in the amount produced at this point, Q_1, when we derive the marginal revenue curve (see Fig. 2). At the point of the kink in the demand (average revenue) curve, the marginal revenue curve becomes discontinuous. Since profit maximization occurs where the marginal cost and marginal revenue curves cross each other, the company will still produce Q_1 for maximum profit, despite potential changes in cost conditions (represented by marginal cost curves MC_1 to MC_2).

In the real world the kinked demand curve means that oligopolistic firms seek out other ways than price to improve their market dominance and profits, often by advertising and branding, which can increase demand for their products, or perhaps by seeking reductions in costs through, say, better practices or new technology.

KONDRATIEFF CYCLE This is a long-term economic cycle (of around 50 years) over which the better-known **business cycles** will be superimposed. They are named after the Russian economist Nikolai Dmitrievich Kondratieff (1892–1931?), who made comprehensive studies of 'long waves' before his interest in objective economics led to his arrest and imprisonment by the Soviets. He later died in prison without ever having been brought to trial.

In 1922 Kondratieff outlined his theories of long waves (expressed in terms of prices), arguing that long cycles were 'probable' for capitalist economies, both in nominal and real terms (especially production cycles). The explanation for the long-run cycles was given in terms of reinvestment cycles of capital goods with relatively extended life spans. This idea is present at a less sophisticated level in **Marx's** description of capital accumulation. These cycles with 'springtide' and 'ebbtide' phases also attracted the attentions of Wicksell (1898), Aftalion (1913) and Lenoir (1913). Kondratieff in his empirical work fitted OLS trends (*see* **regression**, **econometrics**) to per-capita data and moving average corrections to eliminate cyclicality. He found that:

- Upswing phases are longer and gold production seems to increase during them, while wars and revolution are also more frequent.
- Downswing phases are characterized by more frequent depression years, more innovations (inventions), whose large-scale applications prepare the next upswing. Agricultural problems are more intense during downswings and we see markets shrink during the down-turns of the long cycles.

Although later research has shown that some of his conclusions are simply statistical artefacts, his emphasis on discontinuous growth and the periodicity he stressed in cycles are still areas of discussion and research, which make his contribution valuable to economic analysis.

L

LAFFER CURVE The Laffer Curve is a graphical representation of the relationship between **taxation** and government revenues. It shows that as tax rates increase from zero, revenues increase until an optimum is reached. But if tax rates are further increased, they are supposed to discourage extra work, consumer spending, and business **investment**, thereby reducing revenues. In this way the Laffer Curve can guide **fiscal policy** so as to minimize or eliminate a **budget deficit** for a given period. The diagram below show this relationship between tax revenues and tax rates.

From the tax rate 0 to T, it is evident that the government increases its tax revenue by increasing the tax rate. However, any rate higher than T causes a reduction in tax revenues. Thus, the rate T is the optimal rate of tax that a government can impose on

the private sector, as it maximizes revenues.

The Laffer Curve was first introduced by Arthur Laffer, an American economist who is associated with **supply-side economics**. Laffer rejected **Keynesian** theories, and maintained that reducing taxes would encourage business and the rich to invest in taxable activities, rather than parking income in non-productive tax shelters. According to Laffer, governments could expand an economy without incurring a budget deficit by lowering taxes, which would lead to a reduction in prices and increase overall output and government revenues.

Laffer's theories were adopted in the policies of the Reagan administration in the 1980s, whose measures included the deepest tax and budget cuts in US history. While 'Reaganomics' is credited with producing the longest peacetime boom in history,

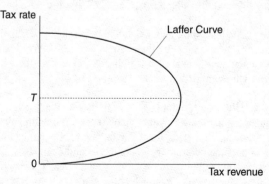

Laffer Curve

many have criticized it for its neglect of the poor, deterioration of infrastructure, and massive budget deficits financed by foreign borrowing. And some have argued that it was those deficits which helped created the boom, rather than any Laffer effects.

LEAKAGES These are flows out of the **circular flow of national income**, representing net reductions in output/production/demand. They are the opposite of injections.

Typical examples of outflows (leakages) are the total direct taxation on income (T), savings (S) and imports (M). We treat them as outflows because taxation reduces the disposable income (Yd) to households, while savings take out of circulation the saved portion of income. Imports, finally, represent a decrease in an economy's trade surplus since funds travel abroad to pay for goods and services bought from abroad. The sum of leakages ex post (= after the event) should identically equal the sum of inflows, i.e.

$$S + T + M = G + I + X$$

where G is government spending, I is the investment demand in the economy, and X is exports. This is not an identity in ex ante (i.e. planned or intended) terms, because it is the result of a series of decisions made by different (though sometimes overlapping) agents for different reasons. Importantly, **Keynes** pointed out that it need not hold ex post either, because of variations stemming from the demand side of the economy.

Hence leakages only equal injections when the economy is in equilibrium,

and again, according to Keynes, that may or may not be at full employment. Keynes' views were a flat contradiction of **Say's** Law, which put simply says that supply creates its own demand (or that prices are assumed to be such that the value of commodities produced is equal to spending (i.e. demand) on all commodities). Keynes described this as a major error which had pervaded Classical economics and economic policy. (*See* **Classical economics**.)

LIBOR This is the acronym for the London Interbank Offered Rate, the interest rate at which large **banks** will borrow and lend the dollar and Eurocurrencies. It is important because it is a good indication of other interest rates charged to commercial or individual customers. LIBOR is a short-term rate, used as a basis for calculating the rate used by all banks for lending for periods of up to two years. When the lending interval exceeds two years the borrower will be charged a rate of interest higher than LIBOR. This is achieved by 'rolling over' the borrowings, i.e. re-borrowing for smaller intervals during the total duration of the loan. LIBOR is used as a basis for determining the terms of loans to emerging economies by such institutions as the **IMF** and the World Bank. (For a discussion of long-term interest rates, *see* **bonds**.)

LIFFE This acronym, which stands for the London International Financial Futures Exchange, is a market for **futures** and **options**, which are forms of **derivatives** whose popularity has exploded over the past couple of decades. As the world's capital markets have become more global and deregulated, so the possibilities have increased speculation and hedging on financial instruments as well as traditional commodities. LIFFE has been one of the fastest growing financial markets to cater for the new demand.

LIFFE was set up in 1982 after similar successes in Sydney (1979) and Chicago in establishing financial futures markets. LIFFE originally traded **currency** and **interest rate** futures, but over the years added options and futures on stock indices, **bonds**, and **commodities**. It is based on an 'open outcry' trading pit, but has now included electronic trading once the pit trading has closed for the day.

LIFFE is centred on a clearing house system through which all transactions pass. The clearing house acts as a financially independent guarantor and regulator of the exchange. The Bank of England also has a regulatory role.

LONG/SHORT-RUN Economists have long understood the importance of different time frames and how they present different solutions, especially in examining various states of equilibrium. As with so much else, the British economist Alfred **Marshall** (1842–1924) is generally credited with refining the implications of time frame. Earlier economists had noted the tendency of variables eventually to reach their 'natural levels'. Adam **Smith** had applied it to the level of average wages, profits, rents and prices. Deviations from this level are self-correcting due to the stability

properties of the market. A special case in the classical era is **Marx**, who also applied the 'long-period position method' to analyse the level of the average rate of interest – refraining from any determination associated with 'material' laws or metaphysical notions, such as the 'just price', that occupied some of his predecessors. In Marx's approach the notion of *average* plays the role of the long-run position of equilibrium for all variables. Any market position (i.e. any short-run behaviour of a variable) gravitates towards its long-run equilibrium state.

The distinction between long-run and short-run methods was also used by economists such as **Walras**, Menger, Jevons, Bohm-Bawerk, Clark and Wicksell. Equilibrium variables are always linked to the level of capacity utilisation and the technological conditions of **production**. Marshall in his writings is the first to analyse the adjustment to equilibrium in a single market (i.e. the notion of partial equilibrium). His effort opposed the Walrasian attempt to produce a general equilibrium theory of all markets. Marshall utilizes the following three terms: short-period equilibrium, long-period equilibrium and temporary equilibrium. The element that differentiates the three is the condition of the corresponding supply function. Temporary equilibrium deals with a completely fixed supply. The short-period equilibrium analysis assumes that there is some flexibility in changing a product's supply, but with the capital factor fixed for the specific industry, so that technology is given and the production potential of the industry is fully determined. In the long-run analysis there is no fixity of supply due to the flexibility of all factors of production. So any size of production is possible.

The long-period analysis tends to 'normal profit rates', since quasi-rents disappear. In the short-run as well as in the case of temporary equilibrium, abnormal profits/losses are feasible. (*See* **theory of production costs, theory of consumer demand**.)

Keynes, a trenchant critic of the **Classical** and **neo-Classical** traditions, denied the validity of many long-run analyses. He is famous for the following phrase:

> This long-run is a misleading guide to current affairs. In the long run we are dead. Economists set themselves too easy, too useless a task if in tempestuous seasons they can only tell us that when the storm is long past the ocean is flat again.
>
> (*A Tract on Monetary Reform*, 1923, p. 65)

Following Marshall's approach in defining the short-run framework of all economic activities, Keynes generalized the concept of the fixity of capital goods from the industry level and applied it to the total economy. The attempt to explain the main forces affecting the level of employment and its fluctuations turned Keynes to questions such as accumulation and the role of effective demand in it. In his *General Theory* (1936), he emphasized the notion of an 'under-employment' equilibrium. This is a condition in which market forces have not exhausted their influence. However, long-run considerations

are not absent from his world and still remain a point of debate regarding Keynes's contribution to the analysis of a market economy. His sharp distinction, though, has affected greatly the realm of economic policy. **Neo-Keynesian** 'fine tuning' advocates that only short-run active intervention can reconcile or restore imbalances by first correcting their distributive consequences. Demand management brings about full employment and therefore it restores efficiency. Thus, all policy regimes are of a short-run character.

In microeconomics, some modern approaches have abandoned the idea of uniform profit rates that permeates neo-Classical analysis. Instead, they try to develop the distinction between the long-run and the short-run analysis with references to the information available to those in the market at the specific time interval.

In **econometrics**, complete, perfect and zero-sum games have given place to incomplete and imperfect information non-zero sum exchanges. Intertemporal considerations try to refine the long-run aspects while evolutionary dynamics in game theory and in growth analysis are utilized to extend long-run analysis to the case of long-run waves. (This phenomenon was subjected to empirical analysis as long ago as the early 1920s, with the notion of **Kondratieff cycles**, in an effort to encompass long-run periodic movements in technology and production.) The concepts are heavily utilized nowadays in the study of economic growth and the analysis of business cycles. Economic theory today properly distinguishes between short-run and long-run effects of policy implications. And in the realm of economic development the concepts of short and long run are necessary to define the analysis. In every case the short-run elasticities for individual or aggregate functions are lower than the long-run ones.

Modern theorists (such as Malinvaud and Grandmont) have tried to supplement theory with a microeconomic explanation of specific Keynesian concepts, such as the temporary equilibrium and the fix price equilibrium. Instead of a general theory approach they look at quantity adjustments within various time frames, while some of their attempts concentrate on proving persistent disequilibrium behaviour. Essentially this is a process again of refining and restating in modern microeconomics what Marshall began: an understanding of time frames in economic behaviour.

LORENZ CURVE The Lorenz Curve is a graphical representation of a particular type of **concentration measure**. It enables economists to, among other things, plot the extent to which aspects of production are in the hands of a few or many different firms. Mathematically, it illustrates the degree of inequality of a frequency distribution in which the cumulative percentage of a population is plotted against the cumulative percentage of a specific variable. For example, a Lorenz Curve could plot the cumulative percentage of firms in an industry against the cumulative percentage of people employed by those firms in the industry. It could also look at, say, inequalities in income, or in **employment**.

In a frictionless market, the cumulative percentage of the relevant population, be it firms or consumers, would support an equal percentage of variables such as income or employment. The purpose of the Lorenz Curve is to examine different components of markets to measure the extent to which they deviate from equality.

If we take our previous example of firms and employment, place the cumulative percentage of firms on the horizontal axis and the cumulative percentage of employment along the

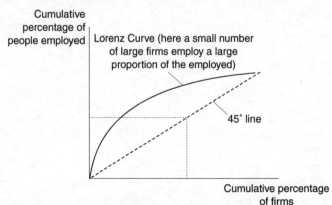

Lorenz Curve

vertical axis, we can observe perfect equality (or a perfectly equal distribution) by drawing a 45 degree line from the axis. By collecting panel data from a census the actual relationship between the variables can be plotted on the graph. The deviation from the 45 degree line will indicate an inequality in the distribution as depicted on the previous page.

Empirically, a typical concentration might be 10 per cent of the top firms employing 10 per cent of the population of the working force. But another economy might have a large number of small firms employing a few people and a small number of large firms employing many people.

This high level of concentration towards large firms would be captured in the curvature of the Lorenz Curve. The greater the curvature in the Lorenz Curve, the greater is the degree of concentration in the market.

A concentration measure which works alongside the Lorenz Curve is the **gini coefficient**. It is measured as the area between the Lorenz Curve and the 45 degree line divided by the area above the 45 degree line. A gini coefficient of 0 indicates equality in the distribution, while a high gini coefficient reveals a high degree of concentration in the market.

M

MALTHUS, THOMAS (1766–1834) An English clergyman and economist whose theories of wages and population made for a gloomy prognosis in the still predominantly agricultural society of his time, Malthus argued that the growth of populations tended to be geometric, whilst the growth in the food supply was arithmetic. This was in stark contrast to the views of other economists of the time, who believed that population growth was associated with increasing levels of wealth. Malthus believed that the population/food problem would be tackled either by external events, such as wars or disease, or by society itself (for example, by encouraging families to have fewer children, to marry later, etc.). His thinking about population, along with the classical economists' notion of the 'wage fund' (*see* **Mill, Ricardo, Marx**), led to the 'iron law of wages', which suggested that wages tended toward the subsistence level in the long term. The level of wages was determined by the value of workers' output minus that surplus taken out by capitalists as profit. If the value of output increased, wages could therefore rise (assuming that the total of profits remained constant). But according to the Malthusian theory this would mean that people would be able to support more children, and this increased population would cause wages to fall (there being many more workers chasing broadly the same number of jobs). They would eventually reach the subsistence level again, and the famine resulting from too many mouths to feed and not enough food would help that process to occur, by reducing the population.

Such a gloomy outlook was shown by events not to be valid: it ignored changes in technology and productivity, and the possibilities opened up by trade and specialization. It is not, however, a history-book quirk: Malthusian theory is still frequently cited nowadays, nearly two hundred years later, as a reason for imposing population controls on developing countries.

MANAGEMENT THEORIES OF THE FIRM This is the body of theory which examines the way companies and business entities approach their basic role – which is to combine the **factors of production** to produce outputs in terms of goods and services in the economy. Management theories often also provide an insight into a firm's **pricing** and output decisions, as well as its strategies in terms of marketing, **R&D**, diversification, and merger activity. Management theories of the firm were founded on microeconomic principles but have implications for macroeconomics as well (such as **fiscal policy** and **governance** of **monopolies** and competitive firms).

Traditionally, firms were seen as behaving in a manner consistent with the notion of profit maximization. This is because managers are accountable to the board of directors, which is voted in by the shareholders of the firm. This means that management is ultimately accountable to the shareholders of the firm, and so any course of action it takes must be in the shareholders' best interests. It is assumed that maximizing profits not only provides greater earnings to be distributed among shareholders in the form of **dividends**, but also improves business confidence and may cause the **share** price of the firm to appreciate.

Elements of this, however, do not fit with the practice in modern capitalism. Therefore, managerial theories of the firm introduce notions such as behavioural theory and organizational theory in addition to profit maximization. The two basic assumptions underlying managerial theories of the firm are as follows:

1. Large **oligopolistic** firms have a separation of ownership from control, which allows management to set the objectives of the firm. This situation, sometimes known as the *Principal–Agent Problem,* arises when a firm is owned by its shareholders (the principal) but is actually controlled by the firm's management (the agent). Traditionally, the average size of individual shareholdings tends to be small – or else shares are owned by institutions whose fund managers may not be interested in the strategy of the firm, but rather in its immediate market performance. Management of the firm is trusted to determine what policies to pursue.
2. Managers are frequently more interested in **revenues** and **asset** goals than in profit maximization. Revenues and assets are taken as symbols of a company's size, and may well have a direct bearing on the salaries and benefits of managers.

One way to develop an understanding of large firms is through behavioural theory. This was pioneered by R. Cyert and J. G. March. It stresses the nature of large companies as complex organizations beset by problems of goal conflict and obstacles in communication. Its aim is to examine these conflicts within the firm, and it proposes that organizational objectives should grow out of interaction among individuals and groups in the firm. This theory recognizes five goals that are relevant to a company's sales, output, and pricing. These goals relate to production, inventory, sales, market share and profits. Each of these goals becomes the primary goal of different managers in the firm, each of whom will try to press his/her specific goal on management. However, conflicts arise and managers have to make concessions in order to achieve satisfactory targets. The theory that firms not only seek 'satisfactory' profits (rather than maximized profits) but other objectives such as increasing sales, market share or size, is referred to as satisficing theory. Thus, behavioural theory attempts to incorporate other characteristics related to firms in order to explain a firm's behaviour in the market place.

Another theory in the behavioural framework of large and complex companies is organizational theory. Traditional economic analysis usually views the firm as a single autonomous decision making agent interested in maximizing profits. Organizational theory suggests that decisions are decentralized and influenced by factors other than pure economic motives. Again, non-optimal or satisficing decisions are the result, rather than profit maximization (*see* **x-inefficiency**). Although behavioural theory is a descriptive approach to explaining firm behaviour, it lacks certain deterministic properties which are necessary to test its hypotheses.

A deterministic alternative to profit maximization is management utility maximization. This theory suggests that firms try to maximise management's utility function (or the *managerial preference function*), which is a function of three parameters: staff, employee benefits, and investments. The role of adding staff can lead to managers receiving higher salaries, because more staff usually require more tiers in the organizational structure, possibly increasing the salaries of those higher up the tiers. Adding staff is also a source of power, status, and prestige which may lead to job security. Employee benefits such as big expense accounts and generous travel budgets are also valued as both a source of direct income as well as projecting prestige and status. Finally, levels of investment over and above that which is economically necessary for the firm enable managers to pursue their own ambitions and increase their status in relation to the physical equipment that they have control

over. Thus all three parameters have a positive influence on the managerial preference function, and the goal of firms is to maximize their own utility functions, subject to constraints in the environment.

A further deterministic alternative to profit maximization is sales revenue maximization. A firm is assumed to seek to maximize its sales revenue subject to some sustainable profit level. The output and pricing strategies will differ to the profit maximizing case, depending on the minimum level of allowable profit. Generally for lower levels of acceptable profit, the sales revenue maximizing principle will tend to produce more units of output. Closely related is the idea of asset value maximization, where growing the size of the firm becomes a predominant goal. Again, this will often bring benefits in status, power, and salaries to the management.

There will be a self-correcting tendency toward profit maximization. If a firm is holding back too much of its profits in order to finance further sales or asset growth, its share value will tend to fall because it will pay out lower dividends. At a certain point the value of its net assets will become greater than its market capitalisation, making it ripe for a takeover. Hence the management will not move too far from an acceptable level of profit. (This can be plotted on a valuation curve for the company – *see* **assets**.)

One question refers back to the principal–agent problem, asking if there can be a 'remarriage' of ownership and control. The explosive growth in **stock market** investment in recent years has increased the pressure for stockbrokers and in particular the fund managers of large **institutions** to be seen to be delivering share performance. Often it is easier to pressurize a firm toward greater profitability than it is to find another vehicle for equity investment. Certainly the major shareholders – the mutual funds, pension companies, and insurance firms – are becoming increasingly articulate in terms of the management and strategy of companies in many countries, and this is a trend which is likely to continue as deregulated markets make global investment more common. In the past few years there has been less opportunity for companies simply to remain 'national institutions' that are run for the benefit of their managers: international investors tend to be less sentimental about such 'sleeping giants'.

(*See also* **asset stripping** and essay 'Changing Trends in Management' by Robert Beynon.)

MARKET STRUCTURE Market structure refers to the way a market is organized. It focuses on those aspects of market structure that have an influence on the behaviour of firms and consumers (as sellers and buyers). In this way market structure is concerned with organizational and other characteristics of markets which affect the nature of competition and **pricing**. In one sense, analysis of market structure is the empirical side of the **theory of production costs** and the **theory of consumer demand**.

Traditionally, the most important features of market structure are the number, size, and distribution of buyers and sellers. This determines the extent to which a market may be close to **perfect competition** or to **monopoly** (or somewhere between the two, for example, **oligopoly**). Often this is determined by the existence or the absence of barriers to entry.

The development of the theory of markets has identified three components that relate to structure, conduct, and performance. These three components influence one another simultaneously rather than sequentially, and allow economists to distinguish one particular market from another.

Structure and conduct are seen as acting together or separately to influence performance. So elements relating to the concentration of buyers and sellers, conditions of entry, nature of the product supplied, as well as the extent of diversification, will all affect the performance of a market. Economists often use **concentration measures** to evaluate a particular structure. These measures, which can be classified as absolute or one-dimensional and relative, indicate the extent to which a particular market is accommodated by a given proportion of sellers. One specific relative concentration measure is the **gini coefficient**, which indicates a high level of concentration (similar to a monopoly) for values close to one (with values closer to zero indicating a more equal distribution).

Generally, performance relates to the efficiency of the market in utilizing scarce resources to meet demand for goods and services in the economy. In some respects, performance is concerned with the ability of the market to contribute to welfare. Performance issues relate to productive, distributive and allocative efficiency, as well as technological progress and a product's 'commercial' performance in the market. Efficiency refers to the relationship between scarce factor inputs and the outputs of goods and services generated from these scarce factors in the economy. This relationship can be measures in physical terms, such as technological efficiency, or in cost terms, such as economic efficiency. The concept of efficiency is used as a criterion in judging how well markets have allocated resources.

In terms of specifying the standards of market structure and conduct that are likely to result in an 'acceptable' market performance, pragmatic or workable competition attempts to provide useful guidelines in applying competition policy to real world markets. Policy makers may aspire to a theoretical ideal of perfect competition, but there are sometimes important operational difficulties involved in stipulating acceptable norms (such as defining a 'fair' level of **profits**). (*See* **regulation**.)

MARSHALL, ALFRED (1842–1924) One of the greatest economists, Marshall helped move the subject out of the **Classical** era into a real understanding of demand, supply and price. Marshall spent most of his career as Professor of Economics at Cambridge University, where he developed the notion of the downward sloping **demand curve**, **elasticities** and the **supply curve**. His work is also important because of its awareness of the time frame in microeconomics. He distinguished between the various changes in factor input in the short, long and very long periods (*see*

long/short-run). He identified the existence of **economies of scale** in the long run. This awareness made his work more flexible than some of the other **neo-Classical** theorists who tended to look at static models of cost and demand.

Marshall was a mathematician by training, and he used calculus to develop his theories of marginal utility and elasticity. In this and in many respects Marshall can be regarded as the first modern economist: certainly his works inspired many of those who have come after him.

(*See* **theory of production costs**, **theory of consumer demand**.)

MARSHALL-LERNER CONDITION If a country devalues its currency to deal with a **balance of payments** deficit, the **devaluation** will only work if exports and imports are relatively price-sensitive (i.e. have high **elasticities** of demand). The Marshall-Lerner Condition states that the sum of the price elasticities has to be greater than unity for the devaluation to succeed, because if the exports and imports are more price-inelastic, the balance of payments deficit remains, but imports are more expensive, perhaps triggering inflation. The M-L Condition is more a rule of thumb than an exact statement, however. Other factors come into account, such as time. It will often take some time for customers abroad to switch into cheaper export goods from the devaluing country, and at the same time those buying imports may take time to change their habits: this is known as the **J-curve** effect. Furthermore, the devaluing country needs to be able to switch more of its production to exports (for the export industries) and at the same time to step up its domestic production for those industries which had previously been import-heavy. That depends on capacity, and on trading relationships (tariffs and other barriers may be a major disincentive to exports, even if they do become cheaper). (*See also* **theory of trade**.)

MARX, KARL (1818–83) German philosopher and economist who predicted the collapse of capitalism and the succession of socialism then communism. Marx was a giant, not because his ideas came true (they didn't, at any significant level) but because he constructed an ambitious and novel framework for analysing history, class, and economics, known as historical, or dialectical, materialism. He argued that at various times in history, one class was dominant, and followed this through primitive communism to slavery, feudalism, and then capitalism. His model had capitalists, the owners of capital, as the dominant model of industrialised society, with the workers creating the value but being paid only at subsistence wages. This allowed the capitalists to take surplus profits, some of which they used to buy extra machines. His argument that it is not possible to exploit capital, only labour, led him to predict that as firms became more **capital-intensive**, the rate of profit would fall. He also argued that fewer workers would be needed, creating unemployment and downward pressure on **wages**. The **business cycle** would eventually create slump and revolution, bringing about the collapse of the system.

Some modern economists have sought to develop Marxist ideas, especially the 'labour theory of value', while others have tried to bring together elements of **Keynes** and Marx (*see* **Cambridge school**). In one sense the collapse of many of the so-called Marxist regimes in Eastern Europe and elsewhere has encouraged economists to re-examine some of the details of Marxian thinking without needing to justify the broader predictions.

MERCANTILISM An economic philosophy of merchants and statesmen during the sixteenth and seventeenth centuries that came about from the growth in trade and the relationship between a nation's wealth and its trade balance. Mercantilism relied on a strong state and extensive **regulation** of economic activity. Mercantilism was characterized not so much by a consistent or formal doctrine, as by a set of generally held beliefs. These beliefs included the ideas that exports to foreign countries are preferable both to trade within a country and to imports; that the wealth of a nation depends primarily on the possession of gold and silver; and that governmental interference in the national economy is justified if it tends to implement the attainment of these objectives.

The mercantilists were in favour of maximizing national wealth partly because the monetary system of the time was relatively primitive relative to the growing needs of economic expansion. Their approach to economic policy first developed during the growth of nation states; efforts were directed toward the elimination of the internal trade barriers prevalent in the Middle Ages in Europe, when a cargo of commodities might be subject to a toll or tariff at every city and river crossing. Because of the primitive monetary system, the treasury of the economy (which primarily consisted of gold bullion) was viewed as the key to the wealth of the state. Foreign trade was regulated in order to obtain a **surplus** of exports over imports. This was done by confining the trade of the colonies to the mother country. Industries were encouraged and assisted in their growth because they provided a source of **taxation** to support the large armies and other equipment of national government. Colonialism was considered a legitimate method of providing the parent countries with precious metals and with the raw materials on which export industries depended. Specifically, exports would be subsidized while imports would be taxed.

Mercantilism, by its very success in stimulating industry and developing colonial areas, soon gave rise to powerful anti-mercantilist pressures. Accordingly, a philosophy of free trade began to take root. Economists asserted that government regulation is justified only to the extent necessary to ensure free markets, because the national advantage represents the sum total of individual advantages, and national well-being is best served by allowing all individuals complete freedom to pursue their economic interests. Adam **Smith** in *The Wealth of Nations* (1776) criticized mercantilist policies because they benefited the producer at the cost of the consumer.

The free-trade system, which prevailed during the nineteenth century, began to be curtailed sharply at the beginning of the twentieth century in what has been seen as a revival of elements of mercantilist philosophy, or neo-mercantilism. High protective tariffs were reintroduced, and for political and strategic reasons, great emphasis was put on national self-sufficiency as opposed to national interdependence and a free flow of trade.

(*See* **comparative advantage, theory of trade, Heckscher-Ohlin factor proportions theory.**)

MERCHANT BANK Merchant banks (US = investment banks) are specialist banks which provide financial services, usually to corporate or institutional clients rather than individual consumers. They perform various roles, including **underwriting** new share issues, managing and advising on mergers and acquisitions, and trading shares and other financial instruments on behalf of clients or on their own account. As traders in financial markets, investment banks are sometimes market makers, a role in which the bank is obliged always to make a price for whatever instrument is being traded.

The role of the investment banks has broadened considerably with deregulation of many of the world's major financial markets. For example, UK merchant banks traditionally made their business in providing foreign exchange and financing international trade, including the issuance of acceptance notes and bills of exchange to companies exporting or importing goods. Separate stockbrokers were active in the equities market, working alongside firms of jobbers who actually placed the transactions. Today all of these activities – foreign exchange trading, equities, **bonds**, **derivatives**, as well as the more traditional banking roles of providing finance for corporate restructuring or mergers – could be part of the work of an investment, or merchant, bank. Such banks are commonly present in all the major global markets, rather than in one or two centres. This trend towards globalization can only gain pace as technological improvements expand the rapid movement, and accurate pricing and tracking, of capital virtually anywhere, 24 hours a day.

MILL, JOHN STUART (1806–73) English economist and philosopher who is sometimes credited with having moved the subject from its **Classical** origins towards the **neo-Classical** theories of **supply** and **demand**. Mill was a supporter of liberalism in economic policy while at the same time arguing for social reforms. Mill developed the work of **Smith**, **Ricardo**, **Say** and **Malthus**, and introduced the idea that supply and demand play a part in defining value. He used this to extend Ricardo's ideas of **comparative advantage** in world trade, being able to use the notion of reciprocal demand to define the terms of trade between two countries.

Mill's views were broadly optimistic about future society: he foresaw a time when the fruits of past economic labours could be enjoyed. This was in sharp contrast to some of the gloomier predictions of economists such as Malthus.

MINIMUM WAGE The idea of a minimum wage rate might be regarded as a **supply-side** measure, although unlike most such measures, its nature is unashamedly interventionist. It is adopted by governments to try to counter the perceived distributive injustices of the wage market. Its opponents argue that the imposition of a floor on nominal wages will lead to a discrepancy between the labour which is supplied and the labour which is demanded at that price, which will in turn lead to unemployment as low-wage workers are 'priced out' of a job. Or, if the economy is near to full **employment**, it could lead to **inflationary** pressures and possibly a **wage–price spiral** (this would be because aggregate demand is strong, and labour is scarce, so employers will continue to produce with the higher-cost labour, probably passing on their costs as higher prices). It is difficult to measure, also, how much the effects of a minimum wage 'feed through' into the **circular flow**, perhaps raising economic activity during a recession, as more lower-paid workers start to have a greater disposable income.

In practice, the most important determinant of the economic impact of a minimum wage rate is where it is set. The lower the level relative to average wages, the smaller its effects will be on the labour market, since it will 'not apply' to the majority of workers.

MODIGLIANI, FRANCO (1918–) Italian-born economist, best known for developing the life cycle theory which examined the propensity to save and consume at various levels of income but, importantly, at various stages of life. His theory was that people would tend to save more when their incomes were high, during, say, early middle age, whilst there would be dis-saving by the retired population. Taking account of all the variations, he argued that the average propensity to save tends to remain constant even as aggregate income rises in an economy.

Modigliani, with M. H. Miller, proposed that the market value of a firm is decided by its expected rate of return, rather than the way it raises money for expansion (*see* **debt**, **asset**, **gearing**). This became known as the Modigliani-Miller Theorem.

MONETARISM Monetarism is a development of **Classical** economics, which looks to various monetary factors to explain the performance of the economy, and in particular the level of prices. It is – in its modern incarnation – strongly associated with the work of Professor Milton Friedman (b. 1912) of the University of Chicago.

Monetarism starts out from the **quantity theory of money**, which holds that the product of the **money supply** and the velocity of circulation is equal to, and the same as, the product of the level of prices and the volume of transactions: $MV = PT$. Monetarists used this to develop a theory of inflation and economic management. The velocity of circulation was taken to be relatively stable, so that money supply clearly has an impact on prices and the level of activity measured by transactions. In this way the money economy acts on the real economy.

The role of the money supply itself is important. Monetarists believe that money is a substitute for all financial and physical **assets**, rather than a substitute for financial assets alone, such as **bonds**, as **Keynes** believed. Therefore an increase in the money supply means that people, on finding they have more money balances than they need, spend it. So money supply can directly affect aggregate demand. Prices, however, will rise, causing the value of the money balances that people are holding to fall (i.e. a reduction in what are known as real money balances), which will then reduce aggregate demand. In that sense the real money supply (measured by people's real money balances) is endogenous, because it depends on prices as well as the desire to hold money or spend it. The interest rate will be a major determinant of whether people hold greater or smaller real money balances. It is also, according to the monetarists, the key factor in deciding investment.

The monetarist prescription therefore sets great store on not allowing the nominal money supply to increase faster than output in the economy. If that should happen, interest rates would fall, money spending would increase (as a substitute for holding money balances), prices rise, and the value of real money balances would fall. In other words, **inflation**.

It is instructive to compare some of the basic tenets of the Keynesian and monetarist theories in the table on the following page.

Some of the economies which embraced monetarist policies during the 1980s (e.g. the UK) were characterized by high unemployment (stable

	Monetarists	*Keynesians*
nominal money supply	exogenous, needs to shadow real output to avoid inflation	exogenous, can affect output and employment
real money supply	endogenous; reflects desire to hold money balances vs. spending	as above
interest rates	the value of return on money and other assets; directly affects spending/saving and investment; close link to money supply through money balances	return for speculative money – rates based on expectations about bonds; no direct link to spending (linked to income) or investment (linked to expectations); not closely linked to money supply (or not at all in case of liquidity trap)
prices	directly linked to nominal money supply through money balances	linked to capacity and aggregate demand; at less than full employment, spending not inflationary

prices were prioritized, and Keynesians argued that the reduction in nominal money supply simply reduced output) and high real rates of interest, which monetarists expected to follow from strict control of the nominal money supply. Inflation did cool, but ironically it proved immensely difficult to control the one variable at the heart of monetarism – the money supply. This is largely because of the problems of defining it and measuring it. Some economists argued that **stagflation** had been a reaction to the oil price increases of the 1970s. Others pointed to the success of the **supply-side** measures (*see* the essay by Patrick Minford). These tended to reduce rigidity, especially in the labour market.

Monetarists have accepted that some of their monetary variables also affect the 'real' economy: for example, it is now accepted that the money supply can directly affect output and employment in the short term, rather than indirectly through the 'real balance' approach. The difference between monetarists and Keynesians over what is a substitute for money is more a matter of degree than anything else. And many monetarists accept the validity of short-term fiscal measures in economic management. The focus of monetarism now has moved toward the notion of 'expectations', and the importance of allowing businesses to make decisions with the maximum amount of information. In the views of some monetarists, governments should do nothing which inhibits the 'rational expectations' of business; once governments do take action, the private sector incorporates that into its 'rational expectations' for the next time – meaning that it is very hard for governments to take any macroeconomic action which has not already been discounted by the pivate sector.

One important outcome of the relatively polarized views of monetarists and Keynesians is the exploration that has followed into the basics and the limits of each school. For policymakers, the likelihood is a continuation of the present range of measures: sometimes with central banks running the monetary policy independent of governments, and in the case of the euro, on behalf of many governments at the same time.

MONETARY POLICY Monetary policy refers to the manipulation by governments of various money variables to control the level of activity and prices in an economy. The money variables are **money supply**, **interest rates**, and **exchange rates**. It is important to realize that whilst it may be possible to target one, or perhaps even two, of these, it will not be possible to target all three because each plays on the others. Monetary policy for many industrialized countries over the past couple of decades has been conducted in the shadow of the debate between the followers of **Keynes** and the **monetarists**. Because they disagree about the workings and effectiveness of monetary variables, and even about their overall relevance as an economic tool, monetary policy has been one of the most contro-

versial areas of economic management.

More detailed exploration of the philosophical differences is given under the relevant entries elsewhere in this book. It is worth an examination here of the various ways in which monetary policy may be conducted.

During the years before the deregulation of international capital markets, governments (or central banks) could control both money supply and interest rates directly, through direct instructions. Commercial banks – whose deposits and the lending against them make up the greatest part of the money supply (*see* **bank credit multiplier**) – could simply be ordered to cap their lending, or instructed to make deposits with the central bank, which would reduce their scope for money creation through the credit mechanism. Loan companies and mortgage providers could be told how much and under what circumstances they could lend. The interest rate could be set by the central bank or the government – notionally by issuing a statement to say at what percentage they would lend to commercial banks or other financial institutions. And the exchange rate was under the **Bretton Woods system** simply fixed against other currencies.

These arrangements, which seem crude in our global economic context, would simply not work today, when it is possible in most economies for an institution or person to borrow money from anywhere in the world, at whatever is the best rate of interest. Exchange rates too are typically allowed to float more or less freely (even in the case of European Monetary Union (**EMU**), the exchange rate of the euro against the rest of the world's currencies will not be fixed). This means that for the most part, the policy maker will rely on open market operations – by actually entering the financial markets to try to alter the monetary variables. The most common method is by buying and selling government **bonds**. In order to reduce the money supply, the government can sell bonds to the public or institutional investors. These are paid for by cheques drawn on the commercial banks, who have to reduce their lending accordingly. The extra financial assets (in this case bonds) which are available on the financial markets will tend to reduce prices, raising their rate of interest. Other rates of interest in the economy tend to follow suit. Governments may still also define the rate of interest at which it will lend to the banks and financial institutions, and because this will usually be a preferential rate compared with the market, it can have some impact for monetary policy.

The international dimension to capital markets means that exchange rate policy is now a very important element in monetary policy. High domestic interest rates, which may be necessary to reduce demand in the economy, often attract large capital inflows, which increase the price of the currency. This makes imports cheaper, perhaps causing consumer spending to rise – the opposite effect to the deflationary intent of the high interest rates. It will also make exports more expensive, encouraging com-panies to switch to domestic produc-tion, again stoking up the **inflationary** pressures. In other circumstances the exchange rate and the domestic inter-est rates can work together to reflate a recessionary economy: allowing the currency to **devalue** after a cut in rates can help to create an export-led recovery.

Many countries allow their central banks to define monetary policy inde-pendently of the government. The usual brief for the bank is the control of inflation. Financial markets tend to prefer this arrangement, because they feel that policy is less likely to be hijacked for short-term political gains. Under European Monetary Union, one central bank will be responsible for setting monetary policy for all the euro member countries. This leaves the national governments the option to use **fiscal** measures to control spending, although their scope will be limited: for example, there are strict rules about operating budget deficits. (*See* the essay by Ian Harnett.)

The effectiveness of monetary policy in controlling the 'real' econ-omy takes us back to the Keynes–monetarist debate. Many economists believe that in today's global econ-omy, fundamentals such as the cost of production and the expertise of the labour force are the key determinants for stable economic growth: these **supply-side** measures, originally associated with ultra-free market thinking, are now part of a broader consensus. (*See* the essay by Patrick Minford.)

MONEY Money is usually defined as having three qualities: it is a medium of exchange, a unit of account, and a store of value. Thus money can enable trade to take place, among individuals, institutions, or countries, with money representing a generally accepted measure of value for all the goods and services that are traded.

The predecessor of money was barter, which was limited mainly because of the difficulty in matching buyers and sellers, each in the market for products for which there was no universal measure of value. Bartering agricultural produce and livestock is one of the oldest forms of trade in the world, but once the need arises for trade in widely different items, often at different times, the need for a universal medium becomes obvious. You might exchange two cows for 20 sheep, but how many sheep would you need for a silk gown, and how would you save up cows to pay for a new plough next year? This problem is known as the 'coincidence of wants', and it led at first to traders who would acquire sheep, or goats, or silk gowns, for trade in the future rather than for their own needs. Gradually they moved toward a money system: once money is introduced, the possibility opens up of large-scale specialization (the gown-maker has enough money to buy food, and the plough-maker can hire a labourer), and real economic activity begins.

In general there are three forms of money:

1. Commodity money is money in the form of precious metals such as gold, silver, or copper, whose value is determined by the value of the material being used. Gold coins used in the United States prior to 1933 are an example of commodity money.

2. Credit money is essentially a promissory note from the issuer (be it a bank or government), which reimburses the creditor the equivalent value in the standard monetary metal.

3. Fiat money is paper money, which is not redeemable in any other form of money and which has a fixed value determined by the central authority in the economy. Coins and notes in circulation in various modern-day economies are an example of fiat money. In general the value of the metal or paper is less than their value as money.

Since money is a store of value and does not have any intrinsic value in and of itself, it requires faith from the agents in the economy in order to remain relatively stable. Creditors are required to accept money in settlement of debts. When the supply of money is not excessive in relation to the level of trade, and the agents are confident that this state will persist, then the **currency** will remain relatively stable. If, however, the supply of money is much higher in relation to the level of trade, then creditors will have less faith in money to settle debts accurately and the value of money will depreciate. (*See* **Gresham's Law**, **inflation**.)

The real value of money is determined by purchasing power (the number of resources someone can acquire with a given amount of money), which in turn depends on the level of prices. According to the **quantity theory of money**, prices depend on the volume of money outstanding in an economy and thus have implications for the role of money in an economy (*see* **monetary policy**).

The basic money of a country into which other forms of money may be converted is referred to as standard money. The monetary standard of a country refers to the type of standard money used in the monetary system (modern-day economies tend to use commodity or fiat money). Usually, the fiat standard is also a managed currency in which the value is generally dependent on the central authorities' management and policies. A question of great concern to economists is whether fiat currency can remain fairly stable for an extended period of time. (*See* **IMF**.)

MONEY SUPPLY Measuring the amount of money in an economy is fraught with difficulty, partly because **money** can encompass such a wide range of instruments, from coins and notes to savings accounts, and partly because it is hard to track whether the same money is circulating faster, or whether more money is circulating more slowly. Over the past few decades the money supply has been central to economic debate, with the **monetarists** differing from the **Keynesians** in their views about how it affects prices and output.

Money supply can be viewed either as 'nominal' or 'real'. The nominal part refers simply to the monetary aggregate M, while the real refers to the real reserves (M/p). M is the money stock and p is the general price level so that M/p is the purchasing power of M in terms of a standard basket of commodities.

The money stock can be defined in various ways. **Central banks** have to decide which monetary aggregates are important for policy purposes, and in terms of which aggregates they should express their targets. Each country has different criteria, but everyone starts with M0 or M1 and increases the number as the 'breadth' of money increases. In the US and the UK, for example, M1 represents mainly cash in circulation plus 'sight' or 'demand' accounts with banks where the money can be withdrawn on demand. M2 is somewhat broader but is still mainly a measure of 'transactions' balances. M3 includes a wider range of deposit accounts, whilst in the UK, M5 is wide enough to include savings accounts and government **bonds**.

Money supply is considered exogenous (i.e. externally controlled) in many economic models. The reason is that it is managed by the central bank. The means by which this is done is termed 'open market operation'. Many Keynesians, however, have tried to endogenize the level of the money supply. They emphasise 'fine tuning' for stability and full employment, and argue that the money supply will tend to follow the other elements at work in economic policy. Recent empirical evidence throws doubt on the monetarist prescription to set rigid rules for the expansion of the monetary base. As the basis for non-inflationary growth in the 1980s and 1990s it tended to fail largely because the set targets regularly were widely missed: on the other hand, inflation levels in general did fall. (*See also* **money supply/aggregate demand linkages**, **monetary policy**.)

MONEY SUPPLY/AGGREGATE DEMAND LINKAGES How the **money supply** relates to aggregate demand in an economy is at the heart of the differences between **monetarists** and **Keynesians.**

Both schools believe that an increase in the money supply will lead to an increase in overall spending (aggregate demand); the key divergence is the question of how much. For monetarists the effect on spending is direct, and the impact on **interest rates** is significant, further increasing consumption and investment. For Keynesians it is indirect, and the impact of interest rates on spending is seen as being less important.

Monetarists believe that if people have access to more money (easier credit, more notes and coins in their pockets or money in their bank accounts), they will spend more on goods and services. They will also tend to buy various financial assets such as **bonds** or **stocks**, whose prices will rise, bringing about a fall in interest rates. This in turn further encourages consumption spending and investment.

For Keynesians the increase in the money supply will tend to mean that many people are more likely to hold what are known as 'idle balances', for speculative and precautionary motives. They might also purchase financial assets such as bonds, whose prices will rise, reducing interest rates. But the effect is less great because, unlike monetarists, Keynesians do not believe that people see all financial assets as being substitutes for holding money balances.

We can contrast the two views in this way: the increase in the money supply for monetarists brings about a sharp fall in interest rates (demand for money, or liquidity preference, is relatively inelastic) whereas for Keynesians the demand for money is more elastic. In this context a rise in the money supply creates only a small reduction in interest rates.

The next stage is the secondary effect on investment spending (*see* **investment**). Monetarists believe that the lower interest rates will have a significant effect on investment spending. In this respect their view is that investment spending is more interest-rate elastic. This then feeds into aggregate demand via the **multiplier** effect. Keynesians accept that lower interest rates will increase investment spending, but they also point to other factors apart from interest rates, such as expectations about future demand, and the amount of spare capacity which exists. So for them the overall effect on aggregate demand is weaker.

Clearly these linkages have a major effect on government **monetary** measures designed to manage the economy through the money supply and interest rates.

MONOPOLY A monopoly is a market condition in which one firm controls the supply of a product for which there are no substitutes. In this context it can dominate the price and output of the product. It is the opposite of **perfect competition**, where no individual firm can control the price.

The monopolist will aim to maximize profit, and the theories of production costs and of consumer demand tell us that this will be at the point where marginal revenue is equal to marginal cost. By setting output at this level (X_1) he or she can realize supernormal profits. The cost C_1 is significantly lower than the price P_1 which exists for that level of output, and the supernormal profits are represented by the rectangle $C_1P_1 \times X_1$ (*see* Fig. 1). This is very similar to what can happen in the short term for a firm in perfect competition. But in a monopoly there are no new entrants, so the monopolist continues to make extra profit.

The supernormal profit is sometimes referred to as a producer's **surplus**. The market for the industry could sustain a lower price – P_2 – which would lead to output at X_2. (The **supply curve** for the industry as a whole is the total of all its firms' marginal cost curves: in this case MC for the one-firm monopolistic industry is the supply curve for the industry as well – see **theory of production costs, perfect competition**.) Under competitive conditions, new entrants would join the market, increasing supply, lowering prices,

and that move would occur. So a monopolist in general produces less at a higher price. The more inelastic the **demand curve** (as would be the case where a monopolist controlled, say, an essential foodstuff or pharmaceutical product) the higher the price the monopolist can charge without sacrificing sales.

For the monopolist there is no motivation to minimize costs, and for this reason, output and prices tend to remain at less efficient levels (*see* **x-inefficiency**). It is for this reason that governments resort to **regulation**, to restrict and control the behaviour of monopolistic firms. Sometimes they impose a monopoly tax as well as other forms of payments.

There are some circumstances, however, where the **economies of scale** achieved by a monopoly, and the extra profits which can be ploughed back into research and development, might allow a greater level of output at a lower price than under more perfect competition. The economist **Schumpeter** put forward a model of monopoly, in which we see the

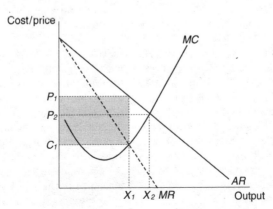

Monopoly, *Fig. 1*

270

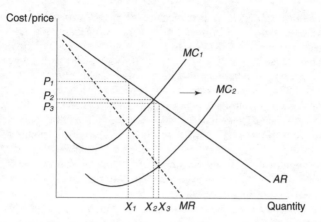

Monopoly, *Fig. 2*

monopolist charging P_1 in the short term for output X_1. If other firms were allowed to enter, the marginal cost of the product would tend to move to a level where it equalled price, giving P_2 at an output of X_2. Schumpeter argued that the monopolist in the long term would be able to reduce costs to shift the marginal cost curve to the right, giving output of X_3 at a price of P_3. The monopolist is still making supernormal profits, but the price is below the more competitive P_2, with higher output.

Whilst it might be difficult to argue that there are 'good' monopolists and bad ones, it is worth distinguishing a natural monopoly from a statutory monopoly. A monopoly based on an overwhelming cost advantage for the leading firm is referred to as a natural monopoly. This situation arises when a firm possesses some unique attribute such as a natural resource or a technological process that others do not possess. Conversely, a statutory monopoly is one where the leading firm's position is based not on some

unique cost advantage, but laws and regulations that preclude possible rivals from entering the industry.

A variation on the monopolist structure that incorporates some of the notion of competition is 'monopolistic competition', where a limited number of sellers exist in a market structure. These sellers believe that prices can be charged as a decreasing function of the quantity sold (it is usually assumed that demand for the product is somewhat inelastic). The producers believe that demand for their product is downward-sloping, yet do not attempt to anticipate the reactions of their competitors in the market like **oligopolies**. Under this scenario firms can expect to make excess profits so long as there are sufficient barriers to entry to exclude new entrants from the profitable venture.

Another type of monopoly, known as a monopsony, is where a single buyer exists for the item sold, with many suppliers. Like the monopolist, the monopsonist also influences the market price, often securing special terms such as favourable credit or payment arrangements as well as a lower basic price.

In practice it becomes increasingly difficult for one firm to control an entire market in today's global trading conditions. Deregulation, and in many countries the sell-off of state monopolies, has reduced monopoly power. Nonetheless the common form of competition in many consumer markets is now the oligopoly, which is itself a long way from perfect competition.

MOST FAVOURED NATION A condition which seeks to ensure equal treatment for all countries in world trade. Members of the General Agreement on Tariffs and Trade (now the World Trade Organization) agree to impose the same tariffs, duties, and regulations on all countries which have MFN status. This applies irrespective of their size or market volume. Similarly if a country negotiates a new trading agreement with one country, it must then conduct its trade with all other MFN countries in the same way. In practice, however, many regions or groups of countries have special arrangements with their main trading partners (e.g. the EU Single Market), which tends to undermine the multilateral nature of the MFN system.

MULTIPLIER This is a cornerstone of **Keynesian** economics. It refers to the fact that an injection, representing an increase in aggregate demand, to the **circular flow of national income**, will eventually bring about a greater increase in income and demand.

Suppose a firm takes on more workers because it expects more demand for its products in the future. The extra wages earned by these new workers will, after tax is deducted, represent an increase in the total disposable income for the economy. Some of this will be spent, some of it saved. The extra spending will increase aggregate demand, as other firms take on extra workers to make extra products, and that in turn will feed into still more spending. It is important to note that this process takes place over time, as the effect of the initial increase in aggregate demand feeds through the economy. Also it is clear from our example that the more of an increase in income that is spent (reflected by the marginal propensity to consume), then the greater the value of the multiplier, and the greater the marginal propensity to save, the lower the mulitplier. Since all of an increase in disposable income will by definition be made up of savings and consumption, then

$$mps + mpc = 1$$

and the value of the multiplier, usually given the letter k, is

$$k = \frac{1}{mps}$$

or alternatively

$$k = \frac{1}{(1 - mpc)}.$$

We can express this using the traditional Keynesian demand–output diagram. Note that the 45-degree line represents all the points where demand and output are in equilibrium (*see* **inflation**), and an increase in aggregate demand from D to D_1

will be shown as a move from curve AD to curve AD_1 (the slope of this curve reflecting the proportion of any increase in income which is spent, rather than saved, i.e. the marginal propensity to consume). A series of moves, which represent the working of the multiplier, bring the level of output up to an eventual new equilibrium, where output rises from O to O_1. If the increase O to O_1 is twice that of the increase D to D_1, then the multiplier has a value of 2.

The steeper the slope of the AD curve, the higher the multiplier.

As well as savings, any increase in aggregate demand will also be subject to **leakages** in the form of taxation and spending on imports. So in the full model, we can express the multiplier as:

$$k = \frac{1}{mps + mpt + mpm}.$$

(*See also* **bank credit multiplier**, **accelerator**.)

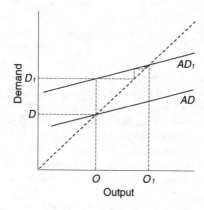

Multiplier

N

NATIONALIZATION Nationalization refers to the public ownership of industry. It is often associated with the thinking of Karl **Marx**, but it has been a widespread phenomenon, occurring in capitalist, socialist, and developing economies. The current trend in macroeconomic practice, from China to Western Europe, is away from nationalization. Some countries (e.g. the UK, and now Germany, Italy, and most of the other EU nations, as well as many of the former socialist countries of Eastern Europe) have vigorously embraced a policy of selling off nationalised industries. This process has been associated both with deregulation, to allow greater competition, and at the same time **regulation** to break up **monopolies**. It has also been seen as a way to broaden equity ownership across a wider range of private investors.

Traditionally, the proponents of nationalization have argued either from an ideological standpoint (that state ownership ensures greater distributive justice and accountability), or from a more pragmatic economic position. In the latter case, some industries may be state-controlled, but the supply and distribution may be undertaken by private enterprise industries operating through the market mechanism.

One of the main economic arguments for nationalization has been the existence of natural monopolies. These are firms or industries which may have a unique advantage in terms of physical resources which cannot be duplicated by other firms. It is often argued that such firms are under no pressure to minimize costs simply because they are able to earn excess profits and as such may abuse their power (*see* **x-inefficiency**). At the same time, certain industries such as gas and telephone require an interlocking of supply, and so competition in such an industry may result in an unnecessary duplication of resources at an extra expense. Against that, the free enterprise position would be that every economic activity benefits from competition, and that provided regulators are effective in breaking up monopolies where necessary, pricing and investment decisions will maximize the efficiency and allocation of scarce resources. In addition, allowing governments to interfere in microeconomic activity is seen as being ultimately detrimental to the consumer.

As markets become more global, there is now a growing awareness that one-country industries will find it increasingly difficult to compete successfully with multinational companies which have access to greater capital resources and considerable **economies of scale**.

(*See* essay on stakeholding by Justin Urquhart Stewart.)

NEO-CLASSICAL ECONOMICS The neo-Classical school in economics is an extension and a systematization of the **Classical** analysis. It is often seen as being in the opposing corner to **Keynesian** and **neo-Keynesian** thinking. The works of Adam **Smith**, David **Ricardo**, Robert **Malthus**, Jean Baptiste **Say** and Karl **Marx**, along with the contributions of the Marginalist school of thought (**Marshall**, **Walras**, and Jevons), have all helped to shape neo-Classical economics. More recently, Arrow, Debreu, and Mackenzie developed certain aspects, including the model which is now the reference point for general equilibrium analysis. An outline of the basic tenets of the neo-Classical paradigm is as follows.

1. Economic activities are in the final instance supply-determined. This premise stems from Say's Law. It implies that the demand side is under-determined by the structure and function of the supply side of the economy. Thus, all fluctuations emanate from, or are dominated by, the behaviour of aggregate supply. Therefore, the structure of all economic progress is deeply rooted in supply phenomena. (*See* **supply-side economics**.)

2. There exists a sharp distinction between nominal and real economic variables. This assumption is called the 'Classical dichotomy'. Nominal variables are those aggregates measured in pecuniary or monetary terms. They are expressed in dollars, pounds, marks, yens, or whatever is the country's monetary unit. Real variables, on the other hand, take into account the general price level prevailing in the economy. They represent purchasing power with reference to a standard basket of goods and services. The Classical dichotomy states that all disturbances related to nominal variables will be confined in the nominal sector of the economy. Therefore, there exists no channel of communication between real and monetary phenomena, especially in the **long-run** analysis. The transmission mechanism of relative prices is perceived to be the adjusting means through which disturbances are communicated between the nominal and real economy.

3. The **quantity theory** of money holds and money is neutral. That means that changes that in the quantity of money will have an impact only on the price level and not on the level of production, at least for the long run. A refinement of this position led to the idea of the 'superneutrality' of money, which involves equiproportional changes of M (money) and P (prices) through time, i.e. equality of the rates of growth of **money supply** and **inflation**.

4. The velocity of money circulating is assumed to be fixed for any particular economy, given its institutional structure and the historical development of its production process.

5. The free-enterprise market system has an intrinsic property of stability. The innate characteristic of any market, especially when viewed from a general equilibrium standpoint, is its ability to reach

clearing or equilibrium levels. This property of market clearing is best summarized in the proposition known as **Walras's Law**. This states that all excess demands for all agents and markets in an exchange/production economy will tend to zero. Associated with the notion of the existence of a unique and stable general equilibrium solution is the concept of individual rationality. All individuals are assumed to look after their self-interest, and in doing so they utilize all social resources optimally. This aspect of the market system is sometimes referred to as the 'invisible hand', a concept derived from Adam Smith.

6. The role of the market is twofold. It allocates scarce resources amongst competing alternative needs (social and individual) and distributes returns for the factors involved in the production process. Two major issues prevail: the problem of production efficiency (technical and allocational) and the problem of distributive justice. For the neo-Classical school the most important is the first one. In the long run the market system is considered to solve also optimally the problem of distribution.

7. As for economic policy, priority is given to all regimes aiming to combat inflation. Distributive issues such as unemployment are thought of as residually resolved by the system in the long run. Hence, the focus of economic policy ought to be the attempt to reduce inflation so that private investment and growth will be encouraged.

8. Expectations play an important role in the development of economic activities. Therefore, in order to reduce inflationary expectations monetary policy should abide by rules and should not be discretionary. Policy instability induces uncertainty and increases the likelihood of divergence from equilibrium behaviour.

9. The general equilibrium approach is preferred as a means of analysis, and small-scale econometric models with emphasis on their predictive performance are utilized. The competitive equilibria reached are optimal, i.e. **Pareto** optimality exists. Justifications rely on fixed-point theorem arguments.

10. The market of loanable funds is assumed to clear with the appropriate adjustment of the **interest rate**. Savings are considered to depend positively on the interest rate – contrary to Keynesian conceptions, which treat savings as a part of, and a function of, disposable income.

11. Government intervention in the market is considered inefficient and therefore unwarranted. The role of the state is to guarantee the unobstructed function of the market as the ultimate device to allocate property rights in an efficient and just way. Anti-trust policies and **regulation** which counter the menace of **monopoly** power are viewed as one appropriate form of state intervention.

12. In the long run, 'parasitic' phenomena such as systematic speculation, arbitrage, or informational asymmetries/inadequacies are considered eliminable. Appropriate release of information by the state

guarantees that the first best properties of the general equilibrium solutions will be preserved with the reduction or elimination of uncertainty.

13. Trade-offs identified by relations such as the **Phillips Curve** are arbitrary from an analytical point of view, since: (a) no microeconomic underpinnings are provided for this aggregate behaviour; and (b) long-run empirical evidence is inconclusive, so the assumed trade-off does not hold.

14. Analytical tools and abstractions such as the aggregate production function or the social welfare function are utilized in an effort to supplement formal theory with the treatment of normative issues. All normative evaluations should, however, take seriously the constraints imposed by Arrow's Impossibility Theorem, which sets logical limits to how individuals can act together to produce a consistent set of preferences for the group as a whole.

(*See also* **theory of production costs, theory of consumer demand**, and the essay by Paul Ormerod.)

NEO-KEYNESIAN ECONOMICS In one sense, the debate which scorched the academic earth between the followers of **Keynes** and the **monetarists** has been fought out. There are still differences in certain sections of the frameworks, such as the demand for money and the **money supply/** spending linkages. There are still empirical grey areas, and a major taxonomic problem with **money** itself. But for today's Keynesians, the neo-

Keynesians, the debate centres much more about what is equilibrium. They reject the **neo-Classical** synthesis (*see* **IS/LM** model) which sought to reestablish the links between the money economy and the 'real' economy of output and **employment**. Attempts have been made to characterize states of recession and chronic unemployment as anomalies from the equilibrium of cleared markets, and modern neo-Classical economists have pointed to wage stickiness and liquidity traps as being possible reasons why economies do not – in the short term – move towards a full capacity equilibrium.

This is all vigorously rejected by the neo-Keynesians. In essence, their position can be summarized as follows:

1. The market system has a tendency towards a non-market-clearing state. Markets do not clear, and this is a common feature of all market economies. This is evident from real world problems such as unemployment (an indication of non-clearing factor markets or under-employment of capital resources), speculation in financial markets, arbitrage (either at a domestic or international level) and widespread poverty or unequal distribution of international economic growth and development. All these empirical issues point towards one major deficiency of the **Classical** tradition's approach: the market-clearing assumptions associated with **Walras's Law**. Neo-Keynesians consider the equilibrium approach an unfruitful and operationally meaningless concept in the light of the history of modern

western economies. Conditions of disequilibrium or off-the-equilibrium behaviour may and do arise very often in today's economies.

2. **Say's** famous law (that supply creates its own demand) is rejected, following Keynes's lead. The economic system is demand-driven. The fluctuations of the demand side are dominant. They are attributed to the time-instability of **investment** demand as well as to the relatively lower, but not negligible volatility of the government sector's demand for consumption and investment goods on the one hand and the variance of private **consumption** on the other.

3. The **quantity theory** explanations of monetary phenomena are deemed unsatisfactory. The equation $MV = PT$ does not hold, or it is unstable through time given the variability of the velocity of money. Empirical evidence seems to favour this remark, since velocity shocks are common in the recent economic history of many countries.

4. Money is not 'neutral' and changes in the monetary base can be transmitted to the real sector of the economy via transmission mechanisms (for example, the interest rate) that bridge financial and real markets. The potency of monetary policy increases in proportion to the size of certain crucial parameters. These include the fiscal characteristics of the economy (i.e. the structure of its income taxation and the nature of its tax rates), its marginal propensity to save, and the responsiveness of private investment plans to changes in interest rates.

5. **Inflation** is considered a microeconomic phenomenon and its explanation should incorporate issues such as:
   (a) the level of profit or the mark up structure in a particular industry;
   (b) the ratio of direct to indirect taxation for a specific product;
   (c) the growth of marginal productivity of factors and resources used in a specific production process;
   (d) the proportion of the product's value that is imported. Prices of imported resources and factors play a crucial role (leading to the notion of imported inflation).

6. Private investment is unstable. The theory of marginal efficiency of capital may be utilized to analyse the level of investment demand, but factors such as 'animal spirits' (the term was coined by the post-Keynesian Joan Robinson) are important in the stimulation of the overall investment behaviour.

7. The market of loanable funds has two sides: **demand** (i.e. aggregate investment) which is affected by the rate of interest; and **supply** (i.e. overall savings) which is determined by the disposable income. Therefore, this market does not necessarily clear either ex ante or ex post.

8. Employment and income are determined at the macroeconomic level.

Following on from and developing the above points, we can see that for neo-Keynesians various policy prescriptions hold. Demand management and 'fine tuning' are endorsed for both the level of government expenditure (*G*) and for the money supply (*Ms*). For this reason both *G* and *Ms* are viewed as endogenous variables – contrary to the monetarist/neo-Classical positions. Neo-Keynesians favour active and ongoing intervention and therefore take the side of discretion in what is known as the 'rules vs. discretion' debate (compare with the 'rule' of maintaining the growth of money supply in line with growth of output). Only the **short-run** dimension is important for the analysis of economic phenomena (as Keynes pointed out, in the long run we are dead). And the problem of distributive justice takes priority over that of productive efficiency. Thus, economic policies aiming at combating high unemployment rates are appropriate. A demand stimulus corrects the distributive justice first and facilitates afterwards the restoration of efficiency in production.

It should be pointed out that some economists argue that neo-Keynesianism is a misnomer for an elaboration or in some cases a development of the views of Keynes, and that it does not represent a separate body of thinking. One area that could claim itself to be a definite new strand has been the use of microeconomic theory to explain various forms of 'stickiness' in wages and prices, thus giving an indication of why markets do not clear. The implicit contract theory and efficiency wage models examine why wages may remain higher during periods of recession and lower during periods of labour shortage than they otherwise would. In essence, this is attributed to labour and employers both benefiting from more constant wages. Similarly, the 'shopping model' developed by Okun points to the desire of shopper and shopkeeper, or supplier and client, to maintain a relationship, often at the expense of flexibility in prices. (*See also* essay on relationship marketing by Adrian Payne and Sue Holt.)

NEW ISSUE MARKET **Stock markets** buy and sell **shares** and **securities** which have already been issued: the new issue market is a series of mechanisms designed to place new instruments into the trading universe of the stock market. In the process, companies, governments, and other institutions can raise long-term share (or, alternatively, debt) capital. The new issue market is sometimes generically referred to as the primary market, with the main stock market being the secondary market. A company which is offering shares to the public for the first time is said to be making a flotation (US = initial public offering (IPO)).

The largest companies or institutions will often offer their shares directly to the public, usually advertising the IPO widely and printing a prospectus. People can then apply for shares, which, if the issue is oversubscribed, will be allocated by the company or its issuing house (which may be a **merchant bank**), perhaps by favouring certain kinds of investors, or perhaps just by scaling back everyone's applications on a pro-rata basis. If the shares are particularly popular, they will usually start trading at a higher price than the buyers paid for them, so by selling quickly it is possible to realize an immediate profit, a process known as 'stagging'.

The shares may not be so easy to place, and most flotations involve the use of one or more banks or other financial institutions to **underwrite** the issue. That way the risk can be spread.

All of this is a highly expensive process, involving costs for advertising, underwriting, and administering the application and allocation process. If the company already has shares which trade on the stock market, it may choose the simpler and cheaper alternative of a rights issue. This is a process of awarding new shares to existing shareholders. The disadvantage to the company is that the shares will normally be offered at a discount to their current trading price, to encourage the shareholders to pay up for the new issue.

One significant development in new issues over the past decade has been the tendency to place shares simultaneously on a number of big international markets, as well as the 'home' one for the company. That way the issue can reach the widest possible number of private investors and institutions. Deregulation of global capital markets has helped this process, as has the globalization of financial institutions, and indeed companies themselves. If a company is trading globally, it is logical to offer its shares on a global scale.

NORMATIVE/POSITIVE/WELFARE ECONOMICS Positive economics is the area which examines issues and processes which can be verified empirically, whereas normative economics includes some level of value judgement about what is good for society, or the economy, or an economic entity. In practice, most of normative economics leans on positive economics to justify its means, if not its ends. So for example, if stable economic growth with full employment is taken to be 'best' for society, economists can still call on positivism to justify certain types of fiscal or monetary policy. There is often pressure on economists to positivize certain aspects of normative economics, such as welfare policy, or environmental concerns. In this way a calculation may be made of the opportunity cost of building, say, a hospital rather than a road. Or the cost of pollution may be measured by comparing wages or property prices in unpolluted regions, or quantifying the costs to forestry of acid rain, or to the health industry of looking after people made sick by effluent. (*See* **opportunity cost**.)

The complex dynamic and **regression** analysis involved in such processes is very much the realm of **econometrics**. Econometrics is increasingly important as a way of reconciling positive and normative economics, as the sophistication of sampling and testing models develops with more powerful computers. (*See* essay by Paul Ormerod, 'What Economics Is Not'.)

O

OFF BALANCE-SHEET FINANCING If a firm opts to lease or rent an **asset** that is subject to depreciation, rather than buying the asset altogether, then the asset itself will not appear on the firm's balance sheet. However, the rental payments will be taken into account in the profits and losses, and the indebtedness of the company along with the capital employed will be understated.

An example of using an asset by hiring it rather than buying it can illustrate the benefits of off balance-sheet financing. Suppose a printing company decides to install a large press that costs £600,000. Rather than purchase this large fixed asset, the company decides to enter into a lease agreement, agreeing to pay £15,000 per year for five years. Each year, the company allocates £15,000 to the profit and loss account, which does not appear on the balance sheet as a fixed asset because the firm does not own the asset. In essence, the asset simply shows up as an annual operating cost, which may be offset against profit for taxation purposes.

Off balance-sheet financing enables a company to make use of expensive assets without investing large sums of money to pay for them. It also makes use of a company's long-term capital (long-term funds) for as short a period as possible, thus improving its return on capital employed. Not only does off balance-sheet financing enhance a company's accounting ratios (such as the return on capital employed and **gearing** ratio), but it also avoids breaking any agreement between banks with respect to the amount that a company may borrow.

The problems, of course, are that the person who owns the asset such as the printing press will have taken the risk and will therefore require to make a profit, which will usually make leasing or renting more expensive than buying the equipment outright. And off balance-sheet financing also reduces current profits.

OLIGOPOLY An oligopoly is a market characterized by a few firms who have some control over the prices and output of goods they produce. It can be viewed as a hybrid between **perfect competition** and **monopoly**. Three specific characteristics make up an oligopoly: the number of firms, the extent of product differentiation, and barriers to entry.

In an oligopoly, the bulk of the market **supply** is in the hands of a relatively small number of large firms who sell to many small buyers. Although they have some control over the prices charged to customers, they must be wary of prices offered by rivals in the constant struggle for market share. So if one firm reduces its prices in order to gain market share, this may result in greater profits if other firms do not follow suit or it may result in other firms cutting prices as well to protect their market share. In the latter instance all firms suffer through reduced profits. Thus, oligopolistic firms attempt to avoid price competition by employing a price leader strategy where one firm sets the example with prices and other firms 'follow the leader'. This tends to result in a **kinked demand curve**, where the market 'sticks' in the medium term at a certain price.

Another characteristic of oligopolistic markets is the extent to which similar products are differentiated. In most circumstances this is achieved through advertising or branding, allowing prices to remain generally stable.

Oligopolies also tend to be associated with high barriers to market entry. This is the primary reason why they have some control over prices and outputs. It may be that they have achieved a level of technological sophistication that new entrants would find hard to match, or it may be that they can indulge in predatory pricing, reducing profits in the short term to exclude rivals. However, in some cases new firms are drawn into the industry and pursue keen price competition.

A problem that stems from most oligopolies is collusion. This refers to cooperation between independent firms in an attempt to modify competition. Collusion may be explicit in the economy or it may be tacit and involve the fixing of prices at higher levels than at minimum costs. A 'collusive oligopoly' is defined as two or more nearly identical firms pro-

ducing output at levels that are similar to monopolies.

Similar to collusion among firms are cartels among producers. A cartel is an association which regulates prices and output, as well as competition in the market place. Although cartels are illegal in most countries, governments may allow them to operate in order to 'rationalize' output in the economy. In general, however, cartels tend to be unstable because a single member of the association may always be tempted to make excess profits by breaking the terms of the agreement by undercutting the competition. One example of a cartel is the Organization of Petroleum Exporting Countries (OPEC).

In terms of the dynamics of oligopolies, traditional market theory predicts that the resulting output will be monopoly-like, in the sense that it will be below minimum cost levels. Inefficient firms (*see* **x-inefficiency**) are cushioned by excess profits and are reluctant to engage in price competition. They protect their excess profits by high barriers to entry. This is the typical model described by Cournot.

An alternative theory introduced by Bertrand tends to support a more competitive market structure. Bertrand's model is based on two (or more) oligopolistic firms whose behaviour is dominated by the effect of their prices on those of their rivals. This leads to a convergence toward a profit-maximizing price level. It takes little account of the possibility of new entrants.

OPPORTUNITY COST The existence of **scarcity** in economics implies that all of us as individuals, or companies, or governments, must choose between limited resources. It is therefore important to find a way to measure or analyse the implications of making such choices, by looking at the costs and the benefits. Economists search for a comprehensive approach to the costs of activities and so define the opportunity cost of an action as the value of the forgone alternative action. Usually this is described as the best alternative forgone.

Opportunity costs reflect the value of passed opportunities, and in outlining them there are often discrepancies between economic costs and accounting costs. The latter defines costs in terms of monetary outlay. An entrepreneur earning accounting profits of £8,000 without paying himself wages may have much lower profits in economic terms if opportunity costs are considered. For example, if the entrepreneur could be earning a salary working elsewhere, then these wages should also be deducted from the accounting profits. In this way the salary represents the forgone opportunity of earning wages elsewhere. Or a piece of machinery with no scrap value is usually accounted for in terms of its historical cost, when in fact its opportunity cost is zero. In calculating the allocation of scarce resources for public projects, the concept of opportunity cost is developed into social cost-benefit analysis. In an effort to quantify items which do not have a normal market price (such as clean air, or safety), economists have evolved a system of 'shadow pricing' and 'surrogate markets'. So these might try to work out the cost not just of producing certain chemicals in terms of labour, plant, etc., but the possible pollution, noise, etc., that would be associated with them. In this way the 'marginal social cost' is calculated, to be set against the benefits of the project.

OPTIONS/CALLS/PUTS These are forms of **derivatives** that give the buyer (seller) the right to buy (sell) a **security** underlying the **asset** for a given price at a specified time in the future. The given price is referred to as the strike price, and the specified time in the future is called the maturity date. It is important to differentiate this form of derivative from **futures** and forwards in which the buyer (seller) is obliged to buy (sell) the security underlying the asset. The primary benefit of options is that investors can use leverage to their advantage for arbitrage, hedging, or speculating. A call option is the right to buy the security underlying the asset at a specified strike price, whereas a put option is the right to sell the security underlying the asset at a specified strike price.

To understand the dynamics of options, suppose an investor believes that the price of the underlying asset is expected to appreciate some time in the future. The investor can then purchase a call option ('go long in the call') at the given strike price and maturity date. If at the maturity date the price of the underlying asset is greater than the strike price of the call option, the investor will exercise the right to buy, thereby acquiring the asset for less than its market price. The asset could then be sold at the market for a net gain. Call options are bought when the price of the underlying security is expected to appreciate, and put options are bought when the price of the underlying security is expected to depreciate. Combinations of puts and calls can support an infinite number of investment strategies.

The recent work of Black and Scholes in deriving a method of pricing options significantly increased the number of products made in this market. Their work essentially was a method of pricing risk and uncertainty, and was recognized by the award of the Nobel Prize for Economics in 1997. The trading of options has increased rapidly in the past couple of decades, and is part of the global explosion in derivatives, which has led to some concern for governments and regulators.

P

PARADOX OF THRIFT In a nutshell, this explains why **saving** (regarded by most moralists and household economists as 'good') may actually be 'bad' for an economy. If too much disposable income is taken out of consumption, aggregate demand will fall (savings are a **leakage** from the **circular flow of national income**) and the effects of the **multiplier** will mean that the initial leakage will have a greater effect on income than its nominal amount. The injection to the circular flow which corresponds to savings is investment, and saving is regarded as the main source of funds for investment spending by businesses. But savings decisions and investment decisions are made by two different groups of people – they might not necessarily be in equilibrium. (*See* **investment** for a more detailed explanation of the workings of savings and investment at various interest rates and income levels.) If savings are too high, the lack of demand may actually choke off investment; during a period of recovery, that may stall or delay the recovery.

PARETO This is a position where the distribution and allocation of resources in an economy is such that any change to make one person or group better off would at the same time make another person or group worse off.

Vilfredo Pareto, the Italian economist after whom the concept is named, defined 'optimality' in terms of **utility**. This allowed the expression of wants and preferences in terms of marginal rates of substitution between goods, creating an 'indifference curve' which represents the various combinations of goods which provide the same utility (for a fuller explanation of the workings of indifference curves, *see* **Edgeworth Box**). Pareto optimality implies that everyone shares the same ratio of substitution between goods and services; otherwise, by trading, two people could enjoy greater utility without making each other worse off (a Pareto improvement). At the Pareto optimum the same two people would only exchange goods in the same ratio, meaning that the trade would not increase either's utility – or that it would increase the utility of one at the expense of the other.

The big drawback with the notion of Pareto optimality is that, like most tools using comparisons of utility, it is ordinal and does not provide a numerical (cardinal) measure such as price which can be applied across all goods and services. And secondly, it does not address the fact that many real-world economic decisions are based on one person being better off at the expense of another. Nonetheless, the concept has provided a lasting framework for much of welfare economics, where often the decisions (a new hospital, or a new by-pass) are harder to quantify and therefore more likely to be based on notions such as utility. (*See* **opportunity cost**.)

PERFECT COMPETITION The idea of perfect competition is an economic ideal. It reflects the most efficient production in the prevailing market conditions. It rarely exists in practice, but analytically it is important as one extreme of the **theories of production costs** and of **consumer demand**. Four essential ingredients that make up perfect competition.

1. A perfectly competitive market is made up of many buyers and sellers. Essentially they are all too small to have any individual impact on prices. These buyers and sellers are referred to as 'price takers', because they must accept the prices dictated by the law of **demand** and **supply**.
2. Individual suppliers are providing a homogeneous product which cannot be differentiated by consumers.
3. The primary aim of firms under perfect competition will be maximize profits. We shall see why this will lead eventually to each firm making a normal profit.
4. Entry to and exit from the market is freely available, with no barriers as would exist under more monopolistic competition.

If we examine the cost and **revenue** curves for one firm in a perfectly competitive industry, we can see that the price sets a perfectly **elastic** level of demand. The average revenue

(demand) curve is flat, indicating that above the given price, consumers would switch to competitive firms at the original price. Clearly there is no advantage to lowering price, since the individual firm does not produce enough to affect the overall market price, and a reduction would simply undermine profits. Since the revenue from each unit of production remains the same across the demand curve, producing just one more unit will bring in extra revenue equivalent to the prevailing price. So MR is also horizontal at the price P_1. (Compare this to the marginal revenue curve of a more monopolistic firm where marginal revenue at various levels of price takes into account revenue which is forgone at all the higher price levels on the demand curve.)

Suppose that in the short term the marginal revenue and marginal cost curves intersect at the profit-maximizing point of X_1 output. Average cost at this point is C_1, which is lower than the price, allowing the firm to make supernormal profits. These are the rectangle $P_1C_1 \times X_1$ (Fig. 1).

In a perfectly competitive industry, this would attract new entrants. This would increase the supply of the product, causing the industry supply curve to shift to the right. Assuming that demand remained constant, this would result in a lower price, say P_2 (Fig. 2).

The effect would be to squeeze out the supernormal profit – P_2 would eventually be at a new level where $MC = MR$. The individual firm would produce less, reflecting the new entrants to the market, and would make only normal profits. Similarly, if the price fell below P_2, some firms would leave

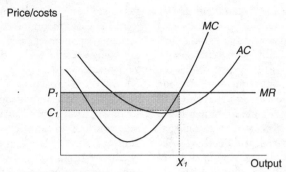

Perfect competition (individual firm in short term), *Fig. 1*

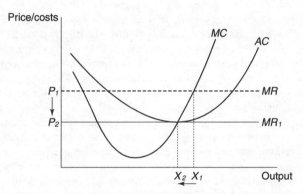

Perfect competition (individual firm in long term), *Fig. 2*

the industry, reducing the supply and shifting the industry supply curve back to the left, raising prices. Thus in perfect competition, individual firms will produce at a level where their technical optimum cost level is the same as the price.

Probably the best examples of perfect competition exist with the supply of certain types of commodity, such as wheat, coffee, or cocoa. There can be major changes (such as crop failures) which shift the supply curve to the left, resulting in higher prices. This would not normally result in supernormal profits, however, as the initial shock would typically have

raised the costs of the firms within the market. Another example of perfect competition is (sometimes) found in the financial markets, where a large number of buyers and sellers make it impossible for one player to set a price. (Although large **institutional** shareholders can often directly affect equity prices, and governments can affect **bond** prices or, through intervention in the currency markets, the **exchange rate**.) (*See* **monopoly**, **oligopoly**.)

Under these conditions it can be said that perfect competition contributes to economic efficiency in the short run as well as the long run. In the short run, because firms are assumed to maximize profits, they set marginal revenue equal to marginal costs (the additional revenue derived from selling a good just covers the additional costs from producing the one more unit of output). If this were not so and marginal revenue was less than marginal costs, then it would pay the firm to reduce production by one unit of output (a similar type of argument can describe the converse scenario). However, we also stated that because firms are price takers they set price equal to marginal revenue. This in turn suggests that in a perfectly competitive industry, price equals the marginal cost of a representative firm. This ensures that no consumer will be deterred from buying something whose value exceeds its cost.

Similarly in the long run, any existing excess profits will entice new entrants, and because of the absence of barriers to entry, this can be done costlessly. As a consequence a greater supply of the product will be available in the market, causing the price to go down. Prices will continue to depreciate until such time as profits are zero. One should not think that this aspect of perfect competition contradicts the assumption of profit maximization. Firms are still maximizing profits, but the zero profit implication indicates that no entrepreneur or factor of production earns more than it just needs to be persuaded into the industry.

Another implication of profit maximization and low barriers of entry is that a firm will produce output at levels where average revenue equals marginal costs as well as average costs.

This implies that average costs coincide with marginal costs in a perfectly competitive industry. This can only occur when costs are minimized.

For the individual firm, this level of homogeneity in a heterogeneous market limits growth. There will therefore be a constant drive to innovate and differentiate to create a product which can command a higher price and more profits: the short-term implications of a greater level of oligopoly or monopoly.

Although a perfectly competitive industry contributes to efficiencies in the short and long run, such frictionless markets are rarely observed in the economy. However, occasionally a situation arises where the buyers and sellers of the market are so numerous that the assumptions of perfect competition actually become realistic. This generally occurs when economies of scale are not present, or if they are present, in terms of the level of output they are negligible relative to the size of the market.

PHILLIPS CURVE In 1958 the British economist A. W. Phillips identified a negative relationship between the relative change in the nominal wage rate and the level of unemployment for the UK over the period 1861–1957. This empirical relationship appears to show a trade-off between **employment** and **inflation**, for higher nominal wage rates can be regarded as an indicator of inflation. If unemployment falls, due to an increase in aggregate demand, then employers will be prepared to pay higher nominal wages (shown in the diagram as a move from U_2 to U_1, leading to a

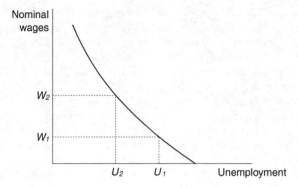

Phillips Curve

move up the curve from money wages at W_1 to the higher W_2 (see figure).

The basic Phillips Curve cannot be considered a solid analytic foundation for economic policy prescriptions. It has several major weaknesses. First, later developments called into question the basic empirical framework. In particular, the period of **stagflation** in the 1970s appeared to show that high nominal wages and inflation could coexist with high unemployment. Secondly, the microeconomic foundations of the Phillips Curve have never been satisfactorily explained, despite the efforts by R. G. Lipsey and E. S. Phelps to provide an explanation of the excess labour supply deemed to be the source of wage changes. Thirdly, **monetarists** such as Friedman argued that in the long run, the Phillips Curve will correspond to the non-accelerating inflationary rate of unemployment (NAIRU), which will be a vertical line in the diagram. Attempts by government to reduce unemployment below this level will lead to higher wages, which will in turn raise unemployment back to its natural level, etc.

This led to a refinement of the Phillips Curve, which became known as the **expectations-adjusted Phillips Curve**.

PIGOU, ARTHUR CECIL (1877–1959) was a British economist who studied under **Marshall** at Cambridge. He is most noted for his contributions to **monetary** theory, **employment** and national income, as well as welfare economics.

Pigou was one of the first economists to enunciate the real balance effect, which subsequently became known as the Pigou effect. In essence it argues that if **wages** and prices are permitted to fall during a recession, there is a resultant increase in the real money supply. This is because the relative value of the money balances people hold (i.e. their *real* balances) increases as prices of labour and **commodities** fall. This rise in wealth will increase consumption and spending, bringing about a reflation of the economy.

The difficulty with this theory is that falling prices and wages usually cause expectations of further falls, bringing about a reduction in spending, rather than an increase.

Although most of his macro-economic theories were superseded by **Keynes**, Pigou is well known for his contributions in welfare economics. His book *Economics of Welfare* (1919) explains how **utility** theory can be applied to sets of groups rather than individuals in the economy, to help governments make policy decisions.

PPP   Purchasing power parity is an element in the theory of trade which holds that the equilibrium exchange rate between trading countries is the rate which prices two identical baskets of goods at exactly the same price in each. Put another way, PPP says that people value currencies for what they will buy.

Formally, the PPP relationship is expressed as:

PPP Exchange rate of currency country X to country Y

$$= \frac{\text{Price of basket of goods in country X}}{\text{Price of basket of goods in country Y}}$$

The table below helps illustrate PPP. For simplicity we assume that the rate of inflation for both countries is zero and the basket of goods in our case is jacket potatoes and french fries.

	Jacket Potatoes	French Fries
United States	$3	$1
United Kingdom	£2	£1

According to the table, the exchange rate under PPP should be 1.33 dollars per £1 ((3+1)/(2+1)).

A variant of the basic PPP is that starting from a basic 'equilibrium' exchange rate, future movements in the rate will be determined by relative price movements in each country. In our example, if the prices in the US changed to $6 for jacket potatoes and $2 for french fries, the PPP exchange rate would be £1 = $2.67 ((6+2)/(2+1)).

Broadly speaking, PPP has been observed not to hold in most cases, because it fails to take into account some of the other factors which determine price differences in different countries, such as differences in incomes, tastes, transportation costs, and government policies.

Probably the most common 'spin-off' from the PPP theory is the so-called 'hamburger test'. Here, the cost of a supposedly universal basic like a hamburger is compared across a number of countries to provide a useful, if crude, guide to living costs. So if the exchange rate is £1 = $1.50 = DM3, but a hamburger costs 80p, $1.50, and DM3.20, life is costlier in Berlin than it is in New York, and it's cheapest in London – if you're living on hamburgers!

PRICE EFFECT/WEALTH EFFECT   An element in the **theory of consumer demand** which examines the effect of a price change on consumer behaviour. A reduction in the price of a product has two implications: first, the consumer has more money to spend on the **product** in question. This is known as the income effect, because it operates in the same way as if the consumer had enjoyed an increase in income. Secondly, there is a substitution effect. The consumer can now spend more on other products, while buying the same amount of the cheaper product, at the same level of income. The two elements in the price effect were identified by the Russian economist Eugen Slutsky. The Slutsky Equation, put simply, says:

price effect =
income effect + substitution effect.

Demand theorists have closely studied the working of the price effect for various goods, and identified that some goods exhibit a proportionately greater substitution effect than others. Put differently, the income effect is negative. This applies particularly to poorer-quality goods, known as inferior goods, which people will prefer to buy less of as their real income increases. The most extreme form of an inferior good is a **Giffen good**, where the negative income effect is so strong that a reduction in price actually means that less of the product will be bought.

(*See* **demand curve**; **upward-sloping demand curve**.)

PRICING PRACTICE In theory, companies will price their products according to the **theory of production costs** and the **theory of consumer demand**, so that marginal revenue equals marginal costs. This is the assumption (in the long term) for **perfect competition**. Firms which enjoy **monopoly** or **oligopoly** positions can be price makers (rather than price takers) and their higher-than-marginal pricing will provide a producer's surplus.

In practice, much pricing will depend on rules-of-thumb, or longer-term marketing and production strategy.

Often companies benefit from the fact that consumers may not always make rational decisions based on perfect knowledge of the market. What is known as 'cost-plus pricing' is usually marginal cost plus 'what the market will take'. This is still pricing for profit maximization, i.e. a situation where marginal revenue equals marginal cost to the best of a company's knowledge.

Other forms of pricing involve price discrimination, which can work when there are different markets with different price elasticities of demand – and no leakage between the two – with the same costs and supply conditions for both markets. Thus airlines operate differential pricing, based, say on business customers and holiday-makers, with the product supply conditions (aircraft seats) the same for each group. 'Peak load pricing' is the term for different prices at different periods of demand: it can apply to utilities such as telephone companies or electricity firms, but it also applies to railways (who may also operate differential pricing, along the lines of the airlines).

Companies which are trying to break into a new market or launch a new product (*see* **product life cycle**) may practise 'penetration pricing' (but may be the victims of 'predatory pricing' by those already in the market). Today's current theories of marketing emphasize the importance of building long-term relationships with customers, and this will also be reflected in pricing practice. (*See* the essay by Adrian Payne and Sue Holt on relationship marketing.)

Industries which are state-controlled may be required by governments or regulators to operate 'marginal-cost pricing', although this may involve their making a loss.

So although the **neo-Classical** price theories form the basis of price in microeconomics, the day-to-day decisions by businesses are more complex, and, because of imperfect market information, somewhat less precise.

PROBABILITY Probability theory is the branch of mathematics that is concerned with measuring the quantitative likelihood that a given event from an experiment will have a particular outcome. This branch of mathematics was developed in an attempt to answer certain questions with regard to games of chance. Although probability theory is attributed to seventeenth century French mathematicians such as Pascal, its roots lie even further back in the study of mathematics and gambling.

Probability theory is primarily based on permutations and combinations, and uses set theory to describe concepts such as probability space, event space, and outcome space. The probability of events is described using any real number between and including 0 and 1. A figure of zero for an event means that there is no likelihood of such an event occurring – it is impossible. Similarly, a probability of 1 implies that the event is sure to occur.

Two important notions of set theory that are employed in probability theory are independence and mutually exclusive events. Two events are independent if, and only if, the probability of both events occurring is equal to the product of the likelihood of each event. The implication is that the likelihood of one of the events occurring has no impact on the occurrence or non-occurrence of the other event. The concept of independence is distinct from mutual exclusivity. Two events are mutually exclusive if the probability of their joint occurrence is impossible. Mutually exclusive events imply that the occurrence of one event necessarily precludes the occurrence of the other event.

The most simple probabilities are the likelihood of a favourable event (x) occurring from a finite number of equally likely events (n). The probability of the event (x) occurring is x/n, where (x/n) is a real number between zero and one inclusive. Rolling a fair dice is an example of a simple probability. The dice has six sides and there is an equal likelihood of any one side turning up. If the favourable event is the likelihood of an even number turning up from one throw, the probability of such an event is 0.5 (the three elements in the event space consist of the numbers 2, 4, and 6 while the six elements in the outcome space consist of the numbers 1 to 6).

Probability theory has laid the foundations for statistics and is used in economics and finance for **utility** theory, pricing and valuation. It is also the basis for **econometrics**.

PRODUCT A product is any form of good or service provided by a firm and distributed in an economy. The functional purpose of a product is twofold: it satisfies a want by the consumer, while providing a means to generate **revenue** for firms.

Companies provide products in an economy through a distribution channel. This is the route used to distribute a product from the manufacturer to the ultimate consumer. Generally, there are three functional parts to a distribution channel.

1. The manufacturing sector creates the product by utilizing **factors of production** such as labour, land and capital.
2. The wholesale sector purchases large stocks of the product from the manufacturing sector to distribute in smaller portions to various retailers and markets.
3. The retail sector purchases the product from wholesalers to provide for the ultimate **consumer** in the market.

Some firms may internalize the entire distribution channel from the initial production to the ultimate consumer in order to reduce transaction costs associated with transport and inventories. This also enables a firm to control various aspects of distribution (*see* **just in time**, **integration**) as well as making better use of marketing strategies.

The product needs to be packaged, partly to protect it during the distribution process, and partly to make it more marketable to consumers. Packaging plays an important role in the marketing of a product and allows a firm to differentiate its product from others.

Product differentiation plays a crucial role in determining the level of revenues and market share for a firm. It is an element of market conduct (*see* **market structure**) and can be viewed as a form of non-price competition. On the supply side, a product may be differentiated according to differences in quality, perform-

ance, originality, or novelty features. These are all a part of the product's design, style, as well as its packaging. On the demand side, however, small or imaginary differences achieved by using advertising and branding can influence a consumer to believe in certain subjective qualities that are 'essential' to the product.

Product differentiation establishes a competitive advantage for firms, particularly in an **oligopolisitic** structure. This is because the market is characterized by a small number of suppliers, all of them reluctant to raise prices for fear of losing customers, none of them wanting to lower prices for fear that the others will follow suit (*see* **kinked demand curve**). As a result, product differentiation is a more efficient means than price competition. In theory, rival firms cannot mimic a differentiated product. It therefore preserves or even enhance a firm's profits and may represent a barrier to entry.

In practice the rival firms will eventually mimic the first company's differentiated product. The firm may then need to focus on product development as a means of generating new revenues. This refers to the process of developing new products which a firm can sell in its existing markets or possibly in new markets. Product development is a necessary part of business for many firms. They experience the tendency of the market to grow then decline over time, requiring new brands to supersede those that are near the end of their **product life cycle**.

PRODUCT LIFE CYCLE A **product** life cycle chronicles the pattern of sales followed by a product from its initial introduction in the market to its decline as management eventually phases out production. It reflects changes in the tastes and preferences of **consumers**, as well as the technological progress that contributes to a greater variety of products in the market.

The product life cycle does not specify a time line, but rather describes four stages which a typical product goes through. The first stage, or birth stage, comes about from development of a new product through successful product innovation and invention from **research and development**. After the launch of a new product, the birth stage is typically characterized by a low level of sales until consumer resistance has been overcome. The primary consumer target at this stage is high-income consumers with adventurous spending habits (sometimes known as 'early adopters').

The birth stage is followed by the growth stage, where the product has gained acceptance into the mass market. This stage usually shows a rapid growth in sales and high volumes. It is typically during this stage that competitors are enticed to enter the market. As more rival products

are introduced, the distinctiveness of the product fades and the firm is obliged to use various marketing and advertising techniques to differentiate its product.

The third stage in the product life cycle, the maturity stage, consists of a large number of sellers and a relatively stable level of sales limited to repeat customers. Competition at this stage is fairly intense and firms have a difficult time differentiating their products. Some may be forced to exit the market as a result of a decrease in **profit** margins brought about from this intense competition. At this stage the market is saturated so that competitors are unable to benefit from any kind of market growth.

Following the intense competition characterized by the maturity stage is the fourth and final stage of the product life cycle, referred to as the decline stage. Here sales begin to decrease as a result of changes in consumer tastes or the introduction of superior products in the market. Management may decide to slowly phase out or completely cease production in order to focus on more profitable ventures.

The diagram below illustrates the typical sales pattern of a product life

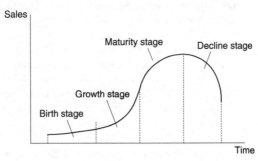

Product life cycle

cycle. The first segment has sales rising at an increasing rate followed by a sharper rise in the second phase (birth and growth). Sales are still rising in the third stage, but at a decreasing rate. Finally, in the decline stage, the level of sales decreases as production is slowly phased out.

One feature of the product life cycle in a global economy is that making and selling the product typically starts in the richer countries, where consumers have greater spending potential and the workforce is more highly trained. As the original life cycle moves through maturity and decline, it may be possible to broaden the market by introducing the product to developing economies, while at the same time benefiting from cheaper labour by moving production (by now standardized) into lower-wage economies. In this way it may be possible to extend the life cycle. This can be observed in particular with the manufacture and sale of some electronic or high-tech goods. Sales of western-brand cigarettes, which are declining in the richer countries, are expanding in poorer nations as the cigarette manufacturers use advertising and branding, as well as low-cost local production, to extend their products' life cycle into the newly growing economies. (*See* essay by Dr Sanjaya Lall on world trade and development.)

PRODUCTION FUNCTION This is the mathematical expression of how the various factors of production combine together to create a given output. At a certain level of technological knowledge, we can say that

$$Q = f(I_1, I_2, I_3, \text{etc.})$$

where Q is the quantity of output, and I_{1-3} are the factor inputs. If increases of, say, x, in the factor inputs create an increase of x in the quantity of output, we can conclude that the firm or entity is experiencing constant returns to scale. If input of x creates less than x of output, there are diminishing returns to scale, and of course if x creates more than an x increase in Q there are increasing returns.

The Cobb-Douglas production function suggests that if there is competition between factor inputs in an economy, particularly between capital and labour, the share of labour input and capital input will be constant, meaning that the two can be substituted in the long term (the proportions, but not necessarily the actual amounts, will remain constant).

(*See also* **capital-intensive, factors of production, theory of production costs**.)

PROFIT Profit is the reward for **investment** or risk-taking in an economic venture. An entrepreneur setting up a business would expect some payment for his time and the risk he has taken, in the same way that a landlord would be paid rent, or an employee would receive wages. In the context of the company or other business units, it is usually seen in terms of a surplus of revenue over costs: a firm's profit is the difference between sales **revenue** and total costs for a given period. This is distributed to those who bear the risks for the enterprise, which in the case of most companies will be the shareholders. Some is retained for further investment in the future of the business.

Gross profits are a broad form of

profits that are measured as the difference between sales revenue and cost of sales. The purpose of gross profits is to determine the costs associated with producing the goods sold (what portion of the revenues are used to 'pay' for producing goods). A narrower form of profits is net profits, which is gross profits minus the selling, administrative, as well as financing costs. This is the profit associated with normal business activity. Net profits are after depreciation (*see* **asset**), interest expenses and **taxes**, and represent the money available either to be reinvested in the firm or distributed among shareholders as **dividends**.

The accumulated net profit from one fiscal period to another is referred to as the 'retained profit'. These funds are normally invested into fixed assets (land, buildings, machinery etc.) and current assets (short term **securities**). Retained profits add value to a firm as they allow it to expand and increase production possibilities.

If firms choose not to distribute dividends or retain profits they may 'share' their profits with their employees in an effort to boost commitment to the firm and increase productivity. **Profit sharing** is a theory advocated in management for the purpose of improving employee relations. The company may simply hand out a portion of the previous year's profits to the employee or create a package that combines **shares** of the company with bonuses. Although a variety of profit sharing schemes have been developed, their impact on employee commitment to the firm and productivity is uncertain.

Profits are also a key element in the **management theory of the firm**. In most economic analysis it is assumed that a firm will behave in a manner that is consistent with maximizing its profits. Public limited companies are owned by the shareholders, who also select members to sit on the board of directors who choose the main management of the company and generally direct company policy. Thus the focus of the company's efforts are directed to please shareholders. Shareholders in turn want value for the money they have invested. This means that they would prefer dividends or an appreciation in the price of the shares held. There are some instances where firms may choose to aim for maximum growth, which may be more desirable for the management, than the maximization of profits, but there comes a point where the asset value of the company is greater than its share price (which may well fall due to lower profits or dividends). This will make the company ripe for a take-over, or perhaps make it the victim of **asset stripping**. (*See also* **governance**.)

One measure of profitability is known as the 'rate of return', which is the profits earned by a firm, measured as a percentage of the assets employed in the business. Another measure is the return on capital employed, which expresses a firm's profits for a given period of time as a percentage of its period-end capital employed.

A firm may also earn 'excess profits', which are profits greater than what is sufficient to ensure that the firm will continue supplying its product or service in the market. In short-term economic analysis, excess profits resulting from an imbalance of market demand and supply may lead to an efficient allocation of resources if it entices other firms to react to this imbalance (*see* **perfect competition**). If excess profits exist in the long run, then it is most likely that the resource allocation is not efficient, and firms are overpricing. Long term excess profits are normally associated with **monopoly** or **oligopolistic** profits, since more monopolistic firms have control over the price they charge customers in the market.

Much of the above refers to accounting or microeconomic definitions of profit. In macroeconomic terms, the economist will always judge profit in the context of **opportunity cost**. If an entrepreneur or shareholder is rewarded by a certain level of profit for taking a risk and investing in a certain firm or industry, the rewards must be counted against what the time, or investment, may have yielded elsewhere.

(*See also* **theory of production costs, theory of consumer demand**.)

PROFIT SHARING Profit sharing is a programme devised to enhance employee commitment to a firm, thus increasing productivity. With a profit sharing programme in place, a company effectively distributes some portion of the **profits** among the employees. There are numerous methods of profit sharing, ranging from a simple cash outlay to a complex package including a combination of **shares** and a bonus.

The most common method of profit sharing used by most firms is the annual year end bonus, whereby the employee receives an annual cash bonus usually based on the previous year's profits. Sometimes the bonus is paid on a weekly or monthly basis after the nominal amount has been determined.

Another type of a profit sharing programme that may be adopted by public limited companies is **options**. Share options give the employee the right to purchase the company's shares at a specified price in the future. The aim is to allow the employee to benefit from future dividend payments made to the shares, as well as being able to purchase shares at a discount if market prices are high. Executive share options are shares sold exclusively to executives of the firm. Some companies may adopt an employee stock ownership plan, which provides company shares in specified increments based on performance and paid for by the company profits.

Although profit sharing is advocated by management in order to improve employee performance as well as commitment to the firm, little evidence in terms of research has proved this.

One issue with share options which is attracting increasing attention is their position as a 'perk', and the ability of the companies issuing them to benefit from the tax benefits they provide. Many countries' accounting rules allow options to be counted against the company's profits for tax, whilst not appearing in the firm's balance sheet as a wage cost. Some economists have argued that this has the effect of inflating the profits of many large multinational firms.

PSBR/PSDR These terms usually

refer to the UK, but the principles apply in any country. The public sector borrowing requirement (PSBR) refers to the excess of public sector spending over its tax receipts. The public sector is comprised of the central government and local authorities, along with the nationalized industries or public corporations (*see* **fiscal policy**). PSBR is a funding flow (i.e. the amount of money which has to be raised by the government to finance the shortfall). It contrasts with the national debt (*see* **public debt**), which is usually expressed as a percentage of GNP and is closely linked to the concept of a stock of capital.

There are several ways for the government to fund the PSBR (*see* **budget deficit**): it can borrow from individuals, from the banks, or from overseas. Each form of borrowing can affect money supply, interest rates, the exchange rate, or inflation.

Running a continuous PSBR is a demand-led way to expand the economy (*see* **Keynes**), and was a cornerstone of many countries' fiscal policy, at least until the 1970s. It was then that the phenomenon known as **stagflation** (high inflation but stagnant growth) helped bring about a move toward balanced budgets (*see* **monetarism**). The opposite of the PSBR is a public sector debt repayment (PSDR), which can also be used as a fiscal tool to slow down an overheating economy.

PUBLIC DEBT Public or national debt is the total owed by a government: the result of borrowing for various reasons such as expansionary **fiscal policy**, major events such as wars, overseas borrowing to maintain a **balance of payments** or **exchange rate policy**, or the various accumulated debts of state enterprises or local authorities.

Public debt may be funded or unfunded (i.e. redeemable at a certain date, or completely undated) and it can be long or short term. Most importantly, however, is the question of whether it is mostly domestically held or based overseas.

If the debt is held domestically (for example, by individuals or **banks** who have bought **bonds** or Treasury bills from the government), then the interest on it (the cost of servicing the debt) is simply a transfer payment in the **circular flow of national income**. It is paid (injection) out of current taxes raised (withdrawal). Obviously, payments to overseas creditors will represent a net outflow and will appear on the balance of payments accounts as an 'invisibles' payment on the current account (with the debt itself appearing in the assets and liabilities section).

Although the stock of debt has no great significance for the performance of economies, and the servicing of it is usually a very small proportion of total government expenditure (less than 10 per cent in the UK), many governments feel it is desirable to keep national debt at or below a fixed proportion of GDP (this was one of the Maastricht Criteria for countries wanting to take part in **EMU**). Whether this was a necessary or sensible condition was the object of much debate among economists and politicians.

If the stock of debt is not a problem for governments, why not fund more spending through debt? Why not lower taxes and issue bonds? This would represent a certain type of fiscal policy, and might have implications also for **monetary policy**. That said, there is lively debate between followers of **Keynes**, and **monetarists** about the benefits or difficulties of long-term **budget deficits**. The key point to remember here, however, is that the current budget deficit represents a funding flow, which may have expansionary or dampening effects on growth, **inflation** and **employment**. The public debt is a stock of indebtedness whose only impact on current economic performance is its servicing.

(*See* Ian Harnett essay for details of national debt under Maastricht criteria.)

Q

QUANTITY THEORY OF MONEY The fixed relation between the quantity of money and the general level of prices has been observed historically by many writers. From the observations of the Greek historian Xenophon of Athens (*c.* 435–354 BC) to the philosopher David Hume (1711–76) and Milton Friedman (1912–), this empirical regularity appears to hold true.

The **Classical** tradition of economic theory has rested its explication of the monetary phenomena on the famous quantity theory equation, which takes the form:

$$MV = PT$$

where M stands for the quantity of money present in a particular economy at some specific point in time and circulating with a velocity V, P represents the general price level and T is a measure of the total output produced in this economy. The equation as it stands holds as an identity, since the left-hand side accounts for the total value of money, while the right-hand side reflects the total value of the output produced. A question arises regarding the definition of money used in this framework. Which of all forms of liquidity is the most suitable to use? The prevailing opinion of current quantity theorists is that we ought to use the monetary base (M0, M1 or M2), also referred to

as 'high-powered money'. An aggregate price index (such as the Consumer Price Index) should also be used to measure P, while T may be a quantity aggregate of production for the time interval in question.

An alternative version that the equation may take is the income form proposed by the economist Irving Fisher:

$$MV = PNy.$$

V now is called the income velocity of money, given the level of the per-capita income y and the population size N. Thus, Ny is the total national income of this economy. This version has a direct reference to the transactions taking place in the economy. The 'cash-balance' approach of the **Cambridge school** has produced another popular version of the quantity theory equation, known as the **Cambridge equation**:

$$M = kPy.$$

This approach may serve as a basis for a comprehensive **demand** theory of money.

On the other hand, the supply point of view of the quantity theory relies on the identity

$$M = B \{[D/R] [1+(D/C)]\} / [(D/R) + (D/C)].$$

The ratio M/B is termed the money multiplier. B stands for the monetary base, M for the total liquidity, D for the level of deposits in the economy's banking system, R for the bank reserves and C for the currency in the hands of the public. (D/R) is the deposit–reserve ratio and (D/C) is the deposit–currency ratio. The determinants of the effects of the two deposit ratios summarized in this expression are called proximate, since their values are determined by other more basic variables under different contexts. Note that in an open economy today the total quantity of the country's high-powered money is directly attached to its **balance of payments**. Modern quantity theorists believe that from this perspective the *nominal* supply of money is influenced by the overall supply of the economy, whereas the *real* supply of money is related primarily to the demand side.

All these various aspects of the quantity theory entail a significant result in terms of rates of change. The following equation must hold as it is deduced from the original $MV = PT$:

$$Gm + Gv = Gp + Gy.$$

In words, this means that the sum of the rates of growth of the quantity and velocity of money are equal to the sum of the rates of growth of the general price level and national income. An important feature of the Classical tradition rests on this expression, the so-called 'neutrality of money'. Assuming that the velocity of money stays constant, at least in the **long run**, and given that the natural

rate hypothesis would also hold (i.e. that the economy will tend toward a full equilibrium market-clearing position), then:

$$Gm = Gp.$$

This says that the rate of growth of the money stock will be matched by the **inflation** rate. Therefore, any attempts to stimulate the growth of income via the application of expansionary monetary policy are doomed, since they are inflationary in nature. Modern quantity theorists, like Friedman, would endorse a fixed policy rule for the expansion of the monetary base so that this process does not encourage inflationary expectations. Hidden in this exposition is the assumption that the transmission mechanism assumed to be operative preserves the Classical dichotomy.

The **Keynesian** school objects to this specification of policy, denying the constancy of the money velocity in the short-run. Empirical evidence, they claim, has recorded velocity shocks in the monetary history of various countries with different monetary arrangements and institutions. The Keynesian tradition favours 'fine tuning' and discretionary intervention, so that stabilization is both feasible (i.e. efficient) and balanced with respect to distributive justice. By doing so they reject the analytic validity of the quantity theory.

Monetarists think that the Keynesian school has overestimated the first-round effects of trying to stabilize economic activity. Furthermore, the analysis of individual choices suffers the defect of not incorporating the wealth (individual or aggregate) explicitly as a determinant of consumption behaviour. As for the volatility in velocity, it is assumed to be pro-cyclical, i.e. it follows cyclical episodes or results from the cyclical behaviour of the main economic variables. Thus, it rises during the expansion phase and falls during the contraction phase. In addition, fluctuations in monetary growth play a major role in severe depressions. Strong evidence suggests that inappropriate contractionary monetary policy is responsible for such crises, or for their aggravation.

Keynesians tend to incorporate in their explanatory scheme factors such as the coordination failure of the applied policies. They invoke arguments that there are innate instabilities in the free enterprise market system.

However, the **neo-Classical** economists (Lucas, Sargent, Wallace, Barro, and McCallum) have shown in their work of the early 1980s, that under the rational expectations hypothesis, fine-tuning procedures of demand management are unreliable. They not only fail to stimulate the economy even in the short-run, but may have even graver consequences such as the simultaneous increase of unemployment and inflation (for example, the **stagflation** of the 1970s). The neo-Classical approach undermines the general credibility of economic policy (especially when it is pre-announced). This conclusion is known as Lucas Critique. The quantity theory, however, remains unaffected in their conception of the monetary phenomena.

One thing is certain. Despite all these controversies the quantity theory approach remains an operationally important analytical tool whose validity will continue to generate agreement, debate and scientific analysis in the design of new policy options for many years to come.

R

REGRESSION This is an important part of **econometrics**, but has a more general relevance in economics. Essentially it plots the relationship between dependent and independent variables, allowing this relationship to be expressed in a mathematical form. It is especially important in the complexities of economic forecasting.

As a simple example, let us observe the relationship between income and consumption, (the **consumption function**). We can treat income (Y) as the independent variable, and consumption C as the dependent variable. Assuming a simple linear relationship, we can plot various levels for Y giving us various readings of C. In order to find an equation for the relationship, we plot a line which most nearly fits the actual readings. This is usually done using a method known as ordinary least squares, which gives us the minimum value for the sum of the vertical distances from the line. (How closely the line fits the readings is given by the correlation coefficient.)

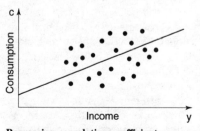

Regression correlation coefficient

We arrive at a consumption function which gives us $C = (a+b)Y$, where the numerical values of a and b will provide us with the position and the slope of the line.

A more complex relationship might also involve observations about, say, interest rates, so that both income and interest rates (I) are independent variables whose relationship we want to describe with the dependent variable C. We might well come up with an equation like $C = (a+b)Y + (x+y)I$, where x and y represent our observations about interest rates and various levels of consumptions. Graphically we would need to create a three-dimensional display, with a separate axis to measure interest rates against consumption. This is known as multiple linear regression.

Sometimes the relationships with the independent variables are themselves co-dependent (income and interest rates working on each other as well as on consumption). This is known as multicollinearity.

If the relationships are not linear, we would see a non-straight line function. We might have an equation like $C = (a)Y^N$, to represent a power function (it could also be an exponential relationship).

Regression analysis will normally incorporate an element to account for errors: sometimes a series of error terms are themselves correlated (auto-correlation), and other methods (apart from ordinary least squares) will be used to calculate the relationship. We can also introduce time series into the analysis, rather than plotting a static (timeless) relationship.

There is a detailed discussion about how regression analysis – and particularly the kind of calculations we can make with today's computers – can call into question some of our assumptions about economics in the essay by Paul Ormerod, 'What Economics Is Not'.

REGULATION Regulation refers to the supervision and control of the economic activities of firms or economic entities. This is usually by governments, or by government-appointed agencies within a country, or international regulatory bodies with the support of governments, such as the World Trade Organization (WTO). The purpose of regulation is to increase efficiency, as well as open competition, health and safety within economic activity.

Traditionally, regulation has been applied to various market structures and prices (anti-trust or anti-monopoly bodies and legislation still exist in most economies). Other kinds of regulation may look after the interests of employees and shareholders. The growth of regulation in the economy has led some economists to study the effects in terms of cost-benefit analysis, by attempting to measure the social benefits created by regulation and comparing them to the costs of implementation.

The crucial question is when do regulators become anti-competitive and protectionist. Naturally enough, this depends on your point of view. Regulation in international trade has often been used as a means of protectionism, where a country might impose quotas, or certain kinds of production criteria, on goods and services which are offered for sale. The effect is usually to restrict imports and protect home industries. Organizations such as the WTO may then act as super-regulators to reduce barriers on behalf of all of their members.

In recent decades governments in many advanced countries have attempted to dismantle 'natural **monopolies**'. In some cases this has involved deregulation, where new firms are allowed to compete in areas which have traditionally been the realm of one firm or one group of firms. An example would be the deregulation of telecommunications, media, and computing, so that cable TV companies may be allowed to offer telephone or Internet connections, or telephone companies can offer TV and Internet access. In other countries there has been a break-up of state-controlled monopolies, often in the transport and utilities sectors (*see* **supply-side economics**). Ironically, the effective break-up of monopolies (deregulation) often requires a greater level of regulation, to ensure that barriers to entry and predatory pricing are not used by the former monopolists.

As economic activity becomes more global, the difficulty of regulation becomes more complex. This is partly because regulators have to work across borders, often in countries with different legal and regulatory frameworks, and partly because the actual mechanics of tracking business and money flows globally is harder than if firms were predominantly active in just one country. Airline mergers and joint ventures in Europe and North America have posed problems for US and EU regulators. Attempts to keep track of capital flows in largely deregulated global financial markets have proved almost impossible, sparking fears for example about the dangers to investors of the use of **derivatives**, and fears that various shifts in financial flows could cause problems for **banks**.

In general the trend is set for a growth in international regulators, perhaps representing a group of countries within one geographical area (NAFTA, the EU, and ASEAN are examples of some free-trade regional regulatory bodies), or else global bodies such as the WTO, the IMF, and the World Health Organization. It is also likely that the huge explosion in individual share ownership and investment which has occurred in most industrialized economies will lead to an upsurge in 'consumer-based' regulators.

RESEARCH AND DEVELOPMENT The commitment of resources by a firm to pure and applied scientific research is referred to as R&D (research and development). The process of R&D results in the refinement and modification of research ideas and prototypes with the intention of developing a commercially viable process for **products**.

Two characteristics of R&D are invention (more closely associated with the research side of R&D) and innovation (associated with the development of new products). The former deals with the act of discovering new methods and techniques of manufacturing new products, while the latter deals with the task of bringing these inventions to the market place. In terms of resource allocation, invention requires little, as it is often an inspirational process undertaken with limited facilities. Innovation, however, is resource intensive and requires a substantial capital outlay in order to explore methods of bringing a product to the market place. Unfortunately not all methods of product innovation result in introducing a successful product line. It is due to these conditions that larger firms with greater capital resources are able to prosper by investing in R&D. Such firms are able to pool risks and undertake a large number of projects simultaneously to take advantage of R&D. Thus, the market structures that tends to facilitate R&D the most are **monopolies** and **oligopolies** (simply because such firms can yield excess profits and as such are more highly motivated towards product differentiation).

The benefits reaped by an economy from firms investing in R&D include economic growth and a greater variety of products for the consumer. R&D can contribute to economic growth as resources of the economy are put to more efficient use. At the same time, firms can increase revenues and expand their consumer base by successfully introducing new products. As such, many countries attempt to foster technological growth by granting patent rights to reward the efforts of inventors. There may be costs too, in addition to the investment outlay. Among the social costs might be the development of an education system which provides the right kinds of skills to invent and innovate, and the provision of an infrastructure which encourages firms to certain countries where R&D is easier (for example, the provision of a modern telephone and IT backbone). (*See* essay by Lall on world trade and development.)

REVENUE (COMPANY) Revenue refers to returns from the sale of goods or services. For any firm or economic entity, if revenues exceed costs, then **profits** are made. The exact relationship between revenue and costs is examined in the **theory of consumer demand** and the **theory of production costs**.

A company's revenues can be looked at as a function of the entire output (average revenue), or in terms of the revenue that is created by producing just one more unit (marginal revenue). Marginal revenue is particularly important as a way of measuring how much a company should produce to maximize profits. Total revenue is calculated as the total sales multiplied by the average revenue (which is normally the same as the price). Revenues for a particular firm can perform differently under varying conditions of competition: under **perfect competition**, for example, the firm has no way of controlling the price, so that the average revenue will remain at the prevailing price level however much is produced. On the other hand, a more **oligopolistic** or **monopolistic** firm will have enough 'clout' in the market to affect demand by changing the price. For these firms, revenue

calculations will be closely linked to **elasticity** (i.e. to what degree sales will fall if price is increased, or rise of price is reduced, which obviously has a direct bearing on total revenues).

In accountancy terms, **turnover** has a similar meaning to revenue. Turnover refers to income generated before taxes and costs. Government revenue is normally raised through taxes, but will also include the sale of assets such as the privatization of industries. (*See* **budget deficit, fiscal policy**.)

REVENUE (TOTAL, MARGINAL, AVERAGE) A key part of the **theory of demand** as applied to firms and other economic entities concerns revenue. Along with an examination of price **elasticity**, it allows us to find the points where revenues are maximized, and with the **theory of production costs**, it helps us to find the point of production where **profit** maximization occurs.

Take a company or business unit which makes product X and can have some influence over price. Its standard demand curve shows the various quantities of X which will be demanded (sold) at various prices. Total revenue is simply the price multiplied by the quantity sold: in this case $P_1 \times Q_1$, which is the rectangle in Figure 1. The important question for the firm is whether a reduction in price, say to P_2, will result in increased revenues. It will certainly mean more sales, Q_2, but only by knowing the elasticity of the demand curve from P_1 to P_2 will we know the impact on total revenue. This is where the concepts of average revenue and marginal revenue are useful.

Average revenue is simply the total revenue divided by the number of units sold. Looked at another way,

$$\text{average revenue} = \frac{P \times Q}{Q} = P.$$

So price *is* average revenue. (Since all the units will be sold at a given price, a higher price means a higher average revenue and a lower price a lower average revenue. Total revenue will take into account the changes in quantities sold.)

Marginal revenue is described as the additional total revenue derived from producing just one more unit of a product. The marginal revenue curve shows the revenue at various given prices, minus the revenue derived from those units which would otherwise have been sold at a higher price. Mathematically its gradient is exactly twice that of the average revenue (demand) curve. Crucially, when total revenue is increasing, marginal revenue must by definition be positive, and when total revenue is falling, marginal revenue is negative (one extra unit either brings in more revenue, adding to the total, or one extra unit impacts negatively on the total). When marginal revenue is positive, the demand curve's elasticity is more than unity (a reduction in price (P_3 to P_1, say) causes total revenue to increase ($P_1 \times Q_1$ is greater than $P_3 \times Q_3$). When marginal revenue is negative, the demand curve's elasticity is less than unity, so a price cut causes a fall in total revenue ($P_2 \times Q_2$ is smaller than $P_1 \times Q_1$). When marginal revenue is neither positive nor negative (i.e. at zero, where it cuts the X axis – corresponding in the diagram to price P_1 and output Q_1), the demand curve's elasticity is unity, and total revenue is maximized.

It therefore will not make sense for the firm to cut price below P_1, for marginal revenues will be negative and total revenue will fall. In practice

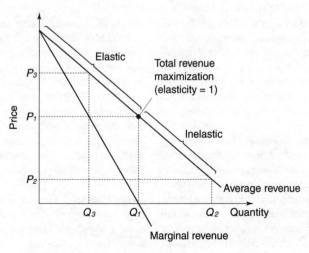

Revenue, *Fig. 1*

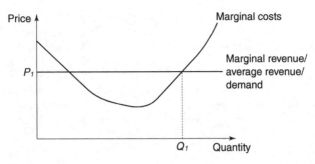

Revenue, *Fig. 2*

the firm needs also to take into account its marginal costs, and since these are rarely zero or negative, its output may well be higher up the demand curve than Q_1, at a higher price than P_1. (*See also* **oligopoly**, **kinked demand curve**.)

In conditions of **perfect competition**, where an individual firm is unable to influence price, the average revenue and the marginal revenue curves in the short term will be the same, indicating that each additional unit will bring in the same additional revenue as all the others produced (see Fig. 2). The curve will be horizontal (infinitely elastic), showing that the smallest rise in price will drive all customers away, while the smallest reduction in price will reduce marginal revenues below marginal costs and make the output non-viable.

RICARDO, DAVID (1772–1823) English economist who developed the theories of economic rent, **diminishing returns** and **comparative advantage** in trade. Like **Malthus**, Ricardo argued that a rising population would put pressure on natural resources to feed it. He believed that more marginal land would be cultivated to grow

food, and that the current, relatively superior land, would confer a rent payment on landlords and profit to farmers. Rising rent payments would mean higher costs of production, leading to demands by workers for higher wages. Profits would be eroded. Furthermore, wages would never rise above a subsistence level in the long term, because as wages rose, workers would have more children, eventually adding to the labour supply and forcing down wages.

All of this led Ricardo to seek the solution in importing foreign grain. His theory of comparative costs first showed how all countries can benefit from free international trade. His views helped spearhead the campaign to repeal the Corn Laws, which had prohibited cheap imports.

Ricardo is probably the greatest overall theorist of the **Classical School**, and parts of his thinking have been embraced by **neo-Keynesian** economists some two centuries later.

RISK CAPITAL Any new venture requires capital to start it up, whether it's a one-person business in which the proprietor puts personal savings or time into a small enterprise, or a large company or government which might turn to a **merchant bank** or the **stock market** or **bond** market to finance a major project. Generally the higher the risk, the higher the yield investors will require in return. Sometimes risk capital will be needed for a merger or take-over, and the highest-risk acquisitions (such as leveraged buy-outs) may be financed using high-yielding debt such as **junk bonds**. Start-up businesses will often look for **venture capital**, in which investors carry some of the risk of providing capital in exchange for some of the equity.

An important component of risk capital is the use of **investment** appraisal techniques. Those who finance any venture with risk want to be able to evaluate each alternative by reducing as much of the systemic risk as possible in order to make a sound decision. There are numerous techniques, the three most common of which are as follows.

1. Payback period. This is one of the simplest investment appraisal techniques, whose basic criterion is a calculation of the number of periods it will take for the investment to pay for itself. Specifically, with the payback method, in order for a project to be undertaken the period within which the cumulative net revenue from an investment project equals the original investment must be deemed acceptable by the investor. For example, if a project is to cost £25,000 and the firm is aware of the project contributing revenues of £19,000 the first year and £10,000 the second year, then it will be accepted if manage-

ment's target payback for its ventures is two years. The main disadvantage with the payback method of evaluating investments is that it is one-dimensional. It does not incorporate any type of flow analysis by taking into consideration the time value of money, or cash flows over the whole life of the project.

2. Net present value (NPV). One of the most popular techniques, NPV adds the dimension of the time value of money in choosing between different investments. NPV may consider the **profits**, or the cash flow generated by a particular venture compared to its associated costs. It works on the principle that a project is acceptable if, over its entire life, the total discounted revenues exceed or are equivalent to the total discounted costs. For example, assume a firm is considering purchasing equipment with an initial cost of £10,000 and with estimated servicing costs of £2,000 in the second year and £3,000 in the fifth year. If the equipment is expected to generate revenues of £2,500, to last for seven years and the **interest rate** is 5 per cent, should the equipment be purchased? We can summarize this information in the table on the next page and then apply discounted cash flow analysis to determine whether this project is worthwhile.

Thus, at an interest rate of 5 per cent the firm can expect to make a profit of £301, and so would consider purchasing the equipment. If a firm wanted to do sensitivity analysis on this project it could vary the interest rate as well as the

	Expected revenues	Expected costs
Year 0		£10,000
Year 1	£2,500	
Year 2	£2,500	£2,000
Year 3	£2,500	
Year 4	£2,500	
Year 5	£2,500	£3,000
Year 6	£2,500	
Year 7	£2,500	
Total discounted at 5%	**£14,465**	**£14,164**

Discounted cash flow

time of the project and the expected revenues.

NPV is applied to many different types of ventures as well as individual projects undertaken by firms. The essential requirement to ensure that NPV is accurate is correct forecasts of revenues and costs, as well as a discount rate correctly applied.

3. Cost–benefit analysis. Cost-benefit analysis is the general technique for evaluating the total social costs and social benefits associated with an economic project. It is similar to NPV in its comparison of costs and benefits associated with a project. But it is broader in that it may be applied to a greater number of projects. Cost-benefit analysis is generally used by public agencies when evaluating large-scale public investment projects such as major new railway lines or power stations in order to assess the welfare or net social benefits which will accrue to the nation from these projects. This generally involves the sponsoring bodies taking a broader long-term view of a project than would a company concentrating on project profitability alone.

S

SAVINGS Saving is the difference between income and **consumption**. It is a withdrawal in the **circular flow of national income**, and corresponds to the injection of investment. Saving can be carried out by individuals, or by companies who hold on to their **profits** rather than investing them or distributing them to shareholders, or by governments in the form of a budget surplus (*see* **fiscal policy**).

The greatest proportion of saving is by individuals (or households). **Keynes** argued that households save more as incomes increase, and that principle allows us to plot the savings schedule, which we derive from the consumption schedule and the 45 degree line where consumption and disposable income are equal. At low levels of income, more is consumed than earned, leading to dis-saving, whilst higher up the schedule we see positive saving.

Savings go on to provide funds for **investment** spending, and it is the actions of the financial markets which ensure that the two are matched. **Monetarists** and **Keynesians** differ about how sensitive investment (and consumer spending) is to the **interest rate**, with monetarists arguing that interest rates (and therefore **monetary policy**) are a major determinant. Thus a reduction in interest rates will, according to the monetarists, increase consumer spending, reducing saving, but also increase investment spending, potentially bringing inflationary pressures if savings are not matched

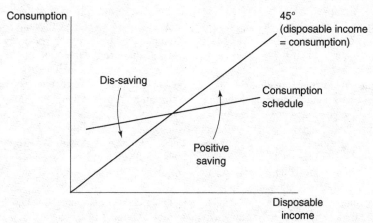

The savings schedule

311

to investment (too much money chasing too few goods, in the traditional phraseology).

One analytic tool which tries to bring together the real and the monetary aspects of the macroeconomy is the **IS/LM** model, which relates interest rates and various levels of income to define an equilibrium point where supply and demand for money, and savings and investment, are equal.

SAY, JEAN BAPTISTE (1767–1832)

A French economist, primarily known for developing the market theories introduced by Adam **Smith**.

Among his published works, the two most noted are *Traité d'Économie Politique* (1803) and *Cours Complet d'Économie Politique Practique* (1829). It is in the first that Say develops the notions of market theory that he is best remembered for. He argues that since every product exchanges for another product in the market, this necessarily implies that every product put on the market creates its own **demand**, and every demand exerted in the market creates its own **supply**. Thus he argues that there is no under-utilization of resources in the economy. This idea is developed in Say's Law, which is the principle that states aggregate supply creates its own aggregate demand.

Because aggregate supply creates its own aggregate demand, the very act of producing a given level of national output generates an amount of income exactly equal to the output that has been produced. Thus, in order to reach the full employment level in an economy, all that needs to be done is to increase aggregate supply. Say's Law implicitly assumes that the economic

system is supply-led, and all income generated must be spent in the economy. It has been used to deny the possibility of economic problems resulting from an overproduction of goods and services, and to suggest that the national economy will function at close to full employment (without requiring any government intervention).

Keynes, however, argued that some income is saved and invested by households, and that market expectations also affect demand, so we cannot simply assume that supply will necessarily generate its own demand.

Many economists argue that Say's Law applies to economies in equilibrium, as well as to barter economies.

The initial concept of the entrepreneur is also attributed to Say, as well as the division of the **factors of production** into the three components of labour, land, and capital.

(*See also* **supply-side economics**.)

SCARCITY One of the fundamental concepts underlying economics, scarcity is defined as insufficiency of amount or **supply**. In the realm of economics, however, the pursuit is the management of scarce resources. Recognizing that the supply of resources in an economy is finite, economists are concerned with different methods of managing these resources. The study of economics would be futile if there were an infinite supply of resources, simply because one would not need to be concerned with methods of distribution.

The classic Robinson Crusoe model, though simple in form, is a perfect example that highlights the significance of scarcity in economics. Suppose that we consider a one-consumer economy. The agent is a **profit**-maximizing producer who produces a consumption good from labour inputs and is simultaneously a **utility**-maximizing consumer who owns the profit-maximizing firm. Crusoe is the sole economic agent on an island whose daily routine consists of making decisions between how much time he should spend picking bananas for survival and how much time for leisure. Here we can observe the three essential ingredients that make up an economy: labour (Robinson Crusoe), land (the Island), and **capital** (bananas). Recognizing that there is a fixed amount of labour (Crusoe can work up to a maximum of 24 hours in a day), a fixed amount of land (the island has fixed boundaries), as well as a fixed amount of capital (only so many bananas can be picked in a given period of time), Crusoe must choose how much of these scarce resources to consume.

Having recognized the significance of scarcity, economists are primarily concerned with an appropriate distribution mechanism of the scarce resources. Economists are also interested in methods of production that will minimize scarcity of resources for future generations.

The concept of scarcity has also created a much-debated issue in economics with regards to the concept of efficiency (**Pareto** optimality) and the concept of fairness (distributive justice). Often economists disagree not only on the definitions of these concepts but also on acceptable levels of efficiency and fairness. Unfortunately not all efficient allocations are fair, and not all fair allocations are efficient. More often than not, improving the allocation in terms of one of the concepts requires sacrificing the other.

SCHUMPETER, JOSEPH A. (1883–1950) Austrian-born economist best known for his analysis of trade cycles and economic development over the long term. He used empirical study of trade cycles from the eighteenth century to the twentieth to identify short-, medium-, and long-term fluctuations (*see* **long/short-run, Kondratieff cycle**). He regarded the role of technological innovation as critical to growth, arguing that without it the economy would become stuck in a static equilibrium. He also believed that capitalism would eventually give way to a form of socialism, because firms would become ever larger and more bureaucratized. This would lead to their being nationalized. (*See* **management theories of the firm**, Beynon essay on management.)

As well as being an important economist, Schumpeter is regarded, like **Galbraith**, as a highly talented and enjoyable writer on economic and sociological topics.

SECURITIES In the broadest sense, securities are documents giving title of property or claims on income to the bearer. More specifically, however, securities are financial **assets** such as stock, equities, debentures and some short-term assets such as bills. The rate of income earned on the amount invested in a security is usually referred to the rate of **interest**.

The essential characteristic of a security is that it is saleable. It can be traded in various financial markets, most typically a **stock market**.

Usually securities can be found in three forms.

1. Fixed income securities offer a stated fixed income and come in the form of debentures, preferred **shares**, stocks, or **bonds**.
2. Variable income securities have fluctuating incomes, which are usually driven by investor expectations in the market. Ordinary shares in a company are the most typical form.
3. Other types of securities include bills of exchange, assurance policies, and warrants.

In order to issue securities in the stock exchange, a corporation must register with an organized member, and normally uses a **merchant bank** to make a flotation (US = IPO). In most cases the bearer of the security becomes a shareholder in the corporation. As a shareholder, the bearer has certain voting privileges which translate into the strategic objectives of management. However, this role is distinct from that of creditors, to which the corporation has greater legal obligations. Thus, funds must be distributed to creditors first before any income may be distributed to the shareholders.

Securities may also be classified as redeemable or non-redeemable. Redeemable securities may be repurchased by the issuing corporation. The main purpose of redeemable securities is for a corporation to attempt to keep the market price of a security somewhat in line with the value. This is because variable and other types of securities tend to follow investor expectations. By reducing the number of securities outstanding in the market, the issuing corporation can create value.

As the price of securities moves up or down, the real interest rate paid will vary separately from the **dividend**, which is payable on the face value or coupon value of the security. So a security with a dividend of, say, 10 per cent, would pay out £10 on every £100 batch of stock which was owned. If the price fell to £80, the payout would still be £10, but the yield would have risen to $10/80 \times 100\% = 12.5\%$. So yield = dividend/price.

There is a secondary market in many securities, which allows investors to trade instruments such as calls, puts, and **options**. These confer the right, but not necessarily the obligation, to buy or sell the underlying security at a certain point in the future at a fixed price. As such, they derive their own saleability from the underlying security, and for that reason are known as **derivatives**. Derivatives are an important way of hedging and arbitrage in securities markets.

SHARE PRICE INDEX　A share price index is a measure of **stock market** activity. Specifically, it is an index number which indicates changes in the average prices of selected **shares** (**securities**) on the stock exchange, compared to a base period. (An index number is simply a weighted average of a number of statistical observations (selected share prices in this case) as a percentage of a similar weighted average in an earlier period (usually referred to as the base period).)

These selected shares may be used as a proxy for the entire exchange, or they may represent a specific segment of the market, such as utilities, metals, or technology stocks. The chosen shares are usually referred to as 'blue chips', because of their solid market position and investor confidence, these desirable traits making them suitable to be used as proxies to describe share price behaviour in a specific part of the market, or the market as a whole.

Roughly speaking, the share price index shows the percentage change in market value of a portfolio compared with its value in the base year of the index. It is published in several daily newspapers as it is calculated on all major exchanges throughout the world. Generally speaking, the larger the exchange, the greater the variety of share price indices for different sectors in the exchange.

It is possible to trade **options** and **futures** on a share price index. These **derivatives** can be used to hedge exposure to individual shares, or for arbitrage by betting that the market as a whole will move in certain direction. In addition, some unit trusts (US = mutual funds) actually track the stock price index by investing solely in its component shares. These 'tracker funds' are based on confidence about a whole sector or stock market, rather than the performance of individual companies. Their managers would argue that since most of the companies which make up the index will be reliable blue-chips, the risks are low.

SHARES, SHARE CAPITAL Shares are a type of **security** which effectively confer on the shareholder parcels of ownership of a company. Shareholders have a proportion in the rights to the nominal capital and entitlement to a proportion of the distributed profits. If a company is liquidated, shareholders have a claim on the residual value based on the type of share held, after all **debts** have been paid. In the same way, they are only liable for the price paid for their shares, not for the full debts of the company. This is what is known as limited liability. For a company, issuing shares is a way of raising capital without taking on debt in the form of loans or overdrafts. The money is raised by initially placing the shares for sale (known as an offer for sale or sometimes a flotation or initial public offer). After that, the shares may be bought or sold, meaning that the ownership of the company can change, but there is no further inflow of funds to the company until the next offer for sale.

The amount of share capital a company can raise is set out in its articles of association. A company can choose whether it wants to raise money from shares, or by the issue of long-term loan capital, known as debentures. Debentures tend to pay a fixed rate of **interest**, unlike the **dividends** on shares, which depend on the firm's profits. As loans, they are cheaper than, say, bank loans or overdrafts. For the investor they are safer than shares, but they do not confer any ownership rights. The relationship of share capital to loan capital defines the company's **gearing**.

Shares may be bought and sold in an open market such as a **stock** exchange or, in the case of a non-public company, they may be traded privately. The stipulations for trading shares of a private company are much more strict and require them to be offered to existing shareholders first, to ensure control of the company can remain among the interested parties.

Shares may have voting rights attached to them, and may be fully or partly paid: companies are obliged to keep a public record of the rights attached to each class of shares. Generally there are two classes of shares that a corporation may offer to the public: preferred shares and ordinary shares. Preferred shares precede ordinary shares and supersede debtors in the payment of dividends and return to capital in the event that the company is liquidated. They normally entitle the holder to a fixed rate of dividends and have limited voting rights attached to them. Cumulative preferred shares carry forward the entitlement to preferred dividends if they are unpaid from one year to the next. Ordinary shares, however, are shares in the equity capital of the corporation. Holders are entitled to all the distributed profits after debtholders and preferred shareholders, and usually have greater voting rights. Preferred shares are usually held as a long-term investment, while ordinary shares are often held with the hope of benefiting from a company's shorter-term growth or performance.

Shares that are partly and fully paid are referred to as paid-up capital. Sometimes a company will require a portion of the coupon value of the share to be paid when the shares are issued, with the remainder to be paid in set instalments at specified later dates. In an offer for sale, companies often allow existing shareholders special prices or discounts in the new issue (known as a rights issue).

Sometimes a company's reserves of capital will have built up over a number of years, and the company may want its share capital to be more in line with what the company is worth. In this instance it will issue free shares to existing shareholders. This is known as a scrip or bonus issue. Often for the company it will increase confidence, making it easier to raise capital in the future. It might also make it more attractive for a takeover. For the investor, the value of the existing shares will fall, reflecting the added supply of shares, but there is usually the hope that they will eventually move back to where they were trading originally, as the company is now worth more in terms of equity capital, and perhaps more attractive to possible acquisition suitors.

If the shares in a company are simply trading at a very high price in the market, firms will often introduce a share split. Unlike a scrip issue, this does not represent any real change in the value of the company, in terms of its balance sheet. Suppose it has 100,000 ordinary shares with a coupon value of £1, capitalizing it at £100,000, with the shares trading at £12 a share. It issues instead 200,000 ordinary shares with a coupon of 50p. The share capitalization is the same, but the price would fall to £6, which is more convenient for brokers and investors. With more shares in the market, the shareholding base may also widen, bringing in fresh investors to the company and perhaps providing more people ready to provide funds in the next offer for sale.

(*See also* **unit trust/mutual fund**.)

SMITH, ADAM (1723–90) An economist who is acknowledged as the founder of much of what became British **Classical economics**. Smith's *Wealth of Nations* was the first serious attempt in the history of economic thought to separate the study of political economy from the related fields of political science, ethics, and jurisprudence. Much of his writing examined economic growth; he used such notions as laissez-faire, natural law, and division of labour to try to explain how economies operate. Born in Scotland and educated at Oxford, Smith held a teaching post in the University of Glasgow from 1751 to 1763, before becoming the private tutor of Henry Scott, third Duke of Buccleuch.

His first major work, *The Theory of Moral Sentiments* (1759), was a study of ethics. But it was the *Inquiry Into the Nature and Causes of the Wealth of Nations* (1776) that gained him the greatest acclaim. It is a penetrating analysis of the processes whereby economic wealth is produced and distributed, and demonstrates that the fundamental sources of all income, that is, the basic forms in which wealth is distributed, are rent, **wages**, and **profits**. The central thesis of *The Wealth of Nations* is that capital is best employed for the production and distribution of wealth under conditions of governmental non-interference, or laissez-faire, and free trade. In Smith's view, the production and exchange of goods can be stimulated, resulting in an increase in the standard of living, only through the efficient operations of private industries with a minimum of regulation and control by governments. To explain this concept of government maintaining a laissez-faire attitude toward commercial endeavours, Smith proclaimed the principle of the 'invisible hand': in pursuing his or her own good, every individual is led, as if by an invisible hand, to achieve the best good for all. Therefore any interference with free competition by government is almost certain to be injurious.

It is important to note that Smith's belief in every individual's pursuit of self-interest in no way excluded the notion of society. On the contrary, Smith's arguments relied on the fact that, as humans, we have a general inclination to identify ourselves with society. The concept of the invisible hand combines what is best for the individual with what is best for society. Having individuals define themselves in terms of the societies they constitute – while enabling the market to dictate the actions of people and businesses – will result in efficiencies and consequently raise the standard of living.

Although this view has undergone considerable modification by economists in the light of historical developments since Smith's time, many sections of *The Wealth of Nations*, notably those relating to the sources of income and the nature of capital, have continued to form the basis for theoretical study in the field of political economy. *The Wealth of Nations* has also served, perhaps more than any other single work in its field, as a guide to the formulation of governmental economic policies.

SOLOW GROWTH MODEL This model for economic growth, developed by the US economist Robert Solow, is a **neo-Classical** theory which is in contrast to the **Harrod-Domar** version. Solow's model assumes that the long-term growth rate in an economy and the 'natural' growth rate (required to maintain the population in full employment) will come together because of changes in the capital–output ratio, which is the proportion of total income used for capital investment.

Whereas Harrod and Domar assumed that the capital–output ratio was constant, Solow argued that **diminishing marginal returns** would tend to mean that as income increases, each extra unit of capital investment will yield a smaller increase in output. On this basis, there is little incentive to a business person to invest more capital, and the capital–output ratio will fall. This will leave more of income for consumer expenditure, which will in turn tend to increase the need for capital as demand increases. (*See* **Keynes**, **accelerator**, **circular flow of national income**.)

Solow went on to argue that investment can affect growth in the short run, but that longer-term, the main factors are the size of the population and technological change (these are exogenous variables in the Harrod-Domar model). Importantly, Solow suggests that the best way to offset the diminishing returns to capital in the long term is improved efficiency through better technology.

STAGFLATION Stagflation is a period of high unemployment with high **inflation**. The classic period of stag-flation for many western economies was the 1970s. A sharp rise in the world price of oil reduced demand and increased inflation, and the inflationary expectations also led to increased wage demands and cost–push inflation.

What was important to economics was that this (at the time) baffling phenomenon brought about a questioning of some of the major tenets of the last 40 years. **Keynesian** demand management had always argued that unemployment represented a shortfall in **demand** which could therefore not coexist with inflation, usually experienced in periods of excess demand. Policy-makers in many countries began examining alternatives such as **monetarism** or supply-side measures. Monetarists argued that the major determinant for prices was the **money supply**, and that its control was more important than managing demand. Supply-siders argued that freeing up markets, particularly the labour market, would increase productivity.

Governments did try to track the money supply, although that proved harder to measure and control than some had hoped. Markets in many economies were liberalized. Stagflation went away. But Keynesian theories did not. Current Keynesians embrace elements of **supply-side economics**, and agree with a more monetarist attitude to interest rates, always seen by monetarists as a key determinant of investment levels. Many monetarists too agree that crude targeting of the money supply is not sufficient in itself to achieve steady growth. Some would argue that stagflation would have disappeared anyway, because it was a temporary phenomenon, and that once western economies had absorbed the shock of the oil price rise, partly by changing production and consumption habits (becoming less oil-reliant for energy, for example), a return to the normal trade cycle would occur naturally.

Nonetheless, for economics, stagflation provided an opportunity for a thorough re-examination of conventional wisdom, a process which is still continuing today.

STOCK MARKET A stock market is the business transacted at a stock exchange. Generally it is a place where company stocks, government **bonds**, and other **securities** are bought and sold. In Europe, a stock market is also referred to as a bourse.

The market, like all financial markets, provides liquidity to encourage investors, and a way for companies or governments to raise money.

Stock markets have grown hand in hand with capitalism, and exchanges can be found in most financial cities. The world's largest are in New York, London and Tokyo. Many of the formerly communist countries of the Soviet bloc have opened stock markets during the past few years, and still-communist China also has a stock market in Shanghai.

Stock exchanges first developed from informal meetings in coffee houses where 'shares' of companies were traded. The first exchange ever to be set up was in Amsterdam (1602), which primarily traded shares of the United East India Company. The British Stock Exchange (1698) is considered the first true stock market. Nowadays many markets are based on electronic trading (e.g. London), and many stock markets with a trading pit also have electronic trade after the main exchange has closed (e.g. Frankfurt). In some centres, second and third exchanges have grown up, specializing in particular types of shares (e.g. the NASDAQ in New York is the 'over-the-counter' exchange for many new, high-tech companies).

Different markets adopt differing forms of **regulation** and trading systems. London, for example, is based on market makers who are obliged to quote a price at any time for a stock, as well as stockbrokers, who trade on behalf of their clients. Similarly there are varying requirements for companies wishing to obtain a listing. Such a company would first enter the **new issue market**, where the sale of its shares might require a **merchant bank** to act as an **underwriter**. Once on the market, its shares can be bought and sold by private investors (whose numbers are growing in North America and most European countries) or, more likely, by **institutional investors**.

There are as many investment strategies as there are investors, some more rational than others. Markets may be described as being dominated by the **bulls** or by the **bears**, depending on whether they are rising or falling. Overall trends can be tracked in the **share price index** (most markets have several of them). Investors look at, among other things, yields, dividends, past performance, sector performance, and company/market/economic fundamentals. Some try to use information they should not have, or that they should not trade on: there are stiff penalties for this

insider trading, although it is often difficult to find the culprits.

As with other financial markets, stock markets are becoming increasingly global, partly through increased deregulation (driven by a need to stop the business flowing elsewhere) and partly through the kind of electronic trading that allows 24-hour international trading. This naturally leads to greater inter-connectivity between markets, greatly increasing the fears of a global crash if sentiment suddenly turns bearish. Some argue that the increase in private investment in stocks and shares would broaden the economic implications of such a downturn; others say that private investors are more likely than institutions to hold onto their shares, reducing volatility. Economists have yet to fully understand the macroeconomic implications of wider share ownership on, for example, the **money supply**, **fiscal policy**, and **savings**. This is an area which is set to become one of the most important areas of economic management, if the popularity of stock market investment continues to grow.

STRUCTURAL UNEMPLOYMENT This is the type of unemployment that is associated with the 'real' structure of a specific economy. Those who are 'structurally unemployed' either possess the wrong skills, or live in the wrong place to respond to existing job vacancies.

The 'asymmetry' of aggregate demand in the **long run** is blamed for creating a production structure that cannot absorb a substantial portion of the labour force. The notion is linked to the idea of 'sectoral shifts' that

occur during the business cycle. From a **Keynesian** point of view, structural unemployment may be viewed as an extreme case of frictional unemployment, and can be only marginally affected by aggregate demand management. Its reduction would require the design and implementation of industrial policies that would change the structure and orientation of the private and public sector production. The **Classical** tradition instead blames social and legal impediments in the labour market (**minimum wage** laws and unemployment compensation) for deviations from the natural rate of unemployment. (*See* **supply-side economics**.)

Many economists argue that structural unemployment is by definition short-term, and that growth and consequent changes in the labour market will correct it. Nevertheless current changes in the nature of production, trade, and capital markets are likely to make the *type* of labour a key element of factor endowment in the future. This puts a premium on education, and often highly specific labour skills. As economies attempt to develop these skills in an increasingly global market, we can anticipate the presence of significant pockets of structural unemployment, especially in developing countries. (*See* essay by Sanjaya Lall.)

SUPPLY CURVE Supply refers to the amount of a product made available for sale. The total supply of a product at various prices is reflected by its supply curve. Supply comes together with demand in markets to determine the equilibrium prices where consumers and producers will trade. The traditional supply curve indicates how much a producer will supply at various price levels, and generally slopes 'upwards', because more will usually be supplied at higher prices.

Any discussion of supply curves will, however, depend on the market conditions. If companies are able to 'make their own prices' in conditions of **monopoly** or **oligopoly**, the supply curve will not be relevant. In conditions of **perfect** (or near-perfect) **competition**, the supply curve for an industry is the sum of the supply curves for all the firms operating within it. The **theory of production costs** is that for an individual firm the supply curve will be the marginal cost curve above the level that revenue (or price) exceeds average costs.

In general a firm's supply curve will slope upwards because the marginal costs of producing extra units will rise as more units are produced (the law of diminishing returns). For an industry the upward slope will also reflect the fact that higher prices will attract more entrants in the hope of higher profits. The gradient (slope)

of the supply curve indicates the price **elasticity** of supply: if supply is inelastic (steeply sloping curve), a small rise in price can result in very few extra units of production being made available to the market, whereas elastic supply means that a price rise brings proportionately more units into play.

If the cost conditions change significantly (from, say, a technological improvement or a hike in the price of raw materials), the whole supply curve may shift to the left or right, from S to S_1 or S_2 in the diagram.

The term 'excess supply' refers to a situation where the state of the market for a commodity is such that more of the commodity is available for purchase than consumers choose to buy at the prevailing price. This usually leads to a price fall so that excess supply eventually disappears. Excess supply can be observed in circumstances where governments maintain a minimum price control.

(*See also* **theory of consumer demand**, **demand curve**, **supply-side economics**.)

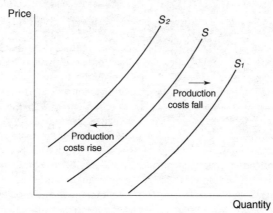

The supply curve

SUPPLY-SIDE ECONOMICS Neo-
Classical microeconomics teaches us
that price is determined by the interaction of **supply** and **demand**, and
that an increase in supply (a shift in
the supply curve to the right) will
mean that more is supplied at a given
price. Much of post-**Keynesian** macroeconomics has concentrated on the
workings of aggregate demand; the
so-called aggregate supply curve is
drawn as a 45 degree line against output and demand, customarily becoming vertical at the full employment
output level. Supply-siders extrapolate their aggregate supply curve as a
total of all the microeconomic supply
curves in the economy. To them, the
trick is to shift it to the right, supplying more at a constant price, and
moving from S to S_1 or S_2. This
reflects a series of falls in the costs of
economic activity. (It may not be
especially relevant to plot the aggregate demand curve in this context; it
might be seen as downward-sloping,
demonstrating that as prices fall, more
goods and services are purchased.)

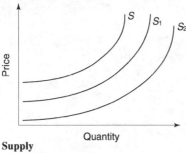

Supply

For most supply-side economists
the most effective way to achieve
more output at the same price level,
i.e. without **inflation**, is to tackle the
rigidities within the economy, and
especially within the labour market.

Rigidities may arise from trade
unions determining wage levels above
their 'free market' level; they may
occur from a lack of occupational or
regional mobility; they may exist because of a statutory **minimum wage**.
(In his essay on supply-side policies,
Patrick Minford tries to show that
reducing rigidities that arise from the
operation of the benefits system has
the effect of reducing the so-called
natural rate of unemployment: *see
also* **expectations-adjusted Phillips
Curve**.)

There are other inhibitions to more
efficient production, according to
supply-siders. Heavy tax burdens act
as a disincentive to employment or
enterprise. (The **Laffer Curve** is a
representation of how government
revenues too can fall as the tax burden
becomes higher.) So are tariff barriers, and over-regulation of capital
markets. The advantages of freeing
up world trade are clear to most
economists and policy-makers, and
many believe that today's international capital markets have helped
to create an expansion of investment.

Is supply-side economics just a
prescription for governments to stay
out of the economy, and therefore a
move simply to the market-clearing
economics of the neo-Classical economists? Partly – certainly this was one
of the key features of the policies
practised in the US during the
Reagan presidency, which became
known as Reaganomics. But freer
markets imply a greater role for
the (usually government-appointed)
regulators, as they also require that
monopolies and **oligopolies** should be
challenged as another 'rigidity'. This
is especially true in countries which

have adopted the supply-minded policies of taking some of their state industries into the private sector, where the regulators have an important role in clearing the way for new entrants into what were previously public monopolies.

The biggest supply-side element at present is the technological revolution, which can be seen as relatively politically neutral. The implications of new technologies are examined by Richard Lander in his essay. In the context of new technology there is a role for the state in providing training and infrastructure (noted by Sanjaya Lall in some of the more successful Asian economies – see his essay).

Supply-side measures are not mutually exclusive to demand management, despite the close association of many supply-siders with **monetarist** policies. Many of today's governments have stripped away some of the early polemical zeal of this branch of economics and embrace it as another useful tool of growth.

SURPLUS Economics is the study of the distribution of **scarce** resources. Sometimes, however, far from being scarce, a resource may actually be in abundant **supply**. Thus, a 'surplus' in the general sense refers to any amount supplied in excess of the amount **demanded** at a specified price, so that there is a more than sufficient level of the commodity available in the economy.

In economics, a distinction is usually made between types of surplus, depending on the sector of the economy being observed. Sometimes a surplus refers to earnings of a production factor in excess of the amount required to put it into production. It may also refer to an excess amount received for a production factor relative to the price of supplying it. Here, for example, a surplus could result from a producer receiving an excess from labour compared to the wages it pays.

The most common form of surplus in economics, however, refers to the value received by consumers and producers in comparison to the price established in the market. A **consumer** surplus is the amount by which the consumer values a product over and above the price paid in the market. Alternatively, a producer surplus is the excess of the price received by a supplier of a commodity over the minimum amount the supplier would

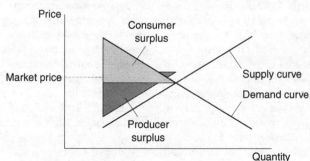

Producer and consumer surplus

be willing to accept to maintain the current level of output. These concepts can be viewed graphically in a market depicting demand and supply for a given commodity.

Consumer surplus in the above market can be observed as the area between the demand curve for the good and the going market price. Alternatively, producer surplus is the area above the supply curve for the good and the going market price. A **monopolistic** firm may sometimes be able to use price discrimination to charge different prices for the same commodity. It can therefore extract most of the consumer's surplus when the demand function is known. This is because the firm can charge exactly the price each successive consumer is willing to pay.

(*See also* **perfect competition**, **oligopoly**.)

SWAPS Swaps are a means by which companies or institutions change the way they finance their **assets** or **debts**. Typically they involve swapping **interest rates**, or **currency** payments, and since they are instruments derived from the underlying debt or asset, they are a form of **derivative**.

An interest rate swap is an agreement between two parties for the exchange of a series of cash payments, usually where one of the payments is based on a fixed rate of interest while the other is based on a floating rate of interest. The purpose is to apportion the fixed interest rate to the party which anticipates large volatility in the interest rate market, and the variable or floating rate to the party which anticipates a fall in interest rates. This is just one example – an

abundance exist. The key point is that investors either in different markets or with different perceptions of the market can swap certain properties of investments to suit their expectations. For example, a **building society** with assets consisting of long-term fixed rates and short-term deposits as liabilities faces a risk of a rise in interest rates. An interest rate swap could reduce this exposure to risk.

With currency swaps, the two debt service flows are denominated in different currencies. Thus the currency swap is a means by which a borrower can exchange the type of funds most easily raised for the type of funds required, usually through the intermediary of a **bank**. For example, a UK firm may find it easier to borrow funds in the UK when it really wants Canadian dollars to pay a debt. If a Canadian company is in exactly the opposite circumstance (that is, it seeks sterling but can borrow Canadian dollars more efficiently), then a currency swap will be advantageous to both parties.

Generally, interest rate swaps and currency swaps are transactions performed by large companies for hedging purposes in international markets. However, it is not uncommon for speculators to enter this type of transaction as well. Swaps are sometimes one element in custom-designed exotic derivatives, with perhaps elements of stock price **options** also included. The idea is to reduce risk to the company, or else to realize speculative profits by taking advantage of its position in the financial markets. Some blue-chip firms have come famously unstuck in this kind of speculation over the past decade.

T

TAP ISSUE A tap stock applies to British government **bonds**, known as gilt-edged **securities**. These are offered to the market by tender, where they go in general to the highest bidders. Bonds not taken up are later offered back into the market by the Bank of England in quantities and at prices that suit monetary policy at the time. Like a tap they can be turned on or off. If the government wants to raise **interest rates**, it can turn on the tap by offering bonds at a lower price, thereby raising the yield, which is the effective interest rate.

A tap issue usually refers to an issue of government bonds or bills of exchange which are offered either to other government departments without going through the market (to facilitate government book-keeping) or which are effectively non-tradable in the financial markets (such as National Savings Certificates). Again, all of these can be turned on or off, according to policy.

Generally, the British government may borrow money in the form of a promissory note that repays principal plus interest as a tender issue or a tap issue. The primary distinction between the two is that the former involves the money market, while the latter bypasses the money market. A tender refers to an offer of supply at a fixed price. Thus a tender issue is government borrowing in the form of

issuing short-term treasury bills (the promissory notes) at a fixed price (a tender) through the money markets. When the government bypasses the money market and issues these treasury bills to government departments and other market makers at a fixed price, it is then termed a tap issue.

Thus, tap issues allow the government to influence the price as well as the quantity of gilts. Gilts are any type of fixed interest security or stock issued by the British government. They are generally viewed as a safe and sometimes conservative investment vehicle, as it is highly unlikely that the British government will default on its interest payments. Tap issues are referred to as such because of the government's ability to control the volume and prices like turning a tap on or off. For example, increasing the volume through a tap issue will increase the quantity of gilts circulating. In order to entice more market makers to acquire these gilts, their prices must be reduced, which is essentially the same as increasing the rate of interest.

TAXATION Taxation is the system through which governments obtain **money** from the private sector of people and corporations. It is a means for raising **revenue** (although the government has access to various other methods of securing revenues in order to support itself as well as to provide public services such as defence and social security) (*see* **bonds**, **monetary policy**, **circular flow of national income**). A government may use taxation for a variety of reasons – macroeconomic management (*see* **fiscal policy**), but also redistribution, control of social habits (eg tobacco smoking), or to fund major costs such as wars. Generally speaking, although taxes are compulsory them is no guarantee that taxpayers will derive the equivalent value in terms of public services to the extent that they pay taxes.

In medieval times, taxes were paid in terms of labour rather than money, and although taxation has evolved greatly over time, its fundamental pattern has remained the same. The government designates a tax base (be it income, property holdings or a given commodity), then applies the tax through a tax schedule which specifically states the amounts levied for different levels of the tax base, and finally collects the tax. An established criterion for government revenue-raising was developed by Adam **Smith**: it is still used by policy makers as the principle of taxation. It sets out four fundamentals which are needed for a tax to serve its purpose to both the public and the private sectors.

1. The principle of fairness: the tax must be applied to individuals according to their relative ability to pay, and in terms of the benefits received by the taxpayer.
2. Clarity and certainty, so as not to create any ambiguities.
3. Convenience in its application to the private sector.

4. Efficiency in terms of being administered economically (*see* **Pareto**).

Taxes perform differing functions depending on the responsibilities expected of the enacting government. In general, lower levels of government tend to levy taxes solely on property, having limited powers as to what can be taxed. Higher levels of government have the opportunity to reach a much broader tax base, and can manipulate fiscal policy as a way to manage the economy.

Taxes may be classified as proportional, progressive, or regressive. A proportional tax is levied according to a certain fixed percentage that the taxpayer is able to pay. Progressive taxes are taxes whose rates increase in proportion to increases in taxpayers' income. Regressive taxes disregard the ability of the taxpayer to pay (a sales tax which is applied to goods in an economy is an example of a regressive tax as it is applied evenly to rich and poor people alike).

The notions of average and marginal tax rates are measures of taxation, and help define different classes of taxes. The average tax rate is defined as the total taxes paid, divided by the gross income. In this way progressive tax rates can be characterized as a positive relationship between changes in the average tax rate and changes in income (as income goes up, so does the tax rate, while as income falls, so does the tax rate). Conversely, with regressive tax rates, the relationship between changes in the average tax rate and income are opposite.

The marginal tax rate, on the other hand, is the share of additional income that is taxed away. Specifically it is defined as the change in the total taxes paid, divided by the change in the gross income.

Two popular forms of taxation are quantity taxes or value taxes. Quantity taxes mean that consumers have to pay a certain amount to the government for each unit of the good purchased. Value taxes, or *ad valorem* taxes, are taxes on the value or the price of the good.

The concept of taxation is tightly connected to the notion of redistribution of the wealth of the economy from one group to another. In terms of households this is generally done through income taxes, which are taxes on the level of income of the individual.

Although the different tax schemes described above could be applied, most income taxes tend to be progressive. In fact a 'negative' income tax is sometimes also used by a government as a means to eliminate the 'poverty trap'. This is the situation whereby those entering low-income employment tend to remain in categories of standard tax because of rigidities in the tax structure. The poverty trap can mean that leaving the benefit system or 'black economy' and taking up official employment is not worthwhile at low levels of income. So by literally adding to income, rather than deducting money from it, the trap can be eliminated – or at least raised to a higher income level.

In terms of firms we sometimes see negative taxes in the form of a '**monopoly** tax', which is a means to eliminate the deadweight loss (or producer surplus) created by monopolies and their pricing structure.

The 'polluter pays' principle is another tax scheme which attempts to redistribute benefits from producers to consumers. Here, a company is taxed according to the level of pollution it contributes into the environment.

TECHNOLOGICAL GAP THEORY A **theory of trade** which seeks to explain changes in the patterns of international trade over time, based on technological changes and product innovation. According to the theory, technologically advanced countries with a high propensity to innovate are able to achieve trade advantages by being able to offer sophisticated new products to the world markets. So products which incorporate new technologies will be exported, until the importing countries eventually copy them and export them onto the world market themselves. The technology gap theory differs from the **Heckscher-Ohlin factor proportions theory**, because it suggests that trading patterns are dynamic.

The technological gap theory can be seen as a justification of trade in its own right. Economies which focus on **research and development** will introduce products into the world market that are initially unobtainable from other sources. Not only does the technologically advanced country benefit from trade, but consumers in the world market benefit from the availability of the new products. In countries where demand for the product is sufficiently high, the new production technique or technology will be copied. The extra competition will tend to reduce prices, and if the new producers start to export their home-made versions, they will help to move their countries' foreign trade accounts back toward balance with the original innovating country. In the mean time the world economy has grown and a greater number of consumers have been exposed to the new product.

In today's increasingly global economy, many new products will be introduced in all the countries in which a multinational company operates (for example, in the computer, entertainment or pharmaceuticals industries). This means that a simple 'technology gap' is less likely to exist. It might however mean that it is more difficult for other firms to emulate the innovation, because the innovating company may have such a strong global presence that it can raise barriers to entry within the market (*see* **oligopoly**). In certain cases firms may benefit from patents which are granted to justify the cost of the R&D which goes into creating new products. One common feature of today's innovations is that production may start in **capital intensive**, high labour-cost nations, but move to cheaper areas of production as the process becomes more established. The profits from this shift in production will not necessarily stay within the newly producing countries, whose trade accounts therefore will not necessarily move into balance.

THEORY (BENEFITS) OF TRADE The basic principle of trade derives from the principle of **comparative advantage**: countries will always benefit from trade if they export goods in which they have a comparative advantage in factor production. It applies between two countries even if country A has an absolute advantage in the production of its goods: A and B will benefit if A and B specialize in the goods in which each has the greater comparative advantage. From this work, which originated with David **Ricardo** and even in its earliest form, Adam **Smith**, grew the theory of trade. The **Heckscher-Ohlin factor proportions theory**, and further work by Paul Samuelson, outlined the relationships between factors of production endowment and comparative trading advantage. Various **trade bodies** such as GATT and the WTO have been set up to promote and police free trade across the world. The figures are clear: trade growth has far outstripped GDP growth over the past half century. (During the period from 1950 to 1996 world output by volume grew six times, and world output of manufactures grew nine times. For the same period there was a 16-fold increase in merchandise trade and a more than 30-fold increase in world trade in manufactures.)

One of the difficulties now facing world trade **regulators** is how to monitor and control trade in such intangibles as intellectual property, which in a technological world are often worth very much more than mere goods and services. There is also the problem of how to keep track of the movement of information and ideas via, say, the Internet. Furthermore, many interest groups (trade unions or environmental groups) or regional trading blocs (such as the EU) may have strong arguments against completely free trade, making trade negotiations a complex process of compromise and partial progress.

(*See also* the essay by Sanjaya Lall on trade and developing countries.)

THEORY OF CONSUMER DEMAND Demand, in its simplest terms, is about how much of a given product is purchased at various prices. That in itself indicates that demand is the study of the **consumer**, and how he or she 'ticks', in an economic sense. The theory of demand is one of the twin pillars of traditional (**neo-Classical**) microeconomic theory, the other being the **theory of production costs**, which tell us about the firm (or any other economic entity), and how much it produces (the **supply** rather than the demand side).

Demand starts with an intuitive observation: it would seem natural enough that the cheaper something is, the more of it will be consumed. What economists and business planners are interested in is the interplay with other factors, such as different goods, income and time. But the most basic observation about consumer behaviour is the **demand curve**, which indicates how much of a given pro-duct the consumer will buy at a given price. Its slope tells us about **elasticities** (how sensitive the demand for a product is to price, but also to income, and to the demand for other products). For a company it is an indication of **revenues**, based on how much it will be able to sell at a given price. The relationship of demand to supply can give a company its **profit**-maximizing output level, and the price at which that can be achieved. To derive our demand curve, we return again to the consumer, and indifference curves and budget lines.

An indifference curve is a way of expressing a person's preferences between two goods, called X and Y. The graph shows that a person may choose, for example, ten units of X and ten of Y, or six units of Y and seventeen of X, in order to be equally happy. Thus, any position on indifference curve A represents equal **utility**. The gradient of the indifference curve *A* at any given point expresses the marginal rate of substitution of goods X and Y. Note that toward the end of curve *A*, at, say, point *Aa*, the con-

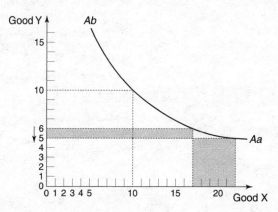

Demand Theory, *Fig. 1*

sumer will require significant additional amounts of X in order to forgo one unit of Y. The same applies in reverse at the other end, say at point *Ab*. This shows that the more of something we have, the less additional satisfaction we will derive from one more unit relative to other goods. This is known as the law of diminishing marginal utility.

Suppose that for some reason the consumer were suddenly able to have larger quantities of X and Y. This may be because the price of either or both is reduced, or because the consumer's income has increased. We would then need to plot a second indifference curve, B, further out from the origin than *A*. This represents a higher level of satisfaction throughout; curve *C* represents even higher satisfaction. But although the dream of moving out to an infinitely distant indifference curve may be attractive, it is obvious that in the real world that is impossible, since we only have limited resources, and all goods have a price. We bring in the real world through an understanding of 'budget lines'. These allow us to examine the effects

of changes in income (the income effect) and prices (the price effect).

Let's assume that the prices of X and Y are constant, and that our consumer's income is also constant. It is easy to work out the various permutations of X and Y which the consumer could potentially afford (in this case, say 15 units of X and none of Y, or 20 units of Y and none of X). The gradient of the budget line *BL* thus represents the ratio of the prices of X and Y. This is, simply, what the consumer can afford. If we now add in the consumer's 'wish list', in the form of our outward-marching indifference curves, we can find the point at which the consumer enjoys the maximum satisfaction at a given income level, and this must be the point at which the furthest indifference curve touches the budget line (in this case, where B coincides with *BL*, at D_1). A higher indifference curve, *C*, is desirable but unaffordable since it is at all points higher than budget line *BL*. A lower indifference curve, *A*, is certainly affordable, but leaves resources unused and represents a lower level of satisfaction. Only D_1 is said to

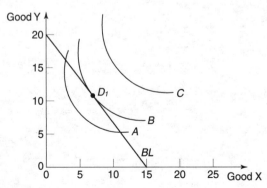

Demand Theory, *Fig. 2*

represent consumer equilibrium, and since the gradients of the two curves are at this point identical, we can say that consumer equilibrium is the point where the marginal rate of substitution (as described by indifference curve *B*) is equal to the ratio of prices for X and Y (as described by budget line *BL*).

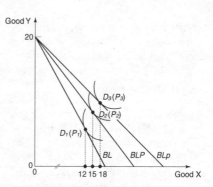

Demand Theory, *Fig. 4*

Just as we can construct a series of outward-marching indifference curves, so we can develop various budget lines. If the prices of X and Y remain constant, the gradients of the budget lines remain constant, but successive increases in income mean that we can move outward to budget lines *BL₁* and *BL₂*, which give us new positions of consumer equilibrium (*D₂* and *D₃*).

So D_1 represents our original price for X, and we can call that P_1. We can see the numerical value – 12 units of X. A lower price, P_2, takes us to D_2, which is 15 units of X, and lower still, price P_3, is at D_3, which is 18 units of X. We can replot that as price against amount consumed and we have derived a demand curve for product X.

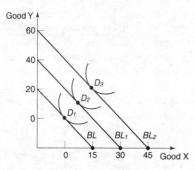

Demand Theory, *Fig. 3*

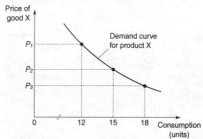

Demand Theory, *Fig. 5*

Similar things occur if the price of one of the goods, say X, is reduced at a given level of income. The budget line *BL* swings outwards to *BLP*, i.e. its gradient changes, because the ratio of prices has changed, and the consumer is able to buy more units of X all along the line relative to Y. The consumer moves to a new equilibrium, *D₂*. If the price falls more, we move to *D₃* on *BLp* (see Fig. 4).

In the real world, not all goods respond in the same way to changes in price. Some goods, such as luxuries, will tend to be very price-sensitive, because they will be the first things that consumers will stop buying if prices increase. We characterize this by comparing the gradient of the demand curve – the steeper it is, the less price sensitive (or inelastic) the demand; the flatter, the more price sensitive (or elastic). (For a more mathematical explanation, *see* **elasticities**.) Furthermore, some goods are affected by changes in the price of others in different ways. A fall in the price of one newspaper may mean a fall in the sales of a rival journal, as consumers switch from the 'Daily Bugle' to the 'Daily Trumpeter'. These products are known as substitutes. But a cut in the price of the 'Daily Trumpeter', and its consequent increase in sales, may mean an increase in demand for newsprint. Such products are known as complementary.

We also know that consumers benefit from changes in the price of a given product in a number of ways. When the price of X fell, we moved from D_1 to D_2. This happy event has two elements. First, we have an income effect. This means that we have relatively more resources, to spend both on X and Y at a given level of income – to this extent, it is as though the income itself had risen, represented by the outward rotation of the budget line to *BLP*. But there is

also a substitution effect: that more units of X can be purchased right along the budget line *BLP*, relative to the amount of Y. This is characterized by the change in gradient (the ratio of prices) in the budget line. We can express this by drawing *BLS*, whose gradient is parallel to that of *BLP* but at the same income level as *BL*. So for a normal good, the substitution effect is the shift from D_1 to *DS* and the income effect is the shift from *DS* to D_2. Both mean more of X is demanded (see Fig. 6).

For certain goods, known as 'inferior goods', the income effect is negative – these are products which will be discarded for 'better' ones as purchasing power increases (even from a price cut). Take X and Y and suppose that X is inferior. The cut in the price of X will still mean a move to budget line *BLP*. But importantly, the position of our indifference curve has shifted to IC_2, with a consumer equilibrium at ID_2. The substitution effect is once again shown by the move from D_1 to *DS*. Income effect is negative (*DS* to ID_2 means less of X is

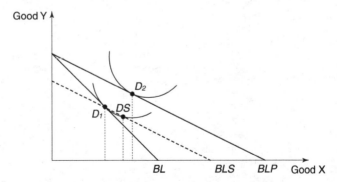

Normal good: Income effect = move to D_2 on *BLP*
Substitution effect = move from D_1 to *DS* on *BLS*

Demand Theory, *Fig. 6*

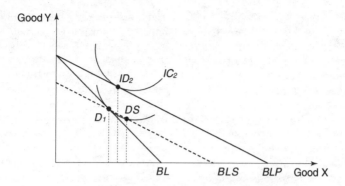

Inferior good: Negative income effect is outweighed by substitution effect so at *ID₂* a little more X is demanded

Demand Theory, *Fig. 7*

demanded). But the change of gradient still means that slightly more of X will be demanded at ID_2 than at D_1. So the demand curve is steep, but it still slopes backwards, representing higher quantities demanded as prices increase (see Fig. 7).

The most extreme example of an inferior good is a **Giffen good**, where the income effect outweighs the substitution effect. If X were a Giffen good, the consumer equilibrium for *BLP* would be at a tangent to the wildly shifted indifference curve *GC*,

indicating a consumer equilibrium at GD_1, where *less* of product X is consumed, despite a cut in its price. (The substitution effect is once again the move from D_1 to *DS*. But in this case D_1 to *DS* is smaller – in terms of demand for X – than *DS* to GD_1, the negative income effect). It's clear from this that the demand curve for a Giffen good would slope forwards.

An alternative way to derive a consumer's demand curve is the theory of revealed preference, developed by the economist Paul Samuelson. This

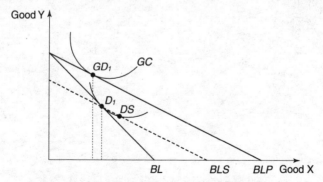

Giffen good: Negative income effect outweighs substitution effect so less of X is demanded despite lower price

Demand Theory, *Fig. 8*

ignores utility, and works from the premise that consumers will behave rationally and consistently. In particular, rational consumers will always choose more of something if they can, spend all of their incomes, and will be transitive in their choices: so that if they prefer A to B, and prefer B to C, they must therefore prefer A to C, sparing the need to go through an individual indifference analysis of A to C. From that we can examine demand for product X compared with money, which effectively represents all the other products available instead of X.

The consumer is on budget line YX, choosing to buy x at a given price, and to have y amount of money to spend on other things. If the price of X falls, the budget line rotates outwards to YX_1, just as it does in indifference curve analysis. The increase in the quantity of x demanded, which is now x_1, is the income effect, leaving the same amount (y) of money. (The substitution effect is the new budget line Y_2X_2, representing the new relationship between X and money (i.e. Y_2X_2 shows for various given

levels of X, how much money will be left over, taking into account the new price). The consumer will purchase, say x_2, leaving y_2 money left over.)

Effectively the consumer is revealing a preference of X relative to everything else (= money): the result is the same, and we can go on to plot various levels of consumption of X against various prices exactly as we did for the indifference curve analysis above.

THEORY OF PRODUCTION COSTS This is one of the two pillars on which much of microeconomic theory is based. It deals with how much a firm, or economic entity, should produce, at what price, and over what time period. It is, in a sense, the 'other side' of the **theory of consumer demand**, which concerns itself with how consumers make decisions to buy, how much they buy, and at what price.

Much of what follows is known as **neo-Classical** economics. Its basic assumption, that firms will always try to maximize their profit, has been challenged by some of the modern

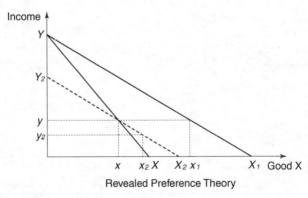

Revealed Preference Theory

Demand Theory, *Fig. 9*

management theories of the firm. The actual behaviour of certain fundamental elements, such as marginal cost, has been questioned after empirical research into how companies really operate. And it should be seen always in the context of what kind of market is under examination (*see* **perfect competition**, **oligopoly**, and **monopoly**). Nonetheless, it can be taken as a reasonable start to understanding the way individual firms or business units operate in the economy.

We start with a definition of costs: they are payments made to employ the **factors of production** (land, labour, capital and enterprise). A firm pays rent for land, wages for labour, interest on money borrowed for capital and profit for enterprise. Therefore the costs of a firm will include all of these payments, including an allowance for 'normal' profit. (For a fuller description of various kinds of profit, *see* **profit**.) The aim of the exercise is to maximize revenues and minimize costs, allowing the firm to maximize its profits.

It is important to distinguish between the two types of cost – fixed costs and variable costs, which are involved in any production process. Fixed costs are those which do not rise according to how much is produced: for example, the rent paid on a factory, or the interest paid on the plant in it. Variable costs will increase as more is produced. They could be labour, or raw materials. What's important is the rate at which they increase.

Naturally for fixed costs, the more that is produced, the lower is the cost to each unit. So the average fixed costs for a firm over a gradually increasing level of output will tend to fall continuously. With variable costs the picture is more complicated. If a firm adds labour in a factory, or raw materials, it will expect to produce more. Since the production process is already under way, adding more variable factors to it is likely to make it more efficient (it is better in general to run a factory with 20 people than with two). Therefore the average variable cost (the variable cost attributable to each unit of output) will tend to fall. It will start to rise again, however, once **diminishing marginal returns** set in. There will come a point when adding extra people or raw materials to the production process makes it less, rather than more, efficient. In the factory, another hundred people may not add much more to the output than 20, but they are still a cost. So, beyond the technical optimum output we would expect average variable costs to rise.

Add together the average fixed costs and the average variable costs and we get the average total costs. This is clearly the key number for a company in making decisions about how much to produce. It is unlikely to want to continue adding to output if its total average costs are rising. For a more sophisticated understanding of how average total costs will rise or fall, it is necessary to introduce the concept of the margin. Marginal cost is the cost attributable to producing one more unit of output at that level of output. Obviously marginal cost will, like average variable cost, reflect diminishing returns. In fact it will anticipate them by turning upward before the technical optimum output is reached. The reason is that the extra output produced by adding just one more variable factor to the process will gradually reduce. In fact the marginal cost curve is rising for the entire time that the average variable cost curve is flattening off. It cuts the average variable cost curve at its lowest point (the technical optimum output). Beyond this, the cost of producing one more unit is higher than the variable cost per unit.

Relating this to the average total cost, we note that the marginal cost curve also cuts the average total cost curve at its lowest point (Fig. 1). Logically the total average costs must be falling if marginal cost is below them, whilst if it is above, then total average costs must be rising, being 'dragged higher' by the greater marginal costs.

It is now time to add in the revenue side of the equation, to assess whether at a given level of costs the firm can make a profit. A moment's thought will bring us to the conclusion that profit (revenue minus cost) must be maximized when marginal revenue equals marginal cost. If making one more unit costs less than the marginal revenue it produces, it's worth mak-

ing it. If making one more unit costs more than the attributed revenue, it's not worth making it. So $MR = MC$ gives us the level of output which would maximize profit.

But there is no reason to suppose that the market demand conditions will allow that amount of output to be sold at a price which ensures a profit. Suppose that the MR curve were in the position shown in Figure 2, with the demand (average revenue) curve shown by AR. Although PM is the profit maximizing level of output, it corresponds to a price (average revenue) of P_1. That is below the average variable cost at that level of output, and well below the average total cost. The firm would not be in existence for very long if it continued producing at that price!

In fact we can extrapolate a key point at the technical optimum output level. The price P_2 has to be at this level of cost or above it for the firm to continue in production even in the short term. Below it, even the average variable costs are not being covered: each new labourer or unit of raw materials is costing more than it

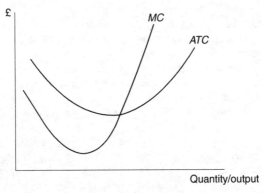

Production Costs, *Fig. 1*

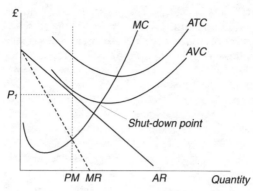

Production Costs, *Fig. 2*

brings in in revenue. It is the short term shut down point. Longer-term, the firm would expect to more than cover its average total costs, at P_3 or above.

We can now plot the supply curve of the individual firm. Since the firm will produce extra units only if the cost of making each one is covered by the revenue (= price) the supply curve is in fact the section of the marginal cost curve above the shut-down point. (This kind of supply curve assumes that the firm is operating under conditions of perfect competition. If it is a monopoly or oligopoly, it can 'make its own price' in the market. Under perfect competition the supply and demand curves for the firm will be different than for the industry as a whole.)

It should now be pointed out that in the long term, *all* costs are variable. This is because a whole factory can be shut down, or plant can be bought or sold. And in many discussions on how efficiently a company can produce, it is the long-term cost curve which is analysed. This represents the technical path for maximum efficiency. If

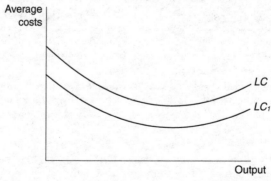

Production Costs, *Fig. 3*

a firm is operating below LC, then clearly it has realized efficiencies which allow its long-term cost curve to be redrawn at, say, LC_1 (Fig. 3). If it is above LC it is operating inefficiently. Its costs are higher than they technically need to be, and it will make lower profits or perhaps be the victim of a take-over. (This is known as **x-inefficiency** – see entry for a fuller discussion.)

TRADE BODIES Trade bodies exist to encourage free, or freer, trade, globally or regionally. The most important trade body is the World Trade Organization (the WTO), the successor to GATT (the General Agreement on Tariffs and Trade). These bodies are generally credited with having helped to open up world trade over the past 50 years, so that growth in trade has outstripped growth in production many times over on all the measures. They conduct their work by complex and byzantine negotiations, involving a little off a tariff here and a general reduction in duties there; their main power derives from their membership. Being in the club requires that all the members abide by the rules: even if they may not support every one of them, they are there because the general benefits to their economies outweigh the short-term pain of having to free up trade. More than 130 countries are currently members of the WTO, dozens more are hoping to join, including behemoths like China and Russia. One of the greatest challenges now facing the WTO is the advance of technology, with its associated issues of intellectual property and free trade on the Internet (*see* essay by Lander).

Other trade bodies tend to be regional, such as NAFTA (the North American Free Trade Association) or ASEAN (the Association of South East Asian Nations), or the EU (European Union). The WTO has a '**most favoured nation**' clause, which means that the tariff advantages it grants to its 'most favoured' trading partners must be guaranteed to all the rest. This is designed to avoid bilateral and regional tariff regimes from developing into exclusive trading blocs. The regional trading groups have therefore tended to concentrate, on creating single markets in their regions, with a minimum of customs formalities and a completely free flow of labour, goods and services. Nonetheless, it is clear that some of the interests of regional groups may be in opposition to those of global multilateral trade, another challenge likely to face the trade bodies in the next decade as world trade and regionalization develop.

TRANSFER PAYMENTS A mechanism of **fiscal policy** through which grants and other payments involve the transfer of income from one group of individuals (taxpayers) to other groups of individuals (for example, state pensions). Transfer payments from a government are not made in return for a productive service. Thus, transfer payments are a form of income redistribution, not a return to a **factor of production**. For this reason transfer payments are not included in the national accounts, which is a money measure of **value added** in the economy.

Transfer payments are, in general,

made to specified groups classified by the government. They include:

- the unemployed: a basic income to people who are officially unemployed for a specified time;
- low income individuals or families: welfare provisions or income support are provided;
- state pensioners, one of the largest categories: they receive annuities from trusts set up for employed individuals;
- others: recipients of social services as well as other income support (including charitable donations made by companies).

The aim of transfer payments is twofold, in that they are tied to a notion of welfare economics and also serve as a stimulant in the economy. Transfer payments redistribute income and aim to provide for individuals in need. At the same time, as part of a deficit budget, they can be injected into an economy that is sluggish, the purpose being to entice households to increase their expenditures on goods and services. (In this case the total taxation – or withdrawal – would be less than the total of the injection – or payments.)

TURNOVER Turnover is the total sales for a firm or an economic entity in a given period. Assuming that each unit sold is profitable for the firm, maximizing turnover can be an important goal (and in some cases is used as a goal in preference to profit maximization – *see* **management theories of the firm**).

Turnover in a more specific sense also measures the rate of sales. In this accounting context, turnover refers to the number of times a particular stock of goods is sold and restocked during a given period. It is a measure of the overall benefit of a good to a producer's product line. Thus, a high turnover implies that a good is frequently bought in the market as well as frequently made by the producer. This high level of turnover relates to two attractive qualities of a product: efficient production capabilities and frequent trade in the market. A product that is produced in large quantities will benefit from **economies of scale**. It will usually accommodate demand in the market by having a production line which can easily be scaled up or down. Similarly, a product that is frequently used by **consumers** and thus frequently traded has the attractive feature that market demand will be predictable, and perhaps more stable. Both these features can contribute to the overall **revenue** of a firm. An example of high turnover goods would be FMCGs (fast-moving consumer goods, such as detergents, groceries, etc.).

Lower levels of turnover are normally associated with either lower trade, or longer production times. If a product being sold in the market cannot be reused and also is not being depleted, it is likely that trade in the economy of the product will be lower. In extreme cases the good may be a one-time purchase or something which will not be resold for many years (a holiday, perhaps, or a house or a wedding ring). Because of this infrequent trade, although a specific product may have a short production time, it may still have a lower turnover than a good with more frequent trade in the economy. Similarly, if a product is frequently bought by consumers but takes the producer a long time to produce, then it will also have a lower associated turnover. This particular circumstance arises when large backlogs exist in which customers must wait a long period before acquiring the product (for example, a custom-made luxury car).

U

UNDERWRITING The function of underwriting a **security** by a **merchant bank** entails the purchase of an issue of **stock** or **bonds** from a corporation that needs funds. As the underwriter, the merchant bank assumes the financial responsibility of selling the securities to investors, who may be individual or institutional investors.

The bearer of risk in selling these issues in the market is the merchant bank. The corporation in need of funds specifies the amount of funds required and negotiates the issue with the merchant bank for a set price. The merchant bank must then attempt to unload the issue in the market for a price that investors are willing to pay. This price may be greater than or less than the price negotiated by the corporation and the merchant bank. The merchant bank profits when the investors' expectations of the firm's issue are favourable, and the market is willing to offer a higher price for the security. In this sense, pricing of the issue is critical for a merchant bank. Many intricate computer programs have been developed to attempt to price issues accurately.

Sometimes, the risk is too large for a single merchant bank to bear. One alternative is for a syndicate of banks to purchase the issue from the corporation. In this way the risk is diversified among the various banks,

with one lead bank coordinating the transaction (and usually bearing a greater proportion of the risk). Another viable alternative is for the investment bank to agree to sell the issues on a commission basis, thus sharing the risk with the corporation.

UNIT TRUST/MUTUAL FUND These are entities which exist to enable (usually small) shareholders to invest in the **stock market** by buying units in a financial trust which will then buy and sell shares on behalf of all its investors. The investment is managed by fund managers, so the small investor benefits (theoretically) from the strategy of a full-time team of professionals (better portfolio management), as well as realizing **economies of scale** on the actual cost of trade. For this the investor pays a management fee, usually a percentage of the portfolio held.

If the investor wants to sell units, they will be repurchased at a price which represents that value of the trust's total portfolio. So the investor does not actually trade shares, either in the trust or in the shares held by it. This contrasts to the investment trust, where shares are owned in a company whose sole purpose is to invest in the stock market.

Unit trusts/mutual funds usually specialize in particular sectors or stock markets. Some, known as tracker

341

funds, follow a stock price index, simply investing in the companies which make up the index.

With the explosion in individual stock market investment in the past decade, the popularity of unit trusts/ mutual funds has increased in proportion. In certain countries governments encourage private investments by allowing tax breaks on certain managed investment vehicles, so that earnings are free of income or capital-gains tax.

A trust is a legal device under which physical or financial property is placed in the custody of a designated person (referred to as the trustee(s)) to manage on behalf of others. The actions and the method of management of the trustee are regulated by the trust deed. A unit trust is a financial trust formed in the UK to manage a portfolio of **securities**, in which small investors can buy units. The US counterparts of such firms are called mutual funds, and the managers of such mutual funds are referred to as fund managers. As these institutions accrue substantial sums of money to invest in securities, they are also referred to as **institutional investors**.

The primary advantage of unit trusts is that it gives the small investor access to a diversified portfolio so as not to put 'all their eggs in one basket'. At the same time, unit trusts allow less informed investors to worry less in regard to managing a portfolio (although one would want to ensure that the unit trust invested in has managers who are concerned about the performance of the portfolio). Thus unit trusts enable investors to take advantage of strategies that may be beyond their capital restraints, or to rely on the investment strategies of informed fund managers.

As mentioned, the portfolio of investments is chosen by and managed by professional fund managers who seek high capital gains or high yields within the bounds of the trust deed. This is because different types of unit trusts are geared towards different types of investors. Broadly speaking, there are income and growth unit trusts. An income unit trust caters for more risk averse investors, and hence the fund managers must take greater precautions in the types of investments included in these portfolios. The explosive growth of the industry in the 1980s led to a wide array of unit trusts being developed to cater for innumerable types of investors and investment strategies. Investors can now have access to the foreign market if desired.

The trustees in most cases are commercial banks, and are legal owners of the security. They are responsible for ensuring that the fund managers keep to the terms of the trust deed. This way, investors are protected from investment strategies that may conflict with their preferences.

The mechanism by which this process works is quite simple. The unit trust invests funds subscribed by the public in securities, and in return issues units that it will repurchase at any time. These units, which represent equal shares in the trust's investment portfolio, produce income and fluctuate in value according to the interest and dividends paid as well as the stock market price of the underlying securities. It should be noted that the subscriber is not like a shareholder, in the sense that it receives the profits of the unit trust to which it has subscribed.

Finally, the unit trusts themselves generate income in two ways: first, by charging a service fee as a percentage of the income of the trusts' investments; secondly, through the price differential that exists in terms of the prices that it asks (sells) for the units and the actual price that it bids (buys) for them.

UPWARD SLOPING DEMAND CURVE (VEBLEN EFFECT)

Why would anyone buy *more* of something if its price increases, or *less* of something as it gets cheaper? Technically, the reason is that the negative income effect more than outweighs the substitution effect (*see* **theory of consumer demand**, **price effect**). In the vernacular, this amounts either to 'snob value', or else to the fact that a particular product is so poor that people will switch away from it as its price falls and their real income increases.

The former effect, known as 'conspicuous consumption' and identified by the American economist Thorstein Bunde Veblen, identifies certain pro-

ducts as becoming more desirable as they become more expensive. This might apply to some kinds of ultra-luxury goods such as classic motor cars, precious jewels, even scarce tickets to some sporting events. The higher the price, the more highly the product is prized.

The other extreme, the very shoddy product, is the **Giffen good**, observed by the British economist Sir Robert Giffen. He noticed that among the poorest Irish farmers in the nine-teenth century, a fall in the price of potatoes was sufficient to cause a fall in demand as the increase in real income allowed people to buy more nourishing alternative foods.

So at both poles of consumption, we can see a demand curve that slopes upwards, instead of the normal down-ward pattern.

UTILITY

Utility is the starting point in assessing allocation of **scarce** resources in an economy, and in a sense underpins much of the **theory of consumer demand**. It has also helped us to develop theories about how people behave in an uncertain world.

Formally, utility is the capacity of a

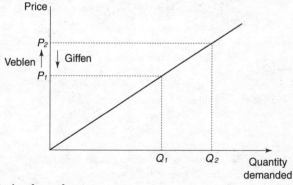

Upward sloping demand curve

good or service to satisfy a human want. Normally it is an 'ordinal' measure – that is, it shows preferences but it does not rank them in absolute quantitative terms (which would be a 'cardinal' measure). It does allow a comparison of various products relative to each other in terms of their desirability for the consumer, and by ing a stage further, allows us to examine marginal rates of substitution. Put simply, do I prefer a chocolate bar to a plate of asparagus? If the answer is yes, then for me a chocolate bar has greater utility than the asparagus. But if I had ten chocolate bars, would I substitute one of them for a plate of asparagus? And if I had two plates of asparagus, would I substitute one of them for eight chocolate bars? Eventually we can construct from such questions an indifference curve, which will show the various levels of substitution of chocolate bars and asparagus which will give me equal utility: I will be indifferent to any of the permutations along the curve.

Modern utility theory has concerned itself with establishing how individuals behave, given choices and risks: this is known as known as expected utility theory. The economists von Neumann and Morgenstern came up with an index which allowed cardinal measurement of utility. It described how consumers will take into account not just their preferences but also the likelihood of their occurring in the future. Their work was tested and challenged by the French economist Maurice Allais, who noted that consumers do not always assess risk in order to maximize utility (the Allais paradox).

The notion of utility is also used to appraise welfare and social projects as part of cost benefit analysis and assessment of **opportunity cost** (*see* **Pareto**).

V

VALUATION Valuation is a method of determining the economic value of firms or business entities. It is used by economists, financial economists, and accountants. It provides a systematic approach to evaluating the worth of various items related to the firm as well as its overall worth.

Many firms invest in long-term capital, also referred to as fixed **assets**. They invest in these assets at some time and use them for a long period to finance operations. Thus it may be simple to value a firm at the moment it invests in these fixed assets, but a standard rule needs to be applied to the valuation of these fixed assets to account for any wear and tear that may have accumulated over time. The standard rule allows stakeholders interested in evaluating different firms to use one established criterion. This is known as the net book value of fixed assets. Net book value is the accounting value of a fixed asset in a firm's balance sheet that represents its historical cost less any accumulated depreciation. It should be noted, however, that the net book value of an asset may not coincide with its market value. It is simply the value of the fixed asset to the firm, whereas the market value of a similar fixed asset represents the value to all interested agents in the economy. So if interested agents value the asset more than the firm, the market value will be greater than the net book value. General factors affecting this discrepancy are primarily inflation, methods of calculating depreciation, as well as expectations.

Valuation may also be applied to the overall worth of the firm. Net worth is the value of the firm according to the balance sheet (*see* **accounts**). It is calculated as the sum of the assets of the firm less its total liabilities or **debts**. This is also the calculation for the shareholders' equity section of the balance sheet. Again, the distinction must be made between net worth and the market value of the company according to shareholders. If the market value of the firm (according to shareholders) is much greater than the actual net worth of the firm, then the firm will be liable for a devaluation in its share price (because it does not have the net worth to back up its high share price). Conversely, if the market value is much less than the net worth of the company then the firm is vulnerable to **asset stripping**, threatening its existence.

VALUE ADDED Value added for a firm or an economy is the total value of output, less the cost of the inputs that are needed for the production process. A firm which makes metal cans will have to pay for inputs in the form of steel, various components, and certain services such as transporting the raw materials to its factory. If the total cost of all these inputs in a given year is x, and its total sales are worth $x + y$, then it will have added a value of y. y represents the value which the company's capital, labour, marketing, and special skills have added to the basic inputs.

It is therefore possible to distinguish between the total, or gross, value of a finished product, and the value added at various stages of its manufacture. In the production process, the outputs of one stage (say, the steel in our example) become the inputs of the next stage. We define intermediate goods as outputs of one set of firms that are used as inputs by another set of firms. Final goods are goods that are not considered as inputs by any other firms (and are usually used up by the ultimate consumer). Value added for a given stage then refers to the value brought about from moving from the preceding intermediate good to the successive intermediate or final good (whichever may be the case).

Value added is one of the methods of measuring the GDP or total output of an economy. As such, it is known as the output approach (two other methods of measuring the size of the economy are the expenditure and income approaches). Specifically, the sum of all the value added in an economy is the GDP. Using the value added principle for measuring GDP is appealing particularly because it avoids double counting and gives a more reasonable indication of total output.

As well as measuring output, the notion of value added has provided a useful indirect **tax** scheme for many governments. Value added tax is a tax on the estimated market value added to a product or material at each stage of manufacturing or distribution. It attempts to give tax receipts to the government at every stage of production. Intermediate producers can claim back the tax they pay on their inputs, but the final consumer generally pays the full amount (*see* **fiscal policy**).

VENTURE CAPITAL Venture capital, also referred to as **risk capital**, is equity and loan capital provided for a new business by people other than the proprietors or managers. Venture capital tends to be focused on entrepreneurs who may be offering an innovative product but who are not able to attract financing through more conventional methods.

There are generally two key characteristics that separate venture capital from other forms of capital. An element of ownership passes to the investor, and the rate of return on such capital tends to be higher. Usually, the equity capital is provided in a package including subordinate and other loans. Thus, the investors of venture capital have a percentage of ownership of the operation and may provide the proprietors with an option to 'buy back' ownership in the future. Entrepreneurs are commonly unable to attract financing for such projects because of the high risks associated with their business proposals, and as a result investors of venture capital require a higher rate of return. Sometimes venture capitalists may take a proactive role in management of the business, in order to oversee the projects of the firm.

W

WAGE–PRICE SPIRAL This is a symptom of **inflationary** pressures arising from the cost side of production, and an extreme form of cost-push inflation. Workers wanting to preserve their purchasing power and standard of living increase their demands for wage increases in an inflationary environment. This increase in the variable and total cost of production will be reflected in the final product's price. As a consequence, consumers will face higher prices and the inflationary process will be reinforced further.

Wage–price inflation is based on 'fixed price' markets in which the changes in prices and wages do not reflect the shift of demand or supply curves but rather, changes in average cost and cost of living. In this sense they tend to be shorter term (*see* **theory of production costs**).

The appropriate response is generally considered to be a restrictive **fiscal** and **monetary policy** in order to shield the economy from accelerating inflation. As is so often the case, the most appropriate nature and mechanism are the subjects of debate.

Monetarists recommended the adoption of a simple rule governing the growth of the money supply. This seems to have led to high short-term unemployment in several economies which have adopted monetarist policies (e.g. the UK in the 1980s,

although it should be noted that the inflation rate did fall). Furthermore there are traditionally problems in measuring and maintaining money supply targets.

The **Keynesian** school proposed 'fine-tuning' as a means of discretionary intervention in the short run. Critics argued that such fine-tuning was often what led to wage–price spirals in the first place, by stimulating aggregate demand rather than allowing economic activity to find its own level. **Neo-Keynesians** are less likely to emphasize large-scale long-term demand management, and reject the traditional Keynesian notion of an incomes policy to control a wage-price spiral.

On the other side, the **neo-Classicals** oppose the pursuit of any demand management policy at all, preferring to encourage governments to provide information so that individuals and firms can develop rational expectations, which will ensure the efficient working of the markets. (*See* essay by Patrick Minford.)

WAGES (LABOUR THEORY OF VALUE) Wages are the reward for labour, one of the factors of production, and throughout the centuries have excited much disagreement and anger among economists, and wage-earners themselves. Early **Classical** economists used the nature of a 'wage fund' which was the stock of resources available to reward the labour force of the economy. This did not necessarily increase with the size of the population, and economists were cast as arguing that wages could never rise above subsistence levels. **Marx** and **Ricardo** developed the concept of the 'labour theory of value', which held that the price of goods was dependent on the value of labour which had gone into producing them. Marx argued that only labour could create value, but that the capitalist class retained some of that value as **profit.**

The **neo-Classical** economists introduced the idea that the going wage represented the value of the marginal product of labour, i.e. what it took to put one extra input of labour into the production process. This meant that labour received a part of the **revenues** from the sales of the goods and services it produced. This notion remains as part of the **theory of production costs**. Wages were thought to operate under the same **supply** and **demand** conditions that governed other elements of the economy. During a period of unemployment, wages would fall, allowing firms to re-employ labour at lower cost and expand the production process.

Keynes was the first to highlight the idea that wages tended to be 'sticky', i.e. they could move upwards during booms but they would tend not to move down during recession. This allowed the economy to reach an equilibrium below full **employment**, a situation which could be remedied by expanding aggregate demand. This would create recovery which would not be inflationary until full employment was reached again.

The period of **stagflation** (high inflation and high unemployment) in the 1970s caused many economists and policy-makers to reassess what was by then a Keynesian orthodoxy. Some governments tried (mostly unsuccessfully) to impose prices and incomes policies. **Monetarists** argued that increases in nominal wage rates were indeed inflationary, and **supply-side** economists argued that allowing wages to reach their natural 'market' level would eventually reduce unemployment (*see* the essay by Patrick Minford). In this respect the wage demands associated with trade unions, or the introduction of a **minimum wage** rate, could lead to 'cost-push inflation' and a '**wage–price spiral**'.

Currently the level of wage increases is monitored carefully by government economists, along with other indicators of possible inflationary trends. Rather than trying to ignore nominal wage rates (early Keynesians believed that as long as real wage rates do not rise, there will be no inflation if there is less than full employment), or trying to impose incomes policies, governments tend to use **monetary** and **fiscal** measures to control activity and regulate prices. During a period of major technological innovation, there is consensus that some flexibility in labour markets is necessary, and that includes the level of wages.

WALRAS'S LAW The nineteenth-century French economist Leon Walras is credited with being a pioneer of the macroeconomic general equilibrium theory, which is the study of the economy as a whole and the examination of whether a set of circumstances can exist in which all markets are stable.

The analysis of general equilibrium is mathematically and conceptually more complex than that of partial equilibrium, where the economist confines the study to one or a few markets, assuming the others to be unaffected by those under review.

Clearly, for governments trying to manage economies, there is a need to look at all markets, and highly sophisticated **econometric** and empirical models are constructed to this end, with varying degrees of accuracy and success.

Walras's Law allowed a level of 'short-cutting' by stating something which is intuitively very simple: in an economy with N markets, if N minus 1 are in equilibrium, then we can assume that the remaining market will also be. It means that, for example, if the markets for money, goods, and labour are in equilibrium, it is not necessary to analyse, say, the **bond** (government borrowing) market, for that, too will 'clear' to equilibrium.

(*See also* **money supply**, **monetary policy**, **circular flow of national income**.)

WILLIAMSON TRADE-OFF MODEL
The Williamson trade-off model is used in merger analysis to evaluate the possible benefits associated with lower costs and the detriments associated with higher prices. It can be used by management as a tool to weigh the costs and benefits of a merger proposal, or it may be used as an application of discretionary competition policy.

The model can be easily illustrated through examining a merger proposal, which would add market power to the firms being merged and prevents the development of a competitive **market structure**. To see the impact of the merger on the competitive nature of the market, let us first examine the market before the merger. Here we will assume for the sake of simplicity that a number of firms produce a homogeneous product with the same cost curves (that is, they have the same average cost). In this market structure the competitive price in the market is identical to the marginal cost, which also coincides with average costs (this is the normal profit equilibrium condition for a competitive market). Now if two or more firms were to merge in this industry, then they might be able to produce at a lower level of constant average costs simply by taking advantage of **economies of scale**. The merged firms will then have to establish a price, not merely in excess of their costs but also in excess of the previous average costs. In such circumstances, a welfare trade-off arises from any price increase in which there is a loss in the consumers' surplus (*see* **surplus**) and a cost saving to the producer from producing at a lower level of costs than previously.

In the event that the loss in consumers' surplus is greater than the cost savings, the most probable course of action would be for the firms not to merge. Alternatively, if the cost saving to the producer is greater than the loss in consumers' surplus, then the firms can merge if they wish to do so. But it should be noted that any benefits gained by the firm will not necessarily be passed on to the consumer. The merged firms may now be in a position to exert **monopoly** or **oligopoly** power, with the ability to make their own price. Clearly in this case the anti-trust **regulator** may act, either to prevent the merger, or to order the new entity to pass on the lower costs.

X-INEFFICIENCY The term x-inefficiency was introduced by the economist Harvey Leibenstein to describe a situation in which firms in a non-competitive market tend to produce at higher than minimum cost levels. In particular, x-inefficiency occurs in a **monopoly** where the ability to control price means that extra (or abnormal) **profits** can exist when the firm is producing at less than its lowest cost. In terms of the **theory of production costs**, the monopoly is producing at a cost level which is higher than the lowest point of **long-run** average cost curve (which represents the technically most efficient point).

X-inefficiencies persist because monopolies exert barriers to entry which make it harder for new competitors to enter the market and force down costs and prices.

Some textbooks bracket 'organizational slack' with x-inefficiencies. Organizational slack often exists in non-competitive environments, although it may exist in a firm which is minimizing its costs of production, i.e. where no x-inefficiency occurs. A monopoly will maximize its (abnormal) profit at an output level which does not correspond to the lowest point on the average cost curve; organizational slack can exist at any point along the average cost curve.

There are three factors that generally tend to contribute to slack:

1. Lack of knowledge. Perhaps the decision makers do not know the exact minimum amount for which a worker may be prepared to work, or else do not know how to operate existing machinery at its maximum potential. Costs will therefore be higher than they need to be.
2. The tendency of firms to be conservative about suppliers. A firm that orders parts from another firm with whom it has established a relationship may be reluctant to 'shop around' for a cheaper deal.
3. A reluctance to invest in new machinery and/or technology. This arises because **investment** in new machinery always involves some risk-taking, which management may shy away from.

Interest groups within a firm can also increase slack by exploiting their potential power. For example, an environmentalist group can urge the company to employ more environmentally friendly methods of production, which may not be the most efficient means. Often, however, these types of costs may be in the interest of the general public.

In recessions, organizational slack tends to decline as companies try to safeguard profits. Since they cannot hope to gain much by raising prices, companies look for alternative means by searching for cost-cutting strategies. So recessions are often accompanied by greater efficiency on the part of the firms which survive, and of course by an increasing number of firms which go out of business altogether.

INDEX